W9-BDH-232

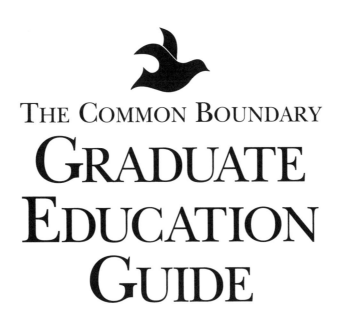

THE COMMON BOUNDARY

GRADUATE EDUCATION GUIDE

8/4/9

Second Edition

THE COMMON BOUNDARY

GRADUATE EDUCATION GUIDE

Holistic Programs and Resources
Integrating Spirituality and Psychology

Written and Edited By

Charles H. Simpkinson, Ph.D.

Douglas A. Wengell, B.A.

Mary Jane A. Casavant, M.A.

Common Boundary, Inc.
Bethesda, Maryland

Published by
Common Boundary, Inc.
5272 River Road, Suite 650
Bethesda, MD 20816
(301) 652-9495

COPYRIGHT © 1994 COMMON BOUNDARY, INC.
All rights reserved. No part of this book may be reproduced or utilized in any form or by
any means, electronic or mechanical, without permission in writing from the publisher.

Printed and bound in the United States of America.

Art Direction: Joseph Yacinski
Design: Jan Zimmeck Design
Electronic Production: Capital Computer Consulting
Cover Photography: Bob Grove

Permission to use the following contributions is gratefully acknowledged:
Bear's Guide to Non-Traditional College Degrees (9th edition) © 1985 by John B. Bear.
"Three Paradigms," by the American Massage Therapy Association and the National
Certification Board for Therapeutic Massage and Bodywork © 1991.

"Folk Psychology and the American Visionary Tradition" © 1994 by Eugene Taylor.

Disclaimer

Common Boundary does not endorse programs or take responsibility for accuracy of
statements supplied by schools. There are degree and nondegree programs listed herein
that offer graduate or postdoctoral programs but are not associated with regionally
accredited institutions. While these programs may offer quality training, users of this
guide are cautioned that a graduate degree earned from a program that is not located in
an institution with full regional accreditation could result in ineligibility for admission to
examination for licensure or certification, if applicable. Licensure, third-party payments,
and the ability to practice independently vary greatly from state to state. Contact your state
government's mental health regulation agency or, in states with a more highly developed
regulatory system, the certification board for mental health professionals.

Ordering information:

To order additional copies directly from the publisher, send a check or money order in
the amount of $19.95 plus $3.50 postage for each copy to Common Boundary,
Department GEG, 5272 River Road, Suite 650, Bethesda, MD 20816. No credit cards
please. Also see order form on page 187.

To add a program:

See form on page 187.

Library of Congress Catalog Card Number: 93-73988
Simpkinson, Charles H., Douglas A. Wengell, and Mary Jane A. Casavant, eds.
The Common Boundary Graduate Education Guide: Holistic Programs and Resources
Integrating Spirituality and Psychology

ISBN: 0-9638795-0-2

The Editors

Charles H. Simpkinson, Ph.D., is publisher of *Common Boundary* magazine and director of its annual conference. He also has a private clinical psychology practice in Bethesda, MD. He is the coeditor of *Sacred Stories: A Celebration of the Power of Story to Transform and Heal* (HarperSanFrancisco, 1993), which is the first book in the Common Boundary Reader series. He received his B.A. from Williams College, studied at Yale Divinity School, and received his Ph.D. in clinical psychology from the University of Tennessee in 1972.

Douglas A. Wengell, B.A., graduated *magna cum laude* from Rutgers University and the Rutgers College General Honors Program in 1993 with a major in English and a minor in psychology. He plans to study the psychology of consciousness in graduate school.

Mary Jane A. Casavant, M.A., is manager of educational programs at Common Boundary. She graduated *cum laude* from Dartmouth College and, after working for several years in education administration, earned a master's degree in religion and culture from The Catholic University of America in 1992.

ACKNOWLEDGEMENTS

MANY PEOPLE, PAST AND PRESENT, CONTRIBUTED TO THE CREATION OF this guide. Historically speaking, Miles Vich, executive director of the Association for Transpersonal Psychology, began the process of cataloging resources in the transpersonal field through a listing of programs that the association publishes every other year, and that provided a piece of the original groundwork for the first edition of this book.

Patricia Ellerd, Ph.D., with the help of Courtney Bennett, developed a prototype that evolved into the first edition. Since its publication in 1991, Wanda Byrd has shepherded a considerable part of the updating process.

As for the significant development of the second edition, we express gratitude to Common Boundary magazine staff members Anne Simpkinson, Rose Solari, and William O'Sullivan for their generous editorial support; Kristen Smith for helping research and fact-check; Darcie Johnston for copyediting the first draft of the manuscript; and Grace Ogden for her marketing expertise. Also, we wish to thank Wanda Tutwiler for helping us choose a printer, and James Morris for advising Common Boundary on how to distribute this book to the people who could most use it.

Last, we are indebted to the many professionals who shared our vision of creating this much augmented second edition and who recognized the importance of outlining the educational opportunities in the psychospiritual and mind-body fields. Contributors include those who wrote portions of this book (as acknowledged after their introductions) and those who provided the editors with up-to-date information from their respective fields. The latter group includes, but is not limited to:

American Psychological Association
Anthony Barton, Ph.D.
Barbara Bernie, L.A.C.
Barbara Bernstein
Greg Blevins, Ph.D.
Alfred Bloom
Bob Brantley, Ph.D.
California State Psychology Association
John Chitty, R.P.P.
Dean Davis, Ph.D.
Barbara Goodrich Dunn
Steve Fahrion, Ph.D.
Cunice Ferreira
Richard Finn, C.T.P.M.
Clyde W. Ford, D.C.
Paul Giblin, Ph.D.
Harriet L. Glosoff, M.A., N.C.C.
Joel Hamaker
Peggy Heller
Institute for Holistic Healing Studies,
    San Francisco State University
Jewish Information and Referral Service
Dwight Judy, Ph.D.
Leslie Kaminoff
Charles Kelley, Ph.D.
Paulo Knill, Ph.D.
George Kousaleds
Ching Lee, Ph.D.
John Lentz
Penny Lewis, Ph.D., A.D.T.R., R.D.T.
Francis Lu, M.D.
Bill McKelve, Ph.D.
Shaun McNiff, Ph.D.
Terence R. Montgomery, C.T.P.M.
Larry Payne
James Price, Ph.D.
Theodore Remley, Ph.D.
Eleanor Sargent, M.A., C.A.C.
Kirk Schneider, Ph.D.
Frank Sherlock
Rabbi Jeffery Silverman
Virender Sodhi, M.D.
Harry F. Swope, N.D., D.H.A.N.P., C.C.H.
United States Department of Education—
    Accreditation and State Liaison Division
Roger Walsh, M.D.
Ruth Warren
Rhea White
Robert Wicks, Ph.D.

TABLE OF CONTENTS

Swedenborgianism
Theosophy
Zoroastrianism

Section III
MIND-BODY STUDIES

PREFACE

I F YOU ARE LIKE MOST AMERICANS LIVING IN THE 1990s, CHANCES ARE THAT YOU OR SOMEONE YOU KNOW HAS HAD A PERSONAL EXPERIENCE WITH alternative therapies. Indeed, according to a 1993 Harvard survey conducted by David Eisenberg, M.D., and reported in *The New England Journal of Medicine*, 34% of Americans have used alternative therapies to improve their health and well-being. The burgeoning interest taking place in the United States in these therapies is a continuation of what Eugene Taylor, Ph.D., calls the long lineage of the "American visionary tradition," a concept that is further outlined in his historically focused introduction. Out of this historical trend has evolved a consciousness movement that now ranges from deep ecology to Zen to socially responsible business. From it, a kind of folk psychology has emerged—an orientation not tied to any particular academic or clinical tradition but rather responding to a grass-roots call for relevance and meaning.

Since the 1960s, there has been a steadily building interest in integrating the traditions of religion and spirituality with such disciplines as psychotherapy, somatic techniques, and the creative and expressive arts. So broad is this folk psychology's spectrum of educational and professional opportunities that not even the name of the overarching field—alternative, holistic, psychospiritual, transpersonal—has been easy to establish. In response, we at Common Boundary are attempting to provide the first comprehensive map of graduate-level programs, nondegree training, and other resources focusing on the nexus of spirituality, psychology, and creativity.

Such psychospiritual programs are rarely found within mainstream educational institutions but instead proliferate and thrive through nontraditional channels. Over the past 30 years a number of pioneers have founded several transpersonal graduate schools and hundreds of nondegree training programs. With the help of a strong network of alternative bookstores, newspapers, and magazines, word is spreading about the availability of holistic workshops, retreats, and conference centers throughout the country. Even mainstream bookstores and publishers can no longer ignore the fact that authors who address themes relevant to the visionary/folk psychology tradition often become best sellers, and more books on alternative topics are being published than ever before.

In assembling this book, we have attempted to weave into a unifying and coherent framework a multitude of rich and often disparate modalities. The guide provides facts about particular retreat centers and universities as well as an overview of how and where your specific interests fit within the field as a whole. We also attempt to introduce some of the hot topics and current conversations in the various emerging disciplines. For example, in the chapter on spiritually sensitive social work, Edward Canda, Ph.D., discusses ethical boundaries in reference to the therapist's difficult task of being sensitive to the spiritual needs of the client without injecting his or her own spiritual agenda or allegiances. In the mind-body section, Don Hanlon Johnson, Ph.D., and the editors discuss some of the many trends in somatic disciplines. In addition, licensure, certification, and third-party reimbursement issues—which are very important to those intending to earn a living within any part of the psychospiritual field—are addressed throughout.

The various professions included in this guide are separated into categories for the sake of structural convenience. Nevertheless, it is interesting to note that the folk psychology movement is dissolving some of the barriers between the various helping and healing professionals—such as clergy, expressive arts therapists, nurses, physicians, psychologists, and somatic therapists. At many holistic conferences and postgraduate (that is, nondegree) professional training programs, for example, the distinctions between the different helping professions are not usually experienced as a barrier. Instead, participants seem to have a unifying interest that overrides their different professional roles.

In all likelihood, the visionary/folk psychology field will continue to grow and reshape itself dramatically in the coming years, as it has already done in the past few decades. One can only speculate about how the emerging health care initiative will influence both the future development and the economic sustainability of alternative therapies in the United States. As the situation evolves, we hope that you will let us know if you discover programs or resources that should be included in future editions, and we encourage your comments and suggestions for how we can better assist you in exploring the farther reaches of psychology, spirituality, and creativity.

Bethesda, MD
September 1994

Charles H. Simpkinson, Ph.D.
Douglas A. Wengell, B.A.
Mary Jane A. Casavant, M.A.

HOW TO USE THIS BOOK

SECTIONS, CHAPTERS, AND SUBCHAPTERS

With convenience and coherence in mind, the editors have divided the material into sections, chapters, and subchapters. In doing so, we made many difficult decisions about grouping and categorizing—an often vexing task, given that these modalities, by their very definitions, steadfastly cross disciplinary boundaries. As with any developing model, however, the guide's organizational categories are a reflection of our best judgment at this moment in history and are open to revision in future editions. The Table of Contents provides a comprehensive overview.

RELEVANT ASSOCIATIONS, ORGANIZATIONS, AND PERIODICALS

We have endeavored to list associations, institutions, organizations, and periodicals (such as journals, magazines, and newsletters) with the modality they best represent. However, if they are interdisciplinary, you may find that they are cross-referenced to other parts of the book or listed only in the Interdisciplinary Resources section.

INDEXES

Please refer to the alpahbetical index if you have trouble locating a particular school, resource, or training center. It may be listed under a name different from the one you might expect. We have also included a geographical index.

PROFESSIONAL TITLES RELEVANT TO THIS GUIDE

THE FOLLOWING TITLES INCLUDE LICENSES (AWARDED BY THE STATE); CREDENTIALS (AWARDED BY CERTIFYING BODIES); AND DEGREES (CONFERRED BY EDUCATIONAL INSTITUTIONS).

A.C.S.W.	Academy of Certified Social Worker
A.D.T.R.	American Dance Therapy Registered
A.T.R.	Registered Art Therapist
Ac. Phys.	Acupuncture Physician
B.C.D.	Board Certified Diplomate (in clinical social work)
B.D.	Bachelor of Divinity
B.S.	Bachelor of Science (generic degree)
B.S.N.	Bachelor of Science in Nursing
C.Ac.	Certified Acupuncturist
C.A.C.	Certified Alcohol Counselor
C.C.H.	Certified in Classical Homeopathy
C.Ht.	Certified Hypnotherapist
C.M.T.	Certified Music Therapist
C.P.C.	Certified Professional Counselor
C.P.T.	Certified Poetry Therapist
C.S.W.	Certified Social Worker
C.T.P.M.	Certified Trigger Point Myotherapists
D.Ac.	Doctor of Acupuncture
D.C.	Doctor of Chiropractic
D.D.	Doctor of Divinity (honorary degree)
D.H.A.N.P.	Diplomate of the Homeopathic Academy of Naturopathic Physicians
D.Ht.	Diplomate in Homeotherapeutics
D.Min.	Doctor of Ministry
D.O.	Doctor of Osteopathy
D.O.M.	Doctor of Oriental Medicine
D.Rel.	Doctor of Religion
D.S.W.	Doctor of Social Work
D.T.R.	Dance Therapist Registered
Ed.D.	Doctor of Education
H.M.D.	Homeopathic Medical Doctor
L.Ac.	Licensed Acupuncturist
L.C.S.W.	Licensed Clinical Social Worker
L.I.C.S.W.	Licensed Independent Clinical Social Worker
L.M.F.T.	Licensed Marriage and Family Therapist
L.M.T.	Licensed Massage Therapist
L.P.C.	Licensed Pastoral Counselor
M.A.	Master of Arts (generic degree)
M.Ac.O.M.	Master of Acupuncture and Oriental Medicine
M.D.	Medical Doctor
M.Div.	Master of Divinity
M.F.C.C.	Marriage, Family and Child Counselor
M.H.C.	Mental Health Counselor
M.S.	Master of Science (generic degree)
M.S.N.	Master of Science in Nursing
M.S.W.	Master of Social Work
N.C.A.C.	National Certified Addiction Counselor
N.C.A.D.C.	National Certificate of Alcohol and Drug Counseling
N.D. or N.M.D.	Naturopathic Medical Doctor
O.M.D.	Oriental Medical Doctor
Ph.D.	Doctor of Philosophy (generic degree)
Psy.D.	Doctor of Psychology
R.Ac.	Registered Acupuncturist
R.D.T.	Registered Dance Therapist
R.M.T.	Registered Music Therapist
R.N.	Registered Nurse
R.P.T.	Registered Poetry Therapist
S.T.D.	Doctor of Sacred Theology
S.T.M.	Master of Sacred Theology
T.E.P.	Trainer, Educator, and Poetry Therapy Practitioner
Th.D.	Doctor of Theology

KEY TO ACCREDITING ORGANIZATIONS

AAMFT	American Association for Marriage and Family Therapy
AAPC	American Association of Pastoral Counselors
ACA	American Counseling Association
APA	American Psychological Association
ATS	Association of Theological Schools in the United States and Canada
CACREP	Council for Accreditation of Counseling and Related Educational Programs
CAMFTE	Commission on Accreditation for Marriage and Family Therapy Education
CCNASC	Commission on Colleges of the Northwest Association Schools and Colleges
CCSACS	Commission on Colleges of the Southern Association of Colleges and Schools
CIHE	Commission on Institutions of Higher Education
CSWE	Council on Social Work Education
MSACS	Middle States Association of Colleges and Schools
NBCC	National Board for Certified Counselors
NCA	National Counseling Association
NCACS	North Central Association of Colleges and Schools
NCATE	National Council for Accreditation of Teacher Education
NEACSS	New England Association of Colleges and Secondary Schools
PASC	Pacific Association for Schools and Colleges
SACS	Southern Association of Colleges and Schools
USCCCCA	United States Catholic Conference Commission on Certification and Accreditation
WASC	Western Association of Schools and Colleges

THE SPECTRUM OF HOLISTIC HEALING MODALITIES

THE EDITORS HAVE TAKEN THE LIBERTY OF PLACING THE FOLLOWING DISCIplines, therapies, and fields within the category they best appear to represent. However, just as there is a range of modalities, so are there individual practitioners of each modality who, despite their specialized training, integrate other concepts of mind, body, and spirit into their practice. Therefore, we encourage you to use this graph more as a tool to help visualize the epistemological and philosophical relationship between the evolving disciplines outlined in this guide than as a definitive classification.

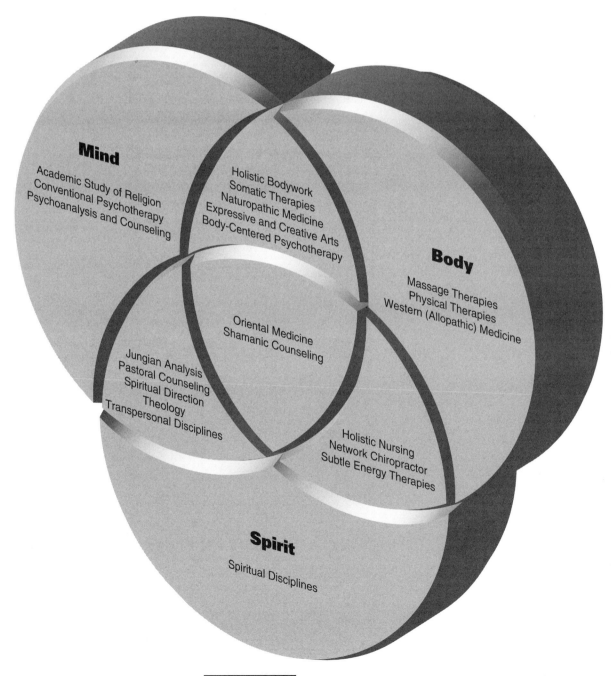

Mind
Academic Study of Religion
Conventional Psychotherapy
Psychoanalysis and Counseling

Holistic Bodywork
Somatic Therapies
Naturopathic Medicine
Expressive and Creative Arts
Body-Centered Psychotherapy

Body
Massage Therapies
Physical Therapies
Western (Allopathic) Medicine

Oriental Medicine
Shamanic Counseling

Jungian Analysis
Pastoral Counseling
Spiritual Direction
Theology
Transpersonal Disciplines

Holistic Nursing
Network Chiropractor
Subtle Energy Therapies

Spirit
Spiritual Disciplines

HISTORICAL INTRODUCTION

Folk Psychology and the American Visionary Tradition

Eugene Taylor, Ph.D.

ODAY WE ARE PRIVILEGED TO WITNESS THE BREAKTHROUGH OF AN EDUCA-tional ideal that is destined to influence all aspects of modern culture. This ideal has been called education for transcendence—a means by which one gains not only skills for a vocation but also tools for life-long psychological development and spiritual growth. Its nature is self-knowledge; its end is nothing less than the transformation of consciousness.

The influence of this educational ideal is already far-reaching; everywhere it seems to be gradually reshaping many of our most staid and traditional institutions. Mind-body medicine, ecological awareness, lifetime spiritual disciplines, and holistic management strategies are but a few examples of its ever-widening effect on fields as varied as psychology, religion, health, and learning.

But, while changes in our social institutions themselves may be new, the integration of psychology and spiritual development is not. It is not merely the product of recent social events from the 1960s. It did not just appear on the scene yesterday. It is not simply an infant gadfly fluttering around the edges of the giant mammoth of mainstream culture that once swatted would be gone; and it is neither superficial, naive, nor New Age.

Rather, the single most important fact about the relationship between psychology and spirituality is that it has a long and venerable history. According to some interpreters, the fusion of these two domains lies at the heart of an alter-native reality tradition in the West that is more mystical than analytic, intuitive rather than rational, and inwardly directed toward consciousness rather than outwardly directed toward what is material, physical, and concrete. For example, the cosmological worldview of the Egyptians required a detailed understanding of those parts of the soul that could return from the dead. Priests in the Grecian temples of Asclepius based their healing techniques on interpretation of a patient's dreams. Gnosticism and Neoplatonism, which helped shape the theology and sacraments of the early Christian church, provided elaborate teachings linking purification of the soul with an awakening to the experience of divinity within the inward life of the person. Western religious classics such as *The Cloud of Unknowing, The Philokalia,* and the *Spiritual Exercises of St. Ignatius* prescribe detailed steps toward the inward perfection of personality. From the spiritual visions of the medieval mystics to the later ideals of the Rosicrucians and hermetic scholars, the goal has always been to transform the baser elements of personality into the more noble.

In the United States, an intuitive, mystical, and visionary psychology of character development has always defined the core of American folk culture. Such a psychology draws on the long heritage of American self-sufficiency and self-help. It has combined the ideals of progress with evolution and thus is profoundly optimistic. It continues to be characterized by its emphasis on multiple realities, by its view that personality is shaped by dynamic forces of the unconscious, and by its aim toward an understanding of extraordinary states of consciousness and expanded human potential. It is also known by its intense attraction to the natural environment and by its hint that there is some fundamental relationship between a return to nature and the recovery of basic values. It can be identified by its millennial vision of world peace. In its search for parity between science and spirituality, folk psychology rests on the assumption that mental healing is an integral part of physical health and that there is healing to be found in community. It promotes the paranormal as an integral part of human functioning, and it takes seriously dream images, personal symbols of one's destiny, and religious visions.

Although it has become more visible today than ever before, this visionary tradition has asserted itself from the earliest days of the American experience. It might be characterized as emerging across six general periods:

SPIRITUAL COMMUNITIES

While Puritan Calvinism dominated ecclesiastical church life after the founding of the American colonies, numerous mystical communities also flourished. The Dutch Labadists who settled as contemplative farming communes in the New World left their mark today as the Amish and Mennonites. William Penn, promoting the deeply personal experience of the Inward Light, launched his Holy Experiment in Pennsylvania, which gave refuge not only to the English Quakers but also to droves of Christian Pietists who settled Germantown and sites along the Wissihicken River. One among them was the Ephrata Cloister, the oldest monastic community on the American frontier.

By the time of the American Revolution, spiritual communities, believing in the power of internal prayer and mystical awakening, had become a permanent part of the American landscape. Beginning in the 1780s, the Shakers, led by Mother Ann Lee, practiced collective trance rituals

and through divine ordinance established settlements on the East Coast. They began to cultivate extensive tracts of organic produce. They grew large quantities of herbs and seeds. They built religiously inspired furniture and crafts, and they developed a widespread distribution network for their wares. In all this they blended religious values with the qualities of thrift, economy, beauty, and grace, and produced large,

---

An intuitive, mystical, and visionary psychology of character development has always defined the core of American folk culture.

---

innovative, and economically successful communities.

The Shakers were soon followed by an explosion of other utopian social experiments. Thomas Lake Harris and Robert Dale Owen started groups in rural areas of the East Coast. Followers of Etienne Cabet, founder of the Icarian colonies, settled on the midwestern frontier. Hundreds of such settlements, based on every kind of belief system imaginable, dotted the American landscape. The ecstatic visions of Joseph Smith created the present day Mormon church. Those of the prophetess Ellen White led to the Seventh-Day Adventists. Even the New England Transcendentalists started communities such as Fruitlands in Harvard, Massachusetts, and Brook Farm in West Roxbury. The long-awaited millennium, the Coming of the Lord's Kingdom on Earth, appeared to be at hand in the form of transformed personalities and renewed societies. All this caused the Concord sage Ralph Waldo Emerson to declare that as far as the New Dispensation was concerned, there was not a man among us without a blueprint in his waistcoat pocket.

In this first phase of the American visionary tradition, charismatic individuals who had ecstatic experiences, liberal-

ly interpreted in a Christian context, moved hundreds and even thousands of people to follow them and to have visions of their own. This led to a remarkable era of experiments in charismatic healing and utopian socialism that proved to be some of the most successful in the world for what they tried to achieve.

THE MIND CURE MOVEMENT

In the second phase of the American visionary tradition, beginning in the opening decades of the 1800s, a cultural filter began to emerge that reshaped psychospiritual ideas from elsewhere into a uniquely American indigenous folk psychology. This indigenous psychology blended religious experience with an intuitive psychology of character development that soon became widespread throughout the 19th century.

Homeopathy, an alternative medical system based on administering drugs that mimicked the symptoms of illness, came to America from Germany in 1825. Phrenology, an alleged science of character development that assessed personality by measuring bumps on the skull, was imported from Vienna in 1832. Hypnotism, then called Mesmerism, after its founder Franz Mesmer, came to New England from France in 1838 and allowed for the alteration of consciousness as a form of parlor entertainment. These systems became indigenized once they had been absorbed into the religious framework of American folk psychology as they were taken up by popular culture. Collectively they provided an inner language, a cognitive map of the territory, and mind-body techniques for the exploration of personal consciousness. Educated readers became extensively involved with these psychospiritual systems, and entrepreneurs mined them for all the commercial value they were worth.

By the mid-19th century, nostrum vendors, traveling mesmerists, trance speakers, and mental healers crisscrossed the continent on a nationwide lecture circuit connected by a network of underground newspapers. Miraculous healings were reported in these papers.

Individual healers such as Phineas Parkhurst Quimby and Andrew Jackson Davis claimed inordinate powers, cured thousands, and had many followers.

Theosophy developed after the Civil War, bringing to the folk culture important tools for self-knowledge. The Christian Science church, which brought us *The Christian Science Monitor,* continues as a strong voice for spiritual healing in a blatantly scientific and skeptical age. New Thought produced the Unity School of Christianity, Divine Science, and the Today Church, all unique expressions of American religious life that blend spiritual development with material prosperity. The Theosophical Society inspired the esoteric teachings of Alice Bailey, the Waldorf Schools of Rudolf Steiner, and the remarkable educational ministry of Jiddu Krishnamurti, a native-born Indian philosopher trained in the spiritual teachings of the East, who became an important influence on the modern American counterculture movement.

THE TRANSCENDENTALISTS

A third phase of the American visionary tradition centered around Ralph Waldo Emerson, Henry David Thoreau, and the Concord Transcendentalists. From the spiritual contemplation of the Transcendentalists came the idea that God speaks directly to us through nature. Thus, knowledge of the working of the mind, the preservation of the environment, and the internal awakening of the spiritual sense became the goals of successive generations of readers who followed them. Through the Transcendentalists a body of writing soon developed depicting this spiritualized folk psychology in terms of a coherent and inspired popular philosophy. Meanwhile, numerous writers such as Margaret Fuller, Louisa May Alcott, and Nathanial Hawthorne helped a new literary genre emerge that was for the first time identified as uniquely American.

Through them, innovative educational experiments in character development were also undertaken. The editors of the Transcendentalist publication *The Dial* introduced American readers to the ideas of Hindu, Buddhist, and Confucian philosophy. Margaret Fuller helped launch the women's movement with her conversations, which invited intelligent women together to discuss the most controversial questions of the day. Both Frank Sanborn and Bronson Alcott started schools to teach Transcendentalist ideas to young children. James Freeman Clarke wrote a best-selling book called *Self-Culture,*

By the time of the American Revolution, spiritual communities...had become a permanent part of the American landscape.

---

which blended the teachings of phrenology with Transcendentalism.

The great Emerson wrote on the Oversoul, while Thoreau awakened us to a consciousness of the American wilderness. In all, they defined a popular psychospiritual philosophy of the era that persists to this day.

SCIENTIFIC PSYCHOTHERAPY AND THE RELIGIOUS PSYCHOLOGIES

In the fourth phase of the American visionary tradition an attempt was made, using the objective techniques of the fledgling mental sciences, to investigate and interpret this folk psychology and to abstract from it what could be empirically verified. Physicians, astronomers, physicists, and psychologists, largely from the ranks of the American Association for the Advancement of Science and from Harvard University, banded together to form the American Society for Psychical Research. Their express purpose was to test the claims of the spiritualists and mental healers using the most advanced techniques of scientific experimentation. While they did not confirm the existence of life after death, the most important result of their investigation was an understanding of dynamic principles of the subconscious. Their discoveries led to the development of the so-called Boston School of Psychotherapy around figures such as William James, Richard Cabot, and James Jackson Putnam.

The Boston School of Psychotherapy was essentially defined by an important cycle of events. First, techniques of hypnosis, crystal gazing, and automatic writing borrowed from the mental healers were tested in the university laboratory for their ability to induce and take away neurotic symptoms by suggestion. Under the name of psychotherapeutics, these techniques were then adapted in the outpatient departments of local hospitals in the treatment of the psychoneuroses. As a result, Boston became the center of developments in scientific psychotherapy in the English-speaking world between 1889 and 1920 and was known for its major contributions to the development of one-to-one psychotherapy, group psychotherapy, psychiatric and medical social work, and more.

At the same time, a wave of popular religious psychotherapies also resulted from the new medical psychology. The Emmanuel Movement, which began in Boston in 1906 in the Episcopal church, blended the techniques of scientific psychotherapy with Christian teachings of character development. Frank Buchman's Oxford Group, which started in Hartford, Connecticut, a little later, incorporated dynamic conceptions of the subconscious with the methods of public testimony and automatic writing to bring on transcendent awakening. By the 1930s these efforts helped to set in motion historical conditions that led to the development of Alcoholics Anonymous and, later, other 12-Step programs.

PSYCHOANALYSIS

A fifth phase of the American visionary tradition was the era dominated by psychoanalysis. In this period, more than a half century passed during which the reality of the transcendent was almost completely denied by established institutions of Western civilization. This denial was encouraged in no small measure by scientific, technical, and economic advances in American culture. While psychodynamic ideas were kept alive within psychoanalysis, the ethic of transcendence was driven underground, where it was nurtured at the popular level of folk psychology. Asian spiritual teachers such as Jiddu Krishnamurti, Georges Gurdjieff, and Paramahansa Yogananda occasionally appeared on the scene and attracted small but appreciative audiences. Psychics such as Minna Crandon, Arthur Ford, and Edgar Cayce became well-known and continued to stimulate a burgeoning psychic underground. This was also the era of Norman Vincent Peale and his power of positive thinking, as well as Napolean Hill, who adapted New Thought techniques to prosperity in business. Outwardly, however, psychoanalysis continued to prevail in the arena of American high culture, eventually becoming influential enough to control almost all clinical teaching in psychology and psychiatry between 1945 and 1964.

But psychoanalysis also had its own underground. The German psychoanalytic émigré Wilhelm Reich developed radical theories linking sexual liberation to political reform. His ideas of orgone energy, while too extreme for Freud, led to Reichian body work, which became an important part of the 1960s counterculture. Carl Gustav Jung, who propounded a depth psychology based on the idea of a collective unconscious, joined Freud briefly but broke with him in 1912. Jung's ideas later became a major influence on the counterculture psychotherapies. Another unorthodox voice was Victor Frankl, who came out of the Nazi concentration camps and declared that psychoanalysis was irrelevant to a full understanding of human experience because it had no spiritual dimension. His antidote was existential psychoanalysis, which became a moving force behind the development of humanistic psychology. Still, another voice was Erik Erikson, a pioneer in child psychoanalysis who transformed Freud's ideas by emphasizing the social aspects of identity and by extending the

explanatory power of psychoanalysis across the entire life span. In fact, his psychology became most emblematic of the American brand of psychoanalysis practiced today.

THE COUNTER-CULTURE PSYCHOTHERAPIES

A sixth phase of the American visionary tradition dawned with the counterculture movement of the 1960s. During

---

A body of writing soon developed depicting this spiritualized folk psychology in terms of a coherent and inspired popular philosophy.

---

this period, successive generations of young people experienced a collective opening of the doors of perception, initiated largely by psychedelic drugs that first made their way into the folk culture through the CIA and other branches of the American intelligence community. The CIA had developed psychedelics as a so-called truth serum to disorganize and break down enemy agents. Many of the psychiatrists who worked with them were interested in these chemicals because their effects seemed to mimic psychosis. The folk culture, however, showed that they could be used for the expansion of consciousness. Through this younger generation of psychonauts, modern depth-psychology met boiling undercurrents of the American visionary tradition, and psychedelic drugs soon replaced psychoanalysis as the chief bridge mediating inner and outer realities in popular folk culture.

While it has been generally recognized that traditional religious institutions currently have a considerably diminished impact in modern society, the scientific outlook that replaced traditional religious forms has also shown itself to be inadequate in addressing vital dimensions of human experience. At the same time, the nascent folk psy-

chology within the alternative reality tradition emerged as a new cultural force, reawakening widespread interest at the popular level in the transcendent through a science of consciousness. Holistic health, alternative medicine, altered states of consciousness, and new conceptions of personality became the vogue.

As this subculture matured, psychedelics, in turn, were largely displaced by meditation and spiritual practice. Still grossly misunderstood by the reigning pundits of high culture and the various government drug czars, a remarkable transformation and collective self-healing was being undertaken. A spiritual psychology emerged which acknowledged that once one had fixed the vision of higher consciousness before the mind through psychedelics, one had to begin working on the realization of this vision over a lifetime. Self-renewal, periods of ascetic discipline, the re-evaluation of relationships, purification of the body, stints of selfless service, a sense of nurturing the earth, and the polishing of consciousness were ideals that replaced psychedelics and quickly became part of a permanent lifestyle change for many young people of the postwar generation.

Within this milieu, a psychotherapeutic counterculture emerged. Humanistic psychology, originally an intellectual movement within academic psychology led by such lights as Carl Rogers and Abraham Maslow, conceived a new scientific model of the person, based not on psychopathology or statistical normality but on positive concepts of health and growth. Next, transpersonal psychology, devoted to understanding states of consciousness, grew out of the humanistic psychology movement. Soon, a network of holistic growth centers emerged offering a smorgasbord of meditation, body work, and expressive and creative arts therapies. A flood of new spiritual teachers from non-Western religions also appeared on the American scene and catalyzed this process.

Subsequently, more attention has been devoted to the relationship between the mind and the body and between ordinary consciousness and spiritual awakening. This holistic way of viewing reality has produced widespread interest in the healthful effects of acupuncture, hypnosis, yoga, meditation, and biofeedback. It has spawned new interest in non-Western systems of healing, and it has drawn our attention to such new categories as subtle energies, holistic health, physics and consciousness, and mind-body interaction. Perhaps the most heretical field from the standpoint of orthodox science is psychoneuroimmunology, the possibility that through relaxation techniques and the right kind of guided mental imagery the mind can influence the body's immune system.

These developments were also accompanied by major political and social changes that also came to the surface in the 1960s. The civil rights movement, the women's movement, a sexual revolution, and protests against the immorality of the Vietnam War all intermixed. Issues of free speech and the pursuit of spiritual experience independent of control or coercion by traditional institutions became the focus of a new politics of consciousness.

Based on these experiences, successive generations of young Americans—beginning with those youthful participants of the 1960s counterculture who are now well into middle age—have launched a new ethic that has become a significant and apparently permanent force for social change.

AN ETHIC OF THE 21ST CENTURY

The most significant aspect of the present changes occurring in American social consciousness is the radical difference between the myths guiding the different generations. By this I mean that technology and the rational tradition of the intellect have spawned a milieu in which each generation now differs from its immediate predecessor not arithmetically but exponentially. People born before 1945 simply do not think the same way as those born after. Unless they are truly united in the life of the spirit, it is as if they live in completely different worlds, although sharing the same physical space.

Similarly, those born after the advent of the modern computer revolution even in their youth have skills far beyond the first children of the Atomic Age. They also confront social problems as their first and most immediate experience, problems that may be far more dire and immediately life-threatening than previous generations. Children

---

The young men and women of tomorrow will continue to foster attitudes profoundly distrustful of standardization, bigness, mass registrations, and oaths of fealty to fossilized ideologies.

---

born now will be the adults of a new millennium. Their joys, disappointments, and opportunities will surely be unlike anything we are presented with today. Even though we may live to see that same world, we will not see it with their eyes.

For this new generation we have the *Common Boundary Graduate Education Guide*. First published in 1991, it was popular enough to go into the present second edition. While the information it contains will need to be continually updated, it is a handbook for the student of the future, and the educational ideal it embodies is an ethic of the 21st century. It forecasts a worldview that will be grounded in the transcendent, yet at the same time demand that integrated personalities master the details of technological progress. It tells us that the new view will be pluralistic and multicultural in outlook, at once inward and at the same time tremendously appreciative of native differences between individuals, family, and clans. It tells us that the young men and women of tomorrow will continue to foster attitudes profoundly distrustful of standardization, bigness, mass registrations, and oaths of

fealty to fossilized ideologies. Moreover, it fosters an outlook that is set on positioning science and technology in their proper place: not as the main reasons for living, but as adjuncts to the continuing mystery of human experience, as tools for human growth, especially in the sense of spiritual development.

This volume, which has been so painstakingly prepared, is a doorway to the possibility of self-realization. Pointing toward avant-garde training programs in graduate and professional education, spiritual practice, innovative therapeutic methods, the expressive and creative arts, spiritual retreats, and other resources, it represents one means by which the inward process of personality transformation itself is gradually transforming traditional ideas about learning in Western society.

—Eugene Taylor holds an A.B. and M.A. in psychology and comparative religions and a Ph.D. in the history and philosophy of psychology. He is a Lecturer in Psychiatry at Harvard Medical School, Consultant in the History of Psychiatry at the Massachusetts General Hospital, and author of William James on Exceptional Mental States *(University of Massachusetts Press/Amherst, 1984). He is also the director of the Cambridge Institute of Psychology and Religion and teaches the history of psychology course at Saybrook Institute. His new book on the American visionary tradition will appear through Addison-Wesley in the spring of 1995.*

SECTION I

MENTAL HEALTH DEGREE PROGRAMS WITH A SPIRITUAL COMPONENT

In This Section:

➤ COUNSELING

➤ EXISTENTIAL AND HUMANISTIC PSYCHOLOGY

➤ HOLISTIC NURSING

➤ TRANSPERSONAL AND SPIRITUALLY ORIENTED PSYCHIATRY

➤ RESIDENTIAL PSYCHOLOGY DEGREE PROGRAMS

➤ NONRESIDENTIAL PSYCHOLOGY DEGREE PROGRAMS

➤ SPIRITUALLY SENSITIVE SOCIAL WORK

➤ SUBSTANCE ABUSE COUNSELING

CALIFORNIA INSTITUTE OF INTEGRAL STUDIES

I
N RECENT YEARS MANY MENTAL HEALTH GRADUATE SCHOOLS HAVE RESPONDED TO THE DEMAND FOR GREATER ACKNOWLEDGMENT OF SPIRI-tuality in their psychotherapy training programs, just as in the past many theological schools have added mental health components to their curricu-la. In theological education, the spiritual and psychological interface is known as pastoral psychology. Similarly, each of the different mental health disciplines refers to this nexus by a particular title. The most numerous and highly developed psychospiritual programs began in the field of psychology, mostly in the form of alternative schools offering "transpersonal psychology" graduate degrees. Next came programs in "holistic nursing," "spiritually sen-sitive social work," and most recently, "transpersonal psychiatry."

As subsequent sections explain, what was once conventional may now be considered alternative, and vice-versa. Before allopathic medicine became the standard Western medical model, for example, the field of medicine in the United States included an array of healing modalities such as homeopathy, which is now classified as an alternative medicine. Social work began as a religiously motivated and affiliated service, but removed spiritual topics from its standardized curriculum in the last several decades, and just recently is beginning to return to its spiritual roots. Psychology, seeking to be more like the physical and biological sciences, separated from its origins in philosophy, theology, and the study of the mind in the 19th century. However, because of the rise of transpersonal-oriented graduate schools in the last two decades, alternative psychology has provided the leadership that has brought a spiritual dimension back into the professional study of mental health in the United States.

Perhaps this shifting within the mental health field shouldn't be surprising: History has shown time and again that just as a culture's worldview changes over time, so does its system of education. Modern models of education have generally excluded spiritual values (e.g., subjectivity, higher meaning, sacredness). It is no wonder, then, that alternative educational models in general not only threaten this society's modern pedagogy but also call into question the epistemological foundations on which our culture's scientific worldview is based.

As we approach the 21st century,

these conventional and alternative models—represented by individual activists, social movements, and lobbying organizations—will in all likelihood continue to compete for cultural dominance that brings with it prestige, endowments, and high-paying and respected jobs. The American Psychological Association (APA), for example, in its effort to compete on an equal footing with psychiatry, continues to lobby state legislatures to require standardized training programs in psychology that emphasize (like psychiatry) the empirical dimensions of human experience. Some psychologists are even beginning to lobby for the right to prescribe medication. Similarly, professional mental health counselors seek the same advantages as psychologists and social workers. In the coming years, the federal government will become a larger player in the health-care marketplace. The impact of this new factor will be significant, but in ways that are difficult to predict at this time (see page 167).

In deciding between a mainstream or an alternative program, you are (to a certain degree) being asked to consider your own values; the audience you want to address; and the position from which you want to influence, help, and interact with others. As Jim Fadiman, Ph.D., elucidates in his psychology subchapter introduction, psychospiritual graduate programs fall on a continuum between more and less established programs. It is up to you to find out where you want to situate yourself. Following an alternative educational route doesn't always mean you are less likely to achieve your goals or get a particular job; instead, it may

LICENSURE ISSUES

LICENSURE, THIRD-PARTY PAYMENTS INSURANCE, AND THE ABILITY TO PRACTICE independently vary greatly from state to state. Without even considering how the new health-care reforms will change the mental health field, state and federal laws will continue changing. It is important to learn how the regulations (applicable to your state of residency) affect your rights and responsibilities as a prospective practitioner. Contact your state government's mental health regulation agency or, in states that have a more highly developed regulatory system, the certification board for each mental health profession.

require that you demonstrate your professional competence rather than rely on a conventional program's reputation. However, in so doing, you allow yourself to follow a career path consonant with your most deeply felt values.

COUNSELING

In 1972, the Virginia State Board of Psychologist Examiners sued a professional counselor for conducting a private practice in career counseling (*Weldon v. Psychologist Examiners*), arguing that he was practicing psychology and that the level of formal training needed to do this effectively required at least a doctoral degree. The verdict: unprecedented recognition by the Virginia Supreme Court that counseling was a profession separate from psychology. Since this decision, the American Counseling Association (ACA) has continued to build on the Virginia ruling.

Since its inception in 1952, ACA has brought together professional counselors, counselor educators, and human development specialists; promoted professionalism; and established an independent accrediting body, the Council for Accreditation of Counseling and Related Educational Programs (CACREP). With

PSYCHOTHERAPISTS BY THE NUMBERS

PROFESSION	NUMBER PRACTICING	NUMBER OF GRADUATES/YR.	NUMBER OF PROGRAMS	MEDIAN FEE
SOCIAL WORKERS	80,000	11,500	106	$ 75
CLINICAL PSYCHOLOGISTS	45,000	1,300	174	90
PROFESSIONAL COUNSELORS	42,000	9,400	230	75
PSYCHIATRISTS	40,000	1,300	199	101
MARRIAGE AND FAMILY THERAPISTS	40,000	n/a	73	80
PSYCHIATRIC NURSES	10,500	643	96	n/a
PASTORAL COUNSELORS	2,100	n/a	104	n/a

Sources: Figures on numbers practicing, graduates, and schools from the respective certifying bodies: American Psychiatric Association, American Psychological Association, Council on Social Work Education, National Association of Social Workers, American Association of Marriage and Family Therapists, American Association of Counseling and Development, American Association of Pastoral Counselors. Figures on nurses from *Mental Health, United States,* 1992, U.S. Department of Health and Human Services. Fees for psychiatrists from *Medical Economics,* April 8, 1991. Fees for others from *Psychotherapy Finances 1992 Survey Report.*

a membership base of approximately 60,000, ACA hopes to widen its scope by inviting similar-minded professions, such as the expressive art therapists, to join its ranks, provided that they meet ACA's education guidelines. ACA also supports the development of a core curriculum of graduate counseling classes, which will help provide prospective practitioners a general counseling foundation on which to build specialized skills (such as school, rehabilitation, or family counseling).

The rift between the American Psychological Association and the American Counseling Association still exists. Their differences, however, seem to be as much political and economic as ideological. The APA tends to support a psychology (and the graduate programs that conform to APA's guidelines) based on the medical model of diagnosis and treatment of disease. The ACA, on the other hand, supports a holistic approach based on a wellness model that includes the diagnosis and treatment of mental and emotional disorders but places more emphasizes on mental *health* than on *illness*.

Nevertheless, the future success of either profession will depend largely on the public's trust in the field's practitioners. In addition, the public may not be willing to pay higher fees for a psychologist who may be more highly trained in academics and research but fails to be sensitive to the humanistic and spiritual dimensions evoked in a client during therapy. According to a recently administered Gallup poll in which 1,000 persons (50 percent male and 50 percent female) were surveyed, 67 percent preferred a professional counselor who recognized the importance of spiritual values and beliefs, and 81 percent preferred to have their own values and beliefs integrated into the counseling process. Yet because state legislatures (indirectly) and insurance companies (directly) regulate which types of mental health professionals receive reimbursement—and in light of APA's defensive reaction against counseling's continued growth—it is not difficult to predict that the struggle for legitimacy will continue to revolve around political and economic issues more than ideology and therapeutic efficacy.

The ACA's 16 divisions confirm the growing variety within this profession. They include institutional, college, school, rehabilitation, multicultural, and religious counseling, as well as counselors in private practice. While individual states with licensing laws for counselors employ various professional titles (such as Licensed Professional Counselor or Licensed Mental Health Counselor), the various degrees and degree programs share a common core curriculum. Approximately 80% of states, plus the District of Columbia, have counseling laws of some kind.

All professional counselors hold at least a master's degree, and most have a B.A. level major in psychology, sociology, or anthropology. Professional counselors provide mental health, rehabilitation, substance abuse, employment, educational, and other counseling services in a variety of settings, including community mental health centers, hospitals, schools, universities, hospices, and government agencies. In 1988, more than two out of three counselors worked in educational settings, mostly in secondary schools. Trends are showing an increase in noneducational settings such as community-based organizations and city agencies.

Whether you choose to attend an accredited program or not, ACA membership requires course work above and beyond the minimum standards for accreditation and licensure set by each state. The ACA's requirements include a minimum of 60 graduate semester hours, including a master's degree in counseling, both based on CACREP's common standards and course work in various specialty areas. (Contact CACREP for a list of approved training programs.) Most states require two years of post-master's supervised experience and successful completion of a written exam before granting licensure.

According to *Money* magazine (April 1993), the counseling profession will continue to grow by 34%; the magazine also reported an average salary of between $14,000 and $35,000 a year.

ADDITIONAL RESOURCES

Accelerated Development, Inc., (800-222-1166) publishes *Programs and Personnel* (8th edition, $34.95), a resource book written by Joseph Hollis and Richard Wantz that provides a comprehensive listing of both CACREP and CORE accredited and nonaccredited schools. Accelerated Development is also planning to publish a supplement on the counseling profession entitled *Status, Trends and Implications.*

M.F.C.C. INFORMATION

Because California's Marriage, Family and Child Counseling (M.F.C.C.) license is generic, many mental health counselors residing in California with a holistic or transpersonal orientation seek it as a way to become eligible for insurance reimbursement.

Associations

American Association for Marriage and Family Therapy (AAMFT)
1100 17th Street, N.W., 10th Floor
Washington, DC 20036
(202) 452-0109

AAMFT lobbies for the advancement of marriage and family therapy at the federal level. Its membership is approximately 21,000—smaller than CAMFT's membership, which represents M.F.C.C.'s only in the state of California. However, AAMFT's numbers are misleadingly small because other licensed therapists (such as clinical social workers, psychiatrists, and psychologists) may practice marriage and family therapy but not join AAMFT. In other words, its not just family therapists who can practice family therapy.

American Counseling Association (ACA)
5999 Stevenson Avenue
Alexandria, VA 22304
(703) 823-9800

Founded in 1952, the ACA is a nonprofit professional and educational organization dedicated to the growth and enhancement of the counseling profession. The association is the largest international counseling organization in existence, with a growing membership of more than 60,000 counselors and human development specialists. The mission of the association is "to enhance human development throughout the life span and to promote the counseling profession." ACA also publishes numerous periodicals. The editors recommend contacting ACA for information about the often confusing licensure laws in your state and about the complex relationship between licensure and the national certification board. Within the Mental Health Counselors Division of the ACA, there is a religion and mental health interest group.

Association of Schools of Allied Health Professions (ASAHP)
1730 M Street, N.W., Suite 500
Washington, DC 20036
(202) 243-4848

ASAHP is a nonprofit professional association for administrators, educators, health care providers, and others who are concerned with critical issues in allied health. Allied health professions, according to ASAHP, include art, dance, music and creative arts therapists; substance abuse counselors; and general counselors. The association serves as a forum to link leaders in allied health fields with state and national policy makers in government, business, and industry. ASAHP's diverse membership includes educational institutions, professional organizations, and individuals. It has no formal relationship to the American Counseling Association.

California Association of Marriage and Family Therapists (CAMFT)
7901 Raytheon Road
San Diego, CA 92111-1606
(619) 293-2638

CAMFT is an independent professional organization that lobbies for the advancement of the marriage and family therapy (M.F.C.C.) license in the state of California. With approximately 23,000 members, it is the largest representative of counselors in the United States. CAMFT is independent of the ACA and the AAMFT. It will send you an inclusive list of California state-approved M.F.C.C. programs for $5.

Organizations
Commission on Rehabilitation Counselor Certification (CRCC)
1835 Rohlwing Road, Suite E
Rolling Meadows, IL 60008
(708) 394-2104

The CRCC establishes and oversees national certification requirements for professional counselors who specialize in rehabilitation counseling.

Council for Accreditation of Counseling and Related Educational Programs (CACREP)
5999 Stevenson Avenue
Alexandria, VA 22304
(703) 823-9800 (ext. 301)

CACREP grants accredited status to mas-ter's and doctoral programs in community mental health, school counseling, and marriage and family counseling/therapy. Formed as a corporate affiliate of the American Counseling Association in 1981, CACREP's mission coincides with that of the ACA: to promote the advancement of quality educational programs. It is recognized by the Council on Postsecondary Accreditation (COPA) as a specialized accrediting body. Contact CACREP for a list of accredited schools, as well as a state-by-state listing of necessary credentials for licensing.

Council on Rehabilitation Education (CORE)
P.O. Box 1680
Champaign, IL 61824
(217) 333-6688

Like CACREP, CORE is recognized by COPA and accredits master's degree programs focusing on rehabilitation counseling. It publishes a list of approved programs.

National Board for Certified Counselors (NBCC)
3-D Terrace Way
Greensboro, NC 27403
(910) 547-0607

Recognized by the National Commission for Certifying Agencies, NBCC is an independent nonprofit organization that certifies individual counselors; however, it works closely with the American Counseling Association. It grants the the following titles: National Certified Counselor, National Certified Career Counselor, National Certified School Counselor, National Certified Gerontological Counselor, and Certified Clinical Mental Health Counselor.

Periodicals
Each division of ACA publishes a newsletter; in addition, ACA publishes a total of 14 journals applicable to each respective division. The most relevant to the psychospiritual field are listed below.

American Counselor
American Counseling Association
Quarterly; $18

Counseling and Values
Association for Religious and Value Issues in Counseling (a division of ACA)
American Counseling Association
Three times a year; $12

Guidepost
American Counseling Association
Monthly; $30

Journal of Counseling and Development
American Counseling Association
Bimonthly; $40

EXISTENTIAL AND HUMANISTIC PSYCHOLOGY
Existentialism encompasses several philosophical systems, all centered on the individual's relationship to reality and the conditions of existence. Although philosophers as disparate as Karl Jaspers, Martin Heidegger, Friedrich Nietzsche, and Jean-Paul Sartre are the most famous existentialists, the movement was actually inspired in the mid-1800s by a Danish philosopher named Søren Kierkegaard. Kierkegaard criticized the abstract metaphysical philosophy of his day (as developed by Friedrich Hegel, a German philosopher) and rebuked the complacency of the Danish church. His most lasting contribution was the recognition that the profound ethical and religious demands confronting every individual cannot be sustained by only an abstract intellectual framework but require the subjective involvement of the individual. The searching questions that Kierkegaard posits in regard to the nature of human existence serve as the modern foundation of existentialism. Philosophers who consider the religious implications of existentialism include Jaspers, Martin Buber, Gabriel Marcel, and theologian Paul Tillich.

Existential-oriented therapy addresses how individuals relate to the world and, given the societal realities of the 20th century, how they cope with the debilitating effects of loss of meaning in their lives. Even though not all forms of existential philosophy are considered humanistic, therapists who describe themselves as existentialists frequently hold humanistic values such as honoring the spiritual and mysterious elements of human life. (See page 18 for a brief description of humanistic psychology.) Prolific writers in the existential/humanistic field include Rollo May,

Ph.D., Professor Irving Yalom, M.D., and James F.T. Bugental, Ph.D.

Just as most Jungian thinking and training in the United States takes place outside the university system (with the exception of Pacifica Graduate Institute), so has much of existential psychology. Only a few graduate programs in the United States provide training in existential-oriented psychotherapy. Another training option is to complement your graduate education with a postgraduate nondegree training program in existential therapy. For reasons that are not clear, professionals interested in existential training are psychologists and social workers more often than psychiatrists or psychoanalysts.

Many psychologists who have an existential or humanistic orientation belong to the Association of Humanistic Psychology (AHP) or the Division 32 of the American Psychological Association (APA), or both. It is within this division that transpersonal psychologists have been invited to present papers at the annual APA conventions. This is quite fitting because the Association for Transpersonal Psychology has its roots in the AHP. The AHP publishes a list of graduate schools that offer courses and degrees in humanistic psychology ($5).

Associations and Organizations

Association of Humanistic Psychology
See Residential Psychology Degree Programs.

Bugental Psychology Corporation
24 Elegant Tern Road
Novato, CA 94949-6619
(415) 883-1412
Founded by James F.T. Bugental, Ph.D., the corporation offers programs to practicing mental health professionals and advanced graduate students with some clinical experience. Weekend workshop titles have included "An Introduction to Existential-Humanistic Psychotherapy," "The Art of the Psychotherapists," and "Reclaiming Our Human Roots."

Center for Existential Therapy (CET)
1738 Union Street
San Francisco, CA 94123
(415) 567-5021
The CET, founded in 1987 by Kirk J. Schneider, Ph.D., promotes existential

practice, consultation, and dissemination of referral information about existential-oriented training opportunities.

Division of Humanistic Psychology (Division 32)
American Psychological Association
750 First Street, N.E.
Washington, DC 20002
(202) 336-5500
This division publishes the *Humanistic Psychologist.*

Society for Existential Analysis
Emmy van Deurzen-Smith, Director
Regent's College
Inner Circle
Regent's Park, London NW1 4NS
England

Periodicals

Dialogues: Therapeutic Applications of Existential Philosophy
Glenn Hammel, Ph.D., Editor
937 Shore Point Court, Suite G-313
Alameda, CA 94501
(510) 522-8863
This publication represents the work of the California School of Professional Psychology students.

Humanistic Psychologist
See Periodicals under Residential Psychology Degree Programs.

Journal of the British Society for Phenomenology
Haigh and Hochland Ltd.
The Precinct Center
Oxford Road, Manchester 13
England

Journal of Humanistic Psychology
See Periodicals under Residential Psychology Degree Programs.

Journal of Pastoral Counseling
See Periodicals under Pastoral Counseling.

Journal of Phenomenological Psychology
Humanities Press
165 First Avenue
Atlantic Highlands, NJ 07717
(908) 872-1441
Semiannual; $40

Journal of the Society for Existential Analysis
Contact the Society for Existential Analysis.

Theoretical and Philosophical Psychology
Division 24 of APA
Contact the American Psychological Association.

GRADUATE PROGRAMS
Center for Humanistic Studies
See Residential Psychology Degree Programs.

Duquesne University
Graduate School of Arts and Sciences
Graduate Program in Psychology
210 College Hall
Pittsburgh, PA 15282
(412) 396-6000
The program focuses on insights established by existential and phenomenological philosophy.
General Information: Private, Catholic (nonsectarian)
Degrees Offered: M.A.; Ph.D.
Programs: Psychology
Admission Requirements: Bachelor's degree; GRE; letters of recommendation; personal essay
Application Deadline: March 15 (M.A.); February 1 (Ph.D.)
Contact Person: Director of Admissions
Tuition: $372/semester hour credit
Accreditation: MSACS; Pennsylvania State Board of Education
Year Established: 1878
Faculty: 7 full-time

Naropa Institute
See Residential Psychology Degree Programs.

Saybrook Institute
See Nonresidential Psychology Degree Programs.

Seattle University
Psychology Department
Broadway and Madison
Seattle, WA 98122-4460
(206) 296-5400; (800) 426-7123
General Information: Private, Jesuit, residential
Degrees offered: M.A.
Programs: Existential-phenomenological psychology
Admission Requirements: Bachelor's degree; GPA > 3.0; letters of recommendation; relevant experience
Application Deadline: February 1
Contact Person: Director of Admissions
Tuition: $293/credit hour
Accreditation: Meets Washington State's counseling requirements laws
Year Established: 1981
Faculty: 7 full-time

Sonoma State University
Department of Counseling
1801 East Cotati Avenue
Rohnert Park, CA 94928-3609
(707) 664-2544
See Residential Psychology Degree Programs.

Temple University
See Residential Psychology Degree Programs.

Union Institute
See Nonresidential Psychology Degree Programs.

University of Alberta
Department of Educational Psychology
6-102 Education North
Edmonton, Alberta
Canada T6G 2G5
(403) 492-5245
The members of the basic educational psychology area have a variety of interests, including existential-phenomenological psychology, cross-cultural psychology, and Asian psychology.
General Information: Public, residential
Degrees Offered: M.Ed.; Ph.D.
Programs: Educational psychology
Admission Requirements: Bachelor's degree; letter of recommendation
Application Deadline: February 1
Contact Person: Director of Admissions
Tuition: Contact department
Accreditation: Contact department
Year Established: 1908
Faculty: 40 full-time

University of Dallas
Psychology Department
Robert Kugelmann, Ph.D., Director
1845 East Northgate
Irving, TX 75062
(214) 721-5349
The Department of Psychology is a member of the Consortium of Diversified Psychology Programs. It is in the process of developing a phenomenologically oriented counseling program. Contact the department for up-to-date information.

University of Humanistic Studies
See Residential Psychology Degree Programs.

West Georgia College
See Residential Psychology Degree Programs.

Westchester Institute for Training in Psychoanalysis and Psychotherapy
2 Sarles Street
P.O. Box 89
Mount Kisco, NY 10549
(914) 666-0163

NONDEGREE PROGRAMS
Institute for Dialogical Psychotherapy
See Nondegree Training Programs.

HOLISTIC NURSING
In the last decade, the nursing profession has changed dramatically, and nurses' roles have adapted to these changes. Today, a nurse can exercise her or his own authority and some believe that nurse-run clinics may be on the cutting edge of health care. This emerging role reflects the changing relations between physicians, nurses, patients, and other members of health-care teams. These changes are due to such factors as advances in technology, efforts to restrain escalating costs, confusing payment or reimbursement mechanisms, and changes in patients' expectations, to name just a few.

Equally important in bringing about these changes are social and cultural factors such as the impact of the women's movement and the growing interest in holistic health and spiritual development. Both of these movements recognize the feminine values of relatedness, receptivity, and body consciousness. These values are being explored and legitimized at a time when many are feeling the limits of linear science and reductionism. For example, despite the successes of science, too much separation exists between the world of the health-care team and that of the patient. This has led nurses in the past 20 years to reconsider the "mystery" involved in the practice of nursing.

The development of new educational programs have helped facilitate the reemergence of the nurse as an independent healer. These programs, which began in the 1960s, include the clinical nurse specialist (formerly known as a psychiatric nurse) and the independent nurse practitioner. Each of these fields expands the services and recognition of the nurse in such a way that she or he does not need to leave the profession (i.e., to become a physician) in order to further develop skills and to make more of a professional contribution. These changes give the nurse increased responsibilities, including more managerial functions and more upward mobility and prestige within the health care field. Specifically, there are four functional areas that have expanded the field of nursing: clinical expertise (patient care), patient education, case consultation, and research. By adding the capacity for making assessments and diagnoses, nurses can function more independently.

FORMAL NURSING EDUCATION
There are two avenues to becoming a registered nurse (R.N.). The original path is through a hospital-based training program. The second and longer but higher paid option consists of an academic-based program, which combines hospital (clinical) work and college courses, and leads to a bachelor of nursing science degree (B.S.N.). Both avenues require graduates to sit for a state registered nurse (R.N.) licensing examination (called the National Council Licensure Examination for Registered Nurses).

Nurses may enhance their professionalism in any of several ways. The most common way involves academically based graduate and postgraduate studies, such as those leading to certification as a clinical nurse specialist or independent nurse practitioner. The primary difference between the graduates of these two specialty programs is the ability of the nurse practitioner to prescribe medication, where congruent with state law.

HOLISTIC NURSING
Nursing has always possessed a holistic potential, but scientific advances of the 20th century overshadowed this orientation. The idea of treating the whole patient was in vogue several centuries ago. Florence Nightingale's approach to nursing, for example, was based on what

PSYCHIATRIC MENTAL HEALTH CLINICAL NURSE SPECIALISTS

SINCE 1880 THERE HAS BEEN IN THE UNITED STATES A SPECIALTY KNOWN AS PSYCHIATRIC MENTAL HEALTH (PMH) NURSING. THE PRACtice of psychiatric nursing is conducted at both the basic and the advanced level. Registered nurses with a bachelor's degree in nursing (B.S.N.) who go on to obtain a master of science in nursing (M.S.N.) may specialize in psychiatric mental health nursing. Graduates, after receiving post-master's supervised clinical practice, can take a national examination to be certified as a specialist in adult or child and adolescent psychiatric and mental health problems. Psychiatric-mental health clinical nurse specialists function as psychotherapists and, in some states, have the authority to prescribe medication. They are qualified to practice independently and to offer primary mental health care services in a variety of settings, including agencies, communities, homes, hospitals, or private practice offices. Some of these nurses also prepare themselves as independent nurse practitioners so that they can offer general health care to special populations such as the chronically mentally ill.

Advanced-practice PMH nurses may focus their practice on different populations such as children and adolescents, older adults, and families; on specific mental health problems such as violence, substance abuse, and chronic mental illness; or on different aspects of mental health such as health promotion, illness prevention, and rehabilitation. Some PMH clinical nurse specialists act as consultation-liaison nurses to medical staff who work on hospital medical wards. delivering either direct mental health services or consultation to medical staff.

There are two principal arrangements for the clinical practice of psychiatric nursing: organized care settings and self-employment. Organized care implies an inpatient or outpatient setting; nurses are paid for their services on a salaried, contractual, or fee-for-service basis. Self-employed nurses (or private practice nurses), on the other hand, generally offer outpatient services directly to the consumer, and payment arrangements include direct fee-for-service or reimbursement through third-party payments from an insurance or a managed care company.

The average annual salary for an experienced PMH nurse is about $50,000. The typical private-practice fee varies in different geographic areas, but the average fee is approximately $75 per session.

—*Ernest D. Lapierre, Ph.D., chief nurse at the National Institute of Mental Health's Saint Elizabeth's Center, and Carolyn V. Billings, M.S.N, R.N., C.S., a psychiatric mental health clinical nurse specialist in private practice and the secretary of APNA, contributed to this article.*

we now call holistic principles. Nightingale taught that physical health could not be separated from a balance of psychological and spiritual factors any more than it could be separated from a social context. She was a master practitioner of her own philosophy; for instance, within one two-month period, she reduced the death rate of soldiers in the Crimean War from 42 percent to 2 percent. Holism in nursing has come full circle in the last few decades, with the current interest growing from general clinical nursing programs rather than from psychiatric nursing. This is surprising because one might think that the latter's emphasis on the mind-body interface would have made it the more likely candidate.

Just as health care in general has developed alternative modes of treatment, it is now possible for R.N.s to obtain clinical training in biofeedback, stress reduction, therapeutic touch, healing touch, guided imagery, and massage therapy—all of which are holistic in approach. Also, because nurses have always been legally allowed to touch their patients, they are more receptive to using such complimentary techniques as therapeutic touch than other disciplines. These subjects are generally offered through continuing education programs which, as in other health-care professions, are required to maintain licensure.

Those interested in enhancing their understanding and practice of holistic care may find the American Holistic Nurses Association's offerings beneficial. In order to promote the practice and philosophical premises of holistic care, the association is currently engaged in developing a certifying process specific to the practice of holistic nursing. At the end of this chapter there is a listing of educational resources for continuing nursing education, including programs that place emphasis on holistic principles.

—*This introduction was written by Cara Barker, Ph.D., R.N., C.S., who has dedicated herself to integrating holistic practices into the healing process, first as a health educator, then as a nurse, and currently as a health psychologist.*

ADDITIONAL RESOURCES
Holistic Nursing: A Handbook for Practice
Aspen Publishers, Inc.
(800) 638-8437
Written by Barbara Montgomery Dossey, Lynn Keegan, Cathie E. Guzzetta, and Leslie Gooeding Kolkmeier.

Associations
American Holistic Nurses Association (AHNA)
4101 Lake Boone Trail, Suite 201
Raleigh, NC 27607
(919) 787-5181
Incorporated in 1981, AHNA is a membership, advocacy, and training organization that promotes holistic nursing. It pub-

lishes the *Journal of Holistic Nursing* and the newsletter *Beginnings*.

American Nurses Association (ANA)
600 Maryland Avenue, S.W., Suite 100
Washington, DC 20024-2571
(202) 554-4444

The ANA is a membership and advocacy organization. It represents 2.2 million registered nurses across the United States.

American Psychiatric Nurses Association (APNA)
1200 19th Street, N.W., Suite 300
Washington, DC 20036-2401
(202) 857-1133

The mission of APNA is to promote excellence in psychiatric nursing and to improve psychiatric and mental health care for individuals, families, groups, and communities. APNA is an organizational affiliate of the American Nurses Association.

Homeopathic Nurses Association (HNA)
103 Country Club Road
Greenfield, MA 01301
(413) 773-0888

Established in 1986, the HNA promotes the advancement and refinement of homeopathic nursing.

International Association for Human Caring (IAHC)
University of Texas at Tyler
Division of Nursing
3900 University Boulevard
Tyler, TX 75701
Correspondence offered only by mail.

The central purpose of the IAHC is to serve as a scholarly forum for nurses to advance their knowledge of care and caring within the nursing discipline.

National Association of Nurse Massage Therapists (NANMT)
147 Windward Drive
Osprey, FL 34229
(813) 966-6288

Founded in 1987, NANMT is a nonprofit advocacy organization of nurses who practice massage and other therapeutic forms of bodywork.

National League for Nursing (NLN)
350 Hudson Street
New York, NY 10014
(212) 989-9393

The NLN accredits schools of nursing, sets standards of nursing education, and advances the nursing profession at the local, national, and international levels. It is also involved in promoting a "national health plan on behalf of the nursing community that assures affordable quality care to all Americans."

Nurse Healers and Professional Associates (NHPA)
175 Fifth Avenue, Suite 2755
New York, NY 10010
(212) 886-3776

Incorporated in 1978, NHPA is a membership and advocacy group, as well as a resource for health-care professionals interested in the Krieger/Kunz model of therapeutic touch (see Subtle Energies under Mind-Body studies).

Organizations

American Nurses Center (ANC)
1101 14th Street, N.W., Suite 700
Washington, DC 20005
(800) 274-4262

Those with a master's degree or doctorate in the clinical specialty of psychiatric mental health nursing may apply for specialty credentials in "adult mental health" nursing.

Center for Healing Arts
9032 North 83rd Street
Scottsdale, AZ 85258
(602) 998-7271

Founded by Wendy Miller, Ph.D., and Cara Barker, Ph.D., R.N., C.S., the center provides program development for health-care professionals, institutions, and patients with special attention paid to the healing potential of the creative process.

Center for Human Caring (CHC)
University of Colorado School of Nursing
4200 East Ninth Avenue, Suite C288
Denver, CO 80262
(303) 270-6157

The CHC provides training information about therapeutic touch (see Subtle Energies under Mind-Body Studies).

Holistic Nursing Consultants
878 Paseo del Sur
Santa Fe, NM 87501
(505) 986-8188

Nurses Christian Fellowship (NCF)
P.O. Box 7895
Madison, WI 53707-7895
(608) 274-9001

The NCF describes itself and its mission in the following way: "Since 1948, NCF has brought the ministry of Jesus Christ to nursing students and professionals. By serving the needs of the whole person—spiritual, emotional, professional, ethical, and intellectual—NCF strives to develop nurses who are disciples of Christ, influencing their profession for Him."

TRAINING PROGRAMS

Certificate Program in Holistic Nursing
Contact the American Holistic Nurses Association.

This certificate program is a four-phase program following the progression of identification, exploration, application, and integration of holistic nursing concepts into practice.

Healing Touch
Contact the American Holistic Nurses Association.

The association offers a course of study incorporating a variety of basic to advanced healing methods. This program is sequenced in four levels, allowing participants to move from beginner to practitioner, expert, and instructor.

Therapeutic Touch
Center for Human Caring
See Subtle Energies under Mind-Body Studies.

Westbrook University
Programs: Holistic nursing, M.S., Ph.D.
See Nonresidential Psychology Programs.

Periodicals

Advances in Nursing Science
Aspen Publishers, Inc.
1600 Research Boulevard
Rockville, MD 20850
(800) 638-8437
Quarterly; $60

American Nurse
Contact the American Nurses Association.

Journal of Christian Nursing
P.O. Box 1650
Downers Grove, IL 60515-0780
(708) 964-5700
Quarterly; $17.95

Journal of Holistic Nursing
Sage Publications, Inc.
2455 Teller Road
Newbury Park, CA 91320
(805) 499-0721
Quarterly; $32.40

TRANSPERSONAL AND SPIRITUALLY ORIENTED PSYCHIATRY

Since the days of Carl Jung, who wrote about psychiatry and religion in the 1930s, 1940s, and 1950s, the field of psychiatry has interfaced with issues relevant to religion. In 1961, the Christian Medical and Dental Society formed a psychiatry section that continues to meet during the annual American Psychiatric Association (APA) convention (as does the National Guild for Catholic Psychiatrists). After the formation of the Association for Transpersonal Psychology in 1970, a number of psychiatrists with professional interests in religion or spirituality began to refer to their investigations under the non-sectarian title of transpersonal psychiatry. Transpersonal psychiatry addresses such areas of interest as existential, humanistic, and Jungian therapies; phenomenology; cognitive science; brain research; and the cross-cultural study of consciousness. In addition, transpersonal psychiatry is part of a larger international movement involving interdisciplinary research of non-ordinary states of consciousness achieved through mind-altering techniques such as meditation, biofeedback, and the ingesting of psychoactive substances.

The Food and Drug Administration (FDA) has recently adopted a more open-minded attitude toward the therapeutic application of consciousness-altering substances, and research is currently being conducted on methyleno dioxy methamphetamine (MDMA) at the Harbor-UCLA Medical Center and on dimethyltryptamine (DMT) at the University of New Mexico. A study of the use of lysergic acid diethylamide (LSD) in the treatment of substance abuse has also received preliminary approval from the FDA. The Menninger Clinic in Topeka, Kansas, has been a consistent promoter of transpersonal research, including studies on the relationship between consciousness, mind-body techniques (many of Eastern origin), and optimal health.

Additionally, the importance of non-ordinary states of consciousness is being acknowledged by the traditionally conservative American Psychiatric Association (APA). The fourth edition of its *Diagnostic and Statistical Manual* will include, for the first time, a category for religious and spiritual problems, and the association's 1993 annual meeting featured a dozen presentations on the interface between psychiatry and spirituality. According to Roger Walsh, M.D., professor of psychiatry at the University of California, Irvine, "There is now talk [within some parts of the psychiatric community] of the necessity of a bio-psycho-social-spiritual model or framework to adequately encompass human health and pathology, and to effectively address disorders such as addiction."

Some of the more prolific and noteworthy transpersonal psychiatrists are Jean Bolen, well known for her Jungian writings; Mark Epstein, known for his writing on psychoanalysis and Buddhism; Charles Grob, a leading researcher on the cross-cultural dimensions of psychedelics; Stanislav Grof, a major theorist and researcher; Ann Massion, a researcher of the therapeutic applications of meditation; and Roger Walsh, author and professor at the University of California, Irvine.

A student interested in holistic and transpersonal psychiatry will need to follow the same educational route as any other prospective physician: medical school, internship, and residency. The challenge is to find a medical school (and especially a place of residency) where transpersonal research and ideas are generally accepted or acknowledged. While the following programs as a whole do not have an explicit transpersonal orientation, the interests and support of some faculty members make their programs unique.

Associations

American Medical College (AMC)
Application Service
2450 N Street, N.W., Suite 201
Washington, DC 20037-1131
    All students who seek entrance to medical school must first apply to the AMC.

American Psychiatric Association
1400 K Street, N.W.
Washington, DC 20005
(202) 682-6000
    The APA is a national medical specialty society whose over 38,000 physician and medical student members—throughout North America and in numerous foreign countries—specialize in the diagnosis and treatment of mental and emotional disorders. The oldest medical specialty society in the United States, APA's roots extend back to October 1944, when 13 eminent physicians who specialized in the treatment of mental illnesses gathered in Philadelphia to found the Association of Medical Superintendents of American Institutions for the Insane. The APA publishes the *American Journal of Psychiatry*; the American Psychiatric Press, Inc., publishes numerous books, journals, and reports, including the *Diagnostic and Statistical Manual (DSM)*, the authoritative text on mental illness definitions.

Organizations

Albert Hofmann Foundation (AHF)
P.O. Box 181
Venice, CA 90294-0181
(310) 281-8110
    The AHF was established as a nonprofit organization in 1988 and was named in honor of the man who discovered LSD and the ritualistic use of psilocybin by indigenous cultures. The purpose of the foundation is to establish and maintain a library and world information center dedicated to the scientific study of human consciousness.

Christian Medical and Dental Society
P.O. Box 830689
Richardson, TX 75083
(214) 783-8384
    Founded in 1931, the purpose of the society is to encourage Christians who practice psychiatry to investigate and discuss the relation between their faith and professional work, and to incorporate such examined beliefs into their personal life and daily practice. Since 1961, a psychiatry section of the society has met during the annual American Psychiatric Association conference.

Heffter Research Institute
330 Garfield Street, Suite 301
Santa Fe, NM 87501-2676
(505) 820-6557
    Arthur Heffter, Ph.D. (1886-1925), for whom the institute is named, was the first scientist to systematically study the chemistry and psychopharmacology of a naturally occurring psychedelic. The institute was

established to foster and promote legitimate, rigorous, and ethical research on psychedelics.

Multidisciplinary Association for Psychedelic Studies (MAPS)
1801 Tippah Avenue
Charlotte, NC 28205
(704) 358-9830

MAPS, a nonprofit organization founded in 1986 by Rick Doblin, is a membership-based organization that helps psychedelic-oriented researchers around the world design, fund, conduct, and report on psychedelic research in humans.

National Guild of Catholic Psychiatrists
Taylor Manor Hospital
4100 College Avenue
Ellicott City, MD 21041-0396
(410) 465-3322

The National Guild brings together psychiatrists and other mental health professionals who share a belief in the spiritual dimension of human experience. It advocates the integration of psychiatry and religion through the exchange of clinical experience and knowledge by means of professional meetings and the publication of educational materials. The guild meets during the annual American Psychiatric Association conference.

Program in Medicine and Philosophy
See Allopathic Medicine.

Sanctuary Center
Robert Newport, M.D.
150 Felker Street, Suite G
Santa Cruz, CA 95060
(408) 425-7081

The center is a research organization that is in the process of creating a development plan for a holistic psychiatric hospital based on the spiritual emergence model.

M.D. AND RESIDENCY PROGRAMS
University of California, Irvine
Department of Psychiatry and Human Behavior
College of Medicine
Irvine, CA 92717
(714) 856-5388
Contact Person: Roger Walsh, M.D.

University of California, Los Angeles, at Harbor
Department of Child Psychiatry
1000 West Carlson Street
Torrance, CA 9050
(213) 825-6081
Contact Person: Director of Child Psychiatry, Charles Grob, M.D.

University of California, San Francisco (UCSF)
Director of Residency Training
401 Parnassus Avenue
San Francisco, CA 94143
(415) 476-7724

For general information about UCSF's residency program, contact Marc Jacobs, M.D.

University of California, San Francisco (UCSF)
San Francisco General Hospital
Department of Psychiatry
1001 Potrero Avenue
San Francisco, CA 94110
(415) 206-8984

For specific information about UCSF's residency program and supervision from a transpersonal perspective, contact Francis Lu, M.D.

RESIDENCY PROGRAMS ONLY
Menninger Clinic
Box 829
Topeka, KS 66601-0829
(913) 273-7500
See Research Institutes.

FACULTY IN DEPARTMENTS OF PSYCHIATRY WITH TRANSPERSONAL INTERESTS
Harvard Medical School, Cambridge Hospital
Cambridge, MA 02138
(617) 495-1000

Daniel Brown, Ph.D. (hypnosis, meditation); Jack Engler, Ph.D. (meditation); John Mack, M.D. (global issues)

Menninger Clinic
Elmer Green, Ph.D. (biofeedback); Stuart Twemlow, M.D. (out-of-body experience)

University of California, Irvine
Barry Budner, M.D. (transpersonal psychotherapy); Gordon Globus, M.D. (phenomenology, philosophy, cognitive science); Diane Harris, M.D. (transpersonal

psychotherapy); Larry Howard, Ph.D. (psychology of war and peace); Jim McQuade, M.D. (transpersonal psychiatry); Marlene de Rios, Ph.D. (anthropology); Deane Shapiro, Ph.D. (meditation, self-control, Judaism); Roger Walsh, M.D. (meditation, global concerns)

University of California, Los Angeles, at Harbor
Charles Grob, M.D. (child psychiatry, psychedelics)

University of California, San Francisco
Seymour Boorstein, M.D. (transpersonal psychotherapy); Allan Chinen, M.D. (fairy tales; mid-life issues); Fred Hiatt, M.D. (transpersonal psychotherapy); Francis Lu, M.D. (transcultural); Bruce Scotten, M.D. (Jung); Robert Turner, M.D. (spiritual emergency)

University of Connecticut
School of Medicine
Farmington Avenue
Farmington, CT 06032
(203) 679-2152
Bruce Greyson, M.D. (near-death experience)

University of Louisville
School of Medicine
Health Sciences Center
Louisville, KY 40292
(502) 588-5193
Adam Blatner, M.D. (psychodrama)

University of New Mexico
School of Medicine
Albuquerque, NM 87131
(505) 277-0111
Rick Strassman, M.D. (psychedelics)

University of Virginia
School of Medicine
Charlottesville, VA 22908
(804) 924-5571
Ian Stevenson, M.D. (reincarnation)

RESIDENTIAL PSYCHOLOGY DEGREE PROGRAMS

One of the most difficult choices for a prospective graduate student is whether to attend a traditional or alternative program. In the following essay, James Fadiman, Ph.D., who helped found the Institute for Transpersonal Psychology in Palo Alto, California (one of the first transpersonal programs in the United States), presents some important issues to consider when making this decision.

There are both risks and benefits to attending so-called alternative or nontraditional degree programs, especially those schools with a clear spiritual component. If you want a degree that assures you of the maximum number of job possibilities at the maximum number of institutions, then these schools (with few exceptions) won't meet that need. If, on the other hand, you are determined (while getting a degree) to develop mentally, emotionally, and spiritually, these schools will do a better job than will any traditional program, no matter how famous, endowed, or prestigious.

The re-emergence of these psychospiritual schools will be seen as startling only by those ignorant of history. Originally, private colleges in the United States were founded by religious groups to maintain a literate clergy. State colleges came later and were founded to ensure a population of literate voters. Elimination of the spiritual components from the curriculum came about partly because public funding flowed to nonsectarian education until the secularization of the universities was ubiquitous. Spiritual and moral education withered and eventually almost vanished except for the training of clergy in theological schools.

One may wonder why the spiritual or transpersonal first reemerged in psychology rather than in nursing or counseling or even psychiatry. Perhaps the reason it originated there is that, like a smoldering underground fire, it has always been ready to reemerge when the time was right. For instance, William James, who fathered psychology in the United States, taught and wrote that the discipline included the full range of human experience—from deep psychopathology to the extremes of spiritual clarity and mystical genius. Some time later, for many reasons—some historical and sensible, some hysterical and shameful—academic psychology began to jettison the higher functions of the psyche, including the spiritual and the religious. Psychology began to trail after the hard sciences like an ambitious stepchild, trying in every way to prove that it, too, was able to quantify, replicate, experiment, and reduce complex phenomena to small and manipulatable components (and should be funded for so doing). But all this was soon to change.

If you are secure enough within yourself to want a whole education more than a name-brand, go for the alternative closest to your heart.

The questioning of the basic paradigms of Western consciousness during the 1960s resurrected James's ideas as well as those of the great spiritual traditions. These rediscoveries occurred while mainstream academic psychology was being experienced as arid and unfulfilling. Many of the institutions delineated in this subchapter were founded or envisioned during this period to meet the demands of students and faculty alike for a more meaningful and relevant education.

While the programs described are not mainstream academic, they nonetheless address mainstream human experience. These schools, without exception, acknowledge that the psychospiritual is as importatn (if not more) than the psychosexual and the psychodynamic facets of the psyche. While each of the schools has its own flavor and its own balance between the academic and the experiential, and each takes a different view of what is worth studying in the psychospiritual realm, they all agree on its centrality for a full understanding of one's self and others.

In spite of their broader outlook and the professional success of their graduates (especially those pursuing clinical, counseling, or pastoral degrees), these schools continue to be looked down on by many traditional academics. One possible reason may be the declining prestige of mainstream psychology, whose undergraduate enrollments have declined nationwide over the past decade, while these alternative schools have been thriving. In any case, if you attend one of these programs, don't expect the faculty at your local four-year college or university to fully support your decision.

Prospective students often ask about the differences between the education one receives from, for example, the University of California at Berkeley or Stanford versus one received at one of the many Bay Area alternative schools. My answer is that it is a question of how much of yourself you wish to educate. If you want an easier, less emotionally demanding, more secure, and ultimately more narrow educational experience, go for the mainstream school. However, if you are secure enough within yourself to want a whole education more than a name-brand, go for the alternative closest to your heart. It will be a little light on the academic side, less rigorous in some areas, but far more likely to help you face the emotional and spiritual issues that concern you and will continue to concern you for the rest of your life.

Once you've made that commitment, then you need to sift through the offerings. You can work within the Christian or Jewish tradition; such parochial institutions, however, often teach no more than a smattering of other spiritual traditions. Most of the transpersonal institutions, on the other hand, offer in-depth work in several spiritual and psychological systems, or what Aldous Huxley called "the perennial philosophy," those truths that transcend sectarian limitations.

A large majority of students at all

KEY PSYCHOLOGY TERMS

A NUMBER OF PSYCHOLOGY TERMS HAVE UNDERGONE CONSIDERABLE CHANGES IN DEFINITION WHILE OTHER, NEW ONES HAVE BEEN INTRODUCED to the mental health community in the last 30 years. In response, the editors offer the following definitions in order to help establish a common reference point regarding some of the major fields of study referred to in this chapter and throughout the guide.

HUMANISTIC is a theoretical perspective applied most frequently to the discipline of psychology. Abraham Maslow (1908-1970), one of the major pioneers of the humanistic movement, envisioned a psychology in which the integrity of individual consciousness would be restored. Maslow (and others before him) criticized the then-popular belief that human experience may be reduced into objectively separate and often mechanistic parts—an approach that tends to overlook the perplexing phenomenon of consciousness. In contrast to the classical psychoanalytic theory first proposed by Freud (that certain developmental processes and aberrant experiences are regressive or even pathological), humanistic psychology is based on the assumption that the innate yearning to fulfill one's maximum potential is normal and healthy. Maslow called this process self-actualization and characterized it by placing value on ideals like truth, creativity, beauty, mystery, authenticity, excellence, justice, personal growth, order, playfulness, self-sufficiency, and self-transcendence, and on outwardly engaging oneself in (among other activities) the creation of ultimate meaning and the search for optimum health and wellness. These values can be applicable within a theistic worldview; however, some humanistic psychologists (called "secular humanists") incorporate these values into a nontheistic worldview. Maslow would later conclude that the "farther reaches of human nature" are not ultimately human-centered, but transpersonal.

PSYCHOLOGY (from the Greek word *psyche,* which means "spirit" or "mind") emerged as a distinct, experimental science in the late 19th century. Prior to that point, philosophy and theology addressed those issues that are now considered psychological. Begun primarily with the goal of becoming a science of human behavior, the discipline's formation was significantly influenced by two 17th-century philosophers: Thomas Hobbes, who argued that every phenome-non could be discovered through deductive reasoning, and René Descartes, who suggested that the mind can be analyzed separately from the body. Psychology has since disengaged from theology and philosophy and allied with "scientific" disciplines such as anthropology, sociology, physics, and biology. Also, a number of "schools," or theoretical perspectives (such as behavioral, Gestalt, cognitive, and humanistic), have since widened the field, each defining the mission, philosophy, and methodology of psychology in different and often conflicting ways. Only recently has an alternative movement within psychology returned to an interest in such philosophical concepts as the nature of mind and consciousness.

PSYCHOSPIRITUAL is an umbrella term used to refer to topics or phenomena that present aspects of both the mental health disciplines and any of the numerous and diverse practices and philosophies commonly known as spirituality.

TRANSPERSONAL can refer either to those types of experiences that are deemed "beyond the personal" or to the theoretical approach that attempts to define and study such experiences. The former are considered experiences in which the sense of identity or self extends beyond (*trans*) the individual to encompass wider aspects of humankind, life, psyche, and cosmos. Transpersonal theory, which emerged directly from humanistic psychology, is unique in its adoption of an interdisciplinary epistemology (or way of acquiring knowledge), that includes not only modern scientific methods but also philosophical and introspective ones. It is most often applied to the fields of psychology, psychiatry, anthropology, ecology, and education, among others. Topics of particular interest include the phenomena of consciousness and altered states, mythology, meditation, yoga, mysticism, lucid dreaming, psychedelics, values, ethics, relationships, exceptional capacities, psychological well-being, and motives such as altruism and service. The term also refers to research into transpersonal phenomena and various alternative therapies (most of which are represented in this guide).[1]

1. Drawn in part from the introduction to *Paths Beyond Ego: The Transpersonal Vision* (Jeremy P. Tarcher/Perigee, Books 1993), edited by Roger Walsh, M.D., Ph.D., and Frances Vaughan, Ph.D.

these transpersonal schools choose careers in human service and intend to become therapists, clergy, counselors, or teachers. Graduates from most of these schools find that while getting an initial job is sometimes tough (as their degree sources are not well known), once hired, the quality of their inner development as well as their training give them an edge over their conventionally educated colleagues. Many plan to work as private practitioners, which makes the name of the school they graduate from even less important. Few alumni from the alternative schools have been unable to do the kind of work they intend to do. Obviously, readers pursuing this book are not likely to be wavering between personal development versus business school, so I need not stress that one probably won't make as much money with these degrees as with some others.

Some of these school have "approval," while others are accredited or are becoming so. While each state has its own regulations, approval usually means that the state allows the school to offer degrees. It may or may not mean that its graduates are eligible to be licensed as therapists in that state or other states. If that matters to you, find out. Accredited means that a regional accreditation group agrees that this school resembles the other established schools in the region. This usually means the school is stable enough to last, orthodox enough to be understood, has enough cash in the bank to weather a few bad years, meets all federal guidelines, and so forth. (See the essay on accreditation at the end of this book for more information.) Students at accredited schools or those in the process of completing their accreditation can get federal loans. Check the status of loan programs as the federal rules are constantly shifting. Foreign students usually are not eligible for most loan programs. Tuition and living costs vary enormously, so do your financial homework before you fall in love with a school that you can't afford.

From my own experience as an instructor at a number of these psychospiritual schools, I urge you not to make a final decision on the basis of what the printed materials say or what the faculty or the admissions people have told you. They can't know the actual experiences within their own school unless they are recent graduates of it. Many of these schools are so vital and dynamic that their flavor changes from year to year; the major faculty appear and disappear; and the complexion of the student body changes. Ask to talk with, or even

better, to spend time with students and graduates of any school you are seriously considering.

Also keep in mind that you may not have to physically attend a program to obtain your degree. The postal system and electronic revolution have made it possible to learn in depth without having to relocate. A number of the psychospiritual institutions successfully work with students at a distance, some worldwide. For a more detailed discussion of this, see Nonresidential Psychology Programs.

One final note: Most people who choose a school, by whatever considerations, feel that they have made the right choice. As Rumi, the Persian poet and mystic, said, "There are hundreds of ways to kiss the ground."

—This introduction was written by James Fadiman, Ph.D., who taught at San Francisco State University, Brandeis, and Stanford before helping found the Institute for Transpersonal Psychology in Palo Alto, California. His most recent books are Personality and Personal Growth *(3rd edition, 1994, with Roger Frager) and* Unlimit Your Life *(revised edition, 1994.)*

IMPORTANT TRENDS IN THE PSYCHOSPIRITUAL FIELD

■ In 1982, the California State Psychological Association authorized the organization of a task force on spirituality and psychotherapy. The task force, borrowing from Carl Jung's writings, defined spirituality as "the courage to look within and to trust" and added "what is seen and what is trusted appears to be a feeling of wholeness, belongingness, connectedness, and openness to the universe." The task force then undertook a research study of a sample of 1,440 licensed California clinical psychologists to assess their preparation before and after licensure to deal with their own and their clients' problems of spiritual development. The findings indicated that there was almost no preparation for these issues (other than in theological schools) before licensure.

■ There are 51 divisions representing professional interests under the umbrel-

la of the American Psychological Association. One such interest group is called the Psychology of Religion, or Division 36 (formerly known as Psychologists Interested in Religious Issues). The division recently created a national task force on the topic of religious issues in psychology and clinical training.

■ The American Psychological Association is publishing a book called *Religion and the Clinical Practice of Psychology*, edited by Edward Francis Shafranske, Ph.D., and it is due out in 1995. The publication of this book represents the first formal acknowledgment of the psychospiritual field by APA.

■ In March 1994 the American Psychological Association announced the establishment of a new credentialing mechanism, referred to as the APA College of Professional Psychology, which will issue non-mandated certificates of *proficiency* to licensed psychologists. The APA hopes to position psychologists favorably in a changing and competitive health-care marketplace, as well as to provide increased opportunities for psychologists to earn continuing education credits, which are required by state licensing boards. In this regard, the college will have the authority to issue certificates of proficiency to licensed health service providers in psychology, a marked difference from the APA's traditional role of accrediting only doctoral programs.

The college is now developing procedures for determining which practitioners are qualified to sit for examination in designated proficiency areas. They will also review and select training and continuing educational programs, and adopt standards for the renewal of certificates. Work is already under way on a certificate of proficiency in working with alcoholism and other types of substance abuse; inpatient hospital practice and marriage and family therapy may be included later.

Currently, licensed psychologists with at least five years of experience may be offered an opportunity to earn a diplomate for demonstrated excellence in a specialty sponsored by the American Board of Professional Psychology, an organization separate from the APA. These diplomates cover various areas such as clinical hypnosis and neuropsychology, and include not only treatment but also assessment (i.e., diagnostic) skills. The college's proficiency certificates will differ from the diplomate, however, in that the certificate will be given as an entry-level credential in a proficiency area, which is more specific than a specialty.

■ Most "alternative" psychospiritual schools include self-exploration as part of their academic curriculum, thereby acknowledging the relationship between personal growth (such as required personal therapy) and the capacity to help others. In contrast, even though more conventional, research-oriented Ph.D. programs emphasize the science of psychology more than the art and practice of it, an amazingly large percentage of graduates still enter private psychotherapy practice. Despite these factors, many APA members argue that any specific training in areas like the specialty of psychotherapy should remain postdoctoral. At present, Ph.D. doctoral graduates are not required to specialize in any one field within clinical psychology (except during a year-long internship, which usually allows a student to follow a primary interest, but which may nevertheless have little to do with psychotherapy per se). Thus it should come as no surprise that some graduates of traditional schools planning to go into private practice decline additional training (e.g., attending a nondegree psychotherapy training institute) immediately following the completion of an arduous Ph.D. program. (See Nondegree Training and Postgraduate Programs for examples of postdoctoral psychotherapy training programs.)

The Doctor of Psychology degree (Psy.D.) was developed to allow clinical psychology students to study mostly professionally relevant courses rather than the numerous science-oriented courses usually required for the academic-oriented Ph.D. degree. There are to date, however, only a dozen or so of these programs available in the United States. Contact the APA for a list of these schools.

ADDITIONAL RESOURCES

Getting In: A Step-by-Step Plan for Gaining Admission to Graduate School in Psychology
Published and written by the American Psychological Association, 1993, $14.95.

Associations

American Psychological Association (APA)
750 First Street, N.E.
Washington, DC 20002
(202) 336-5500
APA represents psychologists and the psychology profession.

American Psychological Association (Division 36)
Psychology of Religion
Edward Shafranske, Ph.D.
Pepperdine University
2151 Michelson Drive
Irvine, CA 92715
(714) 833-8221
Founded in 1976 as a division of APA, Division 36 seeks to encourage research in the psychology of religion and to integrate these findings into current psychological theory and professional practice. It publishes a quarterly newsletter and has programs during the annual APA conference. To date, the Division has been dominated by a focus on social psychology from a Judeo-Christian perspective.

Association for Humanistic Psychology (AHP)
1772 Vallejo Street
San Francisco, CA 94123
(415) 346-7929
Founded in 1962, AHP is a worldwide network for the development and application of human sciences that recognize the distinctively human qualities and innate potentialities of each individual. AHP links, supports, and stimulates those who share this humanistic vision of the person. It publishes the newsletter *Perspectives* and the *Journal of Humanistic Psychology*.

Association for Transpersonal Psychology (ATP)
P.O. Box 3049
Stanford, CA 94039
(415) 327-2066
Created in 1970 by Anthony Sutich and Abraham Maslow (who with Stanislav Grof named the field "transpersonal" psychology), ATP is a major voice for the transpersonal movement. It publishes a journal, directed by long-time editor Miles Vich, and holds an annual conference. It also publishes a national listing of professional members and educational programs in transpersonal psychology.

Christian Association for Psychological Studies (CAPS)
Robert King, Ph.D., Executive Director
P.O. Box 890279
Temecula, CA 92589-0279
(909) 695-2277
Founded in 1956, CAPS is an association of Christians in the psychological and pastoral professions. It publishes the *Journal of Psychology and Christianity* and holds annual, regional, and national conventions.

International Transpersonal Association
See International Resources.

National Psychology Advisory Association (NPAA)
c/o The Union Institute
440 East McMillan Street
Cincinnati, OH 45206-1947
(800) 486-3116; (513) 861-6400
The NPAA was begun in 1988 as the sister organization of the Consortium for Diversified Psychology Programs (CDPP). While CDPP is an alliance of accredited traditional and alternative educational programs and professional associations, NPAA is a national organization of individuals committed to pluralistic modes of education and training for a wide range of students, including mid-career professionals and mature learners. NPAA educates state and national officials in the philosophy of alternative educational programs in psychology, monitors national activities in the health-care field, and supports state affiliate organizations in monitoring and revising license-related legislation.

Pre- and Perinatal Psychology Association of North America (PPPANA)
1600 Prince Street, Suite 509
Alexandria, VA 22314-2838
(703) 548-2802
The PPPANA is an educational nonprofit organization dedicated to the in-depth exploration of the psychological dimensions of human reproduction and pregnancy, and the mental and emotional development of the unborn and newborn child. Two basic assumptions govern the association's work. One is the recognition that there is no separation between mind and

body. The other is that life is a continuum that starts not at birth but at conception. Consequently, it is PPPANA's belief that the interplay of physiological, emotional, mental, and spiritual factors during preconception, conception, pregnancy, labor, delivery, and postpartum directly contribute to the psychological health of the mother, child, and family unit. It publishes the journal *Pre- & Perinatal Psychology* and holds a biannual congress.

Organizations

Consortium for Diversified Psychology Programs (CDPP)
c/o Ms. Joan Read, Fielding Institute
2112 Santa Barbara Street
Santa Barbara, CA 93105-3538
(805) 687-1099

CDPP is a consortium of colleges, universities, and national associations whose programs emphasize diverse theoretical and practical knowledge, including but not limited to significant alternative perspectives such as phenomenological, existential, humanistic, and transpersonal approaches to psychology. The National Psychology Advisory Association is the CDPP's sister organization. Consortium members include the Association for Humanistic Psychology; California Institute of Integral Studies; Center for Humanistic Studies; Duquesne University Department of Psychology; Focusing Institute; John F. Kennedy University; National Association for Humanistic Education; National Psychology Advisory Association; National Psychology Internships; Saybrook Institute; Seattle University Department of Psychology; Temple University; Department of Psychoeducational Processes; Union Institute; University of Chicago Psychology Department; University of Dallas Psychology Department; Walden University; and the West Georgia College Department of Psychology.

National Institute for the Clinical Application of Behavioral Medicine (NICABM)
Box 523
Mansfield Center, CT 06250
(800) 743-2226

The NICABM was founded in Connecticut in 1987 to establish practitioner-oriented conferences and seminars for healthcare providers, which focus specifically on issues at the interface between health and psychology. It holds an annual conference.

Periodicals

Biofeedback and Self Regulation
Plenum Publishing Corporation
233 Spring Street
New York, NY 10013-1578
(212) 620-8000
Quarterly; $53

The Humanistic Psychologist
West Georgia College
Psychology Department
Carrolton, GA 30118
(404) 836-6510
Three times a year; $15

This journal is the official publication of the Division of Humanistic Psychology (Division 32) of the American Psychological Association.

Journal of Humanistic Psychology
Sage Publications, Inc.
2455 Teller Road
Newbury Park, CA 91320
(805) 499-0721
Quarterly; $46

This journal was founded by Abraham Maslow and Anthony J. Sutich in 1958 and began publication in 1961. It is the official journal of the Association of Humanistic Psychology. Saybrook Institute also provides editorial support. Topics of special interest are authenticity, identity, personal growth, self-actualization, self-transcendence, I-Thou, encounters, existential and humanistic psychotherapy, community building, humanistic politics, synergy, creativity, and holistic learning.

Journal of Psychology and Theology (JPT)
Subscription Office
13800 Biola Avenue
La Mirada, CA 90639
(310) 903-4727
Quarterly; $38

The *JPT* is an ecumenical Christian journal published by Biola University.

Journal of Transpersonal Psychology (JTP)
P.O. Box 3049
Stanford, CA 94309
(415) 327-2066
Semiannual; $29

Begun in 1969, this scholarly journal addresses the research, theory, and applications of altered states of consciousness, mystical states, and Eastern spiritual practices. It is now the official journal of the Association for Transpersonal Psychology.

Psychotherapy: Research and Practice
3875 North 44th Street
Phoenix, AZ 85018
(602) 952-8656

Quarterly; $60 ($35 student)

This publication is part of the Division of Psychotherapy (29) of the American Psychological Association.

Transpersonal Review (TR)
21821 Burbank Boulevard, Suite 143
Woodland Hills, CA 91367
(818) 888-6690
Biannual; $40

The *TR* publishes critical reviews, summaries, and abstracts of newly released books and journal articles that are relevant to transpersonal studies.

GRADUATE PROGRAMS

Note the key to accrediting organizations on page xix.

Antioch University, Los Angeles
13274 Fiji Way
Marina Del Ray, CA 90192
(310) 578-1080
General Information: Private, nonsectarian
Degrees Offered: M.A. (preparation for M.F.C.C. license)
Programs: Clinical psychology
Admission Requirements: Bachelor's degree; interview; relevant experience
Application Deadline: Rolling
Contact Person: Director of Admissions
Tuition: $2,900/quarter
Accreditation: NCACS; Council for Private Postsecondary and Vocational Education
Year Established: 1972
Faculty: 150 full- and part-time

Antioch University International
Central Administrative Office
Antioch University International
Yellow Springs, OH 45387
(513) 767-6400

Antioch was founded in 1852 as an alternative to existing colleges. It evolved in the 1960s and 1970s into a multicampus University with regional campuses located in New Hampshire, the Pacific Northwest, and Southern California.

Antioch University, New England
Roxbury Street
Keene, NH 03431
(603) 357-3122
General Information: Private, nonsectarian
Degrees Offered: M.A.; M.Ed.; M.S.H.A.; M.S.; Psy.D.
Programs: Clinical psychology; Counseling psychology; dance/movement therapy; marriage and family therapy; substance

abuse/addictions counseling; Waldorf Education teacher training
Admission Requirements: Bachelor's degree
Application Deadline: Rolling
Contact Person: Director of Admissions
Tuition: $11,750 - $17,700/program
Accreditation: American Dance Therapy Association; APA (candidacy status); CAMFTE (candidacy status); NCASC; New Hampshire Postsecondary Commission
Year Established: 1964
Faculty: 48 full-time; 110 associate and adjunct

Antioch University, Santa Barbara
801 Garden Street
Santa Barbara, CA 93101
(805) 962-8179
General Information: Private, nonsectarian
Degrees Offered: M.A.; M.Ed.; M.S.H.A.; Psy.D.
Programs: Counseling psychology; dance/movement therapy; substance abuse/addictions counseling; marriage and family therapy; clinical psychology
Admission Requirements: Bachelor's or master's degree (for Ph.D. program)
Application Deadline: January
Contact Person: Director of Admissions
Tuition: $11,750 - $17,700 (M.A.); $13,500 (Ph.D.)
Accreditation: NCACS; APA (Psy.D.); ADTA (dance/movement therapy); COAMFTE (marriage and family therapy program; candidacy status only)
Year Established: 1964
Faculty: 48 full-time; 110 associate and adjunct

Antioch University, Seattle
2607 Second Avenue
Seattle, WA 98121
(206) 441-5352
General Information: Private, nonsectarian
Degrees Offered: M.A. (Washington State mental health counselor certification)
Programs: Psychology
Admission Requirements: Bachelor's degree
Application Deadline: Rolling
Contact Person: Director of Admissions
Tuition: $11,750 - $17,700/program
Accreditation: NCACS; Washington State Higher Education Coordinating Board
Year Established: 1975
Faculty: Contact department

Atlantic University
67th Street and Atlanta Avenue
P.O. Box 595
Virginia Beach, VA 23451
(804) 428-1512
    The university is associated with Edgar Cayce's Association for Research and

Enlightenment.
General Information: Private, nonsectarian
Degrees Offered: M.A.
Programs: Transpersonal studies (Transpersonal counseling option)
Admission Requirements: Bachelor's degree; GPA > 2.5
Application Deadline: Prior to each semester
Contact Person: Director of Admissions
Tuition: $3,630 for the degree
Accreditation: Licensed by the Commonwealth of Virginia
Year Established: 1985 as a graduate school
Faculty: 1 full-time; 8 part-time

Avalon Institute
3985 Wonderland Hill
Boulder, CO 80304
(303) 443-4363
General Information: Private, nonsectarian
Degrees Offered: M.A.; Ph.D. (in conjunction with other institutions)
Programs: Jungian archetypal psychotherapy
Admission Requirements: Bachelor's degree; interview; relevant experience
Application Deadline: August and February
Contact Person: Director of Admissions
Tuition: $3,600/entire program plus external degree program fees
Accreditation: Through external program institutes
Year Established: 1986
Faculty: 4 full-time

Biola University
Rosemead School of Psychology
Talbot School of Theology
13800 Biola Avenue
La Mirada, CA 90639
(310) 903-6000
    Biola offers graduate study in approximately 20 academic fields to 2,800 students. One of Biola's primary distinctions is its commitment to encouraging students to relate their Christian faith to the study of the various academic disciplines.
General Information: Private, Christian
Degrees Offered: M.A.; Ph.D.; Psy.D.
Programs: Clinical psychology, Ph.D., Psy.D.; pastoral counseling, M.A.
Admission Requirements: Bachelor's degree; five letters of recommendation; GRE, MAT, and MMPI; Personal interview
Application Deadline: January 15
Contact Person: Director of Admissions
Tuition: $11,388/year
Accreditation: WASC; APA
Year Established: 1911
Faculty: 19 full-time

Boston College
Institute of Religious Education and Pastoral Ministry
Chestnut Hill, MA 02167
(617) 552-8440
General Information: Private, Christian
Degrees Offered: Ph.D.
Programs: Interdisciplinary doctorate in religion and education
Admission Requirements: Bachelor's or master's degree; GRE
Application Deadline: Rolling
Contact Person: Director of Admissions
Tuition: Grants and stipend awarded to all admitted
Accreditation: NEACSS
Year Established: 1971
Faculty: 4 full-time; 7 adjunct

California Graduate Institute
Graduate School of Professional Psychology
1100 Glendon Avenue, 11th Floor
Los Angeles, CA 90024
(310) 208-4240
    The California Graduate Institute was founded expressly to expand the scope of traditional graduate study in psychology and psychotherapy. Its founders deemed it essential that students receive instruction from professionals actively practicing their specialties in the field of mental health.
General Information: Private, nonsectarian
Degrees Offered: M.A.; Ph.D.; Psy.D.
Programs: Certificate in behavioral medicine; certificate in psychoanalysis; certificate in psychoanalytic psychotherapy; certificate in psychotherapy; marriage, family and child therapy, M.A.,Ph.D.; psychoanalysis, Ph.D.; psychology, M.A., Ph.D., Psy.D.
Admission Requirements: Bachelor's degree; field experience; pre-application interview; two personal interviews
Application Deadline: Prior to the start of each trimester
Contact Person: Director of Admissions
Tuition: $195/unit
Accreditation: California State approved; National Association for the Advancement of Psychoanalysis; APA categories I and II for continuing education for psychologists
Year Established: 1968
Faculty: 60 full-time

California Institute for Human Science
609 South Vulcan Avenue, Suite 201
Encinitas, CA 92024
(619) 634-1771
    Clinical Psychology M.A. and clinical-counseling psychology Ph.D. degrees meet requirements for clinical psychology and M.F.C.C. licenses in California. Graduate programs can be taken on an independent study basis.

General Information: Private, nonsectarian
Degrees Offered: M.A.; Ph.D.
Programs: Human science, M.A., Ph.D.; integral health science, M.A.; clinical psychology, M.A.; religious studies, M.A.; clinical-counseling psychology, Ph.D. (with specialization in clinical and experimental Biopsychology, holistic health psychology, or parapsychology)
Admission Requirements: Bachelor's degree; letter of recommendation
Application Deadline: Rolling
Contact Person: Director of Admissions
Tuition: $140/unit (M.A.); $180/unit (Ph.D.)
Accreditation: State of California
Year Established: 1992
Faculty: Contact institute

**California Institute of
Integral Studies (CIIS)**
765 Ashbury Street
San Francisco, CA 94117
(415) 753-6100
    CIIS's original emphasis on Asian studies has evolved to include comparative and cross-cultural studies in philosophy, religion, psychology, cultural anthropology, organizational studies, and the arts. M.A. and Ph.D. programs in these areas seek to ground the student in the traditional academic disciplines while encouraging the investigation and integration of the less traditional, esoteric, and Eastern philosophical approaches.
General Information: Private, nonsectarian
Degrees Offered: M.A.; Ph.D.; Psy.D.
Programs: Clinical psychology, Ph.D., Psy,D.; drama therapy, M.A.; East-West psychology, M.A., Ph.D.; expressive arts therapy, certificate; integral counseling psychology, M.A.; integral health studies, M.A.; organizational development and transformation, M.A.; philosophy and religion, M.A., Ph.D.; social and cultural anthropology, M.A.; somatic psychology, M.A.; women's spirituality, Ph.D.
Admission Requirements: Bachelor's degree; Personal interview
Application Deadline: February
Contact Person: Director of Admissions
Tuition: $240-315/unit
Accreditation: WASC
Year Established: 1974
Faculty: 43 full-time; 61 adjunct and visiting

**California School of
Professional Psychology (CSPP)**
System wide Admissions and Financial Aid
2749 Hyde Street
San Francisco, CA 94109
(415) 346-4500
    The CSPP was founded in 1969 as the

nation's first autonomous graduate school of professional psychology. CSPP maintains campuses in four California cities: Berkeley/Alameda, Fresno, Los Angeles, and San Diego.
General Information: Private, nonsectarian
Degrees Offered: M.S.; Ph.D.; Psy.D.
Programs: Clinical psychology; organizational psychology; industrial/organizational psychology; organizational behavior; organizational development
Admission Requirements: Bachelor's degree; personal interview
Application Deadline: December 15 and January 15
Contact Person: Director of Admissions
Tuition: $13,180/year (doctoral program)
Accreditation: WASC; APA
Year Established: 1969
Faculty: 400 full-time and adjunct system wide

Center for Humanistic Studies
40 East Ferry Avenue
Detroit, MI 48202
(313) 875-7440
    The center's programs emphasize theoretical and practical knowledge of humanistic and clinical psychology, training in psychotherapy, and qualitative investigations of human experience.
General Information: Private, nonsectarian
Degrees Offered: M.A., specialist degree (post-master's)
Programs: Humanistic and clinical psychology, M.A., specialist
Admission Requirements: Bachelor's degree; relevant experience; master's degree (for specialist program)
Application Deadline: Prior to fall quarter entry
Contact Person: Director of Admissions
Tuition: $8,800/year
Accreditation: NCACS; State of Michigan Charter
Year Established: 1980
Faculty: 9 full-time

Center for Psychological Studies
1398 Solano Avenue
Albany, CA 94706
(510) 524-0291
General Information: Private, nonsectarian
Degrees Offered: Ph.D.
Programs: Clinical psychology; developmental psychology (individual and organizational)
Admission Requirements: Bachelor's degree; master's degree
Application Deadline: Rolling Admissions

Contact Person: Director of Admissions
Tuition: $330/unit
Accreditation: State of California
Year Established: 1979
Faculty: 8 core; 20 adjunct

Chestnut Hill College
Graduate Division
Philadelphia, PA 19118-2695
(215) 248-7170
    Chestnut Hill is open to students of all religions and creeds.
General Information: Private, Catholic
Degrees Offered: M.A.; M.S.; post-master's certificate
Programs: Advanced study in applied spirituality, certificate; advanced study in pastoral counseling, certificate; counseling psychology and human services (human service counseling; addictions counseling certificate; marriage and family therapy), M.A., M.S.; holistic spirituality/spiritual direction, M.A.
Admission Requirements: Bachelor's degree; interview; MAT or GRE; three letters of recommendation
Application Deadline: Rolling
Contact Person: Director of Admissions
Tuition: $275/credit
Accreditation: MSACS; Commonwealth of Pennsylvania; NBCC and PCACB (counseling program)
Year Established: 1924
Faculty: 25 full-time; 67 adjunct

Chicago School of Professional Psychology
806 South Plymouth Court
Chicago, IL 60605
(312) 786-9443
General Information: Private, nonsectarian
Degrees Offered: Psy.D.
Programs: Clinical psychology
Admission Requirements: Bachelor's degree; GRE or MAT; minimum of 18 semester hours of psychology course work; personal interview
Application Deadline: February 1
Contact Person: Director of Admissions
Tuition: $6,230/semester
Accreditation: NCACS; APA
Year Established: 1979
Faculty: 10 full-time; 24 part-time

Duquesne University
Graduate School of Liberal Arts and Sciences
Pittsburgh, PA 15282
(412) 396-6000
    A Catholic institution operated by the Congregation of the Holy Ghost, Duquesne is open to students of all religions and creeds.

General Information: Private, Catholic (nonsectarian)
Degrees Offered: M.A.; M.S.; Ph.D.; M.A.L.S.
Programs: Liberal studies, M.A.; pastoral ministry, M.A.; psychology, M.A., Ph.D.; theology, M.A., Ph.D.
Admission Requirements: Bachelor's degree; GRE
Application Deadline: One month before entering semester
Contact Person: Director of Admissions
Tuition: $397/credit
Accreditation: MSACS
Year Established: 1878
Faculty: 100 full-time

Emmanuel College
400 The Fenway
Boston, MA 02115
(617) 735-9918
General Information: Private, Catholic
Degrees Offered: M.A.
Programs: Mental health counseling; psychology; rehabilitation counseling
Admission Requirements: Bachelor's degree; GRE or MAT; GRE Psychology; interview; three letters of recommendation
Application Deadline: Rolling
Contact Person: Director of Admissions
Tuition: $358/credit
Accreditation: NEASC
Year Established: 1968
Faculty: 3 full-time; 8 adjunct

Emory University
Graduate Division of Religion
211 Bishops Hall
Atlanta, GA 30322
(404) 727-6333
Founded as a Methodist school in 1883, Emory provides an academic background for teaching. The program does not directly prepare a student in clinical psychology, although this type of training can be incorporated from other programs.
General Information: Private, nonsectarian
Degrees Offered: Ph.D.
Programs: Theology and personality
Admission Requirements: Master's degree or M. Div. or M.S.W.; GRE; three letters of recommendation; writing sample
Application Deadline: January 20
Contact Person: Dr. James Fowler
Tuition: $16,000/year (a stipend and partial scholarship are offered upon acceptance)
Accreditation: CCSACS
Year Established: 1958
Faculty: 5 full-time

Fuller Theological Seminary
Graduate School of Psychology
180 North Oakland Avenue
Pasadena, CA 91182
(818) 584-5400
General Information: Private, Christian
Degrees Offered: M.A.; Ph.D.; Psy.D.; M.F.T.; D.M.F.T.
Programs: Clinical psychology, Psy.D., Ph.D.; marriage and family studies, Ph.D.; marriage and family therapy, M.F.T., D.M.F.T., Ph.D.
Admission Requirements: Bachelor's degree; GRE; letter of recommendation; personal interview
Application Deadline: February 15 for M.F.T.; January 1 for others
Contact Person: Director of Admissions
Tuition: $13,128 (Psy.D., Ph.D.); $186/unit (M.A.); $291/unit (M.F.T.)
Accreditation: WASC; APA
Year Established: 1964
Faculty: 17 full-time

George Fox College
414 North Meridian Street
Newberg, OR 97132
(800) 765-4369
George Fox College's Graduate School of Clinical Psychology provides training through a practitioner model in the context of a Christian worldview. Emphasis is placed on dealing with the spiritual dimension of life in relationship to psychological problems and struggles.
General Information: Public, Evangelical Quaker
Degrees Offered: Psy.D.
Programs: Doctor of Psychology
Admission Requirements: 18 semester credits in psychology; bachelor's degree; four letters of recommendation; GRE; Advanced Psychology GRE; personal interview
Application Deadline: February 1
Contact Person: Director of Admissions
Tuition: $360/semester credit
Accreditation: NASC
Year Established: 1977
Faculty: 10 full-time

George Washington University
Washington, DC 20052
(202) 994-1000
This unique program allows students to integrate the social sciences and the humanities.
General Information: Private, nonsectarian
Degrees Offered: Ph.D.
Programs: Human sciences (interdisciplinary)

Admission Requirements: Bachelor's degree; GRE; letter of recommendation
Application Deadline: March
Contact Person: Director of Admissions
Tuition: $440/credit hour
Accreditation: MSACS
Year Established: 1992
Faculty: Varies (interdisciplinary and self-designed major)

Georgia School of Professional Psychology
Division of the American Schools of Professional Psychology
990 Hammond Drive, Suite 1100
Atlanta, GA 30328
(800) 362-3094
General Information: Private, nonsectarian
Degrees Offered: Psy.D.
Programs: Doctor of Psychology (with a psychology and religion predoctoral minor option)
Admission Requirements: Bachelor's degree; five courses in psychology
Application Deadline: January 15
Contact Person: Director of Admissions
Tuition: $335/credit hour
Accreditation: NCACS; APA (application in process)
Year Established: 1990
Faculty: 11 core; 10 associate

Holy Names College
Institute in Culture and Creation Spirituality (ICCS)
3500 Mountain Boulevard
Oakland, CA 94619-1699
(510) 436-1000
The ICCS was inaugurated to reawaken the Western, Christian mystical tradition with particular emphasis on the creation-centered mystics of the Middle Ages, including Meister Eckhart, Teresa of Avila, John of the Cross, Hildegard of Bingen, and others. Matthew Fox, an outspoken Episcopal priest and intellectual who was expelled from the Dominican Order in 1993, is affiliated with Holy Names College.
General Information: Private, Catholic (ecumenical)
Degrees Offered: M.A.
Programs: Certificate (nine months); counseling psychology, M.A.; sabbatical programs (four months)
Admission Requirements: Bachelor's degree
Application Deadline: Rolling
Contact Person: Director of Admissions
Tuition: $10,600 (M.A.); $10,000 (certificate); $4,800 (sabbatical)
Accreditation: WASC
Year Established: 1977
Faculty: 15 full-time

Illinois School of Professional Psychology
Division of the American Schools of
Professional Psychology
220 South State Street, Suite 509
Chicago, IL 60604
(800) 742-0743
General Information: Private, nonsectarian
Degrees Offered: Psy.D.
Programs: Doctor of Psychology (with a psychology and religion predoctoral minor option)
Admission Requirements: Bachelor's degree; five courses in psychology
Application Deadline: January 15
Contact Person: Director of Admissions
Tuition: $335/credit hour
Accreditation: NCACS, APA
Year Established: 1976
Faculty: 30 core; 11 associate core; 29 associate

Institute of Transpersonal Psychology
744 San Antonio Road
Palo Alto, CA 94303
(415) 493-4430
   The institute's programs balance rigorous intellectual, physical, and spiritual training conducive to the personal transformation that is necessary for the critical understanding and comparative study of human developmental processes and transpersonal experiences.
General Information: Private, nonsectarian
Degrees Offered: M.A.; Ph.D.
Programs: Transpersonal psychology, M.A., Ph.D.; counseling psychology, M.A.; transpersonal studies, M.A.
Admission Requirements: Bachelor's degree; field experience; personal interview
Application Deadline: March 1
Contact Person: Director of Admissions
Tuition: $8,820 (Ph.D.); $4,704 (evening M.A.)
Accreditation: California State Approved
Year Established: 1975
Faculty: 9 full-time; 22 adjunct

John F. Kennedy University
12 Altarinda Road
Orinda, CA 94563
(510) 254-0200
   JFK University is made up of five schools, including a school of psychology and holistic studies.
General Information: Private, nonsectarian
Degrees Offered: M.A.
Programs: Arts and consciousness, M.A.; certificate program (addiction studies, consulting psychology, cross-cultural counseling, expressive arts, grief studies, post-master's clinical training, sport psychology); clinical psychology, M.A. (meets M.F.C.C. requirements); consulting psychology, M.A.; coun-

seling psychology, M.A. (meets M.F.C.C. requirements); holistic health education, M.A.; interdisciplinary consciousness studies, M.A.; sport psychology, M.A.; transpersonal psychology, M.A.
Admission Requirements: Bachelor's degree
Application Deadline: Rolling
Contact Person: Director of Admissions
Tuition: $219/unit
Accreditation: WASC
Year Established: 1964
Faculty: 227 full-time and adjunct

LaSalle University
Human Services Psychology
Box 268
1900 West Olney Avenue
Philadelphia, PA 19141-1199
(215) 951-1767
General Information: Private, ecumenical
Degrees Offered: M.A.
Programs: Human services psychology
Admission Requirements: Bachelor's degree; GRE; letter of recommendation; 15 credit hours in psychology
Application Deadline: Three months before September, January, or May term
Contact Person: Director of Admissions
Tuition: $358/credit hour
Accreditation: MSACS
Year Established: 1988
Faculty: 12 full-time

Lesley College Graduate School
29 Everett Street
Cambridge, MA 02138-2790
(617) 349-8300
   The Holistic Counseling Program provides training for those individuals who view psychology from a holistic perspective and who wish to apply holistic principles to careers in counseling and professional psychology.
General Information: Public, nonsectarian
Degrees Offered: M.A.
Programs: Counseling psychology
Admission Requirements: Bachelor's degree
Application Deadline: Rolling
Contact Person: Director of Admissions
Tuition: $300/credit hour
Accreditation: NEASC; Commonwealth of Massachusetts, Interstate Certification Compact
Year Established: 1953
Faculty: Contact department

Maharishi International University
1000 North Fourth Street, Suite DB1155
Fairfield, IA 52557-1155
(515) 472-1166
   Maharishi International University inte-

grates traditional academic disciplines with Maharishi's concepts of Vedic science and technology. It is associated with the practice of transcendental meditation (TM).
General Information: Private; nonsectarian
Degrees Offered: M.A.; M.S.; Ph.D.
Programs: Neuroscience of human consciousness; psychology; science of creative intelligence
Admission Requirements: Bachelor's degree; GRE; meditation experience
Application Deadline: March 15
Contact Person: Director of Admissions
Tuition: $8,672
Accreditation: NCACS
Year Established: 1971
Faculty: 95 full- and part-time

Marywood College
2300 Adams Avenue
Scranton, PA 18509
(800) 338-4207
General Information: Private, Catholic
Degrees Offered: M.A.
Programs: Clinical services; counseling
Admission Requirements: Bachelor's degree; GRE
Application Deadline: Early March
Contact Person: Director of Admissions
Tuition: $325/credit
Accreditation: MSACS; accreditation of counseling program pending
Year Established: 1922
Faculty: 10 full-time

Massachusetts School of Professional Psychology
322 Sprague Street
Dedham, MA 02026
(617) 329-6777
General Information: Private, nonsectarian
Degrees Offered: Psy.D.
Programs: Clinical psychology
Admission Requirements: Bachelor's degree; GRE and MAT; Relevant experience
Application Deadline: Contact department
Contact Person: Director of Admissions
Tuition: $12,800/year
Accreditation: NEASC; APA
Year Established: 1976
Faculty: 37 part-time; 57 adjunct

Minnesota School of Professional Psychology
Division of the American Schools of Professional Psychology
3103 East 80th Street, Suite 290
Minneapolis, MN 55425
(800) 853-6777
General Information: Private, nonsectarian
Degrees Offered: Psy.D.
Programs: Doctor of Psychology (with a psy-

chology and religion predoctoral minor option)
Admission Requirements: Bachelor's degree; five courses in psychology
Application Deadline: January 15
Contact Person: Director of Admissions
Tuition: $335/credit hour
Accreditation: NCACS, APA (provisional)
Year Established: 1987
Faculty: 10 core; 4 associate core; 18 associate

Naropa Institute
2130 Arapahoe Avenue
Boulder, CO 80302
(303) 444-0202
The Naropa Institute is the only accredited college in North America whose educational philosophy is based on the Buddhist contemplative tradition.
General Information: Private, Buddhist (nonsectarian)
Degrees Offered: M.A.
Programs: Body psychology; Buddhist studies; dance/movement therapy; psychology: contemplative psychotherapy; transpersonal counseling psychology (art therapy concentration available)
Admission Requirements: Bachelor's degree; interview; relevant experience
Application Deadline: Rolling
Contact Person: Director of Admissions
Tuition: $8,000/year
Accreditation: NCACS
Year Established: 1974
Faculty: 22 full-time; 93 adjunct

New College of California
Graduate Psychology Program
777 Valencia Street
San Francisco, CA 94110
(415) 861-4168
General Information: Private, nonsectarian
Degrees Offered: B.A.; M.A.
Programs: Feminist psychology; social-clinical psychology
Admission Requirements: Bachelor's degree; interview
Application Deadline: April 15
Contact Person: Director of Admissions
Tuition: $7,600/year
Accreditation: WASC
Year Established: 1971
Faculty: 7 core; 40 adjunct

Northern Illinois University (NIU)
Department of Admissions
Dekalb, IL 60115-2854
(815) 753-0446
NIU offers a dual Doctor of Education degree in either educational psychology or

in counselor education in conjunction with a master's degree in counseling psychology from Trinity Evangelical Divinity School. See Trinity Divinity School under Theological Training.

Northern New Mexico Community College
El Rito Campus
El Rito, NM 87530
(505) 581-4100
This program is in association with the Elizabeth Kübler Ross Hospice and Grief Counseling Program (see Nondegree Training Programs).
General Information: Public, nonsectarian
Degrees Offered: A.S., certificate
Programs: Hospice and grief counseling, transpersonal grief counseling
Admission Requirements: Bachelor's degree
Application Deadline: Rolling
Contact Person: Director of Admissions
Tuition: $19.50/credit hour
Accreditation: NCACS
Year Established: 1986
Faculty: 1 full-time; 12 part-time

Pacifica Graduate Institute
249 Lambert Road
Carpinteria, CA 93013
(805) 969-3626
The institute incorporates personal/existential, psychoanalytic, Jungian, and behavioral perspectives. All programs emphasize depth psychology. The following programs also prepare students to apply for the California Clinical Psychology license and California Marriage, Family and Child Counseling license.
General Information: Private, nonsectarian
Degrees Offered: M.A.; Ph.D.; M.F.C.C.
Programs: Clinical psychology, Ph.D.; counseling psychology, M.A.; mythological studies, M.A., (Ph.D. program beginning Fall 1994)
Admission Requirements: Bachelor's degree; interview; relevant experience
Application Deadline: June 15
Contact Person: Director of Admissions
Tuition: $6,780
Accreditation: WASC (candidate for accreditation status)
Year Established: 1981
Faculty: 13 core; 10 adjunct

Pepperdine University
Pepperdine University Plaza
400 Corporate Pointe
Culver City, CA 90230
(310) 456-4000
General Information: Private, nonsectarian
Degrees Offered: M.A.; Psy.D.
Programs: Clinical psychology; Doctor of Psychology

Admission Requirements: Bachelor's degree; GRE; relevant experience
Application Deadline: February 15 (Psy.D.); April 1 (M.A.)
Contact Person: Director of Admissions
Tuition: $7,500 (M.A.); $14,000 (Psy.D.)
Accreditation: WASC
Year Established: Contact department
Faculty: 20 full-time

Process Work Center of Portland
733 Northwest Everett
Box 11, Suite 3C
Portland, OR 97209
(503) 223-8188
Process Work is a cross-disciplinary approach to individuals and collective change developed in Zurich, Switzerland, by Arnold Mindell. With its roots in Jungian psychology, Taoism, and physics, Process Work—also known as process-oriented psychology or dream/bodywork—teaches that the solution to a problem is contained in the disturbance itself and therefore provides a practical framework through which individuals, couples, families, and groups may connect with greater awareness and creativity.
General Information: Private, nonsectarian
Degrees Offered: M.P.W.; diploma as certified process worker
Programs: Process work (M.P.W.); various workshops
Admission Requirements: interview
Application Deadline: Rolling
Contact Person: Director of Admissions
Tuition: $300/annual plus student fees
Accreditation: State of Oregon
Year Established: 1990
Faculty: 44 full- and part-time

Rosebridge Graduate School of Integrative Psychology
1040 Oak Grove Road, Suite 103
Concord, CA 94518
(510) 689-0560
Rosebridge's psychology programs include preparation for the M.F.C.C. or Psy.D. state psychologist license.
General Information: Private, nonsectarian, nonprofit
Degrees Offered: M.A.; Ph.D.; Psy.D.
Programs: Clinical psychology; counseling psychology; Doctor of Psychology
Admission Requirements: Bachelor's degree; relevant experience
Application Deadline: One month before admission
Contact Person: Director of Admissions
Tuition: $6,500/year (M.A.); $7,750/year (Ph.D., Psy.D.)

Accreditation: California Council for Private Postsecondary and Vocational Education
Year Established: 1978
Faculty: 35 full- and part-time

Ryokan College
11965 Venice Boulevard, Suite 304
Los Angeles, CA 90066
(310) 390-7560
General Information: Private, nonsectarian
Degrees Offered: M.A.; Psy.D.; Ph.D.
Programs: Accupressure; clinical psychology; counseling psychology; holistic health; nutrition
Admission Requirements: Bachelor's degree
Application Deadline: Rolling
Contact Person: Director of Admissions
Tuition: $5,400 - $12,800/year (depending on program)
Accreditation: California State Approved
Year Established: 1979
Faculty: Contact department

Salve Regina University
100 Ochre Avenue
Newport, RI 02840-4192
(401) 847-6650
General Information: Private, Catholic
Degrees Offered: M.A.
Programs: Holistic counseling
Admission Requirements: Bachelor's degree; GRE or MAT scores; two letters of recommendation
Application Deadline: Rolling
Contact Person: Director of Admissions
Tuition: $230/credit
Accreditation: NEASC
Year Established: 1983
Faculty: 12 full-time

Sonoma State University
School of Social Sciences
Department of Psychology
1801 East Cotati Avenue
Rohnert Park, CA 94928
(707) 664-2411
Sonoma State is one of the 19 colleges in the California state university system. The psychology program is humanistically oriented. Most of the Tamalpa Institute's curriculum in dance therapy can now be used to meet the requirements for an M.A. degree in psychology (see Nondegree Training Programs). Also, Sonoma offers an external master's degree through Natalie Rogers's Person Centered Expressive Therapy Institute in Santa Rosa and the Institute of Transpersonal Psychology in Menlo Park (see Body-Centered Psychotherapy).
General Information: Public, nonsectarian
Degrees Offered: M.A.
Programs: Psychology (with an optional humanistic/transpersonal advisory plan)
Admission Requirements: Bachelor's degree; GRE or Miller and WEPT
Application Deadline: Semester before
Contact Person: Director of Admissions
Tuition: $120/semester unit
Accreditation: WASC
Year Established: Contact department
Faculty: 15 full-time

Southwestern College
P.O. Box 4788
Santa Fe, NM 87502
(505) 471-5756
General Information: Private, nonsectarian
Degrees Offered: M.A.
Programs: Art therapy; counseling
Admission Requirements: Bachelor's degree; interview
Application Deadline: Rolling
Contact Person: Director of Admissions
Tuition: $122/unit; $1,708/quarter full-time
Accreditation: NCASC
Year Established: 1972
Faculty: 14 core; 5 adjunct

St. John's University
Queens Campus
Grand Central and Utopia Parkways
Jamaica, NY 11439
(718) 990-6114
General Information: Private, Catholic
Degrees Offered: Ph.D.
Programs: Clinical Psychology
Admission Requirements: Bachelor's degree
Application Deadline: Rolling
Contact Person: Director of Admissions
Tuition: $324/credit hour
Accreditation: MSACS; APA
Year Established: 1870
Faculty: Contact department

St. Mary's College of California
P.O. Box 4350
Moraga, CA 94575
(510) 631-4705
General Information: Private, Catholic
Degrees Offered: M.A.
Programs: Counseling leadership; marriage and family clinical counselor; school counseling
Admission Requirements: Bachelor's degree
Application Deadline: August 15 (fall); January 15 (spring)
Contact Person: Director of Admissions
Tuition: $290/semester credit
Accreditation: WASC
Year Established: 1976
Faculty: 10 adjunct

Temple University
Counseling Psychology Program
238 Weiss Hall
Philadelphia, PA 19122
(215) 204-3253
Temple's program incorporates humanistic principles and perspectives. The Department of Psychoeducational Processes is a member of the Consortium of Diversified Psychology Programs.
General Information: Public, nonsectarian
Degrees Offered: M.A.; Ph.D.
Programs: Counseling psychology
Admission Requirements: Bachelor's degree; GRE; Advanced Psychology GRE; interview; relevant work experience; three letters of recommendation
Application Deadline: February 15
Contact Person: Director of Admissions
Tuition: $247/unit
Accreditation: APA; NCACS
Year Established: 1948
Faculty: 9 full-time; plus adjunct

United States International University
10455 Pomerado Road
San Diego, CA 92131
(619) 693-4773
General Information: Private, nonsectarian
Degrees Offered: M.A.; Psy.D.
Programs: Counseling psychology, M.A.; Doctor of Psychology with specialization in applied psychology, chemical dependency, clinical psychology, industrial and organizational psychology, marriage and family therapy, or pastoral counseling; marriage and family therapy, M.A., Ph.D.; psychology, M.A.
Admission Requirements: Bachelor's degree; GRE or MAT
Application Deadline: April 15
Contact Person: Director of Admissions
Tuition: $250/per unit
Accreditation: WASC
Year Established: 1952
Faculty: Contact department

University for Humanistic Studies
2002 Jimmy Durante Boulevard
Del Mar, CA 92014-2252
(619) 259-9733
The counseling psychology programs satisfy academic requirements for state licensing as an M.F.C.C. or a psychologist.
General Information: Private, nonsectarian, nonprofit
Degrees Offered: M.A.; Psy.D.; Ph.D.; post-masters certificates
Programs: Psychology with emphases in counseling, transpersonal studies, and health and body-centered psychotherapy,

M.A.; psychology with an emphasis in counseling psychology, Psy.D.; psychology with an emphasis in integral studies, Ph.D.; postmaster's programs in addiction studies and expressive and experiential therapy
Admission Requirements: Bachelor's degree; interview; placement examinations
Application Deadline: Rolling
Contact Person: Director of Admissions
Tuition: $5,500/year
Accreditation: California State Approved
Year Established: 1977
Faculty: Contact department

University of California, Santa Cruz
Division of Graduate Studies and Research
399 Applied Sciences Building
Santa Cruz, CA 95064
(408) 459-4616
General Information: Public, nonsectarian
Degrees Offered: Ph.D.
Programs: History of consciousness
Admission Requirements: Bachelor's degree
Application Deadline: December 15
Contact Person: Director of Admissions
Tuition: $8,122/year (nonresident); $5,041/year (resident)
Accreditation: WASC
Year Established: 1965
Faculty: 8 core

University of Chicago
1116 East 59th Street
Chicago, IL 60637
(312) 702-8859
The Department of Psychology is a member of the Consortium of Diversified Psychology Programs. Also, Eugene Gendlin, Ph.D., the founder of focusing, is a professor in the department.
General Information: Private, nonsectarian
Degrees Offered: Ph.D.
Programs: Psychology (research oriented)
Admission Requirements: Bachelor's degree, letter of recommendation, GRE; statement of purpose
Application Deadline: January 5
Contact Person: Director of Admissions
Tuition: $19,335/year tuition only
Accreditation: NEACSS
Year Established: Call department
Faculty: Call department

University of Notre Dame
217 Hagger Hall
Notre Dame, IN 46556
(219) 631-7706
General Information: Private, nonsectarian
Degrees Offered: M.A.; Ph.D.
Programs: Counseling Psychology, M.A., Ph.D.; developmental psychology, Ph.D.;

social psychology, Ph.D.
Admission Requirements: Bachelor's degree; GRE; relevant experience
Application Deadline: January 15
Contact Person: Director of Admissions
Tuition: $872/credit hour
Accreditation: NCASC; APA (Ph.D.)
Year Established: 1842 (school)
Faculty: 22 full-time

University of San Francisco
School of Education
2130 Fulton Street
San Francisco, CA 94117-1080
(415) 666-6525
General Information: Private, Jesuit
Degrees Offered: M.A.; Ed.D.
Programs: Counseling, M.A. (with emphasis in educational counseling, life transitions counseling, or marital and family counseling); counseling psychology, Ed.D.
Admission Requirements: Bachelor's degree
Application Deadline: Rolling
Contact Person: Director of Admissions
Tuition: $492/unit (M.A.); $542/unit (Ed.D)
Accreditation: WASC, APA (candidacy status of Ed.D.)
Year Established: 1855
Faculty: 8 full-time

University of Santa Monica
Center for the Study and Practice of Spiritual Psychology
2107 Wilshire Boulevard
Santa Monica, CA 90403
(310) 829-7402
The program integrates 36 counseling skills and approaches from various schools of counseling, including: person-centered, Jungian, Gestalt, rational-emotive, Neurolinguistic Programming, and Psychosynthesis. Classes are offered in weekend format to allow for travel to the university.
General Information: Private, nonsectarian, nonprofit
Degrees Offered: M.A.
Programs: Applied psychology, M.A.; counseling psychology, M.A.
Admission Requirements: Bachelor's degree
Application Deadline: August 1
Contact Person: Director of Admissions
Tuition: $9,900 (two-year program in applied); $19,080 (three-year program in Counseling)
Accreditation: California State Full Institutional Approval; PASC
Year Established: 1976
Faculty: 12 full- and part-time

Vanderbilt University
Graduate Department of Religion, Divinity School
Nashville, TN 37240
(615) 322-2776
The purpose of the program is to provide advanced studies in religion and the personality sciences so that students may prepare themselves for careers in teaching, scholarship, and clinical practice.
General Information: Private, nonsectarian
Degrees Offered: Ph.D.
Programs: Religion and personality
Admission Requirements: Bachelor's degree; GRE; interview; master's degree, M.Div or related preferred
Application Deadline: Rolling
Contact Person: Director of Admissions
Tuition: $724/credit hour
Accreditation: SACS
Year Established: 1979
Faculty: 3 full-time

West Georgia College
Department of Psychology
Carrolton, GA 301218
(404) 836-6510
West Georgia College is part of the Georgia State University system of state-operated institutions of higher education. In 1967 members of the Psychology Department sought to move in directions that were more humanistic. The master's program in psychology at West Georgia College was developed with a specific vocational orientation. It includes parapsychology; oriental thought and philosophy; and educational, theoretical, experiential, and phenomenological psychology.
General Information: Private, nonsectarian
Degrees Offered: M.A.
Programs: Psychology
Admission Requirements: Bachelor's degree; GRE; interview
Application Deadline: Quarterly
Contact Person: Director of Admissions
Tuition: $1,700/year; $4,400/year (out-of-state)
Accreditation: National Council for Accreditation of Teacher Education; SACS
Year Established: 1967
Faculty: 12 full-time

World University of America
107 North Ventura Street
P.O. Box 1567
Ojai, CA 93024-1567
(805) 646-1444
The World University offers a unique program directed to personal unfoldment and spiritual growth within the traditional framework of an academic curriculum.
General Information: Private, nonsectarian,

nonprofit
Degrees Offered: M.A.; certificates
Programs: Philosophy, M.A.; psychology, M.A.; religious studies, M.A.; astrology, business, hypnotherapy, meditation, spiritual ministry, thanatology, yoga, certificate
Admission Requirements: Bachelor's degree
Application Deadline: Rolling
Contact Person: Director of Admissions
Tuition: $100/unit
Accreditation: State of California Department of Education Private Postsecondary Education
Year Established: 1974
Faculty: Contact department

Wright State University
School of Graduate Studies
Room 106 Oelman
Dayton, OH 45435
(513) 873-2976
Wright's program offers training and course work designed to develop skills in the holistic counseling process.
General Information: Public, nonsectarian
Degrees Offered: M.S., M.R.C.
Programs: Counseling and guidance, M.S.; rehabilitation counseling, M.R.C.; chemical dependency, M.R.C.
Admission Requirements: Bachelor's degree
Application Deadline: Rolling
Contact Person: Director of Admissions
Tuition: $1,214/quarter ($2,175, nonresident)
Accreditation: CACREP; MSACS; Council on Rehabilitation Education
Year Established: Contact department
Faculty: 15 full-time; 8 adjunct

NONRESIDENTIAL PSYCHOLOGY DEGREE PROGRAMS

External degree programs provide the option of earning a degree without the traditional requirement of attending classes on a university campus. Faculty-student contact is maintained through audiotapes, videos, teleconference calling, computer networks (quickly becoming commonplace), workbooks, and occasional on-sight study groups and workshops conducted by the school's adjunct faculty.

These programs are a pragmatic option for people wishing to earn an advanced degree while maintaining personal and professional job responsibilities. Most "learners," as they are some-

times called, have already acquired their career training but need to finish course work not completed during graduate school, and/or seek to widen their professional or personal education. The average learner enrolled at the Union Institute, a popular nonresidential school, is 46 years old.

There are two types of nonresidential programs: partially flexible curriculum design and self-design. For example, the Institute for Transpersonal Psychology's (ITP) external master's degree program in counseling is a flexible curriculum in that it requires students to fulfill a core marriage, family and child counselor curriculum in addition to choosing electives from the school's transpersonal-oriented courses. The Union Institute program, on the other hand, is completely self-constructed—the learner independently plans, obtains approval for, initiates, and completes an individualized curriculum.

Whatever the structure, all nonresidential programs share the common commitment of providing on-going support to learners while facilitating their progress. ITP offers a mentor to each student; Union students select a core faculty and two adjunct professionals in their chosen area of study. Because of the geographic distance between learners and the main academic campus, external programs also encourage students in common geographical areas to share ideas among themselves, as well as with the professional community in which they live.

Most people who enter a nonresidential program possess a good sense of what they want and have the discipline and commitment to follow the program through to completion. They often hold graduate degrees, which may have helped establish their careers, as well as previous experience in the field they wish to pursue. In addition, it is not unusual for these motivated self-starters to create their own vocation (such as a psychological consultant or writer), or to establish a private psychotherapy practice after graduation (if licensed).

Because accrediting and licensing

bodies remain apprehensive about giving nonresidential programs their approval (for reasons such as lack of coherency, structure, and accountability), prospective students should first ensure that such a degree will provide them with the opportunities they seek. Finally, even though learners are less supervised, do not be deceived into thinking that external programs are less difficult than residential programs; in fact, the self-discipline and motivation required may make these programs the most challenging avenue for graduate education.

The California Institute of Integral Studies, Fielding Institute, Saybrook Institute, and Union Institute offer the only nonresidential clinical Ph.D. programs in the United States that prepare candidates for licensure as a psychologist. These four programs, not surprisingly, require more standardized courses than a self-designed curriculum.

GRADUATE PROGRAMS
American Commonwealth University
2801 Camino del Rio South
San Diego, CA 92108-3801
(619) 298-9040
All learning activities are accomplished through meetings with university-assigned adjunct professors who reside in the learner's geographic area.
General Information: Private, nonsectarian
Degrees Offered: M.A.; Ph.D.
Programs: Humanities; psychology
Admission Requirements: Bachelor's degree
Application Deadline: Rolling
Contact Person: Director of Admissions
Tuition: $275/credit
Accreditation: Council for Private Postsecondary and Vocational Education, State of California.
Year Established: 1979
Faculty: Composed of instructors approved by the university

Antioch University
Individualized Master of Arts Program
800 Livermore Street
Yellow Springs, OH 45387
(513) 767-6322
General Information: Private, nonsectarian
Degrees Offered: M.A.
Programs: Individualized; conflict resolution
Admission Requirements: Bachelor's degree
Application Deadline: Rolling

Contact Person: Director of Admissions
Tuition: $1,290/quarter
Accreditation: NCACS
Year Established: 1852
Faculty: Composed of instructors approved by the university

Atlantic University

67th Street and Atlanta Avenue
P.O. Box 595
Virginia Beach, VA 23451
(804) 428-1512
    See Residential Psychology Degree Programs.

Avalon Institute

3985 Wonderland Hill
Boulder, CO 80302
(303) 443-4363
    See Residential Psychology Degree Programs.

California Institute for Human Science

609 South Vulcan Avenue, Suite 201
Encinitas, CA 92024
(619) 634-1771
    See Residential Psychology Degree Programs.

California Institute of Integral Studies (CIIS)

765 Ashbury Street
San Francisco, CA 94117
(415) 753-6100
    See Residential Psychology Degree Programs.

Center for Psychological Studies

1398 Solano Avenue
Albany, CA 94706
(510) 524-0291
    See Residential Psychology Degree Programs.

Columbia Pacific University

1415 Third Street
San Rafael, CA 94901
(415) 459-1650
    Educational programs are based on a holistic philosophy that emphasizes integration of all aspects of a student's education, work, and individual interests.
General Information: Private, nonsectarian
Degrees Offered: M.A.; Ph.D.
Programs: Arts and Sciences
Admission Requirements: Bachelor's degree
Application Deadline: Rolling
Contact Person: Director of Admissions
Tuition: $1,100/quarter
Accreditation: California State Approved
Year Established: 1978
Faculty: 400 part- and full-time worldwide

Fielding Institute

2112 Santa Barbara Street
Santa Barbara, CA 93105-3538
(805) 687-1099
General Information: Private, nonsectarian
Degrees Offered: M.A.; Ph.D.
Programs: Psychology; human and organizational development
Admission Requirements: Bachelor's degree; relevant experience
Application Deadline: Rolling
Contact Person: Director of Admissions
Tuition: $8,820/year
Accreditation: WASC; APA (candidacy status)
Year Established: 1974
Faculty: 60 located throughout the United States

Goddard College

Plainfield, VT 05667
(802) 454-8311; (800) 468-4888
    Although Goddard offers residential undergraduate programs, all of its graduate programs are primarily nonresidential.
General Information: Private, nonsectarian
Degrees Offered: M.A.
Programs: Interdisciplinary studies; psychology and counseling
Admission Requirements: Bachelor's degree; letter of recommendation; relevant experience
Application Deadline: Rolling
Contact Person: Director of Admissions
Tuition: $7,600/year
Accreditation: NEACSS
Year Established: 1938
Faculty: Composed of instructors approved by the university

Greenwich University

103 Kapiolani Street
Hilo, HI 96721
(808) 935-9934
General Information: Private, nonsectarian
Degrees Offered: M.A.; M.S.; Ph.D.
Programs: Individualized; science of intuition (in conjunction with Holos Institutes of Health®), Ph.D.
Admission Requirements: Bachelor's degree
Application Deadline: Rolling
Contact Person: Director of Admissions
Tuition: $2,500 (M.A.); $3,500 (Ph.D.)
Accreditation: PASC (candidacy status); State of Hawaii
Year Established: 1972
Faculty: 160 adjunct

Institute of Transpersonal Psychology

744 San Antonio Road
Palo Alto, CA 94303
(415) 493-4430
    See Residential Psychology Degree Programs.

Lesley College Graduate School

29 Everett Street
Cambridge, MA 02138-2790
(617) 868-9600; (617) 349-8300
    See Residential Psychology Degree Programs.

Ryokan College

11965 Venice Boulevard, Suite 304
Los Angeles, CA 90066
(213) 390-7560
    See Residential Psychology Degree Programs.

Saybrook Institute

450 Pacific, 3rd Floor
San Francisco, CA 94133
(415) 433-9200; (800) 825-4480
General Information: Private, nonsectarian
Degrees Offered: M.A.; Ph.D.
Programs: Clinical inquiry; consciousness studies; health studies; human science, M.A., Ph.D.; psychology, M.A.,Ph.D.; social philosophy and political psychology; systems inquiry
Admission Requirements: Bachelor's degree (in related field); relevant experience
Application Deadline: Rolling
Contact Person: Director of Admissions
Tuition: $9,000/year
Accreditation: WASC
Year Established: 1971
Faculty: 11 full-time; 32 adjunct

Seattle Pacific University

School of Social and Behavioral Sciences
Counseling and Family Therapy
Seattle, WA 98119
(800) 366-3344
General Information: Private, Christian
Degrees Offered: M.S.; M.F.T.
Programs: Community counseling; counseling and family therapy; marriage and family therapy
Admission Requirements: Bachelor's degree; GRE; letter of recommendation
Application Deadline: March 31
Contact Person: Director of Admissions
Tuition: $290/credit
Accreditation: ACA; AAMFT
Year Established: 1992
Faculty: 1 full-time; 4 part-time

Sonoma State University

1801 East Cotati Avenue
Rohnert Park, CA 94928
(707) 664-2411
    See Residential Psychology Degree Programs.

Southwest University
2200 Veterans Boulevard
New Orleans, LA 70062
(504) 468-2900
General Information: Private, nonsectarian
Degrees Offered: M.A.; Ph.D.
Programs: Counseling/hypnotherapy; counseling psychology
Admission Requirements: Bachelor's degree; related experience
Application Deadline: Rolling
Contact Person: Director of Admissions
Tuition: $77/unit
Accreditation: State of Louisiana (in process)
Year Established: 1981
Faculty: Composed of instructors approved by the university

Summit University of Louisiana
7508 Hayne Boulevard
New Orleans, LA 70127
(504) 241-0227
Summit University honors the International Association for Managerial and Organizational Psychosynthesis (AMOP) program and evaluates, assesses, and provides academic credit leading to an M.A. and a Ph.D. (See AMOP under Psychosynthesis.)
General Information: Private, nonsectarian, nonprofit
Degrees Offered: B.A.; M.S.; Ph.D.
Programs: Open
Admission Requirements: Bachelor's degree; individual assessment
Application Deadline: Rolling
Contact Person: Director of Admissions
Tuition: $2,500/year
Accreditation: Registered with the Louisiana Board of Regents; the university is not accredited
Year Established: 1988
Faculty: Composed of instructors approved by the university

Union Institute
440 East McMillan Street
Cincinnati, OH 45206
(800) 486-3116; (513) 861-6400
Formerly known as the Union for Experimenting Colleges and Universities, the Union Institute was founded by 10 college presidents as an educational research and experimentation organization. The doctoral programs respond to the educational needs of self-motivated adults. The program is designed as an educational alternative specifically for those adults who require more options and flexibility than are usually available in a more traditional university setting.

General Information: Private, nonsectarian
Degrees Offered: Ph.D. only
Programs: Arts and sciences; interdisciplinary studies
Admission Requirements: Field experience desired; master's degree
Application Deadline: Monthly admissions
Contact Person: Director of Admissions
Tuition: $2,484/quarter
Accreditation: NCACS
Year Established: 1964
Faculty: Composed of instructors approved by the university

Vermont College of Norwich University
32 College Street
Montpelier, VT 05602
(802) 828-8830; (800) 336-6794
Vermont's program is derived from the American pragmatists, particularly from the progressive educational theories of John Dewey, which emphasize the testing of theories in practice.
General Information: Private, nonsectarian
Degrees Offered: M.A.
Programs: Counseling and psychotherapy; interdisciplinary; philosophy and religion; psychology
Admission Requirements: Bachelor's degree; interview; relevant experience
Application Deadline: Continuous
Contact Person: Director of Admissions
Tuition: $3,420/semester
Accreditation: NEASC; South Carolina Commission on Higher Education
Year Established: 1970
Faculty: 11 full-time

Walden University
Process Center
801 Anchor Drive
Naples, FL 33940
(800) 444-6795
The Department of Psychology is a member of the Consortium of Diversified Psychology Programs.
General Information: Private, nonsectarian
Degrees Offered: Ph.D.
Programs: Human services
Admission Requirements: Bachelor's degree
Application Deadline: Rolling
Contact Person: Director of Admissions
Tuition: $2,595/quarter
Accreditation: NCACS
Year Established: 1970
Faculty: Composed of instructors approved by the university

Westbrook University
404 North Mesa Verde
Aztec, NM 87410
(505) 334-1115
Westbrook is affiliated with and accredited through Westbrook Theological Seminary.
General Information: Private, nonsectarian
Degrees Offered: M.A.; M.S.; Ph.D.; N.D.
Programs: Addictions counseling, M.A., Ph.D.; counseling psychology, M.A., Ph.D.; Jungian psychology, M.A., Ph.D.; metaphysical counseling, M.A., Ph.D.; mythology, M.A., Ph.D.; naturopathy, N.D.; religious counseling, M.A., Ph.D.; transpersonal psychology, M.A., Ph.D.; holistic nursing, M.S., Ph.D.; holistic science, Ph.D.
Admission Requirements: Bachelor's degree
Application Deadline: Rolling
Contact Person: Director of Admissions
Tuition: $2,700 - $4,710/total, depending on degree
Accreditation: State of New Mexico Commission on Higher Education; International Accrediting Association for Ministerial Education; Association of Fundamental Institutions of Religious Education; National Association of Alcoholism and Drug Abuse Counseling; American Naturopathic Medical Association; International Association of Naturopathic Physicians
Year Established: 1988
Faculty: Composed of instructors approved by the university

SPIRITUALLY SENSITIVE SOCIAL WORK

The profession of social work has always championed a holistic approach to helping people. It has sought to understand individuals in terms of the interplay between biological, psychological, and social aspects. It has emphasized the need to understand people in the context of their social and cultural environments, and it has engaged in a wide range of services, including individual psychotherapy and casework, family therapy and family service, group work, organizational change, community activism, policy development, political action, and international social development. It has advocated the rights and empowerment of the disadvantaged, vulnerable, and oppressed groups even while providing services designed to promote individual adjustment and coping skills, thereby reinforcing the social order. Throughout its professional history, these various concerns have been debated and shifts in priority have occurred, but a commitment to holistic service remains consistent.

Given this orientation, it is natural that social workers would also deal with people's spiritual needs. Early in the history of the profession, the human being was seen as a bio-psycho-social-spiritual being. In fact, the profession in the United States had its origins in Jewish and Christian religious efforts to provide for charity and community support through such projects as the settlement house movement for European immigrants. However, the question of whether social workers should address spiritual needs has been subject to controversy for several decades. Indeed, until recently, the discussion of religion and spirituality has been considered off-limits in most settings of social work education and practice.

Since the early 1980s, there has been increasing effort to retrieve the lost soul of social work. Although the profession arose from explicit spiritual motivation to provide care and service, something severed the tie between this soulful concern and its professional delivery. Lately, a number of scholars and practitioners have been trying to help restore the profession to the wholeness that was its distinctive heritage. (See essay below.)

From the late 1980s, there has been a significant increase in professional publications, conference presentations, and other activities concerning the development of spiritually sensitive social work. In 1990, the Society for Spirituality and Social Work was formed to help network these activities, to make academics and practitioners aware of each others' work, to build the momentum of the movement, and to publish the semiannual publication *The Spirituality and Social Work Journal.* The society also cooperated with the North American Association of Christian Social Workers to generate presentations at national meetings of the National Association of Social Workers and the Council on Social Work Education. These ties prompted the Council on Social Work Education to restore recognition of religion and spirituality as legitimate topics

of concern within the newest revision of the Curriculum Policy Statement used to accredit social work education programs throughout the United States. The American movement to restore the connection between spirituality and social work now has connections with similar efforts in Europe, the Middle East, and East Asia.

There are several clusters of interest within the profession that facilitate the promotion of spiritually sensitive social

---

The student needs to be very self-directed and creative in order to tailor a combined program to suit his or her academic needs and spiritual perspective.

---

work. A national organization known as the Group on Philosophical Issues in Social Work publishes a newsletter and promotes presentations on post-positivist, new-paradigm thinking at the Council on Social Work Education's annual meetings. The global perspective of international social work scholars taps the insights of such spiritual social activists as Mahatma Gandhi. Some feminist social work authors call for a more holistic, contextually oriented way of understanding human behavior which is supportive of spiritual sensitivity. There is also a strong emphasis in the field on designing services that are sensitive to ethnic diversity because it has become clear that religious support systems and ways of healing are very significant to many ethnic and religious groups. A "strengths perspective" on social work is growing, which counters the tendency of professionals to focus on problems, deficits, and pathologies by empowering clients to actualize their self-chosen life goals, develop their talents, and utilize their environmental supports. Social work theory has recently begun to explore insights from

transpersonal psychology and deep ecology that highlight our spiritual connections beyond ego-centered or person-centered boundaries.

These trends have important implications for the profession. Although it is not accurate to say that most social workers are aware of or are in agreement with the return to spiritual concerns, it is clear that this return is happening. This does not mean that a return to sectarian rivalry or worldview competition within the profession is desirable, but rather that some new, not fully predictable vision of human wholeness and holistic human service is emerging.

HOW TO FIND A SPIRITUALLY SENSITIVE SCHOOL OF SOCIAL WORK

Several social work schools allow joint degrees related to theology and social work. These programs generally allow the student to combine course work in two different subject areas without, unfortunately, providing a true integration of both. For example, the Mandel School of Applied Social Sciences at Case Western Reserve University in Cleveland allows for a combined program in Jewish studies and social work. It is also possible for a student to identify one of the many colleges or universities that have both academic religious studies programs and social work programs. For example, the University of Denver has a cooperative relation between the Department of Religious Studies, the Graduate School of Social Work, and the nearby Iliff School of Theology. Many religiously sponsored colleges have social work degree programs and offer an opportunity to mix course work in religion and social work. In any case, the student needs to be very self-directed and creative in order to tailor a combined program to suit his or her academic needs and spiritual perspective.

A student who is serious about finding a program suited to particular interests, such as transpersonal theory or nonsectarian approaches to spirituality, needs to read the social work literature on this subject and identify the relevant authors and their host institutions. This literature can be identified by obtaining bibliographies from the Society for Spirituality and Social Work or by looking in the indexes of *Social Work Research and Abstracts Journal* under the terms *spirituality, religion,* and *church.* Most social work programs do not have a formal focus on spirituality, but committed faculty at some institutions can help the student in this regard. For instance, the University of Kansas in Lawrence is host to several faculty who are working on related areas such as post-positivist philosophy, feminism, and the strengths perspective. It is helpful if a student can identify a faculty person at a potential school who is willing to serve as an advisor or mentor. These suggestions apply at all degree levels.

—This introduction is based on an essay written by Edward R. Canda, Ph.D., professor of social work at the University of Kansas and director of the Society for Spirituality and Social Work.

A HISTORICAL PERSPECTIVE: RETRIEVING THE LOST SOUL OF SOCIAL WORK

Sometimes religiously motivated social services are provided with strings attached. For example, along with an offering of food to the hungry may come pious admonishments and pressures to convert. This insidious linkage of service to proselytization has been rejected by the mainstream profession because it manipulates the very people who are most vulnerable. Thus, despite the laudable contributions of religiously motivated social service, there are important, and often detrimental, effects of sectarianism. Below Professor Canda recounts how social work "lost its soul" yet is now taking steps to retrieve it.

Since the 1920s, the social work profession has turned to psychological and sociological theories and these orientations have taken precedence over the theological perspectives of sin, moral defect, and dependence on divine healing powers. These new theories, it was hoped, would provide scientifically or politically powerful strategies to solve human problems, where religious approaches had appeared to fail in the past. Thus, the profession shifted from a theo-centric to a human-centric view of the human condition.

These trends were reinforced by the rapid expansion of government-based social services that expanded the New Deal reforms of the 1930s in the form of the War on Poverty and the community mental health movement of the 1960s and '70s. As state and federal governments became prominent sponsors and founders of social welfare programs, the constitutional requirement of separation of church and state caused the link

---

The real problem is that the social work profession threw out the baby of spirituality with the bath water of sectarianism.

---

between spirituality and social work to be abruptly severed. Government funding was incompatible with any form of direct or even indirect religious proselytization by social service providers. Even though social work services have continued to be provided through religiously affiliated agencies, such as Jewish Family Services, Lutheran Social Services, and Catholic Charities, such agencies are forbidden to practice religious discrimination or missionizing in any of their government-funded programs. Also, for similar reasons state-university-based social work graduate programs could no longer promote sectarian views and interests in their teaching.

For all of these reasons, the profession of social work has tended to distance itself from sectarian religious ideas and institutions. As a result, most schools of social work have not provided any education about religious or spiritual needs of clients or ways to respond to them. By the early 1970s, the Council on Social Work Education's Curriculum Policy statement dropped references to religion and spirituality as legitimate topics for social work education. Many

social work educators and practitioners (even if sympathetic to spiritual matters) feel at a loss when such topics emerge in work with clients. Therefore, following the general societal tendency toward fragmentation and specialization, rather than holism, they may refer clients to clergy or even treat the clients as though their spiritual concerns are pathological or irrelevant.

Clearly, the profession's fears about the dangers of sectarianism are justified. This, however, is not itself the core threat of a holistic approach to service. The real problem is that the profession threw out the baby of spirituality with the bath water of sectarianism.

All during the history of the profession, people have been aware of religious and spiritual needs. More than 100 articles and books on these topics had been published prior to 1985 by social workers. But these arguments were seldom heard or responded to. Finally, however, during the mid-1980s, the calls for reconsideration increased in intensity. Some well-known and influential scholars joined the chorus, such as Max Siporin of the State University of New York at Albany. This added a sense of legitimacy to the fledgling movement. In 1985, a national conference titled "The Impact of Religious Fundamentalism on Social Work" was held in Cleveland, Ohio, to explore the reactionary backlash of politically conservative religious opponents on social work values. These developments within the profession synchronized with similar developments in the larger society that raised awareness about the importance of spirituality.

As Marilyn Ferguson's book *The Aquarian Conspiracy* pointed out in 1980, and Fritjof Capra's book *The Turning Point* documented a few years later, many influences toward holistic thinking were being felt. These include, for example, the globalization of economies; anxiety over the threat of nuclear annihilation, and environmental damage; feminism, post-modern philosophy, quantum physics, new paradigm holistic social theories; and transpersonal psychology.

Since social workers labor in the trenches of social problems, both practitioners and scholars could no longer ignore such changes. Soul searching within the profession was stimulated and reinforced by the sense of urgency felt by many during this time.

THE NEED FOR A CONCEPTUALIZATION OF SPIRITUALITY SUITED TO SOCIAL WORK PURPOSES

After completing a Master of Arts degree in the cross-cultural study of religions, I decided to pursue a Master of Social Work degree in 1980 in order to apply spiritual insights directly to human service. This educational experience and exposure to social work practice through refugee resettlement work demonstrated the split between social work and spirituality. I decided to pursue further research through a Ph.D. degree in social work at Ohio State University. My research made it obvious that a lack of a conceptualization of spirituality suited to social work purposes reinforced a split. In order to address all the concerns about sectarianism mentioned above, a conceptualization of spirituality for social work purposes must be inclusive of diverse perspectives, but not limited to particular sectarian beliefs. It must provide guidance for how to respond to the spiritual needs of clients, within or outside religious institutional contexts, and it must honor the wide range of alternative and even conflicting spiritual beliefs and practices that exist in a pluralistic society and multicultural world.

In order to develop this conceptualization, I surveyed more than 100 social work writings on the topic and interviewed 18 social work scholars who were major contributors. From this study, I identified six influential spiritual perspectives: atheistic humanist, Christian, existentialist, Jewish, spiritist/shamanist, and Zen Buddhist. All the scholars from these perspectives viewed spiritual needs as central to the human condition, but they varied widely in particular beliefs about reality and human nature. Yet these scholars were very open-minded about the need to establish mutual understanding, acceptance, and cooperation among the divergent spiritual views.

On the basis of their guidance, I developed a conceptualization of spirituality with broad and narrow meanings. In the narrow sense, spirituality involves the basic human need to strive for a sense of meaning, purpose, and moral relatedness with self, other, and ultimate reality, whether or not that reality is viewed in materialist, theistic, animistic, monistic, or in other terms. In this narrow sense, then, spirituality is just one aspect of the person, along with the other biological, psychological, and social aspects.

The broad meaning of spirituality, however, is not limited to any one aspect of the person. Spirituality is the wholeness of what it is to be human and is not reducible to any one aspect. It is the complete gestalt of the bio-psycho-social-spiritual aspects. It is this ineffable entity which has inherent dignity and sacredness, or what the Jewish existentialist Martin Buber calls the "I," irreducible to any object or "it." Spirituality in this sense is a striving to actualize in awareness and behavior the wholeness of each person.

Professional ethics require that each person's right to self-determination of belief and behavior be respected, as long as societal well-being is not damaged in the process. Although many religious traditions claim to uphold the sanctity and inviolable dignity of every person, some religious providers of social service have exhibited a moral condescension and biased judgmentalism—for example, seeing the alcohol-addicted person as a morally defective creature or viewing the poor as deserving of their plight due to a supposed inferiority (or negative karma).

In this conceptualization, spirituality is distinct from religion. All people, religious or otherwise, have spiritual needs and qualities, as noted in the need-hierarchy writings of the transpersonal psychologist Abraham Maslow. Religion, on the other hand, is only the organized, institutionalized, and collective system that provides a structure of beliefs, practices, and community support for a specific form of spiritual development. It is important for the social work field to recognize this distinction if there is to be a spiritually sensitive form of social work.

Associations and Organizations

American Board of Examiners of Clinical Social Work (ABECSW)
8484 Georgia Avenue, Suite 800
Silver Spring, MD 20910
(301) 587-8783

ABECSW is a national nonmembership organization that grants credentials for advanced clinical social workers and offers a diplomate in clinical social work (Board Certified Diplomate, B.C.D.) for those who qualify.

Council on Social Work Education (CSWE)
1600 Duke Street
Alexandria, VA 22314-3421
(703) 683-8080

Since its inception, CSWE has carried the accrediting function for master's and bachelor's degree programs in social work. (The 40 or so doctoral programs, associate arts programs, and minor programs in social work are not accredited by any one body.) As the national accrediting agency for social work education, the council is recognized by the United States Department of Education and the Council on Postsecondary Accreditation. It also stimulates the development of knowledge, practice, and service effectiveness that are designed to promote social justice and further community and individual well being. Contact the council for a copy of the "Directory of Colleges and Universities with Accredited Social Work Degree Programs."

Gandhi Association of Social Workers (GASW)
University of Iowa
c/o Tom Walz
School of Social Work, North Hall
Iowa City, IA 52242
(319) 335-1250

The GASW is an international membership organization of social work faculty and practitioners who are interested in Gandhian thought and its application to the social work profession. Currently, the membership includes about 75 social workers in six countries. Principal activities include sharing research and writing related to Gandhian theory (a broad social and political philosophy) and semiannual development workshops designed to help social work educators apply Gandhian concepts to their teaching. The GASW also publishes a newsletter.

National Association of Social Workers (NASW)
750 First Street, N.E., 7th Floor
Washington, DC 20002
(202) 408-8600
The NASW is a membership association that awards the A.C.S.W. (Academy of Certified Social Workers) credential to M.S.W. practitioners with at least two years of experience. Clinical social workers must also obtain a social work license in the state in which they wish to practice (often indicated by the Licensed Clinical Social Worker, L.C.S.W., designation).

National Federation of Societies for Clinical Social Work (NFSCSW)
P.O. Box 3740
Arlington, VA 22203
(703) 522-4998
The NFSCSW is an advocacy organization that represents clinical social work. Each state has a local society providing professional activities for its members, such as continuing education and advocacy regarding licensing and insurance. These groups also sponsor mentor programs for social work students. The national organization publishes the newsletter *Progress Report*.

North American Association of Christians in Social Work (NAACSW)
Box 90
St. Davids, PA 19087
(215) 687-5777
The NACSW helps social workers integrate their Christian faith with their professional practice. It holds an annual convention and sponsors special gatherings in conjunction with the National Association of Social Workers, the Council on Social Work Education, and the International Congress on Christian Counseling. It also publishes the journal *Social Work and Christianity*.

Society for Spirituality and Social Work (SSSW)
School of Social Welfare
Twente Hall
University of Kansas
Lawrence, KS 66045-2510
(913) 864-4720
Founded in 1990, SSSW is an organization of social workers and other helping professionals dedicated to advancing the appreciation, knowledge, and skills con-

cerning spiritual and religious diversity. It publishes the journal *Spirituality and Social Work*, which includes topics such as Native American spirituality, Christian social work, and spiritual content in social work education. Upon request, the society provides a useful resource, *Topical Bibliography on Religion and Social Work*.

Periodicals

Clinical Social Work Journal
Human Sciences Press
233 Spring Street
New York, NY 10013-1578
(212) 620-8000
Quarterly; $44

Journal of Social Work Education
Council on Social Work Education
Three times a year; $80 (with membership)

Progress Report
National Federation of Societies for Clinical Social Work
Newsletter; $25 (student membership); $125 (licensed membership)

Social Work and Christianity
North American Association of Christians in Social Work
Semiannual; $50 (membership required)

Social Work and Christianity: An International Journal
North American Association of Christians in Social Work
Semiannual; $10

Spirituality and Social Work Journal
Society for Spirituality and Social Work
Semiannual; $8

GRADUATE PROGRAMS
Boston College
Institute of Religious Education and Pastoral Ministry
Chestnut Hill, MA 02167
(617) 552-8440; (800) 487-1167
General Information: Private, Catholic
Degrees Offered: M.A./M.S.W.; D.S.W.
Programs: Doctor of Social Work; joint Master of Arts in pastoral ministry and Master of Social Work; Master of Social Work
Admission Requirements: Bachelor's degree; GRE for Ph.D. program only; letter of recommendation
Application Deadline: Rolling
Contact Person: Director of Admissions
Tuition: $1,236/three-credit course

Accreditation: CSWE
Year Established: 1971
Faculty: 4 full-time; 10 adjunct

Boston University
School of Social Work
264 Bay State Road
Boston, MA 02215
(617) 353-2000
The School of Social Work offers dual degree programs with the Boston University School of Theology
General Information: Private, Christian
Degrees Offered: M.S.W.; D.S.W.
Programs: Clinical social work
Admission Requirements: Bachelor's degree
Application Deadline: February 15
Contact Person: Director of Admissions
Tuition: $6,300/year
Accreditation: CSWE
Year Established: 1839
Faculty: 40 full-time

Brigham Young University
School of Social Work
221 KMB
Provo, UT 84602
(801) 378-4668
General Information: Private, Church of Jesus Christ of Latter-Day Saints
Degrees Offered: M.S.W.
Programs: Master of Social Work
Admission Requirements: Bachelor's degree; three letters of recommendation
Application Deadline: February 1
Contact Person: Director of Admissions
Tuition: $1,860/semester
Accreditation: CSWE
Year Established: 1981
Faculty: Contact department

Case Western Reserve University
Mandel School of Applied Social Sciences
10900 Euclid Avenue
Cleveland, OH 44106-7164
(216) 368-2000
Case Western offers a dual degree program with an M.S.S.A./certificate in Jewish communal service.
General Information: Public, nonsectarian
Degrees Offered: D.S.W.
Programs: Doctor of Social Work
Admission Requirements: Bachelor's degree
Application Deadline: August and January
Contact Person: Director of Admissions
Tuition: $7,260
Accreditation: CSWE
Year Established: 1919
Faculty: Contact department

Catholic University of America
National Catholic School of Social Service
Washington, DC 20064
(202) 319-5000
General Information: Private, Catholic
Degrees Offered: M.S.W.
Programs: Master of Social Work
Admission Requirements: Bachelor's degree;
letter of recommendation; relevant experience; GRE (scholarship applicants)
Application Deadline: July 15
Contact Person: Director of Admissions
Tuition: $6,278
Accreditation: CSWE
Year Established: 1923
Faculty: Contact department

Columbia University
School of Social Work
McVickar Hall
622 West 113th Street
New York, NY 10025
(212) 854-4088
The University offers a dual master's degree combining Jewish studies (**Jewish Theological Seminary**) and a Master of Divinity (**Union Theological Seminary**).
General Information: Private, nonsectarian
Degrees Offered: M.S.W.; D.S.W.
Programs: Master of Social Work; Doctor of Social Work
Admission Requirements: Bachelor's degree
Application Deadline: March 1 (recommended)
Contact Person: Director of Admissions
Tuition: $12,780/year
Accreditation: CSWE
Year Established: 1919
Faculty: Contact department

Drew University
Office of Theological Admissions
Madison, NJ 07940
(201) 408-3111
General Information: Private, Methodist
Degrees Offered: M.Div./M.S.W.
Programs: Master of Divinity/Master of Social Work dual degree
Admission Requirements: Bachelor's degree
Application Deadline: Rolling
Contact Person: Director of Admissions
Tuition: $8,037
Accreditation: Regional, ATS
Year Established: 1866
Faculty: 29 full-time

Iliff School of Theology
2201 South University Boulevard
Denver, CO 80210
(303) 744-1287
General Information: Private, Methodist
Degrees Offered: M.S.W.; M.A. (joint degree

with the **Graduate School of Social Work, University of Denver**)
Programs: Master of Social Work
Admission Requirements: Bachelor's degree
Application Deadline: Rolling
Contact Person: Director of Admissions
Tuition: $305/quarter hour
Accreditation: NCACS, ATS
Year Established: 1892
Faculty: 21 full-time; 23 part-time

Jewish Theological Seminary of America
3080 Broadway
New York, NY 10027-4649
(212) 678-8947
See Columbia University for information on their dual degree program with Jewish Theological Seminary.

McCormick Theological Seminary
5555 South Woodlawn Avenue
Chicago, IL 60637
(312) 947-6317
General Information: Private, Presbyterian
Degrees Offered: M.S.W. (joint degree)
Programs: Master of Social Work
Admission Requirements: Bachelor's degree
Application Deadline: Rolling
Contact Person: Director of Admissions
Tuition: $4,950/year
Accreditation: ATS, NCASC
Year Established: 1960
Faculty: 1 faculty person per 13 students

Pacific Christian College
2500 East Natwood Avenue
Fullerton, CA 92631
(714) 879-3901
General Information: Private, Christian
Degrees Offered: M.F.C.C.
Programs: Marriage, family, and child counseling
Admission Requirements: Bachelor's degree
Application Deadline: Rolling
Contact Person: Director of Admissions
Tuition: $238/unit
Accreditation: WASC
Year Established: 1929
Faculty: 29 full-time; 21 part-time

Pittsburgh Theological Seminary
616 North Highland Avenue
Pittsburgh, PA 15206-2596
(800) 362-5610
General Information: Private, Christian
Degrees Offered: M.Div./M.S.W.
Programs: Master of Divinity/Master of Social Work (via the **University of Pittsburgh, Graduate School of Social Work**)
Admission Requirements: Bachelor's degree
Application Deadline: Rolling
Contact Person: Director of Admissions

Tuition: $5,292/year
Accreditation: ATA, MSACS
Year Established: Contact department
Faculty: 21 full-time; 20 part-time

Presbyterian School of Christian Education
1205 Palmyra Avenue
Richmond, VA 23227
(804) 254-8047
General Information: Private, Christian
Degrees Offered: M.A./M.S.W.
Programs: Master of Arts/Master of Social Work (via the **School of Social Work of Virginia Commonwealth University**)
Admission Requirements: Bachelor's degree
Application Deadline: Rolling
Contact Person: Director of Admissions
Tuition: $5,000/year
Accreditation: SACS; ATS
Year Established: 1914
Faculty: Contact department

Princeton Theological Seminary
CN 821
Princeton, NJ 08542
(609) 921-8300
General Information: Private, Presbyterian
Degrees Offered: M.Div./M.S.W.
Programs: Master of Divinity/Master of Social Work (via **Rutgers University**)
Admission Requirements: Bachelor's degree
Application Deadline: Rolling
Contact Person: Director of Admissions
Tuition: $5,760/year
Accreditation: ATS; NCACS; CSWE (Rutgers)
Year Established: 1812
Faculty: 46 full-time

Servant Leadership School
See Nondegree and Postgraduate Training Programs.

Southern Baptist Theological Seminary
Carver School of Church Social Work
2825 Lexington Road
Louisville, KY 40280
(800) 626-5525
The Carver School's Master of Social Work degree is the nation's only CSWE-accredited M.S.W. program to be granted from a seminary.
General Information: Private, Baptist
Degrees Offered: M.S.W.
Programs: Master of Social Work
Admission Requirements: Bachelor's degree
Application Deadline: Rolling
Contact Person: Director of Admissions
Tuition: $950/semester
Accreditation: CSWE
Year Established: 1984
Faculty: Contact department

Southwestern Baptist Theological Seminary
P.O. Box 22000
2001 West Seminary Drive
Fort Worth, TX 76115-9983
(817) 923-1921
General Information: Private, Christian
Degrees Offered: M.F.C.; M.S.W (in conjunction with the **University of Texas at Arlington**)
Programs: Marriage and family counseling, social work
Admission Requirements: Bachelor's degree
Application Deadline: Rolling
Contact Person: Director of Admissions
Tuition: $100/credit hour (maximum $800/semester)
Accreditation: CCSACS, ATS
Year Established: 1901
Faculty: 105 full- and part-time

Union Theological Seminary
3041 Broadway
New York, NY 10027
(212) 662-7100
See Columbia University (above) for information on their dual degree program with **Union Theological Seminary**.

University of Chicago
School of Social Work Administration
969 East 60th Street
Chicago, IL 60637
(312) 702-1250
A joint degree is offered with the Divinity School and the Chicago Cluster of Theological Seminaries (such as the Chicago Theological Seminary).
General Information: Public, nonsectarian
Degrees Offered: M.S.W.; D.S.W.
Programs: Master of Social Work; Doctor of Social Work
Admission Requirements: Bachelor's degree
Application Deadline: September
Contact Person: Director of Admissions
Tuition: $5,180/quarter
Accreditation: CSWE
Year Established: 1919
Faculty: Contact department

University of Iowa
School of Social Work
308 North Hall
Iowa City, IA 52242
(800) 553-4692
A joint degree is offered with the School of Religion.
General Information: Public, nonsectarian
Degrees Offered: M.S.W.
Programs: Master of Social Work
Admission Requirements: Bachelor's degree
Application Deadline: February 1
Contact Person: Director of Admissions
Tuition: $1,239/semester (in-state); $3,675

(out-of-state)
Accreditation: CSWE
Year Established: 1951
Faculty: Contact department

University of Maryland at Baltimore
School of Social Work
Louis L. Kaplan Hall
525 West Redwood Street
Baltimore, MD 21201
(410) 706-6102
A joint degree is offered with Baltimore Hebrew University in Jewish Studies. See Judaic Theological Training.
General Information: Public, nonsectarian
Degrees Offered: M.S.W.; D.S.W.
Programs: Master of Social Work; Doctor of Social Work
Admission Requirements: Bachelor's degree
Application Deadline: February 15
Contact Person: Director of Admissions
Tuition: $1,935/semester (in-state); $4,105 (out-of-state)
Accreditation: CSWE
Year Established: 1963
Faculty: Contact department

University of Michigan
Project Star
4064 Frieze Building
Ann Arbor, MI 48109-1285
(313) 764-5392
Project Star augments the M.S.W. degree granted by the University of Michigan. Applicants must be accepted to both Project Star and the Michigan School of Social Work.
General Information: Private, nonsectarian
Degrees Offered: M.S.W.
Programs: Master of Social Work with certificate in Judaic Studies and Jewish Communal Service
Admission Requirements: Bachelor's degree
Application Deadline: March 1
Contact Person: Director of Admissions
Tuition: $8,000 (in state)
Accreditation: CSWE
Year Established: 1990
Faculty: Contact department

University of Pennsylvania
School of Social Work
3701 Locust Walk
Philadelphia, PA 19104
(215) 898-5539
General Information: Private, nonsectarian
Degrees Offered: M.S.W., D.S.W.
Programs: Master of Social Work; Doctor of Social Work; a combined M.S.W./certificate is available in Jewish communal services with **Gratz College**, social ministry at **St. Charles Seminary**, and Lutheran social ministry at **Lutheran Theological Seminary**

Admission Requirements: Bachelor's degree
Application Deadline: March 15
Contact Person: Director of Admissions
Tuition: $15,880/year
Accreditation: CSWE
Year Established: 1919
Faculty: Contact department

University of Southern California
School of Social Work
University Park
Los Angeles, CA 90089-0411
(213) 740-2311
A dual degree is offered in Jewish communal service with **Hebrew Union College/Jewish Institute of Religion**. See Hebrew Union College.

Washington University
George Warren Brown School of Social Work
Campus Box 1186
St. Louis, MO 63130
(314) 935-6676
General Information: Private, nonsectarian
Degrees Offered: M.S.W.; D.S.W.
Programs: Master of Social Work; Doctor of Social Work; a dual degree is offered in Jewish communal services with the **Hebrew Union College of Los Angeles**
Admission Requirements: Bachelor's degree
Application Deadline: Contact department
Contact Person: Director of Admissions
Tuition: $458/credit, $17,600/year (D.S.W. program)
Accreditation: CSWE
Year Established: 1928
Faculty: 20 full-time

Yeshiva University
Wurzweiler School of Social Work
Belfer Hall
500 West 185th Street
New York, NY 10033
(212) 960-0810
The clergy plan is designed to assist clergy in becoming professionally responsive to social and psychological needs and is open to clergy of all faiths as well as others affiliated with pastoral society.
General Information: Private, Judaic
Degrees Offered: M.S.W.; D.S.W.
Programs: Doctor of Social Work, Master of Social Work; clergy plan:
Admission Requirements: Bachelor's degree; interview
Application Deadline: Rolling
Contact Person: Director of Admissions
Tuition: $11,994/year
Accreditation: CSWE
Year Established: 1959
Faculty: 27

SUBSTANCE ABUSE COUNSELING

Within the mental health professions, the substance abuse counselors who incorporate a 12-Step approach (which is explicitly spiritual) are the ones who most consistently observe a psychospiritual perspective. There are two paths that lead to a career in alcohol and drug abuse counseling: certification programs (which require two years of practical experience, 270 hours of classroom work, and 300 hours of an internship) and degree programs (which primarily emphasize theory and a 300-hour internship).

Certification programs vary greatly, and the lack of uniformity between the different state programs often results in confusing and sometimes contradictory training requirements. The Project for Addiction Counselor Training (PACT), a federally funded program designed to increase the number of credentialed counselors nationwide, provides a list of requirements applicable to each state. The National Association of Alcoholism and Drug Abuse Counselors (NAADAC) and the National Certification Reciprocity Consortium (two separate organizations) sponsor certification designated as a Nationally Certified Addiction Counselor (N.C.A.C. or C.A.C.). Advantages of certification include quicker access to the profession, guidance from people working directly in the field, and a relatively short training commitment.

The second option, the degree program, offers a more adaptable career route because the student gains more generic counseling and psychology skills; however, this also involves a longer time investment. Degree programs, unlike certification programs, culminate with eligibility for state licensure and board recognition through the National Board for Certified Counselors—the same board that certifies counselors through the American Counseling Association (ACA). While these substance abuse master's degree programs have yet to be officially represented by ACA, the Council for Accreditation of Counseling and Related Educational Programs (the accrediting body for the ACA) is consid-

ering their inclusion. In fact, the ACA already sponsors a division called the International Association of Addictions and Offender Counselors.

While certification and degree programs are separate career paths, consider that 40 percent of NAADAC's members already hold a master's level degree as well as national certification.

Alcoholism and drug abuse counselors work in a variety of settings, including hospitals, health clinics, mental health centers, halfway houses, social service agencies, and alcohol and drug treatment centers. Counselors are paid by salary; the range varies, but an entry level counselor's salary usually starts at approximately $25,000 a year. Many counselors who enter the field are older and more experienced, and have undergone a personal or career transition, and some are recovering from substance abuse themselves. Private practice counselors charge from $50 to $75 per hour.

Associations and Organizations

Association of Schools of Allied Health Professions (ASAHP)
1730 M Street, N.W., Suite 500
Washington, DC 20036
(202) 243-4848

ASAHP is a membership and advocacy organization composed of various health professions, including substance abuse counselors.

Council for Accreditation of Counseling and Related Educational Programs
See Counseling in this section.

International Certification Reciprocity Consortium (ICRC)
Alcohol and Other Drug Abuse
3725 National Drive, Suite 213
Raleigh, NC 27612
(919) 781-9734

ICRC also requires only certification training. It sponsors the National Certificate of Alcohol and Drug Counseling (N.C.A.D.C.).

National Association of Alcoholism and Drug Abuse Counselors (NAADAC)
3717 Columbia Pike, Suite 300
Arlington, VA 22204-4254
(703) 920-4644; (800) 548-0497

NAADAC represents the interests of 30,000 alcohol and drug abuse counseling

professionals in the United States and abroad. NAADAC sponsors competency-based certification (National Certified Addiction Counselor, or N.C.A.C.) specifically for alcoholism and drug counselors which requires relevant experience, coursework, and an examination.

Project for Addiction Counselor Training (PACT)
444 North Capitol Street, N.W., Suite 642
Washington, DC 20001
(202) 783-6868

PACT is a federally funded nationwide program that, in response to the need for additional substance abuse counselors, provides course work and a limited amount of internships for entry-level counselors. Contact PACT for a listing of the legal status of substance abuse counseling in each state, as well as information on training programs and career opportunities.

Periodicals

Counseling and Values
American Counseling Association
Three times a year; $12

Counselor
National Association of Alcoholism and Drug Abuse Counselors
Bimonthly; $36 (nonmembers)

Journal of Ministry in Addiction and Recovery
Haworth Pastoral Press
10 Alice Street
Binghamton, NY 13904-1580
(607) 722-5857
Semiannual; $20

GRADUATE PROGRAMS

Antioch University, New England
See Residential Psychology Degree Programs.

Antioch University, Santa Barbara
See Residential Psychology Degree Programs.

Chestnut Hill College
Graduate Division
Philadelphia, PA 19118-2695
(215) 248-7170
General Information: Private, Christian
Degrees Offered: M.A.
Programs: Counseling psychology and human services (addictions counseling specialization)
Admission Requirements: Bachelor's degree; GRE; interview

Application Deadline: Rolling
Contact Person: Director of Admissions
Tuition: $250/credit
Accreditation: Commonwealth of
Pennsylvania; MSACS; National Board of
Certified Counselors; Pennsylvania
Chemical Abuse Certification Board
Year Established: 1924
Faculty: Contact department

College of William and Mary
School of Education
c/o Dr. Charles Matthews
P.O. Box 8795
Williamsburg, VA 23187-8795
(804) 221-2356

The purpose of Project Taproot, sponsored by the School of Education, is to provide an educational environment that fosters the development of addictions
professionals—counselors and prevention
specialists—in a transpersonal framework.
Project Taproot is unique in its integration
of body, mind, and spirit into a didactic
curriculum.
General Information: Public, nonsectarian
Degrees Offered: M.Ed.
Programs: Addiction counseling
(specialization)
Admission Requirements: Bachelor's degree
Application Deadline: February 1
Contact Person: Director of Admissions
Tuition: $4,414/annual (in-state); $12,604
(nonresident)
Accreditation: SACS
Year Established: 1993 (program)
Faculty: 3 full-time (Taproot)

Governors State University
University Park, IL 60466-3190
(708) 534-4490
General Information: Public, nonsectarian
Degrees Offered: M.A.
Programs: Health science in alcoholism and
drug abuse sciences
Admission Requirements: Bachelor's degree;
Course prerequisites
Application Deadline: Contact department
Contact Person: Director of Admissions
Tuition: $972/trimester (Illinois resident)
Accreditation: NCACS; Council for the
Accreditation of Counselor Education and
Related Programs
Year Established: 1969
Faculty: 160 full-time

Heartwood Institute
220 Harmony Lane
Garberville, CA 95542
(707) 923-2021
Heartwood offers a certificate program
in addictions counseling. Also see Retreat

Centers and Interdisciplinary Somatic
Therapies.

LaSalle University
See Christian Theological Training.

Methodist Theological School in Ohio
3081 Columbus Pike
Delaware, OH 43015
(614) 363-1146
General Information: Private, Methodist
Degrees Offered: M.A.; M.Div.
Programs: Alcoholism and drug abuse min-
istry
Admission Requirements: Bachelor's degree
Application Deadline: Rolling
Contact Person: Director of Admissions
Tuition: $6,400/year
Accreditation: ATS, NCACSS
Year Established: 1985
Faculty: Contact department

National-Louis University
2840 Sheridan Road
Evanston, IL 60201
(708)475-2473
General Information: Private, nonsectarian
Degrees Offered: M.S.
Programs: Human services with a concentra-
tion in addiction counseling
Admission Requirements: Bachelor's degree;
letter of recommendation; interview
Application Deadline: Rolling
Contact Person: Director of Admissions
Tuition: $297/semester hour
Accreditation: NCACS; Illinois Alcohol and
Other Drug Abuse Professional Counselors
Association
Year Established: 1986
Faculty: 1 full-time; 7 adjunct

Northeast Louisiana University
Substance Abuse Counseling
128 Strauss Hall
Monroe, LA 71209
(318) 342-1293
General Information: Public, nonsectarian
Degrees Offered: M.A.
Programs: Substance Abuse Counseling
Admission Requirements: Bachelor's degree;
GRE; GPA > 2.8
Application Deadline: Contact department
Contact Person: Director of Admissions
Tuition: Contact department
Accreditation: NAADC
Year Established: Contact department
Faculty: 9 full-time

Oral Roberts University
7777 South Lewis Avenue
Tulsa, OK 74171
(918) 495-6090
General Information: Private, Christian
Degrees Offered: C.A.D.C.
Programs: Substance abuse disorder
counseling
Admission Requirements: Bachelor's degree;
letter of recommendation
Application Deadline: Rolling
Contact Person: Director of Admissions
Tuition: $160/credit hour
Accreditation: ATS, NCASC
Year Established: 1986
Faculty: 4 full-time; 3 adjunct

Westbrook University
See Nonresidential Psychology Degree
Programs.

Wright State University
See Residential Psychology Degree
Programs.

NONDEGREE PROGRAMS
Westchester Institute for Training in Psychoanalysis and Psychotherapy
2 Sarles Street
P.O. Box 89
Mount Kisco, NY 10549
(914) 666-0161

The Westchester Institute offers a comprehensive training program in the fields
of alcohol and chemical dependency counseling for both professionals and nonpro-
fessionals. The faculty represents a variety
of academic and professional disciplines,
including social work, psychoanalysis, family systems, psychiatry, psychiatric nursing,
art therapy, and group therapy.

SECTION II

SPIRITUAL/RELIGIOUS DEGREE PROGRAMS WITH A MENTAL HEALTH COMPONENT

In This Section:
➤ CHAPLAINCY
➤ PASTORAL COUNSELING
➤ SPIRITUAL DIRECTION
➤ THEOLOGICAL TRAINING

ROBERT FUCCI, 1992

Priceton Theological Seminary
Princeton, NJ

WHEN ONE CONSIDERS HOW MANY BOOKS WRITTEN FROM A PSYCHOSPIRITUAL PERSPECTIVE HAVE REACHED best-seller status, it is hard to deny the growth of the psychospiritual field. But this surge of interest has complex implications, since many of the people expressing such enthusiasm feel alienated from the religious institutions of their childhood and, as a consequence, distrust the idea of exploring spiritual concerns within those same organizations. They have instead sought answers through the commingling of spirituality and personal growth, a perspective that is neither a part of nor dependent upon an organized religion. On the other hand, clergy and other religious leaders are leery of those who remain independent from the grounding of historic and religious traditions, and they dispute claims that a focus on personal growth can be a spiritual process.

How did such a dualism between religion and spirituality come about? Writing in the *Journal of Pastoral Psychology*, Samuel G. Miller states that during the 12th and 13th centuries theological curricula focused on history and intellectual analysis and considered the "spiritual sense" of scripture to be a separate concern, thereby severing the relationship between prayer (i.e., spiritual practice) and theology. Today, this dualism is represented by the field of pastoral counseling, which is largely a theology-based profession, and the discipline of spiritual direction, which is largely spiritually based. Since pastoral counseling was developed within theological schools, it has been primarily concerned with how theological theories (and not spiritual practice) can give direction to counseling. Spiritual direction, on the other hand, emphasizes the use of contemplation and prayer as ways to find moral guidance and to nurture a direct relationship to the divine.

Had it not been for this early theoretical dualism, pastoral psychology might have evolved into a discipline that integrates spirituality and psy-

FROM CLINICAL TO SOCIOLOGICALLY ORIENTED DEGREE OPTIONS IN PASTORAL THEOLOGY

THE TERM *PASTORAL THEOLOGY* RELATES TO THE PROVISION OF PROVIDING CARE. THEOLOGICAL SCHOOLS AND SEMINARIES USE THE term—literally meaning "shepherding the flock"—to refer to the study of human behavior from a theological perspective. The following terms illustrate the wide range of pastoral theology programs offered in American theological schools and seminaries.

CHRISTIAN OR JEWISH CLINICAL PSYCHOLOGY OR SOCIAL WORK

Some theological schools offer Ph.D. degrees in clinical psychology and M.S.W. degrees accredited by the American Psychological Association and the National Association of Social Work, respectively. In such programs, theological study is combined with separate course work in clinical psychology or social work, and additional courses are offered that incorporate both theology and psychotherapy.

PASTORAL COUNSELING/PSYCHOTHERAPY

Some seminaries and graduate schools offer M.Div. and Ph.D. degrees in pastoral counseling. Most seminaries, however, offer only courses or a concentration in pastoral psychology or counseling. Students who graduate from a seminary and want to specialize in pastoral counseling must take additional post-graduate training to qualify for the American Association of Pastoral Counselor's certificate.

CHAPLAINCY

Most theological schools do not offer courses or degrees in chaplaincy. Instead, seminary graduates interested in becoming chaplains may take a year-long internship in clinical pastoral education (C.P.E.) in order to become certified by the College of Chaplains. Nevertheless, many seminaries require all graduates to take at least a summer-long internship in C.P.E., during which they may work in an institution such as a hospital.

PARISH MINISTRY OR PARISH STUDIES (PASTORAL CARE)

Many schools, while not focusing on one-to-one pastoral counseling, offer courses on developing caring networks among parishioners, or other human services that enhance the psychological well-being of parishioners. Sometimes this concentration or major leads, in part, to a Master of Divinity (M.Div.) or a Doctor of Ministry (D.Min.) degree.

PARISH OUTREACH MINISTRY

Some theological programs offer courses in social sciences such as sociology, community organization, and social psychology in an effort to inspire parish leaders to promote structural changes in the church's organizations and other societal institutions. Sometimes, however, outreach is mostly focused on increasing parish membership. Graduate degrees in this area are frequently the M.Div. or D.Min.

SPIRITUAL DIRECTION

Only a small number of theological and independent graduate schools offer an M.A. degree in spiritual direction, although some seminaries (mainly Roman Catholic) offer majors in it, sometimes called spiritual formation. Many seminaries offer a few courses on topics involving spirituality, but not necessarily spiritual direction. There are an increasing number of nondegree training programs for spiritual direction, and there is only minimal discussion among them regarding any future licensing or certification of this field.

chotherapy. Instead, initiative for the integration came from psychologists such as Anthony Sutich and Abraham Maslow, who in the 1960s, under the umbrella of humanistic and, later, transpersonal psychology, provided the original leadership for the emergence of a grass-roots professional movement that combines psychology and spirituality.

Because of consistently increasing interest in transpersonal psychology and consciousness studies, graduate schools such as the California Institute of Integral Studies and John F. Kennedy University were founded. Although these schools continue to advance psychospiritual pedagogy, informal reports indicate that students from leading theological schools are now pressuring faculty to offer some courses from a psychospiritual perspective.

While the Judeo-Christian tradition of pastoral theology in the United States is highly developed and has many different forms of expression, some other major religions are also beginning to develop similar programs. For example, the Kripalu Center holds symposia on the integration of psychotherapy and Hindu disciplines such as yoga; the Karma Triyana Dharmachakra Monastery and Retreat Center has sponsored conferences on the integration of Buddhist meditation and psychotherapy; the Naropa Institute offers a master's degree in contemplative psychology (an integration of Buddhist meditation, bodywork, and psychotherapy); and the American Islamic College integrates numerous disciplines with an Islamic perspective.

RELIGIOUS STUDIES: GENERAL ORGANIZATIONS, AND ASSOCIATIONS

The academic field of religious studies, offered through university or college departments of religion, is generally interdisciplinary in nature and may include courses in sociology, psychology, art history, and anthropology, and, most saliently, it approaches religion from an analytical, historic, and phenomenological perspective. (See the Theological Training introduction for a discussion of the difference between theological schools and academic departments of religion.)

American Academy of Religion (AAR)
P.O. Box 15399
Atlanta, GA 30333-0399
(404) 727-7920

The AAR, founded in 1909, is an academic society and professional association focused on the academic study of religion. The AAR fosters teaching, research, scholarship, and critical awareness of the study of religion as a humanistic and multidisciplinary field of learning. Within the AAR there is an interest group known as Person, Culture and Religion (see below). The AAR publishes the *Journal of the American Academy of Religion*. Write for a list of colleges and universities that have departments of religion.

Person, Culture and Religion (PCR)
Division of the American Academy of Religion
Greg Schneider, Chairperson
Behavioral Science
Pacific Union College
Angwin, CA 94508
(707) 965-6537

A scholarly society affiliated with the American Academy of Religion (AAR), PCR is specifically devoted to providing networking opportunities for scholars involved in the study of religion and religious experience from psychological and social-psychological perspectives. Some 200 academics in North America and Europe subscribe to PCR's newsletter. The organization holds an annual meeting prior to AAR's annual conference.

CHAPLAINCY

The duties of chaplains working in hospitals include counseling patients, staff, and families on a one-on-one basis; facilitating support groups for hospital staff, patients, and families; conducting educational interviews; helping to administer living wills and health-care powers-of-attorney to patients and families; and speaking to the community about psychosocial issues such as cancer, heart disease, grief and loss, stress management,

team building, conflict resolution, spirituality, and death and dying.

The principal mission of a hospital chaplain is to foster a close relationship between clergy (from local churches and congregations) and patients. Some serve on ethics committees in order to assist patients and families in making life-and-death decisions. In addition to holding hospital positions, chaplains also serve in the armed services, prisons, schools, and universities.

A certified Christian chaplain must hold a Master of Divinity degree, have completed four units of clinical pastoral education (CPE), and have obtained an endorsement from his or her religious faith group. A Jewish chaplain usually holds a master's degree in Hebrew Letters and is ordained by a seminary.

There are more and more cases where other religions such as Buddhism and Islam are offering chaplaincy services. For example, the University of California at Berkeley has a Buddhist chaplain for students, and a hospital was recently sued to permit a member of Wicca (an earth-based religion) to be permitted to register as a chaplain.

The College of Chaplains has developed specific certification requirements, but because the field is unregulated, those who lack official certification can be hired. For a candidate who meets the basic requirements for competency, a beginning salary is approximately $35,000.

—*Sara Rose, a chaplain at Belk Heart Center in Charlotte, North Carolina, contributed to this introduction.*

Associations and Organizations
Association of Clinical Pastoral Education (ACPE)
1549 Clairmont Road, Suite 103
Decatur, GA 30033
(404) 320-1472

The ACPE fosters experience-based theological education that combines the practice of pastoral care, qualified supervision, and peer-group reflection within a person-centered approach to religious ministry. The association is recognized as a national accrediting agency in the field of clinical pastoral education (CPE) by the United States Secretary of Education.

Association of Mental Health Clergy (AMHC)
12320 River Oaks Point
Knoxville, TN 37922
(615) 544-9704

The AMHC meets during the American Psychiatric Association's annual conference, where it sponsors presentations and symposia regarding the relationship between religion and psychiatry.

Center for Ethics, Medicine and Public Issues
Baylor College of Medicine
1 Baylor Plaza
Houston, TX 77030
(713) 798-6290

The center was established in 1982 as a cooperative effort of Baylor College of Medicine, Rice University, and the Institute of Religion, which is related to the Texas Medical Center in Houston. Through teaching, the center strives to help medical students and residents better understand the complex ethical issues related to medical care and to train future scholars in the newly emerging field of bioethics. Through research, the center's faculty engage in clinically based and theoretical scholarship about ethical issues arising out of individual patient-physician encounters and out of social policies concerning the delivery of health care. The center publishes the *Journal of Medicine and Philosophy*.

Congress on Ministry in Specialized Settings (COMISS)
Rev. Julian Bryd, President
Methodist Hospital
6565 Fannin Street, Suite D-102
Houston, TX 77030
(713) 790-2381

The COMISS is composed of pastoral care, counseling, and educational organizations, denominations, and faith groups (such as the American Association of Pastoral Counselors, the College of Chaplains, and the Association for Clinical Pastoral Education) who endorse ministers serving in specialized settings as chaplains and pastoral counselors, and who provide health-care services and ministries. Every four to six years, member organizations forgo holding their own annual meetings to attend a COMISS-sponsored "Dialogue" conference, during which issues related to pastoral care and counseling are discussed.

College of Chaplains (CC)
1701 East Woodfield Road, Suite 311
Schaumburg, IL 60173
(708) 240-1014

Founded in 1946, the CC is a membership and advocacy organization that serves chaplains of all faiths and in all types of health and human service settings. The college offers continuing education programs and provides the opportunity for chaplains to be certified as fellows, a designation that represents a high level of competency based on peer review. It publishes two newsletters and a journal, *The Care Giver*.

The Hastings Center
255 Elm Road
Briarcliff Manor, NY 10510
(914) 762-8500

The center, founded in 1970, confronts complex bioethical issues in relation to modern medicine and technology. It sponsors research and education and publishes the bimonthly *Hastings Center Report*.

The Institute of Religion (IR)
Texas Medical Center
P.O. Box 20569
Houston, TX 77225
(713) 797-0600

The IR is related to the Texas Medical Center as an independent, nonsectarian agency for education and service. Since 1955, its affiliated physicians, researchers, ethicists, and theologians have been exploring medical education, patient care, and religious beliefs about life, health, and ethics. The IR also trains clergy for hospital chaplaincy and studies ethical and religious issues in modern medicine.

National Association of Catholic Chaplains (NACC)
3501 South Lake Drive
P.O. Box 07473
Milwaukee, WI 53207-0473
(414) 483-4898

The NACC, founded in 1965, is a professional and advocacy association of pastoral ministers who participate in the church's mission of healing. The association holds an annual national conference and publishes a newsletter.

National Association of Jewish Chaplains (NAJC)
University of California at San Francisco
Mount Zion Medical Center
c/o Rabbi Jeffrey Silverman
P.O. Box 7921
San Francisco, CA 94120
(415) 885-7785

The NAJC is a membership organization of Jewish chaplains.

Society for Health and Human Values
See Allopathic Medicine.

Periodicals

Chaplaincy Today
College of Chaplains
Ten issues a year; $20

Journal of Health Care Chaplaincy™
Haworth Press
10 Alice Street
Binghamton, NY 13904
(800) 342-9678
Semiannual; $28

Journal of Medicine and Philosophy
Center for Ethics, Medicine and Public Issues
Quarterly; $69

Journal of Pastoral Care
Kutztown Publishing Company
P.O. Box 346
Route 222 and Sharadin Road
Kutztown, PA 19530
Quarterly; $20

Journal of Pastoral Counseling
See Pastoral Counseling.

The Tie
College of Chaplains
Bimonthly; $20

PASTORAL COUNSELING

While most pastoral counseling programs are Christian or Jewish, in this chapter we interpret "pastoral" in more broadly defined, nondenominational terms, in part because some psychotherapists with a Buddhist orientation are also labeling themselves pastoral counselors. Even though most graduate programs place pastoral counseling within a strictly denominational context, a few schools define their programs along the same nonsectarian lines as do the transpersonal psychology programs listed in Section I.

The modern-day relationship of religion and psychotherapy began in the 1950s with the collaboration of Norman Vincent Peale, a renowned minister and author of the popular *The Power of Positive Thinking*, and Smiley Blanton, a well-known author and psychiatrist. Peale and Blanton formed the American Foundation of Religion and Psychiatry (now known as the Institutes of Religion and Health), which operated a psychoreligious clinic. During this period, a distinction was made between spiritual

guidance (similar to spiritual direction, discussed earlier) and pastoral psychotherapy, which integrates theology and the behavioral sciences. Today, pastoral psychotherapists maintain this same distinction and work with such clinical and secular problems as depression, family and gang violence, suicide, AIDS, child abuse, and homelessness. Work with spiritual issues, per se, is considered to be more in the realm of spiritual direction.

Pastoral counseling utilizes secular psychotherapy techniques within a theological perspective. In the earlier years, pastoral counselors' search for equality with the mental health professions led to an emphasis on psychological issues more than on spiritual concerns. This partiality toward psychology may soon need to change; according to a February 1992 independent Gallup poll commissioned by the American Association of Pastoral Counselors and the Samaritan Institute, 66 percent of those surveyed prefer a counselor who is sensitive to their spiritual values and beliefs, and 81 percent prefer to have their own values and beliefs integrated within the counseling process.

Pastoral counselors generally work through parish-based counseling centers or in hospitals, clinics, prisons, universities, or religious orders. However, according to Robert Wicks, Ph.D., a pastoral counseling professor at Loyola College in Maryland, a disturbing trend is arising. Some pastoral counselors upon completing a training program are setting up private practices, which effectively separates them from pastoral counseling centers, which in turn isolates them and jeopardizes their ability to make ethical and prudent decisions. Conversely, some pastoral counseling centers not attached to congregations are hiring secular psychotherapists who have no training in theology. It is too early to tell how this situation will affect the future of the field.

The Jewish faith differs in that rabbis are generally considered teachers rather than counselors. Hebrew Union College offers one of the few programs in Jewish pastoral counseling.

The American Association of Pastoral Counselors (AAPC) certifies counselors, accredits pastoral counseling centers, and approves training programs. It is also working for licensing laws to regulate the profession, a long and arduous task that will ultimately require state legislation. While three states currently offer licensure—Maine, New Hampshire, and North Carolina—pastoral counselors in other states may be licensed only through another mental health title, such as professional counselor, clinical psychologist, or social worker. Third-party insurance, in turn, is mainly offered to those with a license, although a select number of insurance companies authorize reimbursement for those possessing a pastoral counseling degree.

There are three routes to certification: obtaining a seminary degree (e.g., Master of Divinity); combining a seminary degree and a master's or doctoral degree in psychology or social work; or, obtaining an M.A. or Ph.D. in pastoral counseling from a seminary or independent training program. In addition, seminaries often offer partial academic credit for various outside nondegree training programs in pastoral counseling.

Pastoral counseling graduate degree programs may be accredited by any of three separate associations, if accredited at all: the American Association of Pastoral Counselors (AAPC); the Council for Accreditation of Counseling and Related Educational Programs; or the United States Catholic Conference's Commission on Certification and Accreditation. As pastoral counseling students continue to demand more academic accreditation, better clinical training opportunities, and further legitimacy, most degree programs may eventually seek university affiliation. The AAPC is in the process of developing a certificate board, even though reaching agreement on psychological standards will be easier than achieving agreement on theological ones! Accordingly, students should seek a program that both fits their theological orientation and

provides a solid foundation in counseling skills. A pastoral counselor's fee is approximately $45 to $65 an hour, although wide variations make this estimation difficult to determine.

—*The staff at the American Association of Pastoral Counselors contributed to this introduction.*

Associations and Organizations

American Association of Christian Counselors (AACC)
2421 West Pratt Avenue, Suite 1398
Chicago, IL 60645
(800) 526-8673

The AACC is an organization of evangelical professional, lay, and pastoral counselors dedicated to promoting excellence and unity in Christian counseling. It publishes *Christian Counseling Today.*

American Association of Pastoral Counselors (AAPC)
9504A Lee Highway
Fairfax, VA 222031-2303
(703) 385-6967

The AAPC was founded in 1963 as an organization that certifies pastoral counselors, accredits pastoral counseling centers, and approves pastoral counseling graduate degree programs. The AAPC represents over 3,200 pastoral counselors and more than 100 pastoral counseling centers in the United States. Its members belong to more than 80 different denominations, including the Protestant, Catholic, and Jewish faiths. The AAPC is nonsectarian and respects the spiritual commitments and religious traditions of those who seek assistance without imposing counselor beliefs onto the client. It publishes a quarterly newsletter.

Association for Clinical Pastoral Education (ACPE)
1549 Clairmont Road, Suite 103
Decatur, GA 30033
(404) 320-1472

The ACPE, a national membership organization incorporated in 1967, establishes standards for clinical pastoral education centers, programs, and supervisors. It supports a person-centered approach to religious ministry by promoting experience-based theological education. The association holds an annual conference and publishes the *Journal of Pastoral Care* and the *ACPE News.*

Congress on Ministry in Specialized Settings
See Chaplaincy.

United States Catholic Conference (USCC)
Commission on Certification and Accreditation
4455 Woodson Road
St. Louis, MO 63134-3797
(314) 428-2000

The USCC, founded in 1983, has designated the Commission on Certification and Accreditation as the agency authorized to accredit pastoral education programs that prepare persons for the ministry in the Catholic Church and to approve the training standards for specialized ministry and certification procedures. The United States Department of Education recognizes the USCC Commission as a national accrediting agency.

Periodicals

Journal of Pastoral Care
1549 Clairmont Road, Suite 103
Decatur, GA 30033-4611
(404) 320-0195
Quarterly; $20

Journal of Pastoral Counseling
Iona College
715 North Avenue
New Rochelle, NY 10801
(914) 636-6623
Annual; $25

Journal of Pastoral Psychotherapy
Haworth Press
12 West 32nd Street
New York, NY 10001
(212) 279-1200
Quarterly; $24

Journal of Pastoral Theology
Iliff School of Theology
2201 South University Boulevard
Denver, CO 80210
(303) 744-1287
Annual; $7

Journal of Psychology and Christianity
See Theological Training in this section.

Journal of Psychology and Theology
See Theological Training in this section.

Pastoral Psychology
Human Sciences Press
233 Spring Street
New York, NY 10013-1578
(212) 620-8000
Bimonthly; $48

EDUCATIONAL PROGRAMS

The schools listed below offer programs in pastoral counseling. To learn what other kinds of curricula are offered by these schools, you may write them for a complete course catalog.

Asbury Theological Seminary
204 North Lexington Avenue
Wilmore, KY 40390
(606) 858-3511
General Information: Private, Christian
Degrees Offered: M.A.
Programs: Parish counseling; counseling
Admission Requirements: Bachelor's degree
Application Deadline: Rolling
Contact Person: Director of Admissions
Tuition: $303/semester hour
Accreditation: ATS; SACS
Year Established: 1923
Faculty: 44 full-time; 15 adjunct

Ashland Theological Seminary
910 Center Street
Ashland, OH 44805
(419) 289-5161
General Information: Private, Christian
Degrees Offered: M.Div.; M.A.
Programs: Pastoral counseling
Admission Requirements: Bachelor's degree
Application Deadline: Rolling
Contact Person: Director of Admissions
Tuition: $1,400/quarter
Accreditation: ATS; NCACS
Year Established: 1878
Faculty: Contact department

Assumption College
500 Salisbury Street
Worcester, MA 01615-0005
(508) 752-5615
General Information: Private, Roman Catholic/ecumenical
Degrees Offered: M.A.
Programs: Pastoral counseling
Admission Requirements: Bachelor's degree
Application Deadline: Rolling
Contact Person: Director of Admissions
Tuition: $726/three-credit course
Accreditation: NEACSS
Year Established: 1983 (program)
Faculty: 6 full-time; 6 part-time

Athenaeum of Ohio
6616 Beechmont Avenue
Cincinnati, OH 45230
(513) 231-2223
General Information: Private, Roman Catholic

Degrees Offered: M.A.
Programs: Pastoral counseling
Admission Requirements: Bachelor's degree; 18 credit hours in both social sciences and theology or religious studies
Application Deadline: Rolling
Contact Person: Director of Admissions
Tuition: $125/quarter hour
Accreditation: ATS; NCACS
Year Established: 1986 (program)
Faculty: 1 full-time; 3 part-time

Boston College
Institute of Religious Education and Pastoral Ministry
Chestnut Hill, MA 02167
(617) 552-8440; (800) 487-1167
   Boston College also offers a joint degree in social work through Boston College's School of Social Work.
General Information: Private, Catholic
Degrees Offered: M.A.
Programs: Pastoral counseling
Admission Requirements: Bachelor's degree; letters of recommendation
Application Deadline: Rolling
Contact Person: Director of Admissions
Tuition: $1,410/three-credit course
Accreditation: NEACSS
Year Established: 1971
Faculty: 4 full-time; 10 adjunct

Briercrest Biblical Seminary
510 College Drive
Caronport, Saskatchewan
Canada S0H 0S0
(306) 756-3200
General Information: Private, Christian
Degrees Offered: M.A.
Programs: Biblical counseling
Admission Requirements: Bachelor's degree
Application Deadline: Rolling
Contact Person: Director of Admissions
Tuition: $252/term
Accreditation: American Association of Bible Colleges; United States Office of Education
Year Established: 1983
Faculty: 4 full-time; 29 part-time

Center for Counseling and Psychotherapy
Southwest Institute for Religion and Psychotherapy
5500 North Western, Suite 200
Oklahoma City, OK 73118
(405) 842-5678
General Information: Private, Christian
Degrees Offered: D.Min.; M.A. through Phillips Graduate Seminary

Programs: Pastoral counseling
Admission Requirements: Bachelor's degree
Application Deadline: June 30
Contact Person: Director of Admissions
Tuition: $280/credit hour
Accreditation: AAPC
Year Established: 1982
Faculty: 10 adjunct

Center for Religion and Psychotherapy of Chicago
30 North Michigan, Suite 1920
Chicago, IL 60602
(312) 263-4368
General Information: Private, ecumenical
Degrees Offered: Certificate
Programs: Pastoral psychotherapy
Admission Requirements: Bachelor's degree
Application Deadline: Rolling
Contact Person: Director of Admissions
Tuition: $6,600/academic year
Accreditation: AAPC
Year Established: 1965
Faculty: 5 full-time; 1 adjunct

Chicago Theological Seminary
5757 South University Avenue
Chicago, IL 60637
(312) 752-5757
General Information: Private, Christian
Degrees Offered: D.Min., Ph.D.
Programs: Pastoral counseling (psychotherapy, family therapy option)
Admission Requirements: Bachelor's degree; GRE
Application Deadline: Rolling
Contact Person: Director of Admissions
Tuition: $874/course (D.Min.); $680/course (Ph.D.)
Accreditation: ATS; NCACS
Year Established: 1855
Faculty: 15 full-time

Christian Theological Seminary
1000 West 42nd Street
Indianapolis, IN 46208
(317) 924-1331
General Information: Private, Christian
Degrees Offered: M.A.; D.Min.
Programs: Marriage and family therapy, M.A.; pastoral counseling, M.A., M.Div.
Admission Requirements: Bachelor's degree
Application Deadline: Rolling
Contact Person: Director of Admissions
Tuition: $3,900/year
Accreditation: NCASC; ATS; AAPC; AAMFT
Year Established: 1958
Faculty: 9 full-time; 25 part-time

Claremont School of Theology
Clinebell Institute
1325 North College Avenue
Claremont, CA 91711-3199
(909) 626-3523
General Information: Private, ecumenical
Degrees Offered: M.Div.; M.A.; Ph.D.
Programs: Pastoral counseling, M.A., M.Div.;
pastoral psychotherapy, M.A., M.Div.; theol-
ogy and personality (emphasis on pastoral
counseling), Ph.D.
Admission Requirements: Bachelor's degree;
GRE
Application Deadline: Rolling
Contact Person: Director of Admissions
Tuition: $260/credit
Accreditation: ATS; WASC; AAPC
Year Established: 1958
Faculty: 28 total

Colorado Christian University
16075 West Belleview Avenue
Morrison, CO 80465
(303) 697-8135
General Information: Private, Christian
Degrees Offered: M.A.
Programs: Biblical counseling
Admission Requirements: Bachelor's degree;
GRE if GPA < 3.0
Application Deadline: Rolling
Contact Person: Director of Admissions
Tuition: $210/semester hour
Accreditation: NCACS
Year Established: 1914
Faculty: 7 full-time; 4 part-time

Columbia Theological Seminary
701 Columbia Drive
Box 520
Decatur, GA 30031
(404) 378-8821
General Information: Private, Christian
Degrees Offered: Th.M.
Programs: Master of Theology with special-
ization in pastoral counseling
Admission Requirements: Bachelor's degree
Application Deadline: Rolling
Contact Person: Director of Admissions
Tuition: $227/credit hour
Accreditation: ATP
Year Established: 1828
Faculty: 34 full-time; 23 adjunct

Earlham School of Religion
228 College Avenue
Richmond, IN 47374
(800) 432-1377
General Information: Private, Religious
Society of Friends (Quaker)
Degrees Offered: M.Div.

Programs: Specialization in pastoral
counseling
Admission Requirements: Bachelor's degree
Application Deadline: Rolling
Contact Person: Director of Admissions
Tuition: $6,608
Accreditation: NCACS, ATS
Year Established: 1960
Faculty: 5 Full-time; 5 part-time

Eastern Mennonite College and Seminary
1200 Park Road
Harrisonburg, VA 22801
(703) 432-4000
General Information: Private, Mennonite
Degrees Offered: M.A. (prepares student for
VA state license)
Programs: Counseling
Admission Requirements: Bachelor's degree;
GRE; letters of recommendation; 18 credit
hours of undergraduate psychology
Application Deadline: Rolling
Contact Person: Director of Admissions
Tuition: $304/semester hour
Accreditation: CACREP
Year Established: 1993
Faculty: 3 full-time

Eastern Nazarene College
23 East Elm Avenue
Quincy, MA 02170-2999
(617) 773-6350
General Information: Private, Christian
Degrees Offered: M.A.
Programs: Pastoral counseling; family
counseling
Admission Requirements: Bachelor's degree
Application Deadline: Rolling
Contact Person: Director of Admissions
Tuition: $4,135/12-credit hours
Accreditation: NEASC, CSWE
Year Established: 1919
Faculty: 73 Full-time

Eden Theological Seminary
475 East Lockwood
St. Louis, MO 63119-3192
(314) 961-3627
General Information: Private, Christian
Degrees Offered: D.Min.
Programs: Pastoral care and counseling
track
Admission Requirements: Bachelor's degree
Application Deadline: Rolling
Contact Person: Director of Admissions
Tuition: $160/credit hour
Accreditation: ATS; NCACSS
Year Established: 1850
Faculty: 13 full-time; 2 adjunct

Graduate Theological Foundation
Donaldson, IN 46513
(800) 423-5983
General Information: Private, ecumenical
Degrees Offered: D.Min., Ph.D.
Programs: Pastoral counseling, D.Min.; pas-
toral psychology, Ph.D.
Admission Requirements: Bachelor's degree;
five years of professional experience
Application Deadline: June 1
Contact Person: Director of Admissions
Tuition: $3,000 (D.Min.); $5,000 (Ph.D.)
Accreditation: None (not desired)
Year Established: 1962
Faculty: 17 full-time

**Hebrew Union College–Jewish
Institute of Religion**
    See Judaic Degree Programs.

Holy Names College
3500 Mountain Boulevard
Oakland, CA 94619-1699
(510) 436-1000
General Information: Private, ecumenical
Degrees Offered: M.A.
Programs: Counseling psychology (emphasis
in pastoral), M.A. (prepares student for
M.F.C.C. license); pastoral counseling,
M.A.; certificate in pastoral counseling
Admission Requirements: Bachelor's degree
Application Deadline: Rolling
Contact Person: Director of Admissions
Tuition: $10,600 (M.A.)
Accreditation: WASC
Year Established: 1977
Faculty: 15 full-time

Iliff School of Theology
2201 South University Boulevard
Denver, CO 80210
(303) 744-1287
General Information: Private, Methodist
Degrees Offered: Ph.D.
Programs: Pastoral counseling
Admission Requirements: Bachelor's degree
Application Deadline: Rolling
Contact Person: Director of Admissions
Tuition: $305/quarter hour
Accreditation: NCACSC; ATS
Year Established: 1892
Faculty: 21 full-time; 23 part-time

Institute of Pastoral Studies
Saint Paul University
223 Main Street
Ottawa, Ontario
Canada K1S 1C4
(613) 236-1393
General Information: Private, Christian
Degrees Offered: M.A.

Programs: Pastoral counseling
Admission Requirements: Bachelor's degree; psychology and theology experience
Application Deadline: Rolling
Contact Person: Director of Admissions
Tuition: $3,050/semester
Accreditation: Member of the Association of Universities and Colleges of Canada
Year Established: 1974
Faculty: 100 full- and part-time

Institutes of Religion and Health

Blanton-Peale Graduate Institute
3 West 29th Street
New York, NY 10001-4597
(212) 725-7850

The institute's main focus is the professional training of clergy in the art of pastoral psychotherapy. The program is the largest clinical training center for pastoral psychotherapists in the world. Special arrangements may be made with degree-granting institutions for dual matriculation. See Institutes of Religion and Health in the Nondegree and Postgraduate Training section.
General Information: Private, ecumenical
Degrees Offered: Post degree certificate
Programs: Certificate in Pastoral psychotherapy; marriage and family residency; pastoral care and counseling ministry; psychotherapy residency
Admission Requirements: Bachelor's degree
Application Deadline: Rolling
Contact Person: Director of Admissions
Tuition: $8,000/year (pastoral psychotherapy); $4,000/year (marriage and family therapy); $1,400 (pastoral studies)
Accreditation: AAPC; AAMFT
Year Established: 1958
Faculty: 40 full-time; 38 adjunct

Iona College

Graduate Department of Counseling
715 North Avenue
New Rochelle, NY 10801
(914) 636-6623
General Information: Private, Judeo-Christian tradition
Degrees Offered: M.S.
Programs: Pastoral and family counseling
Admission Requirements: Bachelor's degree
Application Deadline: Rolling
Contact Person: Director of Admissions
Tuition: $280/credit
Accreditation: MSACS; New York Department of Education
Year Established: 1963
Faculty: 6 full-time; 2 adjunct

Lasalle University

Philadelphia, PA 19141
(215) 951-1350; (215) 991-2000
General Information: Private, Christian
Degrees Offered: M.A.
Programs: Pastoral Counseling
Admission Requirements: Bachelor's degree
Application Deadline: Rolling
Contact Person: Director of Admissions
Tuition: $358/credit
Accreditation: MSACS
Year Established: 1979 (program)
Faculty: 18 adjunct

Loyola College

Loyola College Pastoral Counseling Department
Loyola College Business Center
7135 Minstrel Way, Suite 101
Columbia, MD 21045
(410) 323-1010
General Information: Private, Catholic (Jesuit)
Degrees Offered: M.S., Ph.D.
Programs: Pastoral counseling; certificate of advanced study
Admission Requirements: Bachelor's degree
Application Deadline: Rolling
Contact Person: Director of Admissions
Tuition: $190/credit (M.S.); $320 (Ph.D.)
Accreditation: MSACS; AAPC; USCC
Year Established: 1976
Faculty: 33 full- and part-time

Loyola University Chicago

Institute of Pastoral Studies
6525 North Sheridan Road
Chicago, IL 60626
(800) 424-1238
General Information: Private, ecumenical
Degrees Offered: M.A.
Programs: Pastoral counseling
Admission Requirements: Bachelor's degree; letters of recommendation
Application Deadline: February 1
Contact Person: Director of Admissions
Tuition: $285/credit hour
Accreditation: NCACS
Year Established: 1986
Faculty: 2 full-time; 18 part-time

Lutheran General Hospital (LGH)

1610 Luther Lane
Park Ridge, IL 60068-1243
(708) 518-1800

The LGH pastoral psychotherapy training program is a nondegree program designed for the matriculated or degree-holding student. The hospital, however, is affiliated with Chicago Theological Seminary, Garrett-Evangelical Theological Semi-

nary, Catholic Theological Union, Loyola, the University of Chicago, Illinois Schools of Professional Psychology, and several other Chicago seminaries. Degree credit may be granted from one of the above institutions.
General Information: Private, Lutheran
Degrees Offered: Certificate
Programs: Pastoral psychotherapy training
Admission Requirements: D.Min.; Ph.D.; Psy.D.
Application Deadline: Rolling
Contact Person: Director of Admissions
Tuition: $5,968
Accreditation: AAPC
Year Established: 1971
Faculty: n/a

Marywood College

2300 Adams Avenue
Scranton, PA 18509
(800) 338-4207
General Information: Private, Catholic
Degrees Offered: M.A.
Programs: Pastoral counseling
Admission Requirements: Bachelor's degree; GRE
Application Deadline: Early March
Contact Person: Director of Admissions
Tuition: $325/credit
Accreditation: MSACS; National accreditation of counseling program pending
Year Established: 1922
Faculty: 10 Full-time

Moravian Theological Seminary

1200 Main Street
Bethlehem, PA 18018-6650
(215) 861-1516
General Information: Private, Moravian
Degrees Offered: M.A.
Programs: Pastoral counseling
Admission Requirements: Bachelor's degree
Application Deadline: Rolling
Contact Person: Director of Admissions
Tuition: $3,159/term
Accreditation: ATS; MSACS; CIHE
Year Established: 1807
Faculty: 9 full-time; 15 part-time

Neumann College

Concord Road
Aston, PA 19014
(215) 459-0905
General Information: Private, Catholic
Degrees Offered: M.S.
Programs: Pastoral counseling
Admission Requirements: Bachelor's degree; letters of recommendation

Application Deadline: March 15
Contact Person: Director of Admissions
Tuition: $4,775/semester
Accreditation: MSACSS; NBCC; PA
Department of Education
Year Established: 1980
Faculty: 4 full-time

Olivet Nazarene University
240 East Marsile
Bourbonnais, IL 60914
(815) 939-5291
General Information: Private, Nazarene
Degrees Offered: M.A.; M.S.
Programs: Pastoral counseling, M.A.; psychology, M.S.
Admission Requirements: Bachelor's degree; letters of recommendation
Application Deadline: Rolling
Contact Person: Director of Admissions
Tuition: $145/credit hour
Accreditation: NCACS
Year Established: 1979
Faculty: 8 full-time

Saint Thomas Theological Seminary
1300 South Steele Street
Denver, CO 80210
(303) 722-4687
General Information: Private, Catholic
Degrees Offered: M.A.
Programs: Pastoral counseling
Admission Requirements: Bachelor's degree
Application Deadline: Rolling
Contact Person: Director of Admissions
Tuition: $185/quarter hour
Accreditation: NCACS; ATS; USCCCCA; NBCC
Year Established: 1907
Faculty: 19 full-time; 27 part-time

Southern Baptist Theological Seminary
2825 Lexington Road
Louisville, KY 40280
(800) 626-5525
General Information: Private, Baptist
Degrees Offered: M.Div.
Programs: Pastoral counseling
Admission Requirements: Bachelor's degree
Application Deadline: Rolling
Contact Person: Director of Admissions
Tuition: Scholarship
Accreditation: CCSACS; ATS
Year Established: 1859
Faculty: 46

Temenos Institute
Westport, CT
Also see Conference Centers.
Programs: Pastoral care and counseling training
This nonsectarian program is designed to enrich the pastoral skills of those

engaged in parish ministry, synagogues, chaplaincy, and divinity school education.

University of Puget Sound
1500 North Warner
Tacoma, WA 98416-0221
(206) 756-3211
General Information: Private, Methodist
Degrees Offered: M.Ed.
Programs: Master of Education with specialization in pastoral counseling
Admission Requirements: Bachelor's degree
Application Deadline: Rolling
Contact Person: Director of Admissions
Tuition: $1,250/unit
Accreditation: CCNACS; NCATE
Year Established: 1960
Faculty: 13 full-time

Westminster Theological Seminary
Chestnut Hill, P.O. Box 27009
Philadelphia, PA 19118
(215) 887-5511
General Information: Private, Presbyterian
Degrees Offered: M.A.R.; D.Min.
Programs: Master of Arts in Religion (counseling emphasis); Doctor of Ministry (pastoral counseling emphasis)
Admission Requirements: Bachelor's degree
Application Deadline: Rolling
Contact Person: Director of Admissions
Tuition: $3,300/semester
Accreditation: MSACS; ATS
Year Established: 1812
Faculty: 52 full-time

SPIRITUAL DIRECTION

The practice of spiritual direction has traditionally been understood as a gift or vocation (i.e., a "calling") as opposed to an acquired skill or profession. In fact, training programs for spiritual directors have emerged only recently.

In attempting to distinguish between psychotherapy and spiritual direction, one must consider the type of relationship emphasized in each practice. In general, a psychotherapist focuses on the client-therapist relationship. A spiritual director, on the other hand, acts as a "human midwife," a medium through which a client's relationship to the divine may be explored. If psychotherapy aims to develop psychological integrity and a healthy adaptation to life, then

spiritual direction's aim is to assist individuals in their search for and response to direct experience of the sacred. Whereas therapists help clients solve personal problems, spiritual directors act more as companions than counselors and coach individuals on how to integrate their experience of the sacred into their everyday life.

Just as spiritual direction and psychotherapy differ, so do their respective training programs. The training of a spiritual director usually involves integrating one's inner subjective spiritual experience, whereas the training of a secular therapist relies heavily upon a more prescribed and objectively based program. The Shalem Institute, established in 1978, is one of the oldest and most reputable spiritual direction training centers, and exemplifies such a curriculum. The two-year ecumenical program permits at-home study, practice, and peer group supervision supplemented by two intensive 11-day residencies in the Washington, D.C., area. Eligibility requirements include a willingness to maintain a spiritual discipline, including meeting on a regular basis (usually monthly) with a spiritual director, and having a daily discipline of prayer/meditation, the form of which is up to the individual in consultation with his or her spiritual director. Participants are also expected to have at least two days of solitary retreat during the program year.

Historically, formal spiritual direction has been associated exclusively with Roman Catholic and Anglican (or Episcopal) seminaries and theological schools. A few training programs are ecumenical in nature and operate independently of theological schools. Most spiritual directors do not charge for their services but work through parishes, religious orders, or retreat centers that may or may not offer them financial support. A small number of spiritual directors operate on a freelance, fee-for-service basis.

Trends in the field include an increased interest by those in Protestant denominations such as the Methodists and Presbyterians, who are developing their own spiritual direction training programs. There is also a shift from an exclusive emphasis on the individual's relationship with the divine to an increased effort to consider the social structures that support and affect individuals. Another trend being explored is why the field of spiritual direction has remained largely a Caucasian, middle-class, Christian phenomenon. Spiritual Directors International, a new association, sponsors conferences that address these and other issues.

There are at least two programs in the United States that offer graduate-level degrees in spiritual direction, and at least seven programs in theological schools that permit students to emphasize spiritual direction within a more general degree program. Nevertheless, most training is offered through nondegree programs.

ADDITIONAL RESOURCES
A Code of Ethics for Spiritual Directors
By the Center for Sacred Psychology
Dove Publications
Pecos, NM 87552
(505) 757-6597

Coming Home: A Handbook for Exploring the Sanctuary Within; and *Coming Home: A Manual for Spiritual Direction*
By Betsy Caprio and Thomas M. Hedberg
Paulist Press
997 Macarthur Boulevard
Mahwah, NJ 07430
(201) 825-7300

Associations
Center for Sacred Psychology (CSP)
Box 643, Gateway Station
Culver City, CA 90232
(310) 838-0279

The CSP is a group of psychotherapists and spiritual directors with a Jungian orientation. The center offers personalized intensive experiences and occasional workshops.

Spiritual Directors International (SDI)
c/o Mercy Center
2300 Adeline Drive
Burlingame, CA 94010-5599
(415) 340-7474

The SDI, primarily a networking organization, sponsors two conferences: one for

EASTERN TRADITIONS OF SPIRITUAL DIRECTION

ALTHOUGH SPIRITUAL DIRECTION IS MOSTLY A WESTERN CONCEPT, THERE IS A LONG history of spiritual teaching or guidance outside Judeo-Christian religions and cultures. For example, receiving individual training from a Zen master is called *dokusan* in Japanese. Rather than prescribing a set of requirements that students must pass (as in traditional academic programs), Zen masters award disciples the privilege of *Inka*, or the status of being a Zen teacher, according to their level of spiritual development—surely an elusive standard according to Western models of education. Similarly, *darshan* in the Hindu tradition refers to receiving energy and wisdom through the direct presence of an enlightened person.

practicing spiritual directors; the other for spiritual directors who act as trainers. It publishes a newsletter, *Connections*, and is preparing to publish a journal.

Periodicals
Journal of Spiritual Formation
See Interdisciplinary Resources.

Review for Religious
P.O. Box 6070
Duluth, MN 55806
(314) 535-3048
Bimonthly; $15

This periodical, while addressing a range of issues encountered by people in religious orders, often includes articles directly relevant to spiritual direction.

Spiritual Life
Institute for Carmelite Studies
2131 Lincoln Avenue, N.E.
Washington, DC 20002
Quarterly; $14

This journal includes some articles on spiritual direction from a Carmelite perspective.

The Way
114 Mount Street
London W1Y 6AN
England
Monthly; $46 (air-mail)

The Way includes a section on spiritual direction.

Weavings
Upper Room
P.O. Box 189
Nashville, TN 37202-0857
Bimonthly; $19

This journal has a Protestant flavor and often covers topics relevant to spiritual direction.

DEGREE AND NONDEGREE EDUCATIONAL PROGRAMS
Center for Religious Development
2240 Massachusetts Avenue
Cambridge, MA 02140
(617) 547-4122
Programs: Certificate in spiritual direction

Center for Spiritual Development
Archdiocese of New York
96 Milton Road
Rye, NY 10580
(914) 967-7328
Programs: Two-year program in spiritual direction

Chestnut Hill College
See Residential Psychology Degree Programs.
Programs: Holistic spirituality/spiritual direction, M.A.; supervision of spiritual directors, certificate; training in spiritual direction, certificate

Creighton College
2500 California Plaza
Omaha, NE 68178
(800) 280-2423
Programs: Christian spirituality

Ecumenical Theological Seminary
2930 Woodward Avenue
Detroit, MI 48201
(313) 831-5200
Programs: Certificate in spiritual direction

General Theological Seminary
Center for Christian Spirituality
175 9th Avenue
New York, NY 10011
(212) 243-5150
Programs: Various programs in spiritual direction

Gonzaga University
Religious Studies Department
Spokane, WA 99258-0001
(509) 328-4220
Programs: Pastoral ministry with specialization in spiritual direction, M.A.

Graduate Theological Foundation
Donaldson, IN 46513
(800) 423-5983
Programs: Spiritual direction, D.Min.

Guelph Center
Ignatius College
Guelph, Ontario
Canada NIH 6J9
Programs: Spiritual direction

Institute for Spiritual Leadership
4906 South Greenwood Avenue
Chicago, IL 60615-2816
(312) 373-7953
Programs: Nine-month, full-time training program in "spiritual companioning"

Jesuit Renewal Center
5361 South Milford Road
Milford, OH 45150
(513) 248-3535
Programs: Training in spiritual direction

Loyola House
Box 245
Guelph, Ontario
Canada N1H 6J9
(519) 824-1250
Programs: Degree and nondegree workshops and practicums in spiritual direction

Mercy Center
2300 Adeline Drive
Burlingame, CA 94010
(415) 340-7474
Programs: Nine-month internship in spiritual direction; Spiritual Directors' Institute

Mercy Center
926 Farragut Avenue
Colorado Springs, CO 80909
(719) 633-2302
Programs: National Institute for Inner Healing; teacher training

Neumann College
Concord Road
Aston, PA 19014
(215) 459-0905
Programs: Certificate in spiritual direction

The New Seminary
See Jewish Theological Training.
Programs: Interfaith ministry

On the Way
P.O. Box 390
Iowa City, IA 52244
(319) 351-2357
Programs: Doctoral program in mystical spirituality

This ecumenical organization also provides a self-study spiritual direction program.

Saint Thomas Theological Seminary
1300 South Steele Street
Denver, CO 80210
(303) 722-4687
Programs: Certificate in spiritual direction

School for Charismatic Spiritual Directors
Pecos Benedictine Monastery
Pecos, NM 87552
(505) 757-6415
Programs: Workshops in spiritual direction

Shalem Institute for Spiritual Formation
Mount St. Alban
Washington, DC 20016
(202) 966-7050
Programs: Spiritual guidance

Stillpoint
The Center for Christian Spirituality
P.O. Box 3722
Santa Barbara, CA 93130
(805) 563-2251
Programs: Spiritual direction

Wainwright House
See Nondegree Training Programs.
Programs: Guild for spiritual guidance

Washington Theological Union
9001 New Hampshire Avenue
Silver Spring, MD 20903-3699
(301) 439-0551
Programs: Graduate certificate in spirituality with concentration in spiritual direction

Theological Training

In general, the contemporary study of religion in the United States consists of three basic approaches: the academic study of a religion; the practical training of religious leaders (e.g., ministers, priests, rabbis); and training in a particular theological tradition. The programs listed in this chapter may focus on only one of these three aspects of religious study or on a combination, depending on the goals of the program and the nature of the sponsoring institution. For example, seminaries and theological schools tend to teach theology exclusively, whereas divinity schools, usually associated with a degree-granting university or college, often teach from a wider, more academic perspective. The academic field of religious studies, offered through university or college departments of religion, is generally interdisciplinary in nature and may include courses in sociology, psychology, art history, and anthropology, and most notably approaches religion from an analytical, historic, and phenomenological perspective.

In addition, when studying a particular theological tradition, the assumption is generally that one is approaching the discipline from a faith stance inside that tradition. Departments of religious studies, however, not only abstain from assuming a faith stance, but some even imply that religious faith is detrimental to the detached and objective study of religion.

MEN AND WOMEN IN CHRISTIAN RELIGIOUS ORDERS

The training of novices varies according to the type of religious order. While some orders sponsor an individual's education at a religiously affiliated university or provide training at their own seminaries (which is less formal than a college degree), others provide training and spiritual formation directly from the religious order. Consult the following directories for more information:

The Episcopal Church Annual
Morehouse Publishing
871 Ethan Allen Highway
Ridgefield, CT 06877
(800) 877-0012

This book provides a listing of Protestant religious orders (mostly Anglican and Episcopal) and other Christian religious communities for men and women.

The Official Catholic Directory
P.J. Kennedy and Sons Publishing
Company
121 Chanion Road
New Providence, NJ 07974
(908) 464-6800

This book provides a complete listing of Catholic organizations, including a listing of religious orders for men and women.

EASTERN RELIGIONS

Training for clergy and religious leaders in non-Western faiths (such as Buddhism and Hinduism) mostly takes place outside the realm of formal educational institutions. Training in the United States, therefore, usually involves apprenticeship or intensive study and practice with a recognized spiritual master, as well as direct experience in the native country of the religion. Furthermore, institutes of these religions located in the United States, , tend to focus on the cultural and intellectual history of the religion rather than the direct teaching of its spiritual practices (e.g., the Nyingma Institute and Hindu University).

—Patricia DeFerrari, a doctoral student in the School of Religious Studies at the Catholic University of America, and Carroll Saussy, Ph.D., a professor of pastoral theology at Wesley Theological Seminary, contributed to this introduction.

BUDDHISM

In writing about Buddhism at the time of the first World Parliament of Religions in 1894, William James is reported to have observed that Buddhism would become America's future psychology. There is evidence that his prediction may prove to be correct, for the tenets of Buddhism, its philosophy and practice, continue to receive a warm reception from Western psychotherapists. The reasons for this openness are numerous.

Since Buddhism takes a nontheistic stance (that is, its view of reality does not depend on a creator), its practice is relatively compatible with secular psychotherapy. Also, Buddhism's practical, do-it-yourself philosophy appeals to independent-minded Americans who want a direct religious experience without the need for faith in a deity or the reliance upon an outside mediator. Finally, Buddhism is similar to Western psychotherapy in that it helps individuals understand the nature of mind and attendant emotional experiences.

The various lineages of Buddhism can be traced back to the birth of the Buddha in the sixth century B.C. Becoming a Buddhist of any lineage requires taking refuge in the three basic principles: the Buddha (as a teacher who shows the path), the Dharma (or the teaching), and the Sangha (or the community of practitioners). Those seeking ordination to become a monk or nun, however, typically join an order, study Buddhist texts, and spend long periods of time in meditation. American sanghas typically cannot financially support full-time teachers; as a result, teachers usually support themselves by holding another job.

Those wanting to study Buddhism from a cultural and academic perspective may receive training at various universities and institutes across the United States. The Naropa Institute in Boulder, Colorado, for example, offers a master's degree in Buddhist contemplative psychotherapy. Students seeking more intensive study may travel to southeast Asia to live as a monk or nun for a year or two. Unlike those who take lifetime vows in Western monasteries, these spiritual seekers frequently leave the monastery to return to their homelands.

Monks, nuns, and ordained laypersons perform marriage ceremonies, conduct funerals, provide teaching, operate temples and schools, and offer social services. Most live in monasteries, while those who only practice intensive meditation tend to live in caves or huts and are known as "forest" monks. Typically monks and nuns are celibate, shave their heads, and wear robes. Zen monks may wed, and certain Zen monasteries have both men and women in residence.

Although there are a growing number of psychotherapists and counselors in the United States who consider themselves Buddhists and integrate this perspective into their therapeutic practice, there is as of yet no central organization recognizing and promoting this integration.

—This introduction is based on an interview with Rick Fields, the editor of Yoga Journal *and the author of* How the Swans Came to the Lake: A Narrative History of Buddhism in America *(1990).*

Organizations

America-Bangladesh Buddhist Congress (ABBC)
P.O. Box 10574
Detroit, MI 48210
Correspondence offered only by mail.

The ABBC is a nonprofit sociocultural and religious organization that helps to strengthen the relationship between America and Bangladesh. It is also a regional center of the Inter-Religious Council for World Peace. Its activities are religious teaching, meditation, child development, education, and cultural exchange.

Buddhist Churches of America (BCA)
1710 Octavia Street
San Francisco, CA 94109
(415) 776-5600

The BCA is an incorporated religious organization affiliated with the Jodo Shinshu Buddhist tradition, a form of Mahayana Buddhism.. It publishes a monthly newsletter and maintains a Buddhist bookstore.

Buddhist Peace Fellowship (BPF)
Box 4650
Berkeley, CA 94704
(510) 525-8596

The BPF, a membership organization, was founded in 1978 to bring a Buddhist perspective to the peace movement and the peace movement to the Buddhist community. Buddhists of many traditions are invited to explore personal and group responses to political, social, and ecological suffering in the world. The BPF publishes *Turning Wheel.*

Buddhist Society of Compassionate Wisdom (BSCW)
1710 West Cornelia
Chicago, IL 60657-1219
Correspondence offered only by mail.

The BSCW (formally Zen Lotus Society) is a North American Buddhist Order founded in New York City by the Venerable Samu Sunim in 1967. There are now three Zen Buddhist temples: in Toronto, Ann Arbor, and Chicago. The BSCW provides training in a monastic tradition in three programs called Dharma Worker, Dharma Guardian, and the Maitreya Buddhist Seminary.

Buddhist Women's Network (BWN)
50-62 47th Street
Woodside, NY 11377
Correspondence offered only by mail.

The BWN was formed in 1993 with representatives from 10 Buddhist traditions: Burmese, Cambodian, Chinese, Japanese, Korean, Sri Lankan, Thai, Tibetan, Vietnamese, and Unitarian Universalist Buddhists. Most members live in New York State.

**Center for Tibetan Buddhist
Wellness and Counseling (CTBWC)**
2941 Tilden Avenue
Los Angeles, CA 90064
(213) 477-3877

The CTBWC, a nonprofit educational organization, facilitates integration and promotion of psychological, physical, and spiritual health by incorporating Tibetan healing and Buddhist counseling into conventional psychotherapy. The center offers workshops and healing meditation retreats, and publishes *MindStream.*

Community of Mindful Living (CML)
P.O. Box 7355
Berkeley, CA 94707
(510) 527-3751

The CML was incorporated by students of Vietnamese monk and poet Thich Nhat Hanh to give support to mindfulness practice within the engaged Buddhist tradition. The center offers retreats and a newsletter that lists local sanghas (communities of friends who meet regularly to meditate, practice, and discuss the teachings of Thich Nhat Hanh). It also helps support the social rejuvenation of Vietnam.

Periodicals
Densal
Karma Triyana Dhamachakra
See Retreat Centers.
Quarterly; $14

This newsletter describes the teaching and news of the Karma Kagyu lineage of Tibetan Buddhism.

Inquiring Mind
A Journal of the Vipassana Community
P.O. Box 9999
North Berkeley Station
Berkeley, CA 94709
Correspondence offered only by mail
Semiannual; donation

This journal in newspaper format covers topics relevant to Buddhist meditation and provides a national listing of meditation retreats.

Insight
Pleasant Street
Barre, MA 01005
(508) 355-4378
Semiannual; complimentary

This newspaper offers retreat and class schedules for the Barre Center for Buddhist Studies (see Buddhist Theological Training) and the Insight Meditation Society (see Retreat Centers), and publishes articles of interest to students and practitioners of Buddhism.

Journal of Contemplative Psychotherapy
Naropa Institute
2130 Arapahoe Avenue
Boulder, CO 80302
(303) 444-0202
Sporadic; $20

This journal presents psychotherapy from a Buddhist contemplative perspective.

Lotus
4032 South Lamar Boulevard
Suite 500-137
Austin, TX 78704-7900
(512) 441-9111
Quarterly; $18

Lotus is devoted to exploring inner peace, mindfulness, and compassionate living as a pathway to personal and spiritual growth.

Mindfulness Bell
Community of Mindful Living
P.O. Box 7355
Berkeley, CA 94707
Three issues a year; $12

Each issue includes an article by Thich Nhat Hanh, essays, and experiential accounts by students and others interested in the practice of mindfulness.

MindStream
Center for Tibetan Buddhist Wellness and Counseling
Three issues a year; $15

*Primary Point: An International
Journal of Buddhism*
The Kwan Um School of Zen
528 Pound Road
Cumberland, RI 02864
(401) 658-1476

Shambhala Sun
See Interdisciplinary Resources.

Ten Directions
Zen Center of Los Angeles and the Kuroda Institute
See Retreat Centers.
Semiannual; donation

Tricycle: The Buddhist Review
163 West 22nd Street
New York, NY 10011
Quarterly; $20
(800) 950-7008

Founded by Lex Hixon, the Henry Luce Foundation, Laurance S. Rockefeller, and others as a nonprofit publication, this magazine functions as a national Buddhist platform by offering illustrated essays, news, and book reviews on Buddhism in America.

Turning Wheel
Buddhist Peace Fellowship
Quarterly; $35 (including membership)

EDUCATIONAL CENTERS
Barre Center for Buddhist Studies (BCBS)
Lockwood Road
Barre, MA 01005-9707
(508) 355-2347

The BCBS is dedicated to bringing together teachers, students, scholars, and practitioners who are committed to exploring Buddhist thought and practice as a living tradition. The center's purpose is to provide a bridge between study and practice, between scholarly understanding and meditative insight. The center offers study and research opportunities, lectures, classes, seminars, workshops, conferences, retreats, independent study, and a scholars-in-residence program. In conjunction with the Insight Meditation Society, it publishes a semiannual newspaper called *Insight.*

Green Gulch Farm Zen Center
See Retreat Centers.

Insight Meditation Society
See Retreat Centers.

Karma Triyana Dharmachakra
See Retreat Centers.

Karme-Choling
See Retreat Centers.

Spirit Rock Center
See Retreat Centers.

Upaya Foundation
See Retreat Centers.

Vipassana Meditation Center (VMC)
P.O. Box 24
Shelburne Falls, MA 01270
(413) 625-2160
Considered one of India's most ancient Buddhist meditation techniques, Vipassana, or insight meditation, means "seeing things as they really are." The VMC offers a 10-day course as taught by S.N. Goenka in the tradition of Suyagyi U Ba Khin. There are also centers in North Fork, California; Dallas, Texas; and Ethel, Washington.

Zen Center
See Retreat Centers.

Zen Center of Los Angeles
See Retreat Centers.

Zen Mountain Center
See Retreat Centers.

Zen Mountain Monastery
See Retreat Centers.

DEGREE PROGRAMS
Center for Buddhist Studies
Columbia University, Department of Religion
617 Kent
New York, NY 10027
(212) 854-3218
Most of this center's activities involve scholarship and translation; however, some Buddhist courses are offered in conjunction with the interdepartmental Buddhist Studies program at Columbia. Professor Robert Thurman acts as the director of the center and chair of the interdepartmental program.

College of Buddhist Studies (CBS)
933 South New Hampshire Avenue
Los Angeles, CA 90006
(213) 739-1270
Founded by the Buddhist Sangha Council of Southern California, CBS is the educational arm of the International Buddhist Meditation Center.

General Information: Private, Buddhist
Degrees Offered: Certificate; M.A.; Ph.D.
Programs: Buddhist studies certificate, M.A., Ph.D.; ministerial studies
Admission Requirements: Bachelor's degree
Application Deadline: Rolling
Contact Person: Director of Admissions
Tuition: Contact college
Accreditation: Buddhist Sangha Council of Southern California; State of California
Year Established: 1983
Faculty: 4 full-time

Columbia University
Department of Religion
617 Kent
New York, NY 10027
(212) 854-3218
Professor Robert Thurman, the chairperson, is also the director of the Center for Buddhist Studies at Columbia.
General Information: Private
Degrees Offered: Ph.D.
Programs: Buddhist studies
Admission Requirements: Bachelor's degree; GRE; letters of recommendation; language proficiency
Application Deadline: April 1
Contact Person: Director of Admissions
Tuition: $8,838
Accreditation: NCACS
Year Established: 1988
Faculty: 3 interdepartmental

Institute of Buddhist Studies
1900 Addison Street
Berkeley, CA 94704
(510) 849-2383
The institute is a Jodo Shinshu Buddhist seminary and graduate school sponsored by the Buddhist Churches of America. Its purpose it to train ministers for the denomination. In addition, it provides an accredited nonsectarian graduate program in Buddhist studies through its affiliation with the Graduate Theological Union in Berkeley.
General Information: Private, Buddhist
Degrees Offered: M.A.
Programs: Buddhist studies; Jodo-Shinshu studies
Admission Requirements: Bachelor's degree; GRE; three letters of recommendation
Application Deadline: Rolling
Contact Person: Director of Admissions
Tuition: $125/credit
Accreditation: Through the Graduate Theological Union
Year Established: 1967
Faculty: 3 core; 7 adjunct

The Naropa Institute
See Residential Psychology Programs.

Nyingma Institute
1815 Highland Place
Berkeley, CA 94709
(510) 843-6812
Programs: Foundation Certificate; Nyingma Teachings in Action certificate; six-month human development certificate
The institute, founded in 1973 by the late Tarthang Tulku as a Buddhist education center, also offers some nonresidential courses.

CHRISTIANITY

PROTESTANT

Protestant Christian theological schools and seminaries examine many of the same issues as do religion programs in secular institutions, but do so from a faith perspective. Such study is motivated by questions of how we know God and how faith is mediated in our culture. (Some seminaries are even offering course work in Native American and other indigenous traditions.) Theological study may be undertaken at a seminary or theological school (not always the same thing), a university-based divinity school, or a Bible college. For centuries, formal theological study has tended to be reserved for clergy; only recently has it begun to attract laypersons. The number of female theological students has increased significantly during the last two decades.

The practical training of religious leaders differs according to the denomination in which they will serve. Most Protestant clergy and lay professionals, for example, are trained in seminaries or theological schools. Besides learning patterns of worship specific to their tradition, students study scripture, theology, and preaching. Other training components include spiritual formation, which involves guidance in the practice of spiritual disciplines (such as prayer), and pastoral theology and pastoral care, which concern the practical, social, and interpersonal dimensions of religion.

Entrance into a theological school usually requires a Bachelor of Arts degree; successful completion confers a Master of Divinity (M.Div.) degree. Some lay people pursue the M.A. or M.A.R. degree if ordination is not their goal. The Doctor of Ministry (D.Min.) and Doctorate of Theology (Th.D) are both terminal degrees that first require master's-level training. If you seek the opportunity to teach at a university, a Ph.D. in theology (in conjunction with a university-based program) is generally more favored than the Th.D. Some seminaries also offer the S.T.M. (Master of Sacred Theology), the S.T.D. (Doctor of Sacred Theology), or the D.Rel. (Doctor of Religion) degree.

ROMAN CATHOLIC

The Roman Catholic church has its own hierarchy of ecclesiastical degrees, most of which presuppose an undergraduate university education. There are two tracks to becoming a priest. One is training at a diocesan seminary; the other is affiliation with one of the religious order seminaries (i.e., Franciscan, Jesuit, etc.). There is considerable debate in seminaries of all faiths about the appropriateness of such training because it tends to focus on academic expertise more than nurturing the pastoral qualities needed to work with congregations. While there have not yet been significant changes in the structure of seminary training, these programs have expanded to include courses in religious leadership for people who do not intend to serve as ordained priests. Such students earn certificates and degrees (M.A., M.T.S., M.R.E., D.Min.) in such areas as religious education, liturgical studies, and pastoral care. Many women are enrolled in these programs but are still excluded from training for the priesthood.

Associations and Organizations

American Association of Christian Counselors (AACC)

2421 West Pratt Avenue, Suite 1398
Chicago, IL 60645
(800) 526-8673

The AACC is an organization of evangelical professional, lay, and pastoral counselors dedicated to promoting excellence and unity in Christian counseling.

American Scientific Affiliation (ASA)

P.O. Box 668
Ipswich, MA 01938
(508) 356-5656

Founded in 1941, ASA is a fellowship of over 2,000 Christians in the field of science who seek to integrate their faith and professional calling. ASA would like to see that both science and biblical revelation are treated with integrity. Over 300 of the members are college and university students, and nearly 100 are missionaries. The ASA publishes a bimonthly newsletter, a quarterly journal (*Perspectives on Science and Christian Faith*), and a directory for members, and hosts national and regional meetings throughout the United States.

American Theological Association (ATA)

10 Summit Park Drive
Pittsburgh, PA 15275-1103
(412) 788-6505

The ATA is a membership organization of graduate schools of theology in the United States and Canada. Its 219 member institutions represent the entire spectrum of denominational, ecclesiastical, and theological perspectives evident in North America today, making it the most broad-based religious organization of its kind. The association comprises Protestant, Roman Catholic, and Eastern Orthodox schools of theology, and both university-related divinity schools and free-standing seminaries. Virtually all mainline Protestant denominations are represented as well as the majority of Roman Catholic diocesan and religious order seminaries, a Greek Orthodox seminary, and a seminary of the Orthodox Church in America.

Theological schools seek membership in the ATA for accreditation of their institutions and their various degree programs as well as for ATA's extensive program of services aimed at improving and strengthening theological education in the United States and Canada. ATA is recognized by the U.S. Department of Education as the accrediting agency that sets the standards for quality in North American theological education. In its accrediting reviews of graduate theological schools, the association also works closely with the six regional accrediting agencies for colleges and universities. ATA publishes a "Membership List" of its accredited schools twice a year, following each meeting of the Commission on Accrediting, as well as the journal *Theological Education*.

Association of Christian Therapists (ACT)

14440 Cherry Lane Court, Suite 215
Laurel, MD 20707
(301) 470-2287

The ACT includes mental health therapists, physicians, and clergy, among other professionals.

Christian Association for Psychological Studies (CAPS)

Robert King, Ph.D., Executive Director
P.O. Box 890279
Temecula, CA 92589-0279
(909) 695-2277

Founded in 1956, CAPS is an evangelical association of Christians in the psychological and pastoral professions. The association publishes the *Journal of Psychology and Christianity* and holds annual regional and national conventions.

Free Catholic Church in the Greater Washington Area (FCC)

P.O. Box 32236
Washington, DC 20007
(202) 333-6354

The FCC is affiliated with the International Council of Community Churches, an ecumenical organization. Other than encouraging a ministry that is open to all regardless of gender, marital status, or sexual orientation, the FCC is unusual in that all clergy have degrees and certification in theology, psychology, and psychotherapy.

International Christian Studies Association

2828 Third Street, Suite 11
Santa Monica, CA 90405
(310) 396-0517

ICSA is a multidisciplinary, nondenominational, nonprofit, educational association dedicated to the exploration of knowledge and its integration with Judaeo-Christian ethical and spiritual values. Founded in 1983, ICSA promotes an interdisciplinary and interfaith dialogue.

Monastic Inter-Religious Dialogue (MID)
Our Lady of Grace Monastery
1402 Southern Avenue
Beech Grove, IN 46107
(317) 787-3287

Monastic Inter-Religious Dialogue, originally called the North American Board for East-West Dialogue, was established in 1978 by the Benedictine Confederation to aid third-world monasteries in assuming a leading role in the dialogue between Christianity and the religions of the East. MID's general aim is to foster the contribution of the Christian monastic tradition to the encounter between Eastern and Western contemplative traditions. The organization works in cooperation with other religious people, lay and monastic, who are engaged in this dialogue. It publishes a bulletin three times a year, maintains a monastic persons' network, and participates at national and regional conferences, seminars, and dialogue sessions.

Society for the Study of Christian Spirituality (SSCS)
c/o Bradley Hanson
Luther College
Decorah, IA 52101
(319) 387-1184

The SSCS exists to promote research and dialogue within the growing interdisciplinary field of spirituality.

Institutes

Boston Theological Institute
210 Herrick Road
Newton Centre, MA 02159
(617) 527-4880

The institute is an association that represents nine theological schools in the greater Boston area—Andover Newton Theological School, Boston College Department of Theology, Boston University School of Theology, Episcopal Divinity School, Gordon-Conwell Theological Seminary, Harvard University Divinity School, Holy Cross Greek Orthodox School of Theology, Saint John's Seminary, and Weston School of Theology. The institute publishes a comprehensive catalog of courses available through one or more of the nine membership schools, organized by topic (including the "Sociology and Psychology of Religion" and "Counseling and Psychotherapy.")

Center for Theology and the Natural Sciences
See Research Institutes.

Institute of Religion and Health
See Pastoral Counseling.

Institute on Religion and Democracy (IRD)
1331 H Street, N.W., Suite 900
Washington, DC 20005
(202) 393-3200

The IRD is a nonprofit organization committed to building and strengthening a democratic future, monitoring religious liberty issues around the world, and ensuring that the church focuses on theology more than on politics or sociology. It publishes *Faith and Freedom.*

John Main Institute™
7315 Brookville Road
Chevy Chase, MD 20815
(301) 652-8635

The institute was founded in 1991 to support Christian meditation in the United States and within the international community. The World Community for Christian Meditation, formed during the John Main Seminar in 1991 and a part of the institute, aims to nurture and encourage the practice and teaching of meditation in the Christian tradition as taught by the Benedictine monk John Main (1926-1982). The institute sponsors conferences (from which audiotapes are available) and publishes the *Christian Meditation Newsletter.*

Kanuga Conferences
See Conference Centers.

Kirkridge
See Conference Centers.

Spiritual Life Institute
See Retreat Centers.

St. Benedict Center
See Retreat Centers.

Periodicals

Christian Counseling Today
American Association of Christian Counselors
Quarterly; $35

Journal of Christian Healing
Association of Christian Therapists
Quarterly; $24

Journal of Psychology and Christianity
Christian Association for Psychological Studies
Quarterly; $35

Journal of Psychology and Theology (JPT)
Subscription Office
13800 Biola Avenue
La Mirada, CA 90639
(310) 944-0341 (ext. 5322)
Quarterly; $38

JPT is an ecumenical journal published by Biola University.

Koinonia Journal
Princeton Theological Seminary
P.O. Box 821
Princeton, NJ 08542-0803
(609) 921-8300
Semiannual; $18 ($12 students)

This publication, written by and for theological students, explores emerging areas of interest in the study of religion while fostering an interdisciplinary dialogue.

New Theology Review: An American Catholic Journal for Ministry
The Liturgical Press
St. John's Abbey
Collegeville, MN 56321
(800) 858-5450
Quarterly; $22

Review for Religious
P.O. Box 6070
Duluth, MN 55806
Bimonthly; $18

This Catholic journal provides a forum for a wide exchange of ideas and developments in the spiritual aspects of religious-life communities.

Spiritual Life (SL)
2131 Lincoln Road, N.E.
Washington, DC 20077-0572
Quarterly; $14

SL is a Catholic journal that explores contemporary spirituality.

Theological Education
Association of Theological Schools
Semiannual; $7

DEGREE PROGRAMS

Below we list only those programs that involve both a religion and a social science, such as those offering counseling or family therapy programs from a faith perspective or those that offer programs in culture and personality—that is, the study of religion from both inner (personal self) and outer (societal and social self) perspectives. (For pastoral counseling programs, see the Pastoral Counseling chapter.)

Andover Newton Theological School
210 Herrick Road
Newton Centre, MA 02159-2243
(617) 964-1100; (800) 964-2687 (ext. 272)
General Information: Private, Christian
Degrees Offered: M.A.
Programs: Psychology and religion
Admission Requirements: Bachelor's degree (some exceptions)
Application Deadline: August 13
Contact Person: Director of Enrollment
Tuition: $286/credit hour
Accreditation: ATS; MSACA
Year Established: 1825
Faculty: 23 full-time

Assemblies of God Theological Seminary
1445 Boonville Avenue
Springfield, MO 65802
(417) 862-3344
General Information: Private, Assemblies of God
Degrees Offered: M.A.
Programs: Counseling
Admission Requirements: Bachelor's degree
Application Deadline: Rolling
Contact Person: Director of Admissions
Tuition: $185/semester hour
Accreditation: NCA; ATS
Year Established: 1984
Faculty: 12 full-time

Biblical Theological Seminary
200 North Main Street
Hatfield, PA 19440
(215) 368-5000
General Information: Private, interdenominational
Degrees Offered: M.A.; M.Div.
Programs: Counseling
Admission Requirements: Bachelor's degree
Application Deadline: Rolling
Contact Person: Director of Admissions
Tuition: $126/credit hour
Accreditation: MSACA; ATS
Year Established: 1971
Faculty: 15 full-time

Biola University
Rosemead School of Religion
13800 Biola Avenue
La Mirada, CA 90639-0001
(310) 903-4752
General Information: Private, Christian
Degrees Offered: Ph.D., Psy.D.
Programs: Psychology
Admission Requirements: Bachelor's degree; five letters of recommendation; GRE; Minnesota Multiphasic Personality Inventory; undergraduate experience
Application Deadline: January 15
Contact Person: Director of Admissions
Tuition: $12,012/year
Accreditation: APA
Year Established: 1914
Faculty: 19 full-time; 7 part-time

Boston University School of Theology
745 Commonwealth Avenue
Boston, MA 02215
(617) 353-3050
General Information: Private, Christian
Degrees Offered: M.Div.
Programs: Master's of Divinity (specialization in religion, culture, and personality)
Admission Requirements: Bachelor's degree
Application Deadline: Rolling
Contact Person: Director of Admissions
Tuition: $6,700
Accreditation: ATS; NEACSS
Year Established: 1839
Faculty: 40 full-time

Chicago Theological Seminary
5757 South University Avenue
Chicago, IL 60637
(312) 752-5757

The purpose of this degree is to prepare religious leaders to work at advanced levels in a variety of teaching, counseling, research, and administrative contexts.
General Information: Private, Christian
Degrees Offered: Ph.D.
Programs: The doctor of philosophy degree is offered through two centers, the Center for Theology, Ethics and the Human Sciences and the Center for Jewish Christian Studies
Admission Requirements: Bachelor's degree; GRE
Application Deadline: Rolling
Contact Person: Director of Admissions
Tuition: Contact institution
Accreditation: ATS; NCACS
Year Established: 1855
Faculty: 15 full-time

Christian Theological Seminary
1000 West 42nd Street
Indianapolis, IN 46208
(317) 924-1331
See Pastoral Counseling.

Claremont School of Theology
1325 North College Avenue
Claremont, CA 91711
(714) 626-3521
Also see Pastoral Counseling.
General Information: Private, Christian
Degrees Offered: Ph.D.
Programs: Theology and personality
Admission Requirements: Bachelor's degree
Application Deadline: Rolling
Contact Person: Director of Admissions
Tuition: Contact institution
Accreditation: WASC; ATS; AAPC
Year Established: 1885
Faculty: 38 full-time

Eastern Mennonite College and Seminary
1200 Park Road
Harrisonburg, VA 22801
(703) 432-4260
General Information: Private, Mennonite
Degrees Offered: M.A.
Programs: Counseling
Admission Requirements: Bachelor's degree
Application Deadline: Rolling
Contact Person: Director of Admissions
Tuition: $4,520/year
Accreditation: ATS
Year Established: 1965
Faculty: 8 full-time; 10 part-time; 3 adjunct

Emmanuel School of Religion
One Walker Drive
Johnson City, TN 37601
(615) 926-1186
General Information: Private, Christian
Degrees Offered: M.Div., M.A.
Programs: Master of Divinity, Master of Arts in Religion (with a counseling concentration)
Admission Requirements: Bachelor's degree
Application Deadline: Rolling
Contact Person: Director of Admissions
Tuition: $150/semester hour
Accreditation: ATS, SACS
Year Established: 1961
Faculty: 13 full-time; 8 adjunct

Emory University
Department of Theology and Personality
Graduate Division of Religion
Bishops Hall
Atlanta, GA 30322
(404) 727-4155
Professor James W. Fowler, well-known author of *Stages of Faith*, is the director of

the Center for Research in Faith and Moral Development.

General Information: Private, denominational

Degrees Offered: Ph.D.

Programs: Psychology and religion

Admission Requirements: Bachelor's degree

Application Deadline: February 1

Contact Person: Director of Admissions

Tuition: Each candidate who is admitted receives tuition plus a $10,000 stipend each year for up to four years

Accreditation: SACS

Year Established: 1980

Faculty: 6 full-time

Fuller Theological Seminary

School of Psychology

180 North Oakland Avenue

Pasadena, CA 91101

(818) 584-5520

General Information: Private, Christian

Degrees Offered: M.S.; M.F.T.; Ph.D.; Psy.D

Programs: Clinical Psychology, Ph.D., Psy.D.; marriage and family therapy, M.S., M.F.T., Ph.D.; marriage and family studies, Ph.D.

Admission Requirements: Bachelor's degree

Application Deadline: February 15 for M.S. and M.F.T; January 1 for Ph.D. and Psy.D.

Contact Person: Director of Admissions

Tuition: $277/unit

Accreditation: ATS; WASC; AAMFT; APA (Ph.D. and Psy.D.)

Year Established: 1973

Faculty: 19 full-time

Graduate Theological Union (GTU)

2400 Ridge Road

Berkeley, CA 94709

(510) 649-2400

The GTU is both a consortium of seminaries—the largest and most geographically concentrated theological enterprise in North America—and a graduate school. As a graduate school, the GTU awards M.A., Ph.D., and Th.D. degrees, making available the resources of member schools to doctoral students and providing access to the University of California at Berkeley. In addition, a variety of centers and institutes are affiliated with the GTU, bringing Christians into dialogue with Jewish and Buddhist traditions, raising academic awareness of minority and women's issues, and exploring issues of ethics, science, and methodology.

General Information: Private, ecumenical

Degrees Offered: Ph.D.

Programs: Near-Eastern religions (interdisciplinary religion and mythology option) in conjunction with the University of California, Berkeley; religion and the personality sciences; Jewish Studies; comparative studies

Admission Requirements: Bachelor's degree; GRE

Application Deadline: June 1

Contact Person: Director of Admissions

Tuition: $2,825/semester (M.A.); $4,800/semester (Ph.D.)

Accreditation: ATS; WASC

Year Established: 1893

Faculty: 11 full-time; 6 part-time; 40 adjunct

Hardin-Simmons University

Drawer Z, HSU Station

Abilene, TX 79698

(915) 670-1531

General Information: Private, Baptist

Degrees Offered: M.A.

Programs: Family psychology

Admission Requirements: Bachelor's degree; psychology course work

Application Deadline: Rolling

Contact Person: Director of Admissions

Tuition: $200/hour

Accreditation: SASC

Year Established: 1985

Faculty: 2 full-time; 2 part-time

Iliff School of Theology

2201 South University Boulevard

Denver, CO 80210

(303) 744-1287

General Information: Private, Methodist

Degrees Offered: Ph.D.

Programs: Religion and personality; religion and social change

Admission Requirements: Bachelor's degree

Application Deadline: Rolling

Contact Person: Director of Admissions

Tuition: $305/quarter hour

Accreditation: NCACSC; ATS

Year Established: 1892

Faculty: 21 full-time; 23 part-time

Lasalle University

Philadelphia, PA 19141

(215) 951-1767

General Information: Private, Christian

Degrees Offered: M.A.

Programs: Family treatment of addiction; marriage and family therapy; psychological counseling

Admission Requirements: Bachelor's degree; 12 undergraduate credits in both psychology and religion; GPA > 3.0; interview; letters of recommendation

Application Deadline: Rolling

Contact Person: Director of Admissions

Tuition: $300/credit

Accreditation: MSASC

Year Established: 1974

Faculty: 5 full-time

Louisville Seminary

1044 Alta Vista Road

Louisville, KY 40205-1798

(800) 264-1839

General Information: Private, Presbyterian

Degrees Offered: M.A.

Programs: Marriage and family therapy

Admission Requirements: Bachelor's degree

Application Deadline: Rolling

Contact Person: Director of Admissions

Tuition: $190/credit hour

Accreditation: ATS; CAMFTE

Year Established: 1853

Faculty: 3 full-time; 8 adjunct

Loyola Marymount University

Loyola Boulevard at West 80th Street

Los Angeles, CA 90045

(310) 338-2704

General Information: Private, ecumenical

Degrees Offered: M.A.; M.F.T.

Programs: Counseling; educational psychology; marital and family therapy; school psychology

Admission Requirements: Bachelor's degree; GRE; MAT

Application Deadline: Rolling

Contact Person: Director of Admissions

Tuition: $292/credit hour

Accreditation: WASC; California State Commission on Teacher Credentialing

Year Established: 1918

Faculty: Contact department

Lutheran Northwestern Theological Seminary

2481 Como Avenue

St. Paul, MN 55108

(612) 641-3456

General Information: Private, Lutheran

Degrees Offered: M.A.

Programs: Counseling

Admission Requirements: Bachelor's degree

Application Deadline: Rolling

Contact Person: Director of Admissions

Tuition: $3,600

Accreditation: NCASC; ATS

Year Established: 1869

Faculty: 65 total

McCormick Theological Seminary

5555 South Woodlawn Avenue

Chicago, IL 60637

(312) 947-6317

General Information: Private, Presbyterian

Degrees Offered: M.A.

Programs: Counseling

Admission Requirements: Bachelor's degree

Application Deadline: Rolling

Contact Person: Director of Admissions

Tuition: $4,950/year

Accreditation: ATS; NCASC
Year Established: 1960
Faculty: 1 per 13 students

New College of Berkeley
Center for Christian Studies
   See Conference Centers.

The New Seminary
   See Judaic Theological Training.

North American Baptist Seminary
1321 West 22nd Street
Sioux Falls, SD 57105
(605) 336-6588
General Information: Private, Christian
Degrees Offered: M.A.
Programs: Counseling
Admission Requirements: Bachelor's degree;
letters of recommendation
Application Deadline: Rolling
Contact Person: Director of Admissions
Tuition: $2,975/semester
Accreditation: ATS; NCACS
Year Established: 1858
Faculty: 4 full-time

Olivet Nazarene University
240 East Marsile
Bourbonnais, IL 60914
(815) 939-5291
   See Pastoral Counseling.

Oral Roberts University
7777 South Lewis Avenue
Tulsa, OK 74171
(918) 495-6090
General Information: Private, Christian
Degrees Offered: M.A.; L.P.C.; L.M.F.T.
Programs: Christian counseling; marriage
and family therapy
Admission Requirements: Bachelor's degree;
letters of recommendation
Application Deadline: Rolling
Contact Person: Director of Admissions
Tuition: $160/credit hour
Accreditation: ATS; NCASC
Year Established: 1986
Faculty: 4 full-time; 3 adjunct

Pacific School of Religion (PSR)
1798 Scenic Avenue
Berkeley, CA 94707
(510) 848-0528
   PSR is dedicated to "transcending
denominationalism" by valuing a diverse
faculty that represents numerous denominations and perspectives.
General Information: Private,
nondenominational
Degrees Offered: M.A.; M.Div.; D.Min.

Programs: Concentration in religion and
personality
Admission Requirements: Bachelor's degree
Application Deadline: Rolling
Contact Person: Director of Admissions
Tuition: $5,800/year
Accreditation: ATS; WASC
Year Established: 1866
Faculty: 11 full-time; 2 part-time

Reformed Theological Seminary
5422 Clinton Boulevard
Jackson, MS 39209-3099
(601) 922-4988
General Information: Private, Christian
Degrees Offered: M.A.; M.F.T.; M.Div.
Programs: Counseling; marriage and family
therapy
Admission Requirements: Bachelor's degree;
GRE
Application Deadline: February 1
Contact Person: Director of Admissions
Tuition: $175/credit hour
Accreditation: ATS; CCSACS; AAMFT
Year Established: 1966
Faculty: 20 full-time; 7 adjunct

Regent University
1000 Regent University Drive
Virginia Beach, VA 23464
(804) 523-7400
General Information: Private, Christian
Degrees Offered: M.A.
Programs: Counseling
Admission Requirements: Bachelor's degree
Application Deadline: Rolling
Contact Person: Director of Admissions
Tuition: $175/quarter hour
Accreditation: ATS
Year Established: 1977
Faculty: 73 full-time

Saint Joseph College
The Counseling Institute
1678 Asylum Avenue
West Hartford, CT 06117-2700
(203) 232-4571 (ext. 333)
General Information: Private, Christian
Degrees Offered: M.A.; M.F.T.
Programs: Counseling; marriage and family
therapy; pastoral counseling
Admission Requirements: Bachelor's degree
Application Deadline: Rolling
Contact Person: Director of Admissions
Tuition: $275/credit
Accreditation: AAMFT in process (M.F.T.);
New England Education Board for Higher
Education (counseling)
Year Established: 1987
Faculty: 7 core; 18 adjunct

Saint Mary's College
Minneapolis Center
2510 Park Avenue South
Minneapolis, MN 55404
(612) 874-9877
General Information: Private, Christian
Degrees Offered: M.A.
Programs: Counseling and psychological
services
Admission Requirements: Bachelor's degree
Application Deadline: May 15
Contact Person: Director of Admissions
Tuition: $185/unit
Accreditation: NCACSC
Year Established: 1956
Faculty: 40 part-time

Trinity Evangelical Divinity School
2065 Half Day Road
Deerfield, IL 60015
(800) 345-8337
General Information: Private, Christian
Degrees Offered: M.A.; Ph.D. (via Northern
Illinois University)
Programs: Counseling psychology
Admission Requirements: Bachelor's degree;
inventory examination; prerequisite
courses
Application Deadline: Rolling
Contact Person: Director of Admissions
Tuition: $2,280/quarter
Accreditation: NCACS; ATS
Year Established: 1884
Faculty: 47 full-time

Union Theological Seminary
3041 Broadway
New York, NY 10027
(212) 662-7100
General Information: Private, Christian
Degrees Offered: Ph.D. with certification in
pastoral psychotherapy from the Blanton-
Peale Institutes of Religion and Health
Programs: Psychiatry and Religion
Admission Requirements: Bachelor's degree;
GRE; three letters of recommendation
Application Deadline: Rolling
Contact Person: Director of Admissions
Tuition: $9,950/year
Accreditation: ATS; MSACS
Year Established: 1836
Faculty: 28 full-time

United Theological Seminary
1810 Harvard Boulevard
Dayton, OH 45406-4599
(513) 278-5817
General Information: Private, Christian
Degrees Offered: M.Div./M.A. (via Wright
State University)

Programs: Marriage and family; mental health
Admission Requirements: Bachelor's degree
Application Deadline: January 15
Contact Person: Director of Admissions
Tuition: $6,600
Accreditation: ATS; NCACSS
Year Established: 1954
Faculty: 28 full-time

University of Chicago

The Divinity School
Swift Hall
1025 East 58th Street
Chicago, IL 60637
(312) 702-8217

The University of Chicago offers numerous courses in the psychology and the sociology of religion.
General Information: Private, Christian
Degrees Offered: M.Div.; Ph.D.
Programs: Psychology and sociology of religion (area of study)
Admission Requirements: Bachelor's degree; GRE
Application Deadline: January 5
Contact Person: Director of Admissions
Tuition: $12,660 (M.Div.); $17,835 (Ph.D. first year)
Accreditation: ATS; NCACS
Year Established: 1891
Faculty: 26 full-time

Western Evangelical Seminary

12753 Southwest 68th Avenue
Tigard, OR 97223
(503) 639-0559
General Information: Private, Christian
Degrees Offered: M.A.
Programs: Christian counseling; Christian counseling psychology
Admission Requirements: Bachelor's degree
Application Deadline: Rolling
Contact Person: Director of Admissions
Tuition: $135/quarter hour
Accreditation: ATS; NASC; Oregon Board of Licensed Professional Counselors and Therapists
Year Established: 1947
Faculty: 9 full-time

Wheaton College Graduate School

Wheaton, IL 60187-5593
(800) 888-0141
General Information: Private, Christian
Degrees Offered: Ph.D., Psy.D.
Programs: Clinical psychology
Admission Requirements: Bachelor's degree; four letters of recommendation; GRE

Application Deadline: Rolling
Contact Person: Director of Admissions
Tuition: $350/credit hour
Accreditation: NCACS; APA (provisional)
Year Established: 1977
Faculty: 12 full-time

HINDUISM

Interest in Hinduism continues to develop among Westerners. In terms of educational requirements, there are no official certification or licensing procedures required to enter a religious profession. Nevertheless, the following terms are relevant to Hindu religious vocations.

ASHRAM

A teacher (who may be a swami, a yogi, or a guru) often establishes a teaching center also known as an ashram. The yoga master Amrit Desai, for example, established Kripalu Yoga Centers (ashrams) in Sumneytown, Pennsylvania, and Lenox, Massachusetts; and Swami Paramahansa Yogananda founded Self-Realization Fellowship in Los Angeles. A swami in India may teach from his own home or travel around the country as a freelance teacher. Mahatma Gandhi, who was considered to be a guru and rishi (very wise person), had an ashram in his home.

AVATAR

An avatar is a divine incarnation. Mother Meera, who was born in India and now lives in Thalheim, Germany, is believed by many to be a modern-day avatar.

DEITIES

Because Brahman, the Hindu deity, is considered formless, devotees are permitted to choose their own image or icon that reminds them of God. For this reason, there may be many temples in a single village, each with a different statue inside. These temples are built, owned, and operated by the village elders. Places of worship vary in size from roadside shrines to enormous temples in cities, the latter sponsoring educational centers in which priests learn Sanskrit and Hindu rituals from other priests.

GURU

A guru is a teacher of one of the particular paths for knowing God that exist in the Hindu tradition. In most cases, this path is followed by way of one of the yoga traditions: Bakti Yoga (devotion), Hatha Yoga (purification), Jnana Yoga (knowledge), Karma Yoga (service), Mantra Yoga (prayer), and Raja Yoga (contemplation). Followers typically worship their guru as an earthly manifestation of God. Because students choose their guru and decide whether his or her teachings are of value, the number of teachers practicing is partially market-driven. There are no equivalent professions in the United States, although many in our culture consider people such as Dr. Martin Luther King, Jr., and Mother Theresa to be unique mentors and role models.

PRIESTS

To become a priest one must be a male member of the Brahmin caste (the highest social level). A priest's role is analogous to a justice of the peace in the United States—that is, it is primarily ceremonial. Priests often perform marriages and funerals, bless children, and preside at holiday festivals, for which they are sometimes compensated. However, they are not paid a regular salary and so they typically have another job. Priests may be married. The educational model of India fosters a protégé/professional relationship in which priests teach others who aspire to become priests. However, priests do not provide other forms of teaching or give sermons.

RENUNCIATE

In an ashram, a disciple may take a vow of Brahmacharya (simplicity, obedience, and service) in the order of the teacher. This involves celibacy, charitable work, and a life of simplicity. The oath of simplicity is similar to the Christian monk's or nun's vow of poverty. (In India, this simplicity is very austere. Typically renunciates own a blanket, one change of underwear, a towel, a water pot, and the clothes on his or her back—nothing else.)

SAINT

When miracles, healings, and contagious inspiration happen around a religious leader, his or her devotees may proclaim him or her a saint. If the acclaim grows, other religious leaders quietly ascertain the proclamations' authenticity, and if validated those leaders promulgate the saint's authenticity by visiting him or her and personally offering their respects. Hinduism values living saints, whereas Christianity tends to proclaims saints only after they have died.

SWAMI ORDER

Many years ago Adi Shankara (b. 686 C.E.), a religious reformer, organized the training of religious disciples in regional schools that became known as a "Math," which in some ways is similar to seminaries in the West. These schools teach students in the swami orders subjects like Sanskrit, religious lore, and sacred texts such as the *Bhagavad Gita.* Students are also taught to organize care for the sick, to perform social services, and to even help build water-supply systems.

After acceptance into the order, the swami begins to wear orange robes; practices chastity, obedience, and poverty; and commits him- or herself to serving humanity. Upon graduation, a swami is sent to serve in a place of need. Swamis beg for food and shelter in order to support themselves; however, they are considered mendicants rather than panhandlers by their society. The swamis that endure are the ones whose teachings disciples believe are worth supporting. Established swamis may pick a few disciples to continue their lineage. In India, there are five independent regional centers with a Math attached. Each Math is a headquarters for a master swami order, while each center serves the members of all swami orders in its region.

There are a few female swamis in India. The most famous in the United States is Swami Chidvilasananda, whose ashram is in Fallsburg, New York. She was "tapped," or chosen, by her teacher, Swami Muktananda of the Siddha Yoga lineage.

VEDANTA

Vedanta refers to the *Vedas* and the whole body of literature that explains and elaborates upon their teachings. The *Bhagavad Gita* and the works of Shankara belong to Vedanta. Furthermore, there are 13 Vedanta Societies in the United States and over 125 centers throughout the world, where Vedanta is taught. All are under the spiritual guidance of the Ramakrishna Order, and each center in the United States is a self-supporting unit with a board of trustees made up of Americans. The Vedanta Press, listed below, can supply a complete listing of societies.

YOGACHARYA, JAGADACHARYA, MAHARISHI

These are all titles of honor.

YOGI

Some yogis remain in seclusion like hermits while others engage with society primarily through teaching. Still others both teach and spend part of their time in seclusion.

—This introduction is based on an interview with Gitanand, a renunciate at the Kripalu Yoga Center, the ashram of Yogi Amrit Desai, who is considered to be a guru by his disciples.

Organizations
Vedanta Press
1946 Vedanta Place
Hollywood, CA 90068
(213) 465-7114

Periodicals
Hinduism Today
Himalayan Academy
1819 Second Street
Concord, CA 94519
(808) 822-3152
Monthly; $29
This newspaper-format publication covers various topics concerning contemporary Hinduism in the United States.

International Journal of Hindu Studies
Hindu University of America
Publication is expected to begin in 1994/95.

EDUCATIONAL CENTERS
City of God Retreat Center
See Retreat Centers.

Himalayan International Institute of Yoga Sciences and Philosophy
Rural Route 1, Box 400
Honesdale, PA 18431
(717) 253-5551

Hindu University of America (HUA)
8610 Vesta Terrace
Orlando, FL 32825-7934
(407) 277-5959
Still growing, HUA presently offers graduate programs in Hinduism and yoga, philosophy, and meditation.

Institute of Holistic Health, Music, Yoga, Science and Philosophy
Saraswati Mandiram
76 Ridgewood Street
Dorchester, MA 02122
(617) 287-9094
This institute teaches Hindu and Sanskrit, as well as other disciplines of Indian origin. The institute is currently seeking state board approval of the Swami Vivekananda International School Foundation, a primary school that will address the spiritual self within an interdisciplinary curriculum.

Vedic University of America
10509 Caminito Basswood
San Diego, CA 92131
(619) 578-7289
Founded in 1987, Vedic University is a nonprofit institute carrying out research work in the field of Vedic religion and Indian heritage, and working for the benefit of Indian families residing in the United States and others who are eager to learn Hindi, Sanskrit, Vedic religion, and yoga. It is the only institute in the United States teaching these subjects by mail, fax, phone, and audiocassette tapes. There are about 1,300 students enrolled from around the world.

ISLAM AND SUFISM

Islam is an Arabic word meaning peace, purity, acceptance, and commitment. As a religious and cultural tradition, Islam calls for complete acceptance of the teachings and guidance of God (Allah). A Muslim is one who freely and willingly accepts the supreme power of God and strives to organize his or her life in total accord with the teachings as revealed by the prophet Muhammad in the Qur'an, Islam's most sacred text.

There is no priesthood or any comparable hierarchical structure of authority in Islam. Every Muslim is required to be educated in the religion. However, there are some people who are more educated than others and who act as resources for their communities. A prayer leader (imam) is a man who is responsible for leading others in prayer and answering religious questions. Although an imam does not need any particular academic degree, his responsibility is derived from his advanced studies of Islam and the Qur'an, which may be obtained either through self-study or formal training in specialized institutions. Every major Islamic country has universities that offer programs in Qur'an, Islamic law, theology, and so on. Programs in the United States tend to focus on the history of the Islamic world and Arabic studies.

Sufism is a very broad spiritual movement that is generally defined as a mystical sect of Islam. While mainstream Islam contends that knowledge of God (Allah) and the universe can and should be acquired intellectually, through one's everyday experiences and study of the Qur'an, Sufism asserts that the divine can be known through more subjective experiences, including nonordinary states of consciousness.

Associations and Organizations
Abode of the Message
See Conference Centers.

Institute of Islamic Information and Education
P.O. Box 41129
Chicago, IL 60641-0129
(312) 777-7443

International Association of Sufism (IAS)
25 Mitchell Boulevard., Suite 2
San Rafael, CA 94903
(415) 472-6959
The IAS, a nonprofit organization established in 1983, invites teachers, students, and scholars of all schools of Sufism to join in the common purpose of seeking greater knowledge, mutual understanding, and the dissemination of Sufi principles.

International Institute of Islamic Thought (IIIT) Association of Islamic Social Scientists (AISS)
555 Grove Street, Box 669
Herndon, VA 22070-4705
(703) 471-1133
The IIIT, founded in 1981, promotes Islamic thought and the Islamization of knowledge in contemporary disciplines. The institute publishes scholarly works from its own research programs as well as contributions from scholars around the world. The institute and the AISS jointly publish the *American Journal of Islamic Social Sciences*.

Islamic Academy
23 Metcalfe Road
Cambridge CB4 2DB
England
The academy is a research-oriented, nonpolitical, and neutral religious institution that promotes research in Muslim classics; provides a forum for Muslim scholars; and encourages and assists Muslim communities, countries, and educational organizations all over the world to promote Islamic thought. It also publishes the *Muslim Educational Quarterly*.

Islamic Research Foundation for the Advancement of Knowledge
See Research Institutes.

Islamic Society of North America (ISNA)
P.O. Box 38
Plainfield, IN 46168-0038
(317) 839-8157
The ISNA, a nonprofit membership organization, serves to advance the cause of Islam and Muslims in North America. It provides a range of services to individuals and Islamic centers around the United States, including the Islamic Teaching Center, which offers credit-granting summer classes in Arabic language and Islamic studies, and a correspondence course. Five professional organizations are currently con-
stituents of ISNA: the Association of Muslim Social Scientists; the Association of Muslim Scientists and Engineers; the Islamic Medical Association; the Muslim American Chamber of Commerce and Industry; and the Council of Islamic Schools in North America. Each works to advance ISNA objectives within its respective area of professional competence, and each publishes its own professional journal or newsletter. ISNA also sponsors an annual convention and publishes the journal *Islamic Horizons*.

Sufi Order in the West (SOW)
P.O. Box 30065
Seattle, WA 98103
(206) 782-2001
The SOW, founded in 1910 by Hazrat Inayat Khan as an interfaith approach to spiritual growth, evolved from the spiritual tradition of the Chishti lineage which originated in the East. Khan sought to make the spiritual legacy of Sufism applicable to the needs of our time. Pir Vilayat Inayat Khan is now president. The SOW's classes, seminars, and retreats are open to people of all faiths. It is also an esoteric school offering individual training which is entered into through the process of initiation.

Periodicals
American Journal of Islamic Social Sciences
International Institute of Islamic Thought
Quarterly; $10

Islamic Horizons
Islamic Society of North America
Quarterly; $30 (membership)

Journal of Islamic Studies
Oxford University Press, Inc.
2001 Evans Road
Cary, NC 27513
(919) 677-0977
Quarterly; $93
Published in England, this journal is dedicated to the multidisciplinary study of Islam.

Journal of Sufism
306 West 11th Street
New York, NY 10014
Quarterly; $16
This journal is published in London.

Muslim Education Quarterly
Islamic Academy
Quarterly; $20

Periodica Islamica
22, Jalan Liku
59100 Kuala Lumpur
Malaysia
This journal is an international periodical that covers current issues in the Islamic world.

Sufi Review
Sufi Book Club
Pir Publications, Inc.
Colonial Green
256 Post Road East
Westport, CT 06880
(203) 221-7595
Quarterly; $9
This publication discusses contemporary and classical Sufi mystical thought and teachings, and lists books available through the Sufi Book Club.

Sufism: An Inquiry
International Association of Sufism
Quarterly; $16

EDUCATIONAL CENTERS
American Islamic College (AIC)
640 West Irving Park Road
Chicago, IL 60640
(312) 281-4700

JUDAISM
Leaders of Jewish congregations in America have traditionally been rabbis, teachers, and judges trained in Talmudic study, which consists of the interpretation and application of the Torah. Modern rabbinical training also includes extensive study in Jewish philosophy and history, as well as certain secular studies. Yeshivot, the place where seminary training usually takes place, and other Jewish institutions provide Talmudic education for many students, including women. While orthodox women are not allowed to serve as rabbis, the rule has recently been contested, and women are currently being ordained in conservative and reformed branches. Also, a considerable number of Jewish seminaries offer joint degrees in social work and Jewish communal (i.e., community) service.

ADDITIONAL RESOURCES
Jewish Studies Courses at American and Canadian Universities: A Catalog
Association for Jewish Studies
Ktav Publishing House
900 Jefferson Street
Box 6249
Hoboken, NJ 07030
This book was last published in 1992.

Organizations
Aleph: Alliance for Jewish Renewal
See Conference Centers.

American Jewish Committee (AJC)
165 East 56th Street
New York, NY 10022-2746
(212) 751-4000
The AJC seeks to enrich the quality of American Jewish life and safeguard the rights of Jews by nurturing a pluralistic America in which all faith groups may thrive. The organization commissions and publishes seminal research; plays an advocacy role by articulating its views to government, the media, and the general public; and engages in diplomacy by building and maintaining positive relationships with other groups. There are nearly 50,000 members, representing virtually every profession, political persuasion, and Jewish orientation, and 32 offices in the United States.

Heart of Stillness Retreats
See Retreat Centers.

Kirkridge
See Conference Centers.

Metivta: A Center for Jewish Wisdom
See Retreat Centers.

National Havurah Committee
See Conference Centers.

San Diego Jewish Meditation Institute (SDJMI)
2615 Camino del Rio South, Suite 300
San Diego, CA 92108
(619) 291-4465
Founded in 1992, the SDJMI explores the rich, experiential, inner-contemplative meditative traditions of Judaism as rooted in the Kabbalah, an ancient text of Jewish mysticism. The institute is nonsectarian.

Woodstock Center for Healing and Renewal
See Conference Centers.

Periodicals
Four Worlds Journal
P.O. Box 540
East Meadow, NY 11554
(516) 864-1912
Quarterly; $18

Jewish Social Studies
Indiana University Press
10th and Morton Streets
Bloomington, IN 47405
(812) 855-9449
Three times a year; $35

Journal of Jewish Thought and Philosophy
Academic Publishers
Box 786
Cooper Station
New York, NY 10276
(800) 545-8398
Semiannual; $75
This journal provides an international forum for Jewish thought, philosophy, and intellectual history, with an emphasis on contemporary issues. It covers bibical studies, mysticism, literary criticism, political theory, sociology, and anthropology.

Journal of Psychology and Judaism (JPJ)
Human Sciences Press
233 Spring Street
New York, NY 10013-1578
(212) 620-8000
Quarterly; $42
The *JPJ* is dedicated to exploring the relationship between psychology and Judaism from both a clinical and philosophical perspective.

Kabbalah
41 Palyam Street
Jerusalem 97 890
Israel
Quarterly; $12.75
This newsletter, written in English, addresses current research in Jewish mysticism.

Kerem: Creative Explorations in Judaism
Jewish Study Center Press
2555 Pennsylvania Avenue, N.W., Suite 504
Washington, DC 20037
(202) 223-9405
Annual; $8.50

Lilith: The Independent Jewish Women's Magazine
250 West 57th Street
New York, NY 10107
Quarterly; $16

Moment
Jewish Educational Ventures, Inc.
3000 Connecticut Avenue, N.W., Suite 300
Washington, DC 20008
(800) 221-3148
Bimonthly; $27

New Menorah: A Journal of Jewish Renewal
P'nai Or Religious Fellowship
7318 Germantown Avenue
Philadelphia, PA 19119
(215) 242-4074
Quarterly; $18

Tikkun
251 West 100th Street, Box U
New York, NY 10025
(800) 846-8575
Monthly; $31

Tikkun means "healing and transforming" in Hebrew. Michael Lerner, *Tikkun's* editor, who was recently brought into the spotlight when Hillary Rodham Clinton initiated a discussion referencing his phrase "politics of meaning," argues that the liberal and progressive forces in American politics must move beyond a narrow focus on economics and politics, and attempt to address the psychological, ethical, and spiritual needs of the American people.

Wellsprings
770 Eastern Parkway
Brooklyn, NY 11213
(718) 953-1000
Quarterly; $15

This journal explores issues of contemporary and social concern from a Hasidic perspective, including essays and dialogues on the arts and sciences.

DEGREE PROGRAMS
Baltimore Hebrew University (BHU)
5800 Park Heights Avenue
Baltimore, MD 21215
(410) 578-6922

The Baltimore Institute for Jewish Communal Services offers professional programs through BHU.
General Information: Private, Judaic
Degrees Offered: M.A.; Ph.D.
Programs: Jewish Studies
Admission Requirements: Bachelor's degree; GRE
Application Deadline: Rolling
Contact Person: Director of Admissions
Tuition: Contact department
Accreditation: MSACS
Year Established: 1919
Faculty: Contact department

Baltimore Institute for Jewish Communal Service (BIJCS)
101 West Mount Royal Avenue
Baltimore, MD 21201-5781
(410) 727-4828

The BIJCS offers programs in Jewish Communal Service, Jewish Community Relations, Jewish Journalism, and Jewish Education.

Center for Jewish Studies
Graduate Theological Union
2400 Ridge Road
Berkeley, CA 94709
(510) 649-2482

The center is officially connected with the Jewish Studies Program at the University of California, Berkeley through a cross-registration agreement. See the Graduate Theological Union under Christian Theological Training.
Programs: Jewish Studies, M.A., Ph.D.

Hebrew Union College–Jewish Institute of Religion
School of Jewish Communal Service, Los Angeles
3077 University Avenue
Los Angeles, CA 90007-3796
(213) 749-3424
General Information: Private, Reform Judaic
Degrees Offered: M.A.; M.F.C.C.; certificate
Programs: Certificate in Jewish communal service; Master of Arts in Jewish communal service; double Master of Arts in Jewish communal service and social work (in conjunction with the University of Southern California's School of Social Work; with Washington University's George Warren Brown School of Social Work, St. Louis, Missouri; with San Francisco State University; and with the Univeristy of Pittsburgh School of Social Work)
Admission Requirements: Bachelor's degree; GRE
Application Deadline: Rolling
Contact Person: Director of Admissions
Tuition: $10,000-$13,000/year
Accreditation: MSACS; NCACS; WASC
Year Established: 1954
Faculty: Contact department

Isaac Elchanan Theological Seminary
Yeshiva University
Belfer Hall
2540 Amsterdam Avenue
New York, NY 10033-9986
(212) 960-5344
General Information: Private, Judaic
Degrees Offered: Semikhah Yoreh (traditional ordination)

Programs: Professional opportunities in chaplaincy, counseling, and other communal service
Admission Requirements: Bachelor's degree
Application Deadline: Rolling
Contact Person: Director of Admissions
Tuition: Scholarship based (contact school)
Accreditation: MSACS
Year Established: 1894
Faculty: 10 full-time

Jewish Theological Seminary of America
3080 Broadway
New York, NY 10027-4649
(212) 678-8000
General Information: Private, Conservative Judaic
Degrees Offered: M.A.; M.S.
Programs: Jewish studies and social work (in conjunction with Columbia University); pastoral psychiatry (nonmedical)
Admission Requirements: Bachelor's degree; GRE; letters of recommendation
Application Deadline: Rolling
Contact Person: Director of Admissions
Tuition: $9,612/year
Accreditation: MSACS
Year Established: 1901
Faculty: 78 full-time

The New Seminary
7 West 96th Street, Suite 19B
New York, NY 10025
(212) 866-3795

The New Seminary is considered an innovative concept for the training of interfaith ministers, spiritual counselors, and practitioners to teach, counsel, and work in the community. Its programs are not meant as a substitute for existing religious seminaries but rather as an addition that will support interfaith respect and understanding. Programs include comparative religion, dimensions of psychology, and spiritual healing and counseling. The Jewish spiritual guide program prepares women and men of the Jewish faith to serve both the Jewish and the larger communities as spiritual leaders—teachers of faith, counselors, worship facilitators, and spiritual healers—within a Jewish spiritual perspective. Contact Rabbi Siegal or Rabbi Gelberman at the seminary.
Programs: Jewish spiritual guides/rabbinical ordination; correspondence programs; interfaith ministry, levels I and II; Kabbalistic healing and visual meditation

Yeshiva University
Wurzweiler School of Social Work
See Spiritually Sensitive Social Work.

OTHER SPIRITUAL TRADITIONS

The following traditions, while not as widely known and practiced in this country as Buddhism, Christianity, Hinduism, Islam, and Judaism, also have organized followings. The organizations listed here, some of which are more religiously focused than others, can give you more information about regional groups and educational programs.

ANTHROPOSOPHY

Anthroposophy was founded by Rudolf Steiner (1861-1925) in Dornach, Switzerland, and is now considered an international and interdisciplinary movement that includes Waldorf Education, the largest religious nonsectarian school movement in the world. Anthroposophy, described by Steiner as an "awareness of one's humanity," embraces a spiritual view of the human being and the cosmos, yet focuses on intellectual and intuitive understanding rather than faith.

Steiner drew on the writings of J. W. von Goethe and Hindu concepts popularized by Theosophy. The movement incorporates the sciences of dance, medicine, and agriculture. Its greatest influence has been in German-speaking countries.

Organizations

Anthroposophical Society in America (ASA)
529 West Grant Place
Chicago, IL 60614
(312) 248-5606
The society represents Anthroposophy in America, provides a directory of schools and training programs, and publishes the *Journal for Anthroposophy*.

Physicians Association for Anthroposophical Medicine
See Allopathic Medicine.

Rudolf Steiner Library
R.D. 2, Box 215
Ghent, NY 12075
(518) 672-7690
The national library of the Anthroposophical Society holds 8,000 volumes on Western spirituality and history.

Periodicals

Anthroposophic Press
Rural Route 4, Box 94
Hudson, NY 12534
(518) 851-2054

Journal for Anthroposophy
Anthroposophical Society in America
Quarterly; $12

Degree Programs

Antioch University International
See Residential Psychology Degree Programs.

Rudolf Steiner College
9200 Fair Oaks Boulevard
Fair Oaks, CA 95628
(916) 961-8727
General Information: Private, nonsectarian
Degrees Offered: M.A.
Programs: Arts program; foundation year; Goethean studies program; Waldorf teacher education program
Admission Requirements: Bachelor's degree
Application Deadline: January 1 and August 1
Contact Person: Director of Admissions
Tuition: $6,300/year
Accreditation: Association of Waldorf Schools of North America
Year Established: 1976
Faculty: Contact department

Waldorf Institute of Sunbridge College
260 Hungry Hollow Road
Chestnut Ridge, NY 10977
(914) 425-0055
General Information: Private, nonsectarian
Degrees Offered: M.S. in Education in Waldorf education
Programs: Associate program in early childhood education; Chicago extension program in Waldorf education; early childhood education; orientation year in Anthroposophical studies
speech and drama; Waldorf education, M.S.; Waldorf teacher training
Admission Requirements: Bachelor's degree; interview
Application Deadline: Rolling
Contact Person: Director of Admissions
Tuition: $6,500/year; $9,800/year (master's program)
Accreditation: Association of Waldorf Schools of North America; New York State Department of Education (M.S. in Education only)
Year Established: 1967
Faculty: 32 full- and part-time

JAINISM

Jainism is one of the three religions of the world originating in India. The term *Jain* means a follower of the "Jainas" (Spiritual Victors), human teachers who through their own efforts are believed to have attained "kevalajnana" (omniscience, or infinite knowledge). According to the Institute of Jainology, there are approximately 10 million Jains throughout the world. They practice "ahimsa" (nonviolence) and are strict vegetarians.

Organizations

Institute of Jainology
31 Lancaster Gate
London W2 3LP
England

RASTAFARI MOVEMENT

Named for Crown Prince Ras Tafari, who was crowned as Emperor Haile Selassie of Ethiopia in 1930, this messianic movement originated in Jamaica. Haile Selassie came to be seen as the living God, in fulfillment of the 1916 prophecy of the Jamaican leader Marcus Garvey, who told his followers to "look to Africa where a Black King would be crowned, he shall be your Redeemer."

Today the Rastafari movement exists on other Caribbean Islands and in North America and England. Followers believe, among other things, that Ethiopia is the new Judah or promised land, and that the Black race is the new Israel or favored people who will eventually rise to power. Rastafarians grow their hair in "dreadlocks" so as to resemble a lion's mane and employ the ritual use of marijuana. The musical style known as reggae is a contribution of the Rastafari Movement.

Association of Rastafarian Theologians (ART)
843 West Van Buren Street, Suite 176
Chicago, IL 60607-3521
(312) 752-1071
The ART is the religious division of Roots International Arts Alliance, Inc. Roots was incorporated as a nonprofit organization for cultural, educational, religious,

and scientific purposes in the State of Illinois in 1987. The mission of ART is to promote brotherhood between the races using cultural, educational, and spiritual programs, and to clarify the spiritual agenda of Rastafari through educational religious materials. ART promotes the concepts of an Ethiopian Messiah, the Ethiopian Holocaust of 1935-41, and Ethiopia as the land of Judah. It also networks with other religious organizations that share similar values, and seeks to combine African and Eastern spirituality with traditional cultural practices.

SWEDENBORGIANISM

Born in England, Emanuel Swedenborg (1688-1772) was a scientist, inventor, and religious writer who used his scientific orientation to explore and integrate the world of spirit into the mainstream thought of his day. During his lifetime, he made significant discoveries in astronomy, anatomy, magnetism, mechanics, chemistry, and geology, as well as publishing 30 volumes on theological topics. The Church of New Jerusalem, often called the "New Church," sprang from Swedenborg's writings.

Even though Swedenborg was living in an increasingly materialistic society, he outlined the existence of a spiritual reality, and went so far as to suggest that the invisible world he explored in his mystical experiences has greater metaphysical reality than the visible world explored by science, which he later believed was secondary (yet relevant) to a metaphysical reality. Because of this pioneering work, Swedenborg is considered one of the first modern thinkers to propose a theory integrating spirituality and science, including the social science of psychology, which fully developed only during the 19th century.

Swedenborg's insights into a holistic, universal, and understandable spiritual reality struck a responsive chord in the 19th century—albeit more in literature and the arts than in other traditional religious organizations. For example,

Blake, Coleridge, Emerson, the Brownings, Balzac, Goethe, Thoreau, and Oliver Wendell Holmes found their own worldview supported and broadened by his theology. Theodore Parker, William Ellery Channing, William H. Channing, and Horace Bushnell carried his vision into the pulpits of liberal Protestantism in America, where it has had a lasting impact. New England transcendentalism, spiritualism, Theosophy, and "new thought" have also been profoundly affected by the Swedish philosopher.

The first Swedenborgian church was formed in London in 1787. By the turn of the century, the movement had spread to continental Europe and America. Swedenborg, however, hoped that his writings and interpretation of the Scriptures would eventually become integrated into the already existent Christian Church. He didn't intend to found a church or an autonomous religious denomination, which is exactly what happened after his death.

Swedenborg's influence continues in the 20th century—Helen Keller, Henry James, Sr., William Butler Yeats, Rudolph Steiner, and Jorge Louis Borges represent only a partial list of thinkers influenced by his theology. Outside of Swedenborgian Church circles, his publications and ideas remain relatively unknown.

Organizations

Swedenborgian Church Central Office
48 Sargent Street
Newton, MA 02158
(617) 969-4240

The Swedenborg Foundation (SF)
320 North Church Street
West Chester, PA 19380
(800) 355-3222; (610) 430-3222

The SF was established in 1849 to maintain the availability of books and information about Emanuel Swedenborg. The foundation has accomplished its mission primarily by publishing Swedenborg's own scientific and theological works. The foundation also publishes videos, books, and a journal entitled *Chrysalis*.

Swedenborg Library
79 Newbury Street
Boston, MA 02116
(617) 262-5918

Periodicals

Chrysalis
139 East 23rd Street
New York, NY 10010
(800) 366-7310
Three times a year; $20

Degree Programs

The Swedenborg Foundation
320 North Church Street
West Chester, PA 19380
(800) 355-3222; (610) 430-3222
General Information: Private
Degrees Offered: M.A.
Programs: Swedenborgian studies
Admission Requirements: Bachelor's degree
Application Deadline: Rolling
Contact Person: Director of Admissions
Tuition: $2,700/year
Accreditation: Massachusetts Board of Regents
Year Established: 1866
Faculty: 3 full-time; 3 part-time

Swedenborg School of Religion (SSR)
48 Sargent Street
Newton, MA 02158
(617) 244-0504

The SSR is a graduate-level seminary committed to the education of competent and consecrated Christian ministers for the Swedenborgian Church. In addition to its primary function—preparing qualified candidates for ordination—the SSR offers an M.A. in Swedenborgian studies, a lay leadership program, a one-year certificate program, correspondence courses, and special programs for academically qualified students from any religious tradition.
General Information: Private
Degrees Offered: M.A.
Programs: Swedenborgian studies
Admission Requirements: Bachelor's degree; letters of recommendation
Application Deadline: Rolling
Contact Person: Director of Admissions
Tuition: $2,700/year
Accreditation: Massachusetts Board of Regents
Year Established: 1866
Faculty: 7 full-time

THEOSOPHY

Theosophy (from the Greek *theos*, "god," and *sophia*, "wisdom") is a philosophical system that seeks to learn about reality through mystical experience and to find esoteric meaning in sacred writings. Theosophy claims that all religions stem from the same root of ancient wisdom. This inclusive philosophy is also known to have helped its exponents to introduce Indian religious philosophy to Westerners at the turn of the century.

The primary exponent of Theosophy is the Theosophical Society, an international nonsectarian, nonpolitical, and nondogmatic organization which was formed to revive ancient wisdom and Oriental religion in the West. The international headquarters is now located at Adyar in Madras, India. There are regional societies located in 50 countries, and 138 branches and study centers in the United States—many of which provide classes, lectures, seminars, workshops, and retreats.

Organizations

Theosophical Society in America (TSA)
1926 North Main Street
P.O. Box 270
Wheaton, IL 60189-0270
(708) 668-1571; (800) 669-1571

The TSA was founded in New York City in 1875 by Madame Helena Petrovna Blavatsky, a Russian-born mystic; Colonel Henry Steel Olcott, an American attorney and federal government official; and William Q. Judge, an American attorney. The society states three objectives: to form a nucleus of the Universal Brotherhood of Humanity, without distinction of race, creed, sex, caste, or color; to encourage the study of comparative religion, philosophy, and science; and to investigate unexplained laws of nature and the powers latent in each individual. It publishes the newsletter *American Theosophist*, the journal *The Quest*, and sponsors the Olcott Institute, which offers a nondegree program in Theosophy.

Periodicals

The Quest: A Journal of Philosophy, Science, Religion and the Arts
Theosophical Society in America
Quarterly; $13.97

This magazine explores spiritual and religious experience from a wide range of religious traditions, including Buddhist, Hindu, Islamic, Vedantist, Christian, and Hebrew.

ZOROASTRIANISM

Zoroastrianism is a religious tradition named for its prophet Zoroaster (also known as Zarathustra), whose writings have been dated anywhere from 1000 B.C.E. to 600 B.C.E. Although Zoroastrianism has been at times the official religion of Iran, followers of this religion now number less than one in one thousand in the population of that country. The next largest population of Zoroastrians is in India, where they number about one in ten thousand and are called Parsis. Faith in and devotion to God (known as Ahura Mazda, meaning "the Wise Lord") is central to the religion; however, other lesser deities and spirits—both good and evil—are also acknowledged.

The Zoroastrian priesthood is based on inheritance of eligibility (being born into a priest's family); gender (only males may become priests); and training (generally informal). Fire as a symbol of divine power is very important to the tradition and its rituals; fires burn constantly in "fire temples," and are also used in private homes for ceremonial purposes.

Federation of Zoroastrian Associations of North America (FEZANA)
5750 South Jackson Street
West 56th Street
Hinsdale, IL 60521
(708) 325-5383

The FEZANA is an umbrella organization established in 1987 to coordinate and promote the objectives of the Zoroastrian Associations of North America. The federation publishes the *Journal of the North American Federation* and a youth newsletter, *ZYNA*. The federation's activities include facilitating the emigration of Zoroastrians; conducting censuses and surveys; participating in seminars, conferences, and congresses; and providing limited financial assistance to individuals and institutes. According to the FEZANA, there are approximately 200,000 Zoroastrians around the world, 75% of whom live in India and Iran.

SECTION III

MIND-BODY STUDIES

In This Section:

➤ DEGREE PROGRAMS:

Allopathic Medicine, Naturopathy and Homeopathy, Oriental Medicine, Somatic Therapy, Wellness and Holistic Health

➤ NONDEGREE PROGRAMS:

Ayurvedic Medicine, Body-Centered Psychotherapies, Bodywork and Massage Therapy, Movement Therapy, Network Chiropractic, Reichian-Oriented Therapies, Somatic Therapies, Subtle Energy Therapies

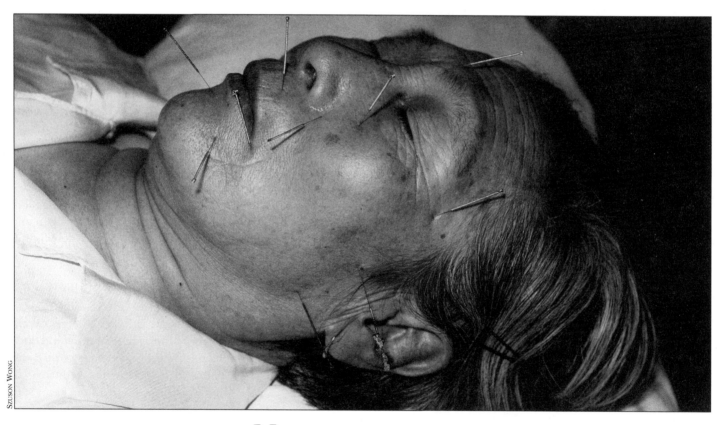

SZUSON WONG

M IND-BODY STUDIES, SOMATICS, ALTERNATIVE MEDICINE, AND HOLISTIC HEALTH ARE ALL USED TO DESCRIBE THE FIELDS OF STUDY AND THERApeutic techniques included in this section The more established disciplines that make up these broad fields include herbology, holistic bodywork, network chiropractic, Oriental medicine (which consists of acupuncture, acupressure, and Qigong), psychophysiology, somatic and psychosomatic therapies (including guided imagery and yoga), subtle-energy methods, therapeutic touch, and transpersonal body-centered therapies.

Some of these methods were derived from ancient Eastern healing traditions; others have a more modern and scientific ancestry. Some were developed over a millennia ago, while others have been "discovered" only in the last 20 years. With such a wide variety of lineages, it is incorrect to assume that the philosophies behind these techniques are similar simply because they share an "alternative" status. In fact, most of them developed from independent philosophical systems that are cultures and centuries apart. What these disciplines do share, however, is a concern for the health and well-being of the whole person, an understanding that the mind, body, and spirit not only are inseparable and interdependent, but also contribute, alone and together, to health and well-being. This approach, often called holistic health or holistic medicine, emphasizes and seeks to enhance the inherent healing ability within each person by empowering him or her to take greater responsibility for his or her personal development, healing, and general health maintenance.

ADDITIONAL RESOURCES
Alternative Medicine: The Definitive Guide
Compiled by the Burton Goldberg Group
Future Medicine Publishing
10124 18th Street Court East
Puyallup, WA 98371
(800) 435-1221

General Organizations
Mind-Body Health Study Group Network
444 North Capitol Street, Suite 428
Washington, DC 20001
(202) 393-2208
Initiated and funded by the Fetzer Institute and based on the Public Broadcasting Service (PBS) documentary "Healing and the Mind with Bill Moyers," the network supports the creation of mind-body study groups throughout the United States.

Planetree
2300 California Street, Suite 201
San Francisco, CA 94115
(415) 923-3696
Founded in 1978, Planetree is a national, nonprofit, consumer health organization that assists other institutions in humanizing and demystifying health care for patients and their families. It also provides programs to help health-care organizations implement patient-centered environments that respond to the needs of the whole person.

The Somatics Society
1516 Grant Avenue, Suite 212
Novato, CA 94945
(415) 892-0617
Founded by the late somatics pioneer Thomas Hanna, the society links educators and bodyworkers from all somatic fields, such as massage therapy, medicine, dance therapy, martial arts, physical therapy, and Rolfing. It publishes the journal *Somatics.*

Study Circles Resource Center (SCRC)
Route 169
P.O. Box 203
Pomfret, CT 06258
(203) 928-2616
Similar to the Mind-Body Health Study Group Network, the SCRC supports the creation of mind-body study groups throughout the United States.

World Research Foundation
See Research Institutes.

General Periodicals
Advances: The Journal of Mind-Body Health
9292 West KL Avenue
Kalamazoo, MI 49009
(616) 375-2000
Quarterly; $39
Published by the Fetzer Institute, this scholarly journal examines research on the mind's influence on the body and discusses the implications for health.

Brain/Mind Bulletin
P.O. Box 42211
Los Angeles, CA 90042
(213) 223-2500
Monthly; $45
Founded by Marilyn Ferguson, author of *The Aquarian Conspiracy*, this newsletter covers research relevant to the mind-body interface, often from a spiritual perspective.

Convergence
See Interdisciplinary Resources.

Somatics: Magazine-Journal of the Bodily Arts and Sciences
The Somatics Society
Semiannual; $25 (with membership)

Mind-Body Degree Programs

ALLOPATHIC MEDICINE
Ever since the 1960s, when Oriental medicine and alternative approaches to healing began to take hold in the United States, there has been considerable progress in pushing beyond the rigid boundaries of allopathic medicine, the dominant approach to medicine in the West (in which remedies produce effects different from or opposite to those produced by the disease.) In fact, a number of American medical schools, research institutes, and hospitals now not only acknowledge the efficacy and usefulness of alternative and non-Western treatment but believe that there is a clear need to practice medicine from a more holistic, multidimensional perspective. This perspective consists of nutrition and lifestyle education, preventative medicine, and the importance of emotional and mental well-being when evaluating one's physical health.

Although many of the following medical schools offer a few nontraditional courses within an already demanding curriculum, a prospective medical student should investigate whether some of the school's faculty in such programs are interested in alternative methods of healing. As the culture's interest (along with formal research) in the mind-body relationship grows, perhaps refined disciplines such as Oriental medicine will one day complement (rather than supplant) the technological wonders of 20th-century science.

While we cannot claim that the following list of medical schools is inclusive (many offer "voluntary" or elective programs in alternative medicine, which are hard to detect from examining course catalogs), the Fetzer Institute in partnership with Pew Health Professions is conducting a comprehensive survey of

American medical and professional schools in order to find the programs that incorporate (or are in the process of incorporating) a psychosocial element into their curricula, including alternative approaches to medicine. The report is being created to help medical schools make decisions about the future of medical school education, and should be available to the public free of charge after August 1994. (Contact David Sluyder at the Fetzer Institute.)

Associations

American Holistic Medical Association (AHMA)
4101 Lake Boone Trail, Suite 201
Raleigh, NC 27607
(919) 787-5146

The AHMA was founded in 1978 to unite licensed physicians who practice holistic medicine. Membership is open to medical doctors, doctors of osteopathy, and medical students studying for those degrees. The association publishes a newsletter and holds an annual conference.

American Medical Association
515 North State Street
Chicago, IL 60610
(312) 464-5000

American Medical Student Association (AMSA)
1890 Preston White Drive
Reston, VA 22091
(703) 620-6600

Founded in 1950, the AMSA is a student-governed, independent association of physicians in training.

Association of American Medical Colleges (AAMC)
2450 North Street, N.W., Suite 201
Washington, DC 20037-1126
(202) 828-0620

The AAMC publishes a useful Medical School Admissions Requirements book ($10 plus $4 shipping).

Physicians Association for Anthroposophical Medicine (PAAM)
Peter Hinderberger, M.D., President
P.O. Box 66609
Portland, OR 97290
(410) 367-6263

PAAM, founded in 1981, is a membership and training organization that promotes anthroposophical medicine in North America. It publishes the *Journal of Anthroposophic Medicine* and holds an annual conference.

Anthroposophical medicine was developed by Rudolf Steiner, a philosopher, scientist, and visionary who not only developed the idea of anthroposophy but also made major contributions to the fields of education (Waldorf Schools), agriculture (biodynamic farming), architecture, the arts, and the social and natural sciences. (See Anthroposophy in Section II.)

Anthroposophical medicine is a holistic and human-centered approach to health care that recognizes and uses the vast information acquired by modern medicine in the fields of anatomy, physiology, biochemistry, and diagnosis. It then adds a knowledge of the laws of the living organism, the psyche, and spirit derived from a spiritual scientific methodology to that which is known by conventional scientific means.

Anthroposophical medicine is not an alternative to but an extension of traditional medicine. Anthroposophical-oriented physicians must undergo conventional medical training and licensure. Intensive postgraduate courses are held annually by PAAM, and concentrated training opportunities are available in Europe, where several large hospitals employ an anthroposophical approach. After meeting the certification criteria, the anthroposophically trained physician may take an exam to become a diplomate of the Board of Anthroposophically Extended Medicine in North America.

Organizations

American Institute of Medical Education (AIMED)
2625 West Alameda Avenue, Suite 504
Burbank, CA 91505
(818) 789-9857

The mission of AIMED is to disseminate medical information, especially related to emotional and psychological factors, to physicians, psychologists, and other health professionals. The institute's target audience is 50 percent physicians who are concerned with the mental health-care problems of their patients and 50 percent psychologists, social workers, nurses, and other mental health professionals. Educational activities and services range from conferences to one-day seminars. Conferences scheduled in 1994 include "Psychological Studies of Art and Artists: Creativity and Madness."

Center for Alternative/Complementary Medicine
College of Physicians and Surgeons at Columbia University
630 West 168th Street
New York, NY 10032
(212) 305-1495

The center is dedicated to providing comprehensive information on less well-known and understood health-care practices and to evaluating scientifically their efficacy. Created and funded in part by the Richard and Hinda Rosenthal Foundation, the center is one of the first such research organizations located in an American medical school.

Center for Ethics, Medicine and Public Issues
See Chaplaincy.

Center for Mind-Body Studies
5225 Connecticut Avenue, N.W., Suite 414
Washington, DC 20015
(202) 966-7338

Directed by James S. Gordon, M.D., clinical professor in the Department of Psychiatry at Georgetown University School of Medicine, the center's projects include the development of a comprehensive model program of mind-body studies for medical students, a community health services program, a mind-body education program for teenagers, and support groups for people with chronic illness. The center acknowledges the biological, psychological, spiritual, and social dimensions of the healing process.

Christian Medical and Dental Society (CMDS)
P.O. Box 830689
Richardson, TX 75083-0689
(214) 783-8384

The purpose of CMDS is to motivate and equip doctors to practice "faith in Jesus Christ" in their personal and professional lives.

Fetzer Institute
See Research Institutes.

Foundation for the Advancement of Innovative Medicine (FAIM)
2 Executive Boulevard, Suite 201
Suffern, NY 10901
(914) 368-9797

Founded in 1986, FAIM was organized as a voice of medicine's innovative professionals, physicians, patients, and suppliers.

The foundation educates the public and professionals in alternative medicine and encourages research and development in promising new approaches to healing.

Hastings Center
See Chaplaincy.

Institute of Religion
Texas Medical Center
See Chaplaincy.

Menninger Foundation
See Research Institutes.

MetaPhysicians
1400 Shattuck Avenue, Suite 7-126
Berkeley, CA 94709
(510) 524-0919
MetaPhysicians is a nonprofit organization that seeks to transform medicine by honoring and acknowledging the interface between spirituality and medicine. It seeks parity between physicians and their patients, and employs and explores various healing systems.

Mind-Body Medical Institute
Behavioral Medicine Program
Mercy Hospital and Medical Center
Stevenson Expressway at King Drive
Chicago, IL 60616-2477
(312) 567-2259
Although this program is designed for patients, its unusual approach may be of interest to prospective health-care providers.

Mind-Body Medical Institute
New England Deaconess Hospital
185 Pilgrim Road
Boston, MA 02215
(617) 632-9525
The institute, founded by Herbert Benson, M.D., is a nonprofit scientific and educational organization dedicated to the study of behavioral medicine, including mind-body interactions and the relaxation response. The institute is directly affiliated with Harvard Medical School.

National Institute for the Clinical Application of Behavioral Medicine
See Residential Psychology Degree Programs.

Physicians Committee for Responsible Medicine (PCRM)
5100 Wisconsin Avenue, N.W.
Washington, DC 20015
(202) 686-2210
Founded in 1985, PCRM promotes preventive medicine through innovative pro-

grams. It publishes the quarterly newsletter *Good Medicine*.

Preventive Medicine Research Institute
900 Bridgeway, Suite 2
Sausalito, CA 94965
(415) 332-2525
The institute offers training programs and conducts clinical research in mind-body medicine for health-care professionals and the general public.

Program in Medicine and Philosophy (PMP)
California Pacific Medical Center
Division of Education
P.O. Box 7999
San Francisco, CA 94120
(415) 202-1562
The PMP, created in 1989, seeks to encourage an understanding of health and healing among both those who provide health-care and those who receive it. The program aspires to serve as a model for other established medical centers. It shares the wisdom of many cultures, encourages collaboration between theory and practice, old values and new ideas, Eastern philosophy and Western thought; and encourages the integration of body, mind, and spirit. Members include physicians, nurses, traditional and complementary health-care providers, theologians, educators, environmentalists, and patients. PMP publishes *Ways of the Healer*.

Society for Health and Human Values (SHHV)
6728 Old McLean Village Drive
McLean, VA 22101
(703) 556-9222
The mission of SHHV is to promote the inclusion of humanities disciplines, curricula, and educational ambiance in health-oriented professional schools. It publishes the journal *Medical Humanities Review* and a newsletter.

Periodicals

Complementary Therapies in Medicine
Churchill Fulfillment Center
5S 250 Frontenac Road
Naperville, IL 60563
(800) 553-5426
Quarterly; $114
Aimed largely at general practitioners, hospital physicians, nurses, and physiotherapists, this United Kingdom journal provides wide-ranging and authoritative information about a variety of complementary therapies.

Journal of Alternative and Complementary Medicine
Mary Ann Liebert Publications
1651 Third Avenue
New York, NY 10128
(212) 289-2300
Quarterly; $65
This new journal is scheduled to begin publication in January 1995.

Journal of Anthroposophic Medicine
Physician's Association for Anthroposophic Medicine
7953 California Avenue
Fair Oaks, CA 95628
Quarterly; $50

Journal of Medicine and Philosophy
Center for Ethics, Medicine and Public Issues
See Chaplaincy.
The journal is a forum for bioethics and the philosophy of medicine.

Medical Humanities Review
Society for Health and Human Values

Mental Medicine Update
Institute for the Study of Human Knowledge
P.O. Box 176
Los Altos, CA 94023
(415) 948-9428
Three times a year; $9.95
Written for both health professionals and laypersons, this newsletter seeks to bridge the gap between research and practice in the fields of behavioral medicine, psychoneuroimmunology, and health psychology. See Research Institutes for more information.

Ways of the Healer
Program in Medicine and Philosophy (see above)
Semiannual; $60 (with membership)

M.D. PROGRAMS

The following medical schools offer, at the very least, elective courses in alternative forms of healing.

Columbia University
School of Medicine, Admissions
630 West 168th Street
New York, NY 10032
(212) 305-3595

Georgetown University
School of Medicine, Admissions
3900 Reservoir Road, N.W.
Washington, DC 20007
(202) 687-1154

Harvard Medical School
25 Shattuck Street, Admissions
Boston, MA 02115
(617) 432-1550

Tufts University
School of Medicine, Admissions
136 Harrison Avenue
Boston, MA 02111
(617) 956-6571

University of Arizona
School of Medicine, Admissions
1501 North Campbell Avenue, Room 2209
Tucson, AZ 85724
(602) 626-6214

University of California, San Francisco
School of Medicine, Admissions
Room C200
San Francisco, CA 94143-0408
(415) 476-4044

University of Louisville
School of Medicine, Admissions
Abell Administration Center
Louisville, KY 40292
(502) 852-5193

University of Maryland
School of Medicine, Admissions
655 West Baltimore Street
Baltimore, MD 21201
(410) 706-7478

University of Virginia
School of Medicine, Admissions
Charlottesville, VA 22908
(804) 924-5571

PHYSICIAN-PATIENT RELATIONSHIP PROGRAMS

The following medical schools have designed programs to enhance the relationship between physicians and patients, and in so doing they nurture the healing process of the patient in a more holistic way.

Harvard Medical School
See M.D. Programs.

Health Communication Research Institute (HCRI)
1050 Fulton Avenue, Suite 105
Sacramento, CA 95825
(916) 483-1583
The HCRI, a nonprofit educational organization, promotes "partnership communication," a language and a relational style that encourages the development of dialogue skills between health-care providers and patients.

Michigan State University
College of Human Medicine
East Lansing, MI 48824
(517) 353-9620

New York University
School of Medicine
550 First Avenue
New York, NY 10016
(212) 340-5290

Picker/Commonwealth Program for Patient Centered Care
Beth Israel Hospital
300 Brookline Avenue
Boston, MA 02215-5491
(617) 735-2388
This program promotes an approach to hospital and health services that focuses on patients' needs and concerns as patients themselves define them.

Tufts University
School of Medicine
See M.D. Programs.

Univeristy of Louisville Medical School
School of Health Sciences Center
See M.D. Programs.

NATUROPATHY AND HOMEOPATHY

Generally speaking, naturopathic medicine employs homeopathy, among other techniques, just as Oriental medicine utilizes specific therapies such as acupuncture.

NATUROPATHY

Naturopathic physicians (N.D.s) are primary health-care physicians, most of whom are in general private practice. Some choose to emphasize particular treatment modalities (such as clinical nutrition, Oriental medicine, or herbology), while others may concentrate in a particular medical field such as pediatrics, gynecology, or allergies. Like M.D.s, N.D.s are trained, licensed, and skilled in the conventional tools of diagnosis such as lab testing, x-ray, and physical exams. Unlike conventional physicians, however, N.D.s are also trained in the use of a wide variety of natural therapeutics, including clinical nutrition, botanical or herbal medicine, homeopathy, acupuncture, hydrotherapy, massage and therapeutic manipulation, and counseling.

Training programs take at least four years and include clinical work. Naturopathic schools are accredited by the Council on Naturopathic Medical Education, an accrediting agency recognized by the Federal Department of Education. To date, N.D.s are licensed to practice in seven states (see box). There are over 17 insurance companies (some as traditional as Blue Cross) that provide up to 80 percent reimbursement. N.D.s should expect to receive approximately one-half the salary of a general allopathic physician.

HOMEOPATHY

The word homeopathy is derived from the Greek words *homos,* meaning "similar," and *pathos,* meaning "suffering." Homeopathy, which can be employed as either a complimentary or primary practice, is a medical and pharmaceutical science that uses minute doses of natural medicines, made from plant, mineral, or animal substances, to enhance the body's defense and immune systems. Homeopathic medicines are prescribed according to the principle of similars; that is, a substance that causes an illness can at the same time cure those same symptoms in a sick person. (Allopathic medicine, in contrast, is a method of treating disease primarily by the use of agents that produce effects different from or opposite to those of the disease treated.) In this regard it is interesting to note that orthodox allopathic medicine incorporates the principle of simi-

LEGAL ISSUES REGARDING THE PRACTICE OF MEDICINE

THE PRACTICE OF MEDICINE IN THE UNITED STATES IS LICENSED BY INDIVIDUAL STATES. NONMEDICAL HEALTH-CARE PROVIDERS MAY OR MAY not be allowed to use homeopathy within the scope of their licenses, depending on the laws of the state in which they reside. Medical doctors (M.D.s) and osteopathic doctors (D.O.s) are the only professionals allowed to diagnose and treat physical illness in all 50 states. Seven states (Alabama, Arizona, Connecticut, Hawaii, Montana, Oregon, and Washington) and the District of Columbia license naturopathic physicians (N.D.s) to diagnose and treat illness. Other professionals such as chiropractors, dentists, acupuncturists, and nurse practitioners may also practice homeopathy in some states.

Homeopathic medicines are prepared in accordance with the *Homeopathic Pharmacopeia of the United States* and are classified as drugs (most are over-the-counter, but some require prescription) by the federal Food and Drug Adminis-tration. The use of homeopathy in the treatment of one person by another may constitute the practice of medicine, depending on the state, and all practitioners must be licensed in a health-care profession.

All licensed physicians (M.D.s and D.O.s) can legally prescribe homeopathic medicines, although three states (Connecticut, Arizona, and Nevada) have separate homeopathic licensing boards granting approval within their jurisdiction. Specialty certification for M.D.s and D.O.s is granted through the American Board of Homeotherapeutics (represented by the title Diplomate in Homeotherapeutics, or D.Ht.); certification for N.D.s is granted through the Homeopathy Academy of Naturopathic Physicians (Diplomate of the Homeopathic Academy of Naturopathic Physicians, or D.H.A.N.P.); and certification for general practitioners of homeopathy is granted through the Council for Homeopathic Certification (Certified in Classical Homeopathy, or C.C.H.).

lars in its use of vaccinations and allergy treatments. Because of the small doses given, such medicines are nontoxic and have few reported side effects.

Most Americans are unaware that homeopathy was a primary medical treatment in the United States from the mid-19th to the early 20th century. Constantine Hering, M.D., a student of German physician Samuel Hahnemann, who is considered the father of homeopathy in the United States, established the first homeopathic medical school in 1835. The American Institute of Homeopathy (AIH), founded in 1884, was the first national medical association in the United States. Three years later the American Medical Association (AMA) was formed. Based on allopathic principles, it denounced homeopathy as a quack remedy. Still, by 1900, there were 22 homeopathic medical schools and almost 100 homeopathic hospitals; approximately 15 percent of the physicians in the United States were homeopaths. During this time the bond between the AMA and pharmaceutical companies solidified: Drug companies paid the AMA to advertise their products in its journal (as they do today), and physicians were paid to promote pharmaceutical drugs and were deluged with complimentary samples. With the AMA's influence over medical school curricula, homeopathy as a viable and accessible form of medicine practically disappeared by the 1950s. Nevertheless, homeopathic medicine has been, and continues to be, an integral part of the health-care system in Europe, where it began.

It may also be gaining ground here in the United States. The Office of Alternative Medicine, sponsored by the National Institutes of Health, recently approved two research grants intended to research homeopathy. According to the National Center for Homeopathy, the sale of homeopathic remedies in the United States is growing by 25 percent per year (reaching $200 million in 1992) and there are an estimated 2,500 homeopathic physicians licensed to practice in this country. However, the low cost of homeopathic remedies (which, at the very least, threatens pharmaceutical profits) and homeopathy's departure from allopathic medicine's orthodox philosophy continue to provoke attacks by the medical establishment.

While there are many training programs and courses in homeopathy, no diploma or certificate from any school or program is recognized at this time as the basis for a license to practice homeopathic medicine in the United States (see box). Since the quality of these programs varies from poor to excellent, the Council on Homeopathic Education was formed in 1982 to monitor and approve the quality of the courses offered for professional training. The National Center for Homeopathy, the largest organization of its kind, can provide a plethora of useful information to the prospective practitioner.

While some learn the practice of homeopathy from books, seminars, and workshops, naturopathic medical schools provide the best education for professionals who need exposure to the theory and clinical practice of classic homeopathy. Bastyr College of Naturopathic Medicine, National College of Naturopathic Medicine, and the Southwest College of Naturopathic Medicine and Health Sciences offer four-year programs leading to an N.D. degree. Those with an N.D. degree are eligible to obtain licenses to practice medicine from a select number of states (see box); all three colleges offer a specialization in homeopathy.

—Staff from the National Center for Homeopathy contributed to this chapter.

Associations

**American Association of
Naturopathic Physicians (AANP)**
2366 Eastlake Avenue, Suite 322
Seattle, WA 98102
(206) 323-7610

The AANP is a professional membership organization that serves naturopathic physicians and promotes naturopathic medicine. It provides information on the licensing of N.D.s.

Homeopathic Nurses Association (HNA)
103 Country Club Road
Greenfield, MA 01301
(413) 773-0888

Established in 1986, the HNA promotes the advancement and refinement of homeopathic nursing.

National Center for Homeopathy (NCH)
801 North Fairfax Street, Suite 306
Alexandria, VA 22314
(703) 548-7790

The NCH, the largest homeopathic membership group in the United States, is a nonprofit membership organization dedicated to promoting health through homeopathy. It provides information and education about homeopathy to laypeople and health-care professionals; publishes a monthly magazine, *Homeopathy Today;* sponsors summer classes; and coordinates a network of 224 study groups around the country. It also publishes an annual directory of homeopathic practitioners, resources, and study groups (available for $6). Membership in the center has grown from 1,000 in 1981 to 7,000 in 1994.

Organizations

**American Board for
Homeotherapeutics (ABH)**
c/o National Center for Homeopathy

The ABH is a certifying (D.Ht.) homeopathic specialty board for licensed physicians and osteopaths who meet the board's prerequisites and pass its examination.

American Botanical Council
P.O. Box 201660
Austin, TX 78720
(512) 331-8868

The council, a nonprofit research and educational organization, publishes various materials on herbal medicine and related topics.

**American Foundation for
Homeopathy (AFH)**
1508 South Garfield Avenue
Alhambra, CA 91801
(818) 284-6565

The AFH, founded in 1924, is a nonprofit organization that promotes homeopathy in the United States.

American Herbalists Guild
P.O. Box 1683
Sequel, CA 95073
Correspondence offered only by mail.

The guild has become a strong force in advocating herbal medicine. It provides a directory of schools and teachers in the United States.

American Institute of Homeopathy (AIH)
1585 Glencoe Street, Suite 44
Denver, CO 80220
(303) 321-4105

The AIH is the oldest national medical professional organization in the United States. It represents the political and professional interests of homeopathic doctors of medicine, osteopathy, and dentistry, and sponsors the Homeopathic Pharmacopeia Convention of the United States. It also publishes the *Journal of the American Institute of Homeopathy.*

**Council for Homeopathic
Certification (CHC)**
Harry F. Swope, N.D., D.H.A.N.P., C.C.H.
1563 Solano Avenue, Suite 162
Berkeley, CA 94707
(415) 389-9502

The CHC is a national certifying organization that currently represents homeopathy practitioners in all relevant professions. The council's objective is to create a single national standard for the practice of "classical homeopathy" (that is, as it was practiced some 200 years ago); it acts in concert with other groups to promote homeopathic education. Practitioners must meet a rigid set of requirements and pass an examination. Successful candidates receive a certificate stating that they are "Certified in Classical Homeopathy." This certification is expected to become the nationally recognized standard for competence in homeopathy.

Council for Homeopathic Education
801 North Fairfax Street, Suite 306
Alexandria, VA 22314
(703) 548-7790

Established in 1985, the council approves courses of homeopathic training and reviews and certifies course material for homeopathic education in the United States.

**Council on Naturopathic Medical
Education (CNME)**
Commission on Accreditation
P.O. Box 11426
Eugene, OR 97440-3626
(503) 484-6028

The CNME is recognized by the United States Secretary of Education to accredit naturopathic medical colleges. Bastyr College and the National College of Naturopathic Medicine are currently accredited. Southwest College of Naturopathic Medicine and Health Sciences is undergoing accreditation procedures.

Herb Research Foundation
1007 Pearl Street, Suite 200
Boulder, CO 80302
(303) 449-2265

This foundation offers research information for laypersons and professionals such as pharmacists, physicians, and scientists.

**Homeopathic Academy of
Naturopathic Physicians (HANP)**
P.O. Box 69565
Portland, OR 97201
(503) 795-0579

Established in 1982, HANP, a specialty society affiliated with the American Association of Naturopathic Physicians, is dedicated to promoting the expertise, practice, and growth of homeopathy. It examines and certifies qualified, licensed naturopathic physicians, called the Diplomates of the Homeopathic Academy of Naturopathic Physicians (D.H.A.N.P.). The academy also sponsors an annual conference and publishes the quarterly journal *Simillimum.*

**Homeopathic Clinical
Research Network (HCRN)**
1154 Montgomery Drive, Suite 1
Santa Rosa, CA 95405
(707) 545-1554

The HCRN is a network that provides clinical sites for homeopathic trials and collaborates on research.

Homeopathic Community Council
c/o National Center for Homeopathy

The council unites the homeopathic community and facilitates the growth of the healing art of homeopathy. It is in the process of producing a directory of homeopathic training programs in the United States.

Institute for Naturopathic Medicine (INM)
66-1/2 North State Street
Concord, NH 03301
(603) 225-8844

The INM is a nonprofit advocacy organization. It promotes education and research in naturopathic medicine.

International Foundation for Homeopathy (IFH)
2366 Eastlake Avenue East, Suite 301
Seattle, WA 98102
(206) 324-8230

The IFH is an educational and membership organization dedicated to promoting public awareness of classical homeopathy, maintaining the highest standards of practice, and working toward the re-establishment of homeopathic medical schools. It also provides a professional training program and publishes a bimonthly magazine.

Periodicals

American Herb Association Newsletter
P.O. Box 353
Rescue, CA 96672
Correspondence offered only by mail.

HerbalGram
American Botanical Council
Quarterly; $25

Homeopathy Today
National Center for Homeopathy
Monthly newsletter; $35

Journal of American Institute of Homeopathy
American Institute of Homeopathy
Quarterly; $35

Medical Herbalism Newsletter
Bergner Communications
P.O. Box 33080
Portland, OR 97233
(503) 231-8257
Quarterly; $29

Natural Health
See Interdisciplinary Resources.

New England Journal of Homeopathy
New England School of Homeopathy (see below)
Quarterly; $40

Resonance
International Foundation for Homeopathy
Bimonthly; $35 (including membership)

Simillimum
Homeopathy Academy of Naturopathic Physicians
Quarterly; $35

TRAINING PROGRAMS

The homeopathic schools listed below may not represent a complete list of training programs; however, the largest and most established homeopathic programs in the United States are included. (Contact the Homeopathic Community Council for an up-to-date directory of training programs.)

Academy for Classical Homeopathy
7549 Louise Street
Van Nuys, CA 91406
(818) 776-8040

American Institute of Homeopathy
1585 Glencoe
Denver, CO 80220
(303) 321-4105

Atlantic Academy of Classical Homeopathy
209 First Avenue, Suite 2
New York, NY 10003
(212) 979-7950

Bastyr College
144 Northeast 54th Street
Seattle, WA 98105
(206) 523-9585
Programs: Naturopathic Doctor (N.D.); nutrition (M.S.); acupuncture (M.Ac.); traditional Chinese herbal medicine (certificate.)

British Institute of Homeopathy and College of Homeopathy
520 Washington Boulevard, Suite 423
Marina Del Rey, CA 90292
(310) 360-5408

Canada College of Naturopathic Medicine
60 Berl Avenue
Etobicoke, Ontario
Canada M8Y 3C7
(416) 251-5261
Programs: Naturopathic Doctor (N.D.)

Center for Preventive Medicine and Homeopathy
111 Bala Avenue
Bala Cynwyd, PA 19004
(610) 667-2927

Clinical Preceptorship
173 Mount Auburn Street
Watertown, MA 02172
(617) 547-7779

College of Homeopathy
520 Washington Boulevard, Suite 423
Marina Del Rey, CA 90292
(310) 306-5408

Complementary Medicine Association
4649 East Malvern
Tucson, AZ 85711
(602) 323-6291

Hahnemann College of Homeopathy
828 San Pablo Avenue, 2nd Floor
Albany, CA 94706
(510) 524-3117

The HCH offers the most extensive course in homeopathy in North America, meeting for four days per month for three years. Participants must have a medical background, including an N.D., M.D., D.O., D.C., L.Ac., D.D.S., D.P.M., R.N., F.N.P., or P.A. license, prior to being accepted to the program.

International Foundation for Homeopathy (IFH)
2366 Eastlake Avenue East, Suite 325
Seattle, WA 98102
(206) 324-8230

Participants must have a medical background, including an N.D., M.D., D.O., D.C., L.Ac., D.D.S., D.P.M., R.N., F.N.P., or P.A. license, prior to being accepted to the program.

National College of Naturopathic Medicine
11231 Southeast Market Street
Portland, OR 97216
(503) 255-4860
Programs: Naturopathic Doctor (N.D.)

Founded in 1956, National College is the oldest naturopathic medical school in North America.

New England School of Homeopathy
115 Elm Street, Suite 210
Enfield, CT 06082
(203) 763-1225

Northwestern Institute of Homeopathy
10700 Old County Road 15, Suite 350
Plymouth, MN 55441
(612) 593-0097

Pacific Academy of Classical Homeopathic
1678 Shattuck Avenue, Suite 42
Berkeley, CA 94709
(510) 549-3475

**Rocky Mountain School of
Homeopathic Medicine**
3122 8th Avenue
Boulder, CO 80304
(303) 838-6315

**Southwest College of Naturopathic
Medicine and Health Sciences**
6535 East Osborn Road
Scottsdale, AZ 85251
(602) 990-7424
Programs: Naturopathic Doctor (N.D.)

Westbrook University
Programs: Naturopathy (N.D.); homeopathy
See Nonresidential Psychology Programs
and Nondegree Training Programs.

ORIENTAL MEDICINE

Traditional Oriental (or Chinese) medicine is a holistic approach to treating the mind, body, and spirit, and includes the many healing modalities that originate from Asian cultures. The techniques involved include herbal blends; acupuncture and acupressure; diet and nutrition; and lifestyle awareness. Body movements and exercises such as Qigong (or chi kung), a deep-breathing and movement practice; Tuina, an Asian-originated therapeutic massage; and tai chi (t'ai chi ch'uan), a system of movements based on the principles of Qigong, are also related to Oriental medicine. In these Oriental systems, the goal of wellness is to maintain a balanced energy system, since it is thought that illness occurs when the pathways of energy, or "chi," become blocked.

The methods associated with Oriental medicine range from the most natural to the most intrusive. Natural healing methods, such as breathing exercises, dietary therapy, acupressure, and herbology, are used as a layperson's form of hands-on, organic healing. If more treatment is needed, however, more complex and manipulative forms of healing such as acupuncture are used, followed by drugs and surgery, which represent the most intrusive interventions.

Although Oriental medicine may be novel to Westerners, it is not only the traditional practice of Asia but one of the most established forms of medicine known in human history. Because these ancient traditions have over the years become less open to change, students may find that the Western somatic versions allow more emphasis on exploration and experimentation.

Students interested in applying a wide range of Asian techniques to their healing repertoire should consider a D.O.M. degree (Doctor of Oriental Medicine; sometimes denoted O.M.D), whereas students interested in specific Chinese modalities, such as acupuncture, may want to consider a more focused training program in that particular technique. In any case, because doctors of Oriental medicine in the United States are still licensed under an acupuncturist's title, learning acupuncture is usually the first step toward establishing a general practice. Also, considering that most Asian doctors study Chinese medicine for 11 years—and that most D.O.M. programs in the United States are only four years in duration—some Americans choose to augment their training in Asia. Approximately 28 states license acupuncturists (and thereby doctors of Oriental medicine); both types of practitioners must pass the same board examination.

More than 20 insurance companies in the United States currently provide third-party insurance reimbursement for acupuncture and Oriental medicine, and this figure continues to increase. Most practitioners work in private practice. Contact the American Foundation of Traditional Chinese Medicine for a comprehensive list of Chinese medicine training programs.

General Organizations
**American Association of Acupuncture and
Oriental Medicine (AAAOM)**
4101 Lake Boone Trail, Suite 201
Raleigh, NC 27607
(919) 787-5181
The AAAOM seeks to educate the public regarding the nature and scope of acupuncture and Oriental medicine, and to facilitate the acceptance of acupuncture as a form of complementary medicine.

**American Foundation of Traditional
Chinese Medicine (AFTCM)**
505 Beach Street
San Francisco, CA 94133
(415) 776-0502
The AFTCM, a nonprofit educational and advocacy organization created in 1982, provides a list of Chinese medicine programs in the United States and Asia. It facilitates an international student and teacher exchange with China for the purpose of increasing the acceptance of traditional Chinese medicine in the United States; fosters scientific research; develops educational programs; and sponsors the International Health Center, an international medical exchange in world healthcare, committed to the treatment and prevention of disease.

Institute of Chinese Herbology (ICH)
3871 Piedmont Avenue, Suite 363
Oakland, CA 94611
(510) 428-2061
The ICH is one of the few American herbology institutes that offer exclusive training in Chinese herbology.

General Periodicals
Gateways
Quarterly; $12
Contact the American Foundation of Traditional Chinese Medicine.

*Qi: The Journal of Traditional
Eastern Health and Fitness*
Insight Graphics
P.O. Box 221343
Chantilly, VA 22022
(800) 787-2600
Quarterly; $18.95

ACUPUNCTURE
According to traditional Oriental medicine, a life force controls the operations of the main organs and systems of the body. This vital force, or chi, as the Chinese call it, circulates from one organ to another along channels or pathways termed meridians, always following a certain route. There are 12 of these meridians in the body, each of them feeding one of the main organs or functions of the body. Chi must be flowing freely and in the correct strength and quality through each of the meridians in order that each and all of these organs

may be healthy. Illness indicates that energy is out of balance. Thus acupuncture treatment (which consists of pricking specific points along the body with fine needles) sets out to correct any imbalance in the energy of a person, thereby curing disease and alleviating pain.

Soon after 1975, when acupuncture was accepted as a legal treatment in the United States, the full scope of traditional Oriental medicine (including the prescribed use of herbs, diet, nutrition, exercise, and massage) also became available legally. Most acupuncturists work in private practice, although a few American hospitals have added acupuncturists to their team of healthcare specialists. A session can last from 15 to 60 minutes (sometimes longer), and practitioners charge anywhere from $25 to $150 per session. In 1985, the state of California required all group insurance plans to offer acupuncture coverage; and in 1989, the state of California required Worker's Compensation insurance to cover acupuncture and to treat acupuncturists as physicians. Now, according to the Pacific College of Oriental Medicine in San Diego, California, insurance patients make up one half of a typical acupuncture practice.

Some 28 states already approve and register, certify, or license acupuncturists (denoted as R.Ac., C.Ac., and L.Ac. respectively). Also, acupuncture schools grant degrees in M.Ac. (master's of acupuncture), D.Ac. (doctor of acupuncture), O.M.D. (doctor of Oriental medicine), and M.O.M. (master's of Oriental medicine). Although the National Accreditation Commission for Schools and Colleges of Acupuncture and Oriental Medicine currently does not accredit schools offering O.M.D. degrees, some U.S. schools may still offer the degree. The title is also sometimes taken by Chinese M.D.s who are licensed in China but not in the United

States and by American practitioners who complete O.M.D. degree programs at foreign schools.

To learn acupuncture's legal status in your area, contact your state's medical board and ask for the acupuncture committee. Contact the Council of Colleges of Acupuncture and Oriental Medicine for a list of accredited training programs; it also publishes the Accreditation Handbook, a guide to state acupuncture laws.

Organizations and Associations

American Association of Acupuncture and Oriental Medicine

See Oriental Medicine.

American College of Addictionality and Compulsive Disorders

5990 Bird Road
Miami, FL 33155
(305) 661-3474

This organization certifies physicians of all allopathic medical specialties in the use of acupuncture for the treatment of addiction and compulsive disorders.

Council of Colleges of Acupuncture and Oriental Medicine (CCAOM)
National Accreditation Commission for Schools and Colleges of Acupuncture and Oriental Medicine

8403 Colesville Road, Suite 370
Silver Spring, MD 20910
(301) 608-9680

Established in 1982 by the CCAOM, the commission is a specialized accreditation agency recognized by the United States Secretary of Education and the Council on Postsecondary Education. It accredits professional master's-level certificate and diploma programs in acupuncture based on the theory of Oriental medicine. These programs must be at least three academic years in length and follow at least two years of undergraduate college-level general education. Contact the commission for a listing of accredited programs. A revised addition of the *Accreditation Handbook*, a guide to state acupuncture laws, is available for $20.

National Acupuncture and Oriental Medicine Alliance (NAOMA)

638 Prospect Avenue
Hartford, CT 06105-4298
(203) 586-7509

The NAOMA is a broad-based professional and lobbying organization that seeks to integrate acupuncture and Oriental medicine into American health care. The alliance accepts individual practitioners and medical colleges as members.

National Acupuncture Detoxification Association (NADA)

3115 Broadway, Suite 51
New York, NY 10027
(212) 993-3100

The NADA provides certificate training for practitioners and the lay public.

National Commission for the Certification of Acupuncturists (NCCA)

1426 16th Street, N.W., Suite 501
Washington, DC 20036
(202) 232-1404

The NCCA offers a test that some states use to verify basic competency in acupuncture. (Although the NCCA is located in the same building as the CCAOM, they are separate organizations.)

Periodicals

Acupuncture Accreditation
Council of Colleges of Acupuncture and Oriental Medicine

American Journal of Acupuncture
P.O. Box 610
Capitola, CA 95010
Correspondence offered only by mail.
Quarterly; $60

Meridians
The Traditional Acupuncture Institute
The American City Building, Suite 100
10227 Wincopin Circle
Columbia, MD 21044-3422
(301) 596-6006
Semiannual; $35

ACUPRESSURE AND SHIATSU

Acupressure, an ancient Asian healing art developed over 5,000 years ago, includes many specific techniques such as Jin Shin Do®, shiatsu (Zen and Barefoot), Namakoshi, Acu-Yoga, and Do-In. Each has distinctive characteristics that incorporate unique ways of touching and interacting with clients. An acupressurist works with the same points used in acupuncture but stimulates the healing points with finger pressure rather than by inserting fine needles.

Although considered older than acupuncture, acupressure tended to be overlooked when the Chinese developed more "technological" methods for stimulating points with needles and electricity. However, using the power and sensitivity of the hands (or in some cases, feet), acupressure is effective in the relief of tension-related ailments, in self-treatment, and in preventive health care. Acupressure can also be combined with massage to increase circulation, reduce pain, and develop all-around health. Practitioners use acupressure as both a primary and an adjunct technique. This technique is eligible for insurance reimbursement only if performed by a licensed professional as a complementary technique.

—*Members of the Acupressure Institute staff contributed to this introduction.*

Associations

American Oriental Bodywork Therapy Association (AOBTA)
6801 Jericho Turnpike
Syosset, NY 11791
(516) 364-5533

The AOBTA is an information and advocacy group that acknowledges and respects all traditions of bodywork therapy, particularly those based in the tradition of Oriental medicine. The AOBTA also sponsors continuing education programs, a national conference, and a quarterly bulletin, and can provide its members with networking opportunities with other masters, instructors, and practitioners of Oriental bodywork. The AOBTA represents 13 Oriental-in-origin modalities: acupressure, Amma Therapy®, Chi Nei Tsang, Eclectic Shiatsu,

Five Element Shiatsu, Japanese shiatsu, Jin Shin Do®, macrobiotic shiatsu, traditional Nuat Thai, Okazaki Japanese Restorative, Shiatsu/Anma, Tuina, and Zen shiatsu.

Periodicals

Acupressure News
Jin Shin Do Foundation for Bodymind Acupressure.

Pulse
American Oriental Bodywork Therapy Association.

Training Programs

There are very few acupressure training programs in the United States. The Acupressue Institute, besides offering their own program, can help you find a training program located near you.

Acupressure Institute
1533 North Shattuck Avenue
Berkeley, CA 94709
(510) 845-1059

Founded in 1976 and approved by the Council for Private Postsecondary and Vocational Education, the Acupressure Institute offers both basic and advanced acupressure training in traditional Oriental bodywork and massage. Even though there are only a few acupressure training programs in the United States, the institute can help you find a training program located near you.

International School of Shiatsu
P.O. Box 187
Buckingham, PA 18912
(215) 340-9918

Founded in 1978, ISS offers a 500-hour training program and a one-year apprenticeship. The school has affiliated locations in North Carolina, Switzerland, Italy, Austria, Belgium, and Holland.

Jin Shin Do Foundation for Bodymind Acupressure™
366 California Avenue, Suite 16
Palo Alto, CA 94306
(415) 328-1811
Programs: Jin Shin Do acupressure

The foundation maintains a directory of authorized teachers and registered acupressurists.

SOMATIC THERAPY

The following introductory essay, written by Don Hanlon Johnson, Ph.D., director of the somatics program at the California Institute for Integral Studies, serves to situate much of the mind-body field in a historical and philosophical context. While Dr. Johnson's essay focuses on somatics, it simultaneously provides a perspective on the mind-body field as a whole. This perspective is possible because somatics, like the holistic health field in general, is interdisciplinary, multicultural, and inclusive of Eastern and Western movement forms as well as the expressive and creative arts.

EMBODIMENT

One of the most comprehensive and widespread Western versions of nondualistic theory and practice is a field that many call "somatics," a word originally coined by the late Thomas Hanna, the founder and editor of the journal *Somatics*. Numbering tens of thousands of practitioners serving a vast population in North and South America, the field also encompasses an equal number of practitioners who are serving an immense population in Asia, Europe, and Australia.

The field includes therapies such as sensory awareness, the F. M. Alexander Technique™, Gerda Alexander's Eutony, Rolfing and its offshoots, Moshe Feldenkrais's Awareness Through Movement and Functional Integration, the Lomi School, Continuum, Aston-Patterning, body-mind centering, Trager work, Hakomi work, Rosen work, process-oriented psychology, the movement work of the late Mary Whitehouse, the extended family of orgonomic and bioenergetic practices based on the work of Wilhelm Reich, and a host of others. Many of the training schools in these methods, some of which are over half a century old, enjoy long-established standards of practice, refined educational programs, and modest empirical studies of their work. Some of the practices (such as bioenergetics, Hakomi, focusing, and process-oriented psychotherapy) use touch, breathing, awareness, and movement to achieve psychotherapeutic goals, while other practices are used more generally to improve our body consciousness.

HISTORICAL BACKGROUND OF SOMATICS

In the popular mind, somatics is viewed as "new age" because it is often believed to have been born at places such as the Esalen Institute during the 1960s and later. The truth, however, is that the field is very old and represents a widespread reaction to the Western-inspired mind-body dualism dating back to the Gymnastik movement. This movement was set in motion by a number of teachers who traveled back and forth between Northern Europe and the Eastern seaboard of the United States during the middle and late 19th century; among them were François Delsarte, Genevieve Stebbins, Bess Mensendieck, Leo Kofler, and Emile Jacques-Dalcroze, to name a few. At the same time, Andrew Still was developing the holistic method of osteopathy in the midwestern United States, a practice whose credibility has been whittled away in this century by the medical establishment.

All these people shared a vision of embodiment that was at odds with the dominant models found in biomedicine, physical education, religion, and classical ballet. Rejecting biomedicine's and religion's separation of the human spirit from a mechanistically conceived body, they envisioned an intimate unity among movement, body structure, health, intelligence, and spiritual consciousness and emphasized a respect for lived experience and the wisdom that can be found through attending to rather than conquering or controlling life processes. At a time when physicians were still engaged in the crudest uses of surgery and medication, and while psychotherapy was just seeing the light of day, the practitioners of various branches of Gymnastik and the new osteopaths were already doing sophisticated healing work using expressive movement, sensory awareness, sound, music, and touch. Instead of imposing a narrow standard of correct form on all bodies, the new practitioners encouraged individual expressiveness and a return to a more "natural" body, thus allowing unique forms of movement to emerge from within. This emphasis on individu-ality is one of the major reasons why there has been such a proliferation of different somatic methods, unlike in medicine where one image of the physical human being predominates.

Unlike physicians and psychologists, the innovators of the somatics field lived within a comparatively silent world of nonverbal practices removed from the vociferous atmosphere of the university and laboratory. Consequently, there have been few books written to articu-

> The emphasis on individuality is one of the major reasons why there has been such a proliferation of different somatic methods, unlike in medicine where one image of the physical human being predominates.

late their work. In fact, it was only the participants in these innovative methods that had access to what was being discovered. Thus, although Wilhelm Reich arrived late in somatics history, he and his heritage captured a disproportionate amount of attention precisely because he was a prolific writer.

The world wars loom large in the shaping of the somatics movement. World War I rent the international and interdisciplinary community, leaving individual somatic schools intact yet isolated and fragmented. World War II dispersed the pioneers in the growing movement, forcing many to put aside the more visionary aspects of their work in order to eke out a living as refugees, marketing their work under the more acceptable forms of physical rehabilitation or psychotherapy.

In the 1960s, the hospitality of the Esalen Institute and a counterculture eager to explore different states of consciousness provided the opportunity for a regathering of strands of the widely shared vision that had been lost 50 years earlier. A new cooperative venture began to form. Some of the old pioneers traveled westward from New York, Tel Aviv, London, and Berlin, gathered large numbers of students, returned to the Northeastern United States, and established new schools. Many even returned to Europe, where their work had been forgotten.

By the end of the 1980s, there were international conferences on somatics in Paris, Zurich, Naples, Montevideo, Montreal, Strasbourg, San Francisco, and New York. At least three international professional organizations now use a version of the name "somatics," and the Association of Humanistic Psychology has recently formed a somatics division. In California, the Coalition on Somatic Practices is a professional group lobbying for state licensing. There are a handful of master's-level graduate degree programs in somatics in the United States and one doctoral program located at Ohio State University.

EVALUATING THE ROLE OF SOMATICS

Many pilot studies and a large body of anecdotal evidence attest to the efficacy of these various methods. Although the medical establishment often criticizes the therapeutic claims of these methods as unsubstantiated, there are nevertheless ongoing efforts among the major private somatic studies institutes to conduct research. The Rolf Institute, the Feldenkrais Guild, and the Guild of F. M. Alexander Teachers are among the groups that have initiated and encouraged investigation of their works by biomedical researchers for over 25 years. With virtually no outside funding, they have managed to complete a number of modest empirical studies.

The uniqueness and diversity of the areas covered by somatics challenge the boundaries of established disciplines such as psychotherapy, education, medicine, physical therapy, and meditation. Consider, for example, the wide range of successful outcomes, which include addressing chronic physical symptoms (back pain, whiplash injuries, various forms of arthritis, scoliosis, the restric-

MIND-BODY STUDIES

tions of cerebral palsy); alleviating emotional and psychological complaints (depression, sexual dysfunctions, body-image problems, substance addictions, intimacy problems); improvement in capacities for focused awareness and stillness required for the practice of meditation; and an increase in everyday flexibility and vitality.

Because of these crossovers into other disciplines, somatics is often associated in the popular mind with such fields as behavioral medicine. However, from a somatics point of view, behavioral medicine retains troubling vestiges of an old dualism, because it contextualizes its strategies (such as visualizations, affirmations, biofeedback devices, and changes in attitude) within a vocabulary of controlling the wayward disease processes of the body even while using the rubric of "mind."

Such an approach is very different from the somatic approach in which one is encouraged to listen to the messages of one's cells, to embrace one's breathing patterns, to follow one's styles of moving and the insights that emerge within an awareness of the movement itself. Thomas Hanna puts it this way: "Somatics is the field which studies the soma: namely, the body as perceived from within, by first-person perception. When a human being is observed from the outside (i.e., from a third-person viewpoint) the phenomenon of a human body is perceived. But when this same human being is observed from the first-person viewpoint of his own proprioceptive senses, a categorically different phenomenon is perceived: the human soma."

The various branches of somatics have always shared an emphasis on the systematic refinement of nonverbal skills, particularly sophisticated methods of touch, breathing, and body-movement instruction. While psychosomatic and behavioral medicine developed out of the marriage between biomedicine and psychoanalysis, from the "top down," as it were, somatic theory developed from the bottom up, by incorporating a wide range of experimental methods (including manipulation,

movement, and body awareness) that evolved outside of universities and clinics. In fact the methods typically developed in response to critical health problems that were impervious to existing medical and psychological treatments.

PHILOSOPHICAL CONSIDERATIONS

In the late 1800s, both F. M. Alexander in Melbourne, Australia, and Leo Kofler in New York were coincidentally afflicted with chronic laryngitis for which

---

While psychosomatic and behavioral medicine developed out of the marriage between biomedicine and psychoanalysis, from the "top down," as it were, somatic theory developed from the bottom up, by incorporating a wide range of experimental methods.

---

physicians could find neither cause nor cure. The two men carried on their healing investigations in widely separated milieus and discovered that as they learned to fully inhabit their body movements, posture, and voice, they were healed. Not surprisingly, they went on to teach this process to others.

Twenty years later, Elsa Gindler contracted tuberculosis in Berlin and was told by her physician that she would never regain the use of one lobe of her lungs. She spent several months devoting herself for hours each day to learning how to inhabit her breathing, eventually regaining full use of the collapsed lobe. In the course of healing, she realized the extent of the healing capacities released by quiet, sustained sensing of bodily activities—without trying to control them with images, affirmations, or programmed strategies. She went on to found a school now known in this coun-

try (through the work of Charlotte Selver) as Sensory Awareness.

Its quiet influence has had an impact on many contemporary forms of psychotherapy and meditation practice. The momentum created by these early pioneers continued with Moshe Feldenkrais, Ida Rolf, Gerda Alexander, Ilsa Middendorf, and countless others who discovered the healing capacities inherent in the cultivation of direct contact with bodily experience—unmediated by images, positive thoughts, or video display terminals.

Despite the mottled and sometimes contentious differences in method and style among the thousands of practitioners who are the heirs of these innovators, today's somatics practitioners share a vision about the nature of reality more akin to older ideas than to modernist European scientific notions. That older vision has to do with the significance assigned to the awareness of natural forms and processes in the life of the human spirit. Bioenergeticists, Rolfers, and Feldenkrais practitioners differ about many things. But they all make the common assumption that sensing, feeling, breathing, moving, postural changes, and excitation are crucial factors in the human search for meaning. Whether one is being probed by a Rolfer's elbow, vibrating under a Reichian's palm, or trying to concentrate on the sensual effects of the disorienting Feldenkrais movements, he or she is constantly reminded that the realities lumped under body or mind are experiential: aching muscles and frayed nerves at one extreme, love and cosmic intuition at the other, with healing taking place in the creative interweaving of these extremes.

For that reason, the soul of somatics is identified as a modern Western version of the ancient psychophysical disciplines—Taoism, Sufism, Buddhism, Greek Orthodox hesychasm (a 14th-century physical method of achieving interior quietness), and so on—whose goal is the attainment of unmediated contact with an experienced reality that is beyond dualistic illusions. Not surprisingly, practitioners and clients of somatics typically have an interest in non-Western disciplines such as hatha yoga or tai chi.

SOMATIC VIEWPOINT AS A RADICAL SHIFT

Even though major differences exist between them, somatic methods are often confused with physical therapy, chiropractic, and massage. In addition to holding a more holistic view of the person, somatics practitioners assert that the various regions and parts of the body are systematically related. For example, bursitis in the shoulder joint or disorders in the lumbar region may be related to torsions in the ankles and knees, chronic back pain may be related to restricted breathing, and carpal tunnel syndrome may be related to muscular tensions in the pelvis. In somatics training, no matter what the particular school, practitioners are taught to see relationships among body parts and layers within any body region and to develop their interventions accordingly.

Somatic methods also differ from other nonconventional therapeutic modalities, such as hypnosis, meditation, and guided imagery. For example, somatics emphasizes body awareness, anatomy, sensory and kinesthetic education, and nonverbal language as the foundations for therapeutic insights, emotional clarity, and spiritual growth. On the other hand, the language of the other nonconventional modalities often reveals a belief that "meaning" or "healing thoughts" come from somewhere other than the depths of flesh, movement, and experience. It is easier for both physicians and members of the public who are brought up within the dominant paradigm of healing to accept hypnosis, imaging, relaxation techniques, biofeedback, and other exotic or foreign methods because it can appear (mistakenly) that these methods do not require a radical and sometimes uncomfortable shift of viewpoint toward the important possibility of finding the source of meaning and healing in the very depths of our flesh. Yet it is precisely this radical shift that constitutes the heart of the various somatics methods:

entering a long, quiet, and demanding journey to contact one's breathing, moving, sensing, pulsing, and feeling. It is the major contribution that somatics adds to these other rich and effective techniques.

People outside the somatics field often comment on the seemingly excessive number of different types of somatic approaches. While there are certainly some negative aspects involved in the extent of this differentiation, the bewil-

> In addition to holding a more holistic view of the person, somatics practitioners assert that the various regions and parts of the body are systematically related.

dering number of approaches represents a healthy resistance to the homogenization of the body that permeates conventional medicine, physical therapy, exercise, and body image teaching, including some highly codified non-Western disciplines such as hatha yoga. In somatics one finds a high regard for the individuality of both teacher and student, and their particular movement style, breathing pattern, and idiosyncratic posture. Somatics does not cut and paste people to fit into a single-sized Procrustean bed. Such a regard for the individual manner of expression and body structure can itself be radically healing.

No one who has practiced these methods for a long time considers somatics a panacea. Rather, the field sees itself as modestly contributing to a more comprehensive model of health care that includes education, exercise, nutrition, relaxation and visualization techniques, mainstream and alternative hands-on techniques, psychotherapy, and group support. Both mainstream and complementary healing methods gain more power when the person who is practicing them has learned to heal

his or her radical split from the direct experience of bodily processes. These are the very internal processes that have been feared and dishonored in a culture whose social, political, and educational structure does violence to the body—at both the personal and collective level. Somatics, when taken for what it is rather than being digested into some more familiar modality, has much to contribute to healing our impoverished relationship to our most intimate home, our body.

—This introduction was written by Don Hanlon Johnson, Ph.D., the director of the graduate program in somatics at the California Institute of Integral Studies in San Francisco. He is the author of The Protean Body: A Rolfer's View of Human Flexibility; Body: Recovering Our Sensual Wisdom, *and most recently,* Body, Spirit and Democracy.

DEGREE PROGRAMS

While there are many nondegree somatics programs, the following list represents the few that offer accredited degrees in somatic therapy. All schools below offer an M.A. degree; only Ohio State University offers a Ph.D. Also see subchapter on nondegree somatic therapy programs.

California Institute of Integral Studies
See Residential Psychology Degree Programs.

Institute for Transpersonal Psychology (ITP)
See Residential Psychology Degree Programs.
The ITP offers electives in somatics.

John F. Kennedy University
See Residential Psychology Degree Programs.

Naropa Institute
See Residential Psychology Degree Programs.

Ohio State University
Sport, Leisure and Somatic Studies
317 Pomerene Hall
1760 Neil Avenue
Columbus, OH 43210-1221
(614) 292-4311; 292-6538
General Information: Public, nonsectarian
Degrees Offered: M.A.; Ph.D.

Programs: Somatic studies area within the College of Education
Admission Requirements: Bachelor's degree; GPA > 2.7.; GRE (900 combined)
Application Deadline: Rolling
Contact Person: Director of Admissions
Tuition: $405/unit hour (nonresident)
Accreditation: NCACS
Year Established: 1980
Faculty: 1 full-time (Professor Seymour Kleinman, Ph.D.); 1 adjunct

WELLNESS AND HOLISTIC HEALTH PROGRAMS

WELLNESS

Wellness, a multidimensional approach that addresses all aspects of health, is a relatively recent addition to alternative and preventive health care. Because of its fledgling status, the practical aspects of the field are difficult to portray. The National Wellness Institute divides wellness into six dimensions—physical, social, emotional, intellectual, spiritual, and occupational—each related to and affected by the others. Often defined as a process emphasizing the enhancement of body, mind, and spirit through the assumption of personal responsibility, wellness aims to improve individual, organizational, and community health and well-being.

Most wellness programs exist within university and college departments of exercise science, sports management, health promotion, or physical education. A few schools (such as Oklahoma State and Ball State Universities) offer a master's degree in wellness. Our limited survey, however, suggests that many health-care professionals (including nurses, counselors, physicians, and teachers) and interested students are more likely to attend wellness conferences, workshops, and continuing education classes and incorporate this knowledge into their established work than they are to seek a separate degree. Ball State University provides a helpful catalog called "Undergraduate/Graduate Degree Programs in Wellness and Health Promotion."

THE USE OF TRADEMARKS IN BODY THERAPIES

THE WORDS PSYCHOLOGIST, PSYCHIATRIST, SOCIAL WORKER, AND SO ON, REPRESENT WELL-ESTABLISHED FIELDS WHOSE PRACTITIONERS ARE LICENSED BY A STATE GOVERNMENT AGENCY. Therapists, therefore, cannot apply these terms to describe themselves unless they have been licensed to do so. The dynamic field of nondegree somatic therapies, however, is less formally regulated; for example, one can call oneself a "bodyworker" without having a specific educational background. For this reason, pioneers who establish new therapeutic techniques, methods, or materials are often eager to protect the integrity of their inventions by ensuring that the name cannot be used loosely or without authorization. When a practitioner creates a service, product, or new artistic expression, there are several ways in which she or he may protect it against imitation and unauthorized usage. The following symbols indicate that the originator of a particular modality has made a proprietary or exclusive claim to its name.

® indicates that the product or service is registered with the United States Patent and Trademark Office. The creator of the product or service is issued a certificate from that government office and is protected against unauthorized usage of his or her mark.

TM refers to products or goods; SM refers to services. TM and SM serve as public notices of claim to trademark or service mark rights and are used with marks that are not registered. These marks therefore do not carry the full benefits of registration with a government agency and are frequently used before a mark is formally registered.

©, or copyright, protects artistic and literary expressions.

HOLISTIC HEALTH

Holistic health is a general term that denotes a philosophy of health rather than a specific practice. In addition to the programs listed here, there are numerous nondegree programs that teach from an implicit holistic health perspective.

Associations
American Holistic Health Association (AHHA)
P.O. Box 17400
Anaheim, CA 92817-7400
(714) 779-6152

The AHHA serves to present the value and methods of a holistic approach through media awareness and educational literature.

National Wellness Association (NWA)
National Wellness Institute
P.O. Box 827
Stevens Point, WI 54481-0827
(715) 342-2969

The NWA, a wellness advocacy group established in 1985, currently serves over 2,100 professionals working in all areas of wellness and health promotion. The institute sponsors the annual National Wellness Conference.

Organizations
Center for Professional Well-Being (CPWB)
Society for Professional Well-Being
Colony West Professional Park
21 West Colony Place, Suite 150
Durham, NC 27705
(919) 489-9167

The CPWB is a nonprofit organization devoted to promoting well-being—the integration of physical, emotional, and cultural aspects of being—and preventing stress among professionals. It annually sponsors a national conference.

National Wellness Coalition (NWC)
P.O. Box 3778
Washington, DC 20007-0278
(202) 298-0949

The mission of the NWC is to promote wellness principles, policies, and practices as the key to affordable, effective health care and a healthy nation. Wellness 2000, NWC's wellness agenda, puts forward a vision for health and well-being in America, calling for a greater emphasis on prevention, self-care, lifestyle changes, and the combined use of proven, cost-effective natural medical and health methods along with conventional medical practices.

Spiritual Wellness Network (SWN)
523 North 66th Street
Wauwatosa, WI 53213-4057
(414) 453-8751

The SWN is a nonsectarian professional organization dedicated to exploring the link between spirituality, health, and well-being. It publishes the *Spiritual Wellness Quarterly*.

Periodicals

There are numerous newsletters that address health and wellness issues. Contact the National Wellness Institute at the National Wellness Association for a list. Other relevant periodicals are listed under Interdisciplinary Resources.

Advances: The Journal of Mind-Body Health
9292 West KL Avenue
Kalamazoo, MI 49009
(616) 375-2000
Quarterly; $39

American Journal of Health Promotion
1812 South Rochester Road, Suite 200
Rochester Hills, MI 48307-9902
(313) 650-9600
Bimonthly; $59.95

Health Values: The Journal of Health Behavior, Education and Promotion
P.O. Box 4593
Star City, WV 26504-4593
(304) 293-4699
Bimonthly; $55

Medicine, Exercise, Nutrition and Health
Blackwell Scientific Publications, Inc.
238 Main Street
Cambridge, MA 02142
(800) 759-6102
Bimonthly; $65

Spiritual Wellness Quarterly
Spiritual Wellness Network
Quarterly; $20 (with membership)

DEGREE PROGRAMS
Ball State University
Fisher Institute for Wellness
Practical Arts Building
Muncie, IN 47306
(317) 285-8121
Programs: M.S. in wellness management

International Academy of Massage Science
The Well-Person Place
P.O. Box 277
Glen Riddle, PA 19037
(215) 558-3140
Programs: M.S. and Ph.D. degrees in holistic health from Susan B. Anthony University

Oklahoma State University
School of Health, Physical Education and Leisure
Stillwater, OK 74078
(405) 744-5493
Programs: M.S. in wellness

NONDEGREE PROGRAMS
College of St. Mary's
2500 South Sixth Street
Minneapolis, MN 55454
(612) 690-7800
Programs: Holistic therapies

Northern Virginia Community College
Loudoun Campus, Continuing Education Office
1000 Harry Flood Byrd Highway
Sterling, VA 20164
(703) 450-2551
Programs: Mind-body studies certificate

This program is a progressive series of seminars that provide participants, through discussion, demonstration, participatory exercise, and study groups, with the knowledge and skills required for self-healing.

Our Lady of Lourdes Wellness Center
900 Haddon Avenue, Suite 100
Collingswood, NJ 08108
(609) 869-3125
Programs: Certification in holistic massage, Christian yoga, shiatsu, foot reflexology, and therapeutic touch

San Francisco State University
Institute for Holistic Healing Studies
1600 Holloway Avenue
San Francisco, CA 94132
(415) 338-1210
Programs: Holistic health minor; holistic

health certificate

The certificate program is for individuals who already have an academic degree and/or are already in a health profession.

Mind-Body Nondegree Programs

AYURVEDIC MEDICINE

Ayurvedic medicine (meaning "knowledge of life power" in Sanskrit) has been practiced in India for over 5,000 years and is apparently the oldest known system of total health. However, unlike acupuncture in the United States, which has recently gained distinction, Ayurvedic medicine still remains a relatively obscure and mysterious science in the West.

Deepak Chopra, M.D., an American-trained but Indian-born physician and popular author, has been the most recent popularizer of Ayurvedic thought. Similar to the philosophy of Oriental medicine, Ayurvedic places equal significance on the body, mind, and spirit; combines natural therapies in conjunction with a client-centered approach to the treatment of disease; considers dietary and lifestyle factors when making a diagnosis; and works to restore internal harmony.

According to the book *Alternative Medicine* (Future Medicine Publishing, 1993), there are 108 Ayurvedic colleges in India (programs consist of five years of vigorous training) and 300,000 Ayurvedic physicians who are represented by the All India Ayur-Veda Congress. Ayurvedic conferences have been held around the world, and both the Soviet Research Center for Preventative Medicine and the National Institutes of Health in the United States are researching the efficacy of Ayurvedic medicine as a prospective complement to our technology-focused health-care system.

Formal Ayurvedic training in the United States is in the same position as was acupuncture about 20 years ago: Training programs are relatively short and general, allowing caregivers to augment their primary practice (such as naturopathic medicine, chiropractic, and acupuncture) with Ayurvedic principles. Licensure is unavailable and, unlike acupuncture, state health boards do not recognize Ayurvedic medicine as a primary discipline. Therefore, insurance is available only through a practitioner's primary modality, assuming that he or she is licensed and therefore eligible for insurance.

TRAINING CENTERS
American Institute of Vedic Studies
1701 Santa Fe River Road
Sante Fe, NM 87501
(505) 983-9385
Programs: Ayurvedic for health-care providers

American School of Ayurvedic Sciences
10025 NE 4th Street
Bellevue, WA 98004
(206) 453-8022
Programs: Training in Ayurvedic for physicians and other health-care providers, as well as laypersons

Ayurvedic Institute
11311 Menaul N.E., Suite A
Albuquerque, NM 87112
(505) 291-9698
Programs: Ayurvedic studies (levels I, II, III); Ayurvedic studies certificate program

The institute was founded in 1984 to promote an understanding of Ayurveda. It offers certificate courses, seminars, and a correspondence course; there is no licensure for Ayurvedic practitioners in the United States. It also publishes the quarterly journal *Ayurveda Today* ($17/year).

College of Maharishi Ayur-Veda Health Center
P.O. Box 282
Fairfield, IA 52556
(515) 472-5866

The center is a referral, educational, and training organization.

Westbrook University
See Nondegree and Postgraduate Training Programs.

BODY-CENTERED PSYCHOTHERAPIES
Just as psychotherapy and bodywork have their own unique dynamics, there are also dynamics specific to the integration of the mind and body. Therefore, while receiving training in a psychotherapy and a body therapy technique may certify you to practice both, a separate understanding of each does not necessarily make you a competent practitioner of both or a body-centered psychotherapist. The following programs were established, in part, to address the need for integrating the two approaches.

Some of the programs listed below require prior experience in bodywork, psychotherapy, or both, and sometimes the need for certification in a body therapy and licensure in a psychotherapy field. Other programs, however, are less demanding. In either case, receiving a certificate of completion from one of these programs does not necessarily entitle you to practice in any given state. Therefore, those who are already licensed in some health-care profession are in the best situation to practice legally and receive third-party health insurance reimbursement.

For a listing of body-centered psychotherapies originating from the theory and practice of William Reich, see Reichian Therapies in the Nondegree and Postgraduate Training section.

General Organizations
There is no association currently representing body-centered psychotherapists in the United States.

Congress of Body-Centered Psychotherapy
Ulrich Fleck
Groner Tor Str. 16
D-3400 Gottingen
Denmark
0551-485520

BODYNAMICS ANALYSIS
Bodynamics Analysis is a psychotherapy system that uses deep states of body awareness to integrate psychological and emotional awareness. The practice's philosophy maintains that people are motivated by a deep drive toward connection with each other; therefore, the central intention of Bodynamics is to help individuals achieve fulfillment in their relationships.

Founded in Denmark by Lisbeth Marcher and her colleagues, Bodynamics has its roots in the Scandinavian traditions of somatic therapy. Marcher has documented the age of activation and psychological content of each muscle and has created a map of seven stages of development that begins with intrauterine and birth states, and progresses through latency and adolescence. This developmental map forms the heart of Bodynamics Analysis.

Techniques unique to Bodynamics include its specific developmental approach to transference in relationships, post-traumatic stress disorder (PTSD), birth trauma, "muscular resignation," "activation of age specific muscles," and "psychomotor movement patterns" (such as rolling, crawling, walking, and grasping).

While Bodynamics is typically a long-term, primary therapy, it is also suitable as a short-term therapy and as an adjunct technique. Referrals come equally from psychotherapists and bodyworkers. The developmental emphasis of Bodynamics is particularly suitable for working with infants and children. Group work is also emphasized.

Professional training includes up to five years of study, beginning with a one-year overview. Curriculum includes intensive anatomy, psychomotor development, character structure theory, body reading, birth and shock trauma, group process, muscle testing, and bodymap interpretation. A two-year practitioner and analytic training program leads to certification.

AVOIDING DUAL RELATIONSHIPS IN THE PRACTICE OF BODY-CENTERED PSYCHOTHERAPY

RESPECT FOR BOUNDARIES AND APPROPRIATE TOUCHING ARE IMPORTANT AND MUCH-DEBATED ISSUES IN ALL OF THE HELPING AND HEALING professions, including the ministry, medicine, teaching, and psychotherapy. However, because the potentially challenging aspect of explicitly combining touch and psychotherapy is inherent in somatic therapies and bodywork, such concerns have become central to these fields. Few if any practitioners would assert that a therapist should never touch his or her clients; however, most would agree that a certain protocol should be followed in such situations. The prevailing code of professional ethics aims at preventing conflicting dual relationships (e.g., combining the roles of therapist, sexual partner, intimate friend, etc.).

Although body-centered psychotherapy draws from the mind-body interface, professional protocol indicates that the multiple roles a practitioner plays must remain separate and be appropriately prioritized. To avoid a dual relationship, then, a psychotherapist may incorporate into her or his practice some form of touch only so long as psychotherapy remains the primary mode of relation. Similarly, a bodyworker may incorporate dialogue into his or her practice so long as bodywork remains the primary mode of relation.

When an individual is both a psychotherapist and a bodyworker, as is often the case, he or she must establish and maintain a primary relationship before establishing a secondary and subordinate one. Some therapists practice both psychotherapy and bodywork. Others, however, use bodywork or psychotherapy to augment their other pre-existing practices. For example, a social worker may use cranio-sacral therapy on her or his clients. In such cases, professionals in the field suggest that the sessions be separate, as should the invoices which are sent to the client's insurance company.

It is important to recognize, however, that some people in the helping and healing professions (notably Episcopal priest Carter Heyward) are challenging the established code of professional ethics, particularly as it pertains to the issue of boundaries. They contend that the creation of rigid boundaries between professional and peer relationships is not only unnecessary and artificial but even damaging and a hindrance to the optimal healing of both practitioner and client. While acknowledging that sexual abuse in therapeutic relationships is very real and dangerous and must not be tolerated, these scholars and practitioners claim that therapists must be careful not to eliminate empathy, intimacy, friendship, vulnerability, and other aspects of mutually healing human relationships from their practices in the interest of maintaining boundaries.

LICENSURE OF BODY-CENTERED PSYCHOTHERAPISTS

The use of somatic techniques within the practice of psychotherapy is governed by the same standards as any other ancillary technique such as hypnotherapy, guided imagery, and behavioral suggestions: The practitioner must have been trained in a professional program whose competencies have public accountability. Moreover, the techniques used should be integrated within an accepted standard of practice—that is, they must not be unethically intrusive, sexually inappropriate, or seductive in form. (See the American Psychological Association's ethical guidelines for a complete description.) As discussed above, conflictive dual relationships are to be avoided. These rules apply in most states. California codes governing psychotherapists, for example, name the body parts that may and may not be touched. Consumer protection laws in California also require all body-centered therapists to be certified in the modality for which they charge fees.

Training Programs
Bodynamics Institute
965 Talbot Avenue
Albany, CA 94706
(510) 524-8090

GENERAL PROGRAMS
Washington Institute for Body Psychotherapy (WIBP)
911 Silver Spring Avenue, Suite 201
Silver Spring, MD 20910
(301) 588-9341

The WIBP offers a two-year training program in body-psychotherapy from a Jungian, organismic, and neo-Reichian perspective.

HAKOMI INTEGRATIVE SOMATICS
Hakomi is a Hopi Indian word that means "How do you stand in relation to the many realms?" However, a modern update might be: "Who are you?" Hakomi was developed by Ron Kurtz, an American, although much of the technique is based on Buddhism and Taoism, particularly concepts such as gentleness, compassion, and mindfulness. Other influences come from general systems theory, which incorporates the idea of respecting the wisdom of each individual as a living organic system, and from modern body-centered psychotherapies such as Reichian work, bioenergetics, Gestalt, psychomotor, Feldenkrais, structural bodywork, Ericksonian hypnosis, focusing, and Neurolinguistic Programming.

After completing the Hakomi training, students may either integrate their knowledge into their ongoing therapeutic work or pursue certification as a Hakomi therapist (C.H.T.). Hakomi certification training is offered in Boulder, Colorado; Portland, Oregon; and Germany. The typical training format consists of four one-and-a-half-day weekends plus skill and peer study groups that meet every four to five months.

Training Programs
Hakomi Institute
1800 30th Street, Suite 201
Boulder, CO 80306
(303) 443-6209

EMOTIONAL-KINESTHETIC PSYCHOTHERAPY (EKP)
EKP emphasizes the relationship between emotional experience, body process, and psychospiritual development. Training integrates skills, concepts, personal healing, community process, and clinical supervision in an apprenticeship training model. The institute offers a three-year, 1,000-hour training program resulting in certification.

Training Programs
Institute for Emotional-Kinesthetic Psychotherapy
3 Central Avenue
Newton, MA 02160
(617) 965-7846

PERSON-CENTERED EXPRESSIVE THERAPY
The person-centered approach to expressive therapy combines movement, art, writing, music, guided visualizations, meditation, drama, and verbal/nonverbal communication skills to facilitate self-esteem and self-expression. The therapy was developed by Natalie Rogers, Ph.D., as an amalgamation of the humanistic psychology of Carl Rogers (her father) and her own explorations of creative expression as a means for personal growth.

Training Programs
Person-Centered Expressive Therapy Institute (PCETI)
P.O. Box 6518
Santa Rosa, CA 95406
(707) 829-8392
Founded in 1985, PCETI offers a four-level intensive training certificate program. An external master's degree program is also offered through Sonoma State University and the Institute of Transpersonal Psychology (ITP). See Residential Psychology Degree Programs for information on Sonoma and the ITP.

PESSO BOYDEN SYSTEM/PSYCHOMOTOR
Cofounded in 1961 by Albert and Diane Pesso, both formally trained dancers, the Pesso System is primarily a group therapy process that combines body and cognitive experience. According to the Pessos, this use of action and touch permits the client to discharge energy held from past events while recreating freer modes of being. The central technique of psychomotor therapy is to have the client experience significant body sensations and emotional states through group role-playing. The "restructuring" that follows helps the client see clearly, understand, and change his or her present state of emotions.

Psychiatrists, psychologists, counselors, and social workers have incorporated psychomotor therapy into their primary practice, and the therapy has been used to treat anxiety, depression, substance abuse, incest, combative families, and chronic pain. The certification program requires practicing psychotherapists to train 26 days per year for three years. Although the therapy was founded in the United States, it has achieved considerable recognition in Europe with the establishment of training centers in Belgium, Denmark, the Netherlands, Norway, Switzerland, and Germany.

Training Programs
Pesso Boyden System/Psychomotor
Strolling Woods
Lake Shore Drive
Franklin, NH 03235
(603) 934-9809 (or 934-5548)

RUBENFELD SYNERGY METHOD
The Rubenfeld Synergy® Method of body-centered therapy emphasizes the use of gentle touch, verbal expression, and movement. It combines techniques used in Gestalt, Alexander Technique, Feldenkrais Method, and Ericksonian hypnotherapy. Like other similar therapies, Rubenfeld Synergy helps open gateways to contacting, expressing, and understanding past memories and current feelings.

Training Programs
Rubenfeld Center
115 Waverly Place
New York, NY 10011
(212) 254-5100
The center, founded by Illana Rubenfeld in 1963, offers a three-year certification training program.

BODYWORK AND MASSAGE THERAPY
In the last few years several preliminary attempts have been made to clarify the scope of the emerging massage/bodywork profession. According to the Job Analysis Advisory Committee of the National Certification Board for Therapeutic Massage and Bodywork (the independent certifying body of the American Massage Therapy Association), there are three fundamental, mutually inclusive, and interrelated paradigms that underlie all forms of massage/bodywork. These three paradigms are called "relaxation," "remediation," and "holistic."

The first paradigm, *relaxation,* includes the practice of massage/bodywork as a personal service. This level of practice is based on the well-documented human biological need for nonthreatening, nurturing touch. This kind of caring touch is noninvasive, relaxing, pleasurable, sensual but not sexual, and stress reducing. Since the practitioner focuses solely on providing a relaxing massage, there is no need for client assessment. Training must include the basics of anatomy and physiology; knowledge about when to refer to other practitioners; and the technical ability to deliver a relaxing, comprehensive, and satisfying massage.

The second paradigm, *remediation,* generally encompasses all of the hands-on healing approaches that seek the correction of dysfunction and alleviation of pain. The application of remediation requires building on the knowledge and skills of the relaxation paradigm, especially in the anatomy and physiology areas, and on the hands-on techniques employed. In addition, skills in assessment and evaluation of the client/

patient's presenting conditions are required. Practice at this level also requires the ability to design and provide treatment based upon clinical assessment, monitoring, and altering one's treatment as appropriate.

The third paradigm, *holistic,* focuses on enhancing, balancing, and transforming the quality of life of the recipient. The welcomed byproducts of the holistic process are the remediation of symptoms, transformational growth, and the prevention of disease. The symptoms of disease are viewed as signaling opportunities for transformation and growth. The holistic paradigm focuses on how the combined healing, evolution, and growth of the body/mind/spirit of the individual can be enhanced in an integrated way. Curing disease is not the focus. The purpose of this paradigm is to enhance the body/mind/spirit's natural tendency to seek a higher order of functioning and well-being.

Holistic practitioners have a fundamental understanding of how their unique approach affects the whole person. They may employ a wide range of therapeutic approaches, each fundamental to the total organization, structure, function and well being of the whole person. For example, energy systems are the focus of the Oriental energetic disciplines while myofascial (soft muscle tissue) systems, with their characteristic relation to gravity, are the focus of Structural Integration™.

Although these paradigms are distinct, each merges into another, forming concentric spheres. Evolving levels are inclusive; in other words, each paradigm includes all of the possibilities of the preceding ones. This means that massage therapists can sometimes just do relaxation massages, and practitioners of the holistic paradigm will sometimes just treat symptoms.

FIVE APPROACHES

A review of the various approaches that lay claim to being considered part of the overall massage/bodywork profession reveals five broad techniques, all of

---

MASSAGE THERAPY AND BODYWORK TRAINING

WHEN CONSIDERING A MASSAGE SCHOOL, CHECK WHETHER THE SCHOOL IS APPROVED for operation in your state (usually through the State Department of Education), whether the school is accredited by the National Certification Board for Therapeutic Massage and Bodywork, and whether the school meets the minimum requirements set by the American Massage Therapy Association, the largest and most influential professional association in the massage therapy field.

---

which share a common theory.

The first category, *traditional massage,* is the form of bodywork based on the five strokes (effleurage, petrissage, friction, tapotemont, and vibration) developed by Johann Metzger of Amsterdam in the late 19th century. In the United States this work was merged with Pehr Ling's Swedish movements and several adjunct modalities to become the well-known Swedish massage of the 20th century.

The second category, *contemporary Western massage/bodywork,* encompasses all of those specialties that are based on Western sciences, such as neuromuscular massage, myofascial release, and positional release. The basic nature of these approaches to bodywork is remedial.

The third category is *structural/function/movement integration.* The various bodywork and movement techniques that address the human relationship to gravity are encompassed here. While these specialties are clearly contemporary Western approaches, they are distinguished from the second category because of the greater depth and breadth of their underlying philosophy. Here the interaction is with the person

---

as a whole and not on parts or symptoms. Examples are Structural Integration and the Alexander Technique.

The fourth approach is called *Oriental bodywork.* The primary focus of treatment is the energy body rather than the physical body, although the physical body is always directly or indirectly affected. This category comprises all the different styles of Oriental bodywork that originally developed throughout Asia. Oriental bodywork is distinguished as a separate category because of its derivation from traditional Chinese medicine, as well as its widespread impact on American bodywork. In this category are such forms as shiatsu, Anma, Amma, and Tuina.

Energetic bodywork is the fifth category. This encompasses all of the approaches to energetic bodywork that have developed throughout the world, and comprises such techniques as polarity therapy and therapeutic touch.

Common to all five basic approaches to massage/bodywork are the variety of adjunct techniques that practitioners use to assist in their work. When based on appropriate education, such techniques (within the scope of all forms of massage/bodywork) are noninvasive. They include, but are not limited to, pressure devices, application of heat and cold, external application of herbal or chemical preparations, electromagnetic treatment modalities, and principles of diet and therapeutic exercise.

Furthermore, all forms of massage/bodywork, regardless of their primary focus, additionally affect the superficial and deep tissues, fascial, myofascial, neuromuscular, musculoskeletal, circulatory, lymphatic, respiratory, digestive, eliminative, and craniosacral systems for the promotion, maintenance, and restoration of health.

The following definitions are proposed for the five approaches to massage/bodywork delineated above.

TRADITIONAL MASSAGE

The treatment of the human body by soft tissue manipulation, using the techniques of effleurage, petrissage, friction, tapotement, and vibration. This approach is based upon traditional Western scientific concepts of anatomy and physiology for the purposes of general relaxation, health enhancement, rehabilitation of muscular injuries, and enjoyment.

CONTEMPORARY WESTERN MASSAGE/BODYWORK

The treatment of the human body using a wide variety of manipulative techniques. This approach is based on modern neurological, psychological, somatopsychic, neuromuscular, biomechanical, or sometimes ancient esoteric concepts of optimal human functioning; all have a broad range of effects including, but not limited to, body/mind/spirit integration, personal growth, physical or emotional relaxation, and the relief of somatic pain or dysfunction.

STRUCTURAL/FUNCTIONAL/MOVEMENT INTEGRATION

The treatment of a human body using a wide variety of manipulative techniques to affect soft tissue (myofascial) or to reeducate the nervous and musculoskeletal systems towards more appropriate and balanced patterns of movement behavior and neuromuscular response. This approach is based upon disciplines that organize, balance, and integrate the body in relation to gravity as an end in itself, and that consequently may have a broad range of applications including, but not limited to, body/mind/spirit integration, personal growth, physical or emotional relaxation, and the relief of somatic pain or dysfunction.

ORIENTAL BODYWORK

The treatment of the human body—including the electromagnetic or energetic field that surrounds, infuses, and brings that body to life—by pressure and/or manipulation. This approach is based upon traditional Oriental medical principles used to assess and evaluate the energetic system, and upon traditional Oriental techniques and treatment strategies that primarily affect and balance the energetic systems as a

means to treat the body, emotions, mind, energy field, and spirit and thus to promote, maintain, and restore health.

ENERGETIC BODYWORK

The treatment of the human body, including the electromagnetic or energetic field which surrounds, infuses, and brings that body to life, by pressure and/or manipulation of the physical body, and the passage or placement of the hands in or through that energetic field. This approach, based upon Ayurvedic, Eastern and Western esoteric, modern therapeutic, or other recognized systems of healing, aims to assess, evaluate, and treat the human body, emotions, mind, energy field, and spirit, and thus promote, maintain, and restore health.

—This essay, reprinted from the Massage Therapy Journal *(Summer 1991), a quarterly publication of the American Massage Therapy Association, was written by staff of the National Certification Board for Therapeutic Massage and Bodywork.*

Associations
American Massage Therapy Association (AMTA)
820 Davis Street, Suite 100
Evanston, IL 60201-4444
(708) 864-0123

The AMTA is a professional membership and advocacy organization. It publishes a directory of approved training programs and the *Massage Therapy Journal.*

Associated Bodywork and Massage Professionals (ABMP)
38677 Buffalo Park Road
Evergreen, CO 80439-7347
(303) 674-8478

The ABMP is an international professional membership organization founded to provide massage and bodywork practitioners with services and information. ABMP members practice a wide variety of massage and bodywork styles, including shiatsu, Rolfing, Alexander, polarity therapy, Feldenkrais, Rosen, Trager, Hellerwork, and Aston-Patterning. It provides a touch training directory, which includes over 500 massage and bodywork schools and organizations worldwide.

Organizations
Care Through Touch Institute (CTI)
Center for Growth in Wholeness
2401 LeConte Avenue
Berkeley, CA 94709
(510) 548-0418
Programs: Certificate in massage and bodywork with sacramental and pastoral applications

CTI draws upon the sacramental dimensions of massage and is known for pioneering an embodied approach to Christian spirituality.

Commission on Massage Training Accreditation/Approval
1313 South East 5th Street, Suite 202
Minneapolis, MN 55414
(612) 379-3826

The commission, which accredits massage therapy training programs, is an administratively independent affiliate of AMTA.

National Certification Board for Bodywork and Massage Therapies (NCB)
P.O. Box 1080
Evanston, IL 60204-1080
(708) 864-0774

The NCB is an administratively independent affiliate of AMTA. In 1988 it initiated the development of a national certification program for massage and bodywork professionals.

Touch Research Institute (TRI)
University of Miami School of Medicine
P.O. Box 016820
Miami, FL 33101
(305) 547-6781

The TRI is the first center in the world for basic and applied research on touch. Its primary aim is to further knowledge regarding the biology of touch in health and development and its role in medicine and the treatment of disease. A multidisciplinary staff of scientists including Ph.D.s and M.D.s with backgrounds in medicine, biology, and psychology are engaged in numerous research projects, including alleviating autistic children's aversion to touch and facilitating mother-infant or caregiver-infant bonding with abused and neglected infants and children.

Periodicals
Journal of Soft Tissue Manipulation
Ontario Massage Therapist Association
950 Yonge Street, Suite 1007
Toronto, Ontario
Canada M4W2J4
(416) 968-6487
Semiannual; $48

Massage
Noah Publishing Company
P.O. Box 1500
Davis, CA 95617
(800) 533-4263
Bimonthly; $22

Massage and Bodywork Quarterly
Associated Bodywork and Massage
Professionals
Quarterly; $15

Massage Therapy Journal
3221 North Main Street
Rockford, IL 61103-3126
Quarterly; $20

Touch Therapy Times
Maryland Bodywork Reporter
13407 Tower Road
Thurmont, MD 21788-1407
(301) 271-4812
Monthly; $25

MOVEMENT THERAPY

While somatics always incorporates movement, the practice of movement therapy may not necessarily incorporate the principles and theory of somatics. Somatics curricula, for example, usually include some form of physical exercises; however, some movement therapy training programs (such as Anna Halprin's, the late Mary Whitehouse's, and Emilie Conrad-Da'oud's) emphasize only movement. It is also considered different from dance therapy, which is primarily employed as an expressive or creative art.

According to the International Movement Therapy Association, a movement therapist uses hands-on repatterning and verbal instruction to teach clients and students to recognize and improve psycho-physical and cognitive-motor movement patterns, as well as stress-related emotional conditions. Practitioners are often licensed in, and hold a degree from, a related field.

Associations
International Movement Therapy Association (IMTA)
P.O. Box 412
Piermont, NY 10968
(914) 353-0521
The IMTA is a nonprofit educational registry and advocacy organization. Accord-

ing to the IMTA's educational standards, graduates from the following programs fulfill all requirements for becoming a Registered Movement Therapist: Alexander Teacher Training, Feldenkrais Training, Bonnie Bainbridge Cohen's Body-Mind Centering, Rubenfeld's Synergy, Gerda Alexander's Eutony (of European origin), Jim Spira's Educational Therapy Training, Laban Institute of Movement Studies Certification, and Tamalpa Institute's Teacher Training programs. Contact the IMTA for recently approved programs, as well as a list of recommended (although not yet IMTA-registered) movement programs.

TRAINING PROGRAMS
Alexander Teacher Training
See Nondegree Somatic Therapies.

Bonnie Bainbridge Cohen's Body-Mind Centering
See Nondegree Somatic Therapies.

Continuum
1629 18th Street, Studio 7
Santa Monica, CA 90404
(310) 453-4402
Continuum was founded in 1967 by Emilie Conrad-Da'oud. A three-year certification program that encompasses body awareness, exercise for increasing longevity, and techniques for rehabilitation and healing is offered.

Feldenkrais Training
See Nondegree Somatic Therapies.

Laban/Bartenieff Institute of Movement Studies
11 East 4th Street
New York, NY 10003
(212) 477-4299
Based on the work of Rudolf Laban (1879-1958) and Irmgard Bartenieff (1900-1981), this certificate-granting institute was founded in 1978. According to the institute, Laban Movement is a theoretical framework and language for describing any movement, from a conversational hand gesture to a complex action. Certified Movement Analysts (CMA) observe, analyze, interpret, and prescribe movement experiences that value individual movement patterns; assess physical and dysfunctional blocks; and guide clients through healthy expressive and functional changes.

ROM Institute
3601 Memorial Drive
Madison, WI 53704
(608) 243-2451
Established in 1987 as a nonprofit organization, the institute provides instructor training, certification, and clearinghouse information on relaxation/pain management and personal health issues, including the ROM (Range of Motion) Dance, a holistic movement and relaxation program based on the principles of tai chi.

Rubenfeld Synergy
See Nondegree Somatic Therapies.

Tamalpa Institute
Teacher Training programs
See Nondegree and Postgraduate Training Programs.

NETWORK CHIROPRACTIC

Chiropractic was developed in the 1890s by Daniel David Palmer, who believed that pressure on the spinal nerves caused disease and that manipulation of spinal vertebrae could help lead to the cure. Donald Epstein, D.C., the creator of network chiropractic, developed this adjunct technique as an amalgamation of general chiropractic and a new method for releasing interference in the nervous system. Practitioners use light touch and taps rather than the more common aggressive manipulations associated with regular chiropractic. The subtle touch technique helps release the emotions of traumatic events—often leaving clients weeping, laughing, or shaking—thereby providing a focus on mental as well as physical health. According to the Association of Network Chiropractic (ANC), there are approximately 500 full-time network chiropractors in the United States and 1,000 who use it as an adjunct technique (compared with an estimated 39,000 general chiropractors nationwide).

Network chiropractors are certified through training modules offered by the Association of Network Chiropractors. In order to qualify for training, a person must be completing their first year of standard general chiropractic training (which generally takes four years to complete). Some insurance companies provide partial reimbursement for network chiropractic (under the title of chiropractor), and most network chiropractors charge about the same fee as general chiropractors.

Associations

American Chiropractic Association (ACA)
1701 Clarendon Boulevard
Arlington, VA 22209
(703) 276-8800

The ACA, a national nonprofit professional and membership organization, has more than 20,000 members and represents the majority of licensed chiropractors in the United States, including students of chiropractic.

Association for Network Chiropractic Spinal Analysis (ANCSA)
P.O. Box 7682
Longmont, CO 80501
(303) 678-8086

The ANCSA offers referrals and support through workshops, seminars, journals, and newsletters. It also provides training programs in network chiropractic. There are, at this time, only periodicals that represent general chiropractic.

Association for Network Chiropractors (ANC)
Innate Intelligence, Inc.
444 North Main Street
Longmont, CO 80501
(303) 678-8086

Contact the ANC for more information on network chiropractic, including a list of training modules and requirements.

International Chiropractors Association (ICA)
1110 North Glebe Road, Suite 1000
Arlington, VA 22201
(703) 528-5000

The ICA, founded by B. J. Palmer (the son of the founder of chiropractic, Daniel David Palmer) is the original association of chiropractors. The organization is primarily concerned with legislation, health-care policy, and public and interprofessional relations.

Organizations

World Chiropractic Alliance (WCA)
2950 North Dobson Road, Suite 1
Chandler, AZ 85224
(800) 347-1011

An international advocacy organization, WCA offers guidance and assistance to professionals and laypeople seeking chiropractic services.

World Chiropractic Federation (WCF)
3080 Young Street, Suite 3002
Toronto, Ontario
Canada M4A2N1
(416) 484-9978

This international federation unites chiropractic organizations around the world. It does not represent individual practitioners.

Periodicals

American Chiropractor
Busch Publishing
5005 Rivera Court
Fort Wayne, IN 46825
(219) 484-9600
Seven times a year; $56

Journal of Chiropractic
American Chiropractic Association
Monthly; $80 (nonmember)

Despite its title, this periodical is more a popular magazine than an academic journal.

Journal of the Neuromusculoskeletal System
American Chiropractic Association
Quarterly; $58

REICHIAN-ORIENTED THERAPIES

Before Wilhelm Reich, M.D., (1897-1957) began developing his ideas about sexology and the mind's relationship to the body during the 1920s, he served as the clinical assistant at Freud's Psychoanalytic Clinic in Vienna. Freud and his followers later vehemently rejected Reich's revisioning of psychoanalysis, which was then itself considered a radical form of therapy. Over the course of his lifetime, controversy followed Reich; his ideas about the connections between the mind and body were banned not only by the governments of Nazi Germany and the Soviet Union but by the United States as well. Reich died in 1957 in a United States federal prison, where he was incarcerated by the Food and Drug Administration for promoting a then-unorthodox approach to cancer treatment. He is buried at his home in Rangeley, Maine, also the location of the Friends of the Reich Museum.

Half a century later, we find that many of Reich's general theories have been incorporated into various alternative somatic therapies. For example, Reich coined the terms "sexual revolution" and "body armor"; developed the first body-centered psychotherapy, called vegetotherapy; described what would later be called subtle energies; and, perhaps most brilliantly, suggested that the body, like a sponge, holds emotional content. Much (but not all) of what has come to be recognized as the field of body-centered therapy may be traced to Reich's prolific writing. (Also see Body-Centered Psychotherapy.)

Although interest in Reich's work waned after his death, those directly associated with him—such as Elsworth Baker, Alexander Lowen, John Pierrakos, and Charles Kelley—eventually organized their own training programs in the United States (see below).

General Resources

Friends of the Reich Museum
P.O. Box 687
Rangeley, ME 04970
(207) 864-3443

Founded in 1959, the Friends of the Reich Museum offers educational programs on Reich's life and work, as well as an exhibit of his laboratory (where he tested his theory of orgone) and various inventions (such as the orgone accumulator). It also provides a bookstore of Reich's published work and makes his unpublished writing available to the public. The nonprofit museum is supported by the Wilhelm Reich Infant Trust, whose director, Mary Board Higgens, holds the copyright to all of Reich's published material.

General Periodicals

Energy and Character: The Journal of Biosynthesis
Abbotsbury Publications
Chesil, London WC1N 3XX
England
Semiannual; $32

This publication is a neo-Reichian journal.

BIOENERGETICS

Alexander Lowen, M.D., and John Pierrakos, M.D., cofounded the Institute of Bioenergetics in 1956 as a nonprofit organization. Dr. Lowen is known for making the practice of orgonomy (see medical orgonomy) less medically oriented and more accessible. In fact, while an orgonomist must be a physician, a bioenergetic therapist may be a psychologist or social worker. Lowen and Pierrakos also made a number of modifications to Reichian therapy, including a departure from Reich's sexual emphasis and a focus on how certain body exercises open up the body and enhance mental health functioning.

Training Programs
International Institute for Bioenergetic Analysis (IIBA)
144 East 36th Street
New York, NY 10016
(212) 532-7742

The institute is devoted to medical research and education in the analytic study of the form and movement of the body. The institute sponsors and directs approximately 45 affiliated bioenergetic societies that offer training in bioenergetic analysis. Societies are located in the United States, Canada, Europe, South America, and New Zealand. A typical curriculum consists of four years of part-time training, personal therapy, and a supervised internship. A certificate is awarded upon successful completion of the program.

Periodicals
Journal of the International Institute for Bioenergetic Analysis
International Institute for Bioenergetic Analysis
Annual; $8

CORE ENERGETICS

John Pierrakos, M.D., separated from Alexander Lowen (his cofounder of the Bioenergetic Institute) in the 1970s and founded Core Energetics with his wife, the late Eva Pierrakos, who was a trance channel. Core energetics is a depth psychology and body-centered psychotherapy that combines Reichian bodywork

with a spiritual discipline called the Pathwork. It also recognizes the body's energy system or aura as a tool for diagnosis as well as healing.

The technique is based on three main principles: The person is a psychosomatic unit; the source of healing lies within the self; and all of existence forms a unity that moves toward creative evolution. Training is grounded in the psychoanalytic concepts of child development, the laws of the unconscious, and especially in the dimensions of energy and consciousness applied to transformation on the physical, mental, emotional, and spiritual levels. However, it should be noted that the program is more focused on practicing therapy from a different perspective than on learning a specific technique. All trainees must have an established therapeutic practice before entering the program such as massage therapy, shiatsu, acupuncture, chiropractic, counseling, and Eastern and Western medicine.

Training is conducted in New York City and at the Institute of Core Energetics West in Mendocino, California. The program consists of infrequent meetings and takes up to four years to complete. There are also several training programs in Europe and one in Mexico.

—Staff from the Institute of Core Energetics West contributed to this introduction.

Training Programs
Institute of Core Energetics East (ICEE)
115 East 23rd Street
New York, NY 10010
(212) 982-9637

Institute of Core Energetics West (ICEW)
P.O. Box 806
Mendocino, CA 95460
(707) 937-1825

Periodicals
Journal of Core Energetics
Institute of Core Energetics
Semiannual; $25

MEDICAL ORGONOMY

Whereas Freud and his followers focused only on the meaning behind verbal content, Reich began moving away from the classical psychoanalytic theories of the 1920s by examining how individuals express, manifest, or suggest latent emotions through observable body movements. From these seminal theories, Reich developed vegetotherapy and its corresponding methodology, character analysis, which measures the health of an individual by observing the interplay of body movements, breathing patterns, and the freedom to express emotions. Later, Reich realized that health and illness are rooted in a delicate balance of a life force he called orgone, and that the related functions of the orgasm, or the ability to experience sexual release, must therefore play a vital role in healthy functioning. Thus, what had been called vegetotherapy evolved into orgonomy. Medical orgonomy, as it is now called, refers to the fact that practitioners who use it must possess a medical degree that includes a psychiatric specialization.

Training Programs
American College of Orgonomy (ACO)
P.O. Box 490
Princeton, NJ 08542
(908) 821-1144

Elsworth Baker founded the ACO with the goal of carrying on Reich's original work.

Orgone Biophysical Research Lab
Jane Demeo, M.D.
P.O. Box 1395
El Cerrito, CA 94530
(510) 526-5978

Periodicals
Annals of the Institute for Orgonomic Science
Box 304
Gwynned Valley, PA 19437
Correspondence offered only by mail.

Journal of Orgonomy
American College of Orgonomy
Semiannual; $40 year

ORGANISMIC PSYCHOTHERAPY

Organismic psychotherapy is concerned with the soul of the individual as it is uniquely expressed by his or her organism. Developed in Europe over the last 20 years by Malcolm and Katherine Ennis Brown, this body-centered psychotherapy weaves together American and European Reichian traditions. It is humanistic in outlook and draws its spiritual underpinnings from the work of Carl Jung, Carl Rogers, Ronald D. Laing, and Gestalt psychologist Kurt Goldstein.

Training Programs
Washington Institute for Body Psychotherapy
Barbara Goodrich Dunn, Director
911 Silver Spring Avenue, Suite 201
Silver Spring, MD 20910

Contact the institute for more information on emerging training programs in the United States.

RADIX

Radix is a body-oriented process involving both individual and group sessions. Developed by Charles Kelley, Ph.D., a student of Reich, and his wife, Erica, radix employs a direct, largely nonverbal approach to loosening muscular armor, resulting in increased emotional freedom. Heavily influenced by Kelley's principal teacher, Wilhelm Reich, the therapy (or educational process, according to radix philosophy) centers around Reich's concept of "orgone," which Kelley now calls "radix."

There are at least 200 radix teachers worldwide, working in Europe, Australia, and Canada, as well as the United States. Instruction involves correspondence, cassette training, and workshops with Kelley, and clinical instruction and supervision with a local radix teacher. Most trainees are mental-health professionals in a related field, but licensure is not required for admission to the program. A rift between Kelley and his students eventually led him to abandon the Radix Institute, which he founded, and

to open the Kelley/Radix Center in Vancouver, Washington.

Associations
Radix Teachers Association (RTA)
Radix Institute

The RTA is a professional and advocacy organization that certifies radix teachers.

Training Programs
Kelley/Radix Center
13715 S.E. 36th Street
Steamboat Landing
Vancouver, WA 98684
(206) 896-4004

Radix Institute
6300 Ridglea Place, Suite 1212
Fort Worth, TX 76116
(817) 738-3638

Periodicals
Journal of Radix Teachers Association
Radix Teachers Association
Linda Glenn, Editor
4 Redbud Drive
Conway, AR 72032
(501) 450-3193
Semiannual; $25

SOMATIC THERAPIES

Also see Don Johnson's essay on somatics, page 77.

The following subchapter represents established teaching centers in the somatics field, all of which provide training programs in the United States, and a central association from which prospective practitioners may request additional information. However, because some somatic methods are informally transmitted from teachers to students outside of a conventional institutional setting, we are unable to provide a comprehensive listing of all somatic techniques. For example, modalities of Eastern origin, such as the martial arts, have resisted standardization and rely heavily upon the student/teacher and disciple/master generational transmission of knowledge. Moreover, training within such unregulated traditions, as karate or aikido, varies as much as the number of masters providing the training. Students must seek out an individual teacher

rather than apply to an institution or training program.

Somatic disciplines that fit this category and provide an example of the field's rich diversity include aikido, Arica, Bowen System, Capoeria, judo, karate, Kung Fu, Lomi, postural integration, Oki yoga, Kundalini yoga, sensory awareness, tai chi (a form of Qigong), Touch For Health, and Trans Fiber. In addition, although we have placed the subtle-energy methods apart from other modalities, each somatic therapy, by its very holistic definition, incorporates some subtle-energy elements.

Nondegree somatic therapies tend not to be covered by third-party medical insurance, although, as with most nondegree modalities, practitioners with a mental-health or related state license may be able to incorporate a somatic therapy as an adjunct to their regular, insurance-reimbursable treatment.

WORK ENVIRONMENTS
Work environments for somatic therapists vary widely and include agencies, offices, clinics, and home visits, as well as group and private practice settings.

FEES
Fees vary according to the practitioner's reputation, as well as according to geography and other market variables. Check with beginning and experienced practitioners located in your area.

ACADEMIC STUDY VERSUS SOMATIC TRAINING PROGRAMS
Trends show that training in somatic therapy is beginning to follow the same model as clinical psychology training. This involves building a general foundation in graduate school before acquiring a more refined specialization from a certificate-granting, postgraduate training program. Rather than viewing these two education models as separate and exclusive, students are being encouraged to pursue both, perhaps concurrently.

As for choosing between a master's or a doctoral degree in somatics, students primarily interested in becoming a practitioner will need only a master's degree, while those interested in teaching and research will need a doctorate. Professionals in the somatics field also recommend garnering some introductory, hands-on experience in a certificate program before beginning a more theoretically oriented graduate program.

CHOOSING A SOMATIC THERAPY TO PRACTICE

You will notice that many, if not most, of the following modalities were developed by the person who either by personal or secondary experience discovered profound healing properties in the method which they now teach. Likewise, as you begin to investigate each practice, talk to various practitioners and experience for yourself, from the client's perspective, the therapies that interest you most.

General Associations

Association of Humanistic Psychology (AHP)
P.O. Box 3327
Saratoga, CA 95070
(414) 258-0635

Among the AHPs many activities and services, it sponsors an interest group called the Somatics Community.

Association International de Somato Therapie (AIST)
Tour Europe
20 Place Des Halles
67000 Strasberg
France

The AIST is an international somatic therapy organization.

General Organizations

The Federation
The Federation is currently comprised of five organizations: the Trager Institute, the American Polarity Therapy Association, the American Oriental Bodywork Therapy Association, the Rolf Institute, and the American Massage Therapists Association. The purpose of the Federation is to protect and advance the collective goals of somatic therapies. The Federation is interested in incorporating other mind-body therapies—such as subtle energy, bodywork, and body-centered psychotherapy—so long as the associations and training programs that represent them subscribe to a set of Federation standards.

SOMATIC THERAPIES: CERTIFICATION VERSUS LICENSURE

DURING THE 18TH AND 19TH CENTURIES, THERE WERE A DIVERSITY OF HEALING THERAPIES IN THE UNITED STATES, MANY OF WHICH WERE GROUNDED IN THE FOLK TRADITIONS OF IMMIgrants and Native Americans. Around the beginning of the 20th century, however, an effort to create a regulated health-care system emerged. Thus were the licensure, certification, and standard-setting organizations such as the American Medical Association (AMA), the American Psychological Association (APA), and the National Association of Social Workers (NASW) created. There were two significant consequences of this development: First, a rift was created between the accepted and the nonaccepted healing methods; second, the accepted methods became more conservative, homogeneous, and hierarchical, while the others, not being restricted by regulation, continued to diversify and develop rapidly. For example, chiropractic and osteopathy, which are both somatic therapies, are now licensed professions; and, while not denying the legitimacy that follows regulation in the form of licensure, many professionals contend that these professions have lost the creative and innovative edge that they originally possessed. Indeed, there are both benefits (e.g., accountability, training standards, societal recognition) and disadvantages to licensing professions.

Meanwhile, the future directions of somatics continue to be debated and discussed among the many somatic therapy groups. Five somatic modalities have formed an organization called the Federation, an advocacy group seeking standard state licensure. Others feel that certification provides enough regulation and consumer protection, and that licensure is therefore undesirable. Still others argue that regulation should be held in the hands of consumers (such as consumer protection agencies) rather than tendentious organizations such as the AMA, APA, and NASW.

Chiropractic, osteopathy, and acupuncture are the only somatic fields currently regulated by licensure. Certification is therefore the primary means by which a somatic practitioner's competency is publicly recognized. As a consequence, most somatic practitioners, who are usually trained through nondegree programs, find themselves ineligible for insurance reimbursement—except for certain instances having to do with the practitioner's additional credentials, the specific modality being employed, the client's diagnosis, and the policy unique to each insurance company or Health Maintenance Organization (HMO).

The Somatics Society
See page 68.

General Periodicals

Most of the training programs listed in this subchapter publish their own journals or newsletters for certified practitioners. The following publication, however, offers a broad overview of the somatics field.

Somatics: Magazine-Journal of the Mind/Body Arts and Sciences
Novato Institute for Somatic Research and Training
1516 Grant Avenue, Suite 212
Novato, CA 94945
(415) 892-0617
Semiannual; $20

ALEXANDER TECHNIQUE

Developed by Frederick Matthias Alexander, an actor and self-taught therapist, the Alexander Technique™ is an educational process that teaches improved use of the mind and body and helps users to identify and change poor and inefficient physical habits, such as posture, which may cause stress and fatigue. The North American Society of Teachers of the Alexander Technique provides a listing of 16 schools offering a three-year post-college program leading to teacher certification. Some practitioners are affiliated with universities (generally through theater arts and music programs), and most use the Alexander Technique as their primary modality in private practice. Insurance coverage is not available. Sessions (or more appropriately, lessons) last approximately 30 to 45 minutes; the average practitioner fee is $30 to $75 per lesson.

Periodicals

Alexander Journal
Society of Teachers of the Alexander Technique
20 London House, 266 Fulham Road
London SW10 9EL
England

Direction
P.O. Box 276
Bondi, New South Wales, Australia 2026
Semiannual; $35;

NASTAT News
Quarterly
  Contact the North American Society of Teachers of the Alexander Technique.

Training Programs

North American Society of Teachers of the Alexander Technique (NASTAT)
P.O. Box 112484
Tacoma, WA 98411-2484
(800) 473-0620
  The society is a nonprofit educational organization that establishes and maintains standards for the certification of teachers and teacher training courses. NASTAT is accredited by the Accrediting Council for Continuing Education and Training. Contact the society for a current list of approved programs and certified teachers.

ASTON-PATTERNING

Developed by Judith Aston in 1977, Aston-Patterning® is an integrated system of movement education, bodywork, and environmental evaluation. Through specifically designed sessions, the teacher and client work together to reveal and define an individual's posture and movement patterns while training the body to reclaim the natural, unstressed structure that lies beneath the layers of unnecessarily held tension. Sessions can include any one or a combination of the following: movement education, which teaches alternatives to stressful habits; massage-like bodywork, which relieves chronic physical and mental stress; and environmental consultation, which modifies the individual's surroundings to suit the body's needs.

  Many Aston-Patterners maintain private practices in which they assist a variety of clients, including athletes, dancers, the elderly, the disabled, and healthy individuals seeking structural and movement enhancement. Practitioners also work in physical therapy, pain management, sports medicine, biofeedback, chiropractic, and psychological and holistic health-care clinics. Sessions last from one to two hours; a primary practitioner's average fee is $50 to $75 per hour.

Training Programs

Aston-Patterning Training Center
P.O. Box 3568
Incline Village, NY 89450
(702) 831-8228
  The center offers basic courses in movement education, three-dimensional soft tissue work, environmental modification, and fitness training for professionals wishing to apply specific Aston concepts in their primary practice. The practitioner certification program (applicable to those who seek to practice Aston-Patterning as a primary technique) is done in five three-week segments over two years.

BENJAMIN TECHNIQUE

The Benjamin System of Muscular Therapy is a combination of treatment and education designed to reduce chronic muscle tension and to promote physical health. This system was created by Ben Benjamin, Ph.D., who founded the Muscular Therapy Institute in 1974. The therapy combines exercise, tension release, and body awareness techniques with an anatomically specific form of massage.

  The two-year core curriculum, designed by the Muscular Therapy Institute, allows students to continue their work while pursuing other forms of education. The training includes classroom coursework, clinical training, and field work. The complete program requires 1,200 hours of training, including 500 hours of practice development. Practitioners often use it as a primary technique.

—Staff from the Muscular Therapy Institute contributed to this introduction.

Training Programs

Muscular Therapy Institute (MTI)
122 Rindge Avenue
Cambridge, MA 02140
(617) 576-1300; (800) 543-4740 (outside Massachusetts)
  The MTI offers a two-year core curriculum and a one-year advanced training curriculum. MTI is licensed by the Commonwealth of Massachusetts's Department of Education and is approved by the American Massage Therapy Association's Commission on Massage Training and the Accreditation Commission for Continuing Education Training.

BODY-MIND CENTERING

Body-Mind Centering™ is a comprehensive educational and therapeutic approach to health and healing. Using a blend of movement, touch, sound, and guided imagery, practitioners help clients learn how to release stress, fear, aches, and pains. Practitioners use the technique independently, although it is often used as a complement to medical, chiropractic, psychotherapeutic, acupuncture, and other physical therapies.

Training Programs

Body-Mind Centering Association (BMCA)
16 Center Street, Suite 530
Northampton, MA 01060
(518) 329-0384

Founded in 1985 by Bonnie Bainbridge Cohen, the BMCA is a nonprofit association of certified teachers, practitioners, and advanced students dedicated to educating the public about Body-Mind Centering. Contact the association for a list of teachers.

School for Body-Mind Centering
189 Pondview Drive
Amherst, MA 01002
(413) 256-8615

The school offers ongoing training and certification under the direction of Bonnie Bainbridge Cohen.

CORE BODYWORK

Core Bodywork is a multiphase system of structural integration that is intended to improve physical alignment and flexibility, and promote optimal performance and self-reliance. Each of the four phases of Core Bodywork focuses on balancing progressively deeper layers of connective tissue and musculature. The technique is an outgrowth of Soma Bodywork.

Practitioners charge approximately $50 to $75 per session and work in alternative health clinics, physical therapy centers, sports/fitness centers, and in private practice.

Training Programs

Core Institute School of Massage Therapy and Structural Bodywork
223 West Carolina Street
Tallahassee, FL 32301
(904) 222-8673

The Core Institute was founded in 1990 in Tallahassee, Florida, by George P. Kousaleos and operates as a graduate training center in Core Bodywork, Core Massage, and Core Myofascial Therapy. The first two phases of Core Bodywork are taught in workshops throughout America and Europe. The final two phases, Core Intrinsic Therapy and Core Integration Therapy, are taught only at the institute in Florida. Combined into a practice, the four phases of training constitute eleven 90-minute sessions. Admission requirements include

licensure or certification in therapeutic massage or bodywork, a personal commitment to the wellness model, a well-rounded knowledge of anatomy and physiology, and an understanding of the importance of combining therapeutic, educational, and developmental techniques.

CRANIO-SACRAL THERAPY

Cranio-sacral therapy originates from the scientific discoveries made by two osteopaths, William Sutherland and John Upledger. According to the Upledger Institute, the cranio-sacral system is the environment in which the brain and spinal cord develop and function. (The term "cranio sacral" is used because the system extends down the spinal cord to the lower end of the spine, known as the sacral, and also involves bones from the skull, face, and mouth, called the cranium.) The rhythm of the system can be felt as clearly as the rhythms of the cardiovascular and respiratory systems; however, unlike these other two body rhythms, palpation is used not only to evaluate a patient's system but to treat the system's dysfunction as well. The therapy consists of evaluation and treatment of the craniosacral system using a gentle form of manipulation. When such movement testing is completed, the restricting obstacle is oftentimes freed, and the system is then said to be able to complete its "self-correction."

Cranio-sacral therapy is used as a complementary technique by a variety of health-care providers, including chiropractors, massage and bodywork therapists, nurses, and physicians.

Training Programs

Upledger Institute
11211 Prosperity Farms Road
Palm Beach Gardens, FL 33410
(407) 622-4334

Founded in 1985 by John Upledger, D.O., the institute is an educational and clinical research center that integrates naturopathic techniques with conventional and well-proven health-care methods. Programs include the six-level Cranio sacral therapy workshop series, as well as training in visceral manipulation, Zero Balancing,

muscle energy, fascial mobilization, applying acupuncture principles to bodywork, Process Acupressure, and Excellence by Design.

EYE MOVEMENT DESENSITIZATION REPROCESSING (EMDR)

EMDR is an interactive technique used by a variety of therapists. From the most basic standpoint, the method consists of asking clients to move their eyes back and forth (with head and body remaining steady), following a therapist's fingers which are rapidly moving from right to left in front of them. The method is said to accelerate the treatment of trauma related to both upsetting past events and present life conditions. According to Francine Shapiro, Ph.D., the founder of EMDR, a controlled study (primarily of Vietnam veterans and rape and sexual molestation victims) offered some evidence that EMDR aids in a rapid desensitization of traumatic memories, including a significant reduction in anxiety, intrusive thoughts, flashbacks, and nightmares. Still, further scientific research is needed to validate the efficacy of EMDR.

Because clinical training is necessary for the effective application of EMDR, training is limited to mental-health professionals who are licensed or certified to provide mental-health treatment. Over 4,000 therapists in America, Israel, and Australia have been trained in the technique. According to Dr. Shapiro, trainees from previous workshops have reported that they have incorporated the technique into modalities as diverse as behavioral therapy, Gestalt, Adlerian, Life Style Analysis, and psychodynamic. Body-centered psychotherapists also use the technique.

Training Programs

Eye Movement Desensitization Reprocessing Institute, Inc. (EMDR)
P.O. Box 51010
Pacific Grove, CA 93950-6010
(408) 372-3900

Workshops last two days and takes place throughout the United States.

FELDENKRAIS METHOD

Developed by Moshe Feldenkrais, an Israeli scientist, the Feldenkrais Method® combines movement training, gentle touch, and verbal dialogue to help people manifest freer, more efficient, comfortable, and healthy movement. The method utilizes aspects taken from neurophysiology, medicine, psychology, acupuncture, the martial arts, yoga, and other modalities. The goal is to create healthy behavioral patterns—thereby reducing stress, alleviating chronic pain, and honing coordination—all the while inhibiting destructive and limiting movements.

The Feldenkrais Method consists of two forms. In the first, called Functional Integration®, practitioners use their hands to guide individual clients to sense differences between habitually limited ways of moving. In the second, called Awareness Through Movement®, practitioners lead a group of clients through specific patterns of simple actions in order to discover new ways to move. Practitioners often use the method as a primary technique.

Training programs, resulting in certification, are held throughout the United States (as well as Canada, Israel, Australia, and Europe). Usually two to four programs begin in the United States each year and span a period of 38 to 46 months, eight weeks a year. A minimum of 800 hours of training over at least 160 days is required.

Training Programs
Feldenkrais Guild
P.O. Box 489
706 Ellsworth Street
Albany, OR 97321-0143
(800) 775-2118; (503) 926-0981
Contact the Feldenkrais Guild for a list of accredited training programs.

FOCUSING

Focusing, developed by Eugene Gendlin, Ph.D., in the early 1960s, is a six-step method for accessing inner body awareness and wisdom, or what Dr. Gendlin calls the "bodily felt sense." The method facilitates mind-body-spirit integration, which in turn helps promote healing. A variety of health-care and other professionals—athletes, bodyworkers, business people, clergy, coaches, educators, psychotherapists, social workers, and teachers—use focusing to enhance their work.

Training Programs
Focusing Institute
29 South La Salle Street, Suite 1195
Chicago, IL 60603
(312) 629-0500
Focusing is taught by the Focusing Institute, a nonprofit organization that can refer you to certified trainers throughout the United States and abroad. Training consists of five weekend workshops, during which basic focusing and empathic listening skills are taught. A certificate is awarded upon successful completion of the program. Additional training is available for prospective focusing teachers. The institute publishes a journal known as *Focusing Folio.*

HELLERWORK

Developed by Joseph Heller, an aerospace engineer who researched the effects of gravity on rockets, Hellerwork consists of deep massage, movement exercises, and verbal expression. The therapy is considered bodywork, not massage; while chiropractic focuses on the vertebrae and other bones, and Swedish massage on manipulating muscles, Hellerwork (like Rolfing, its cousin) focuses on the body's connective tissue, the link between the muscle and the bone. Hellerwork is similar to the Feldenkrais Method of body and mind reorientation in that it restructures both physical and mental patterns.

Training Programs
Hellerwork
406 Berry Street
Mount Shasta, CA 96067
(800) 393-3900
The Hellerwork practitioner certification program requires 1,250 hours of training. Contact the organization for a geographical listing of practitioners and training programs.

INTERDISCIPLINARY/NONDEGREE SOMATIC THERAPY TRAINING

Body Therapy Institute
P.O. Box 202
Saxapahaw, NC 27340
(910) 376-9696
Programs: Graduate level program in somatic therapy
Founded in 1983, the school is licensed by the North Carolina Department of Community Colleges and is approved by the American Massage Therapy Association and the Florida Board of Massage.

Center for Energetic Studies
2045 Francisco Street
Berkeley, CA 94709
(415) 526-8373
The center offers personal and professional education in somatic therapy. Focus is on the body and its connection to the emotional and imaginative aspects of the human experience.

Heartwood Institute
220 Harmony Lane
Garberville, CA 95542
(707) 923-2021
Programs: Breathwork; hypnotherapy; massage and bodywork therapy; polarity; Zen shiatsu acupressure
See also Retreat Centers, Addiction Counseling, and Nondegree Training Programs.

International Academy of Massage Science
The Well-Person Place
P.O. Box 277
Glen Riddle, PA 19037
(215) 558-3140
Programs: Training in a variety of body-oriented therapies

Somatic Institute, Pittsburgh
8600 West Barkhurst Drive
Pittsburgh, PA 15237
(412) 366-5580
The institute provides training in Core-Somatics®, a comprehensive psychophysical-psychospiritual healing modality created by founding director Kay Miller. This synergistic approach uses myth and ritual for renewed self-understanding and for achieving self-actualization. It combines the neuromuscular re-education therapies of the Alexander Technique with the expressive arts, Jungian depth psychology, and Gestalt therapy. The institute offers a two-year professional certification program.

Twin Lakes College of the Healing Arts
1210 Brommer Street
Santa Cruz, CA 95062
(408) 476-2152

Twin Lakes offers various training programs including, but not limited to, massage therapy, shiatsu, Acupressure, and Oriental and Ayurvedic massage.

KINESIOLOGY

Applied kinesiology was founded in 1964 by George Goodheart, D.C., a chiropractor proficient in meridian therapy, osteopathic cranial technique, and nutrition. The therapy is described by the International College of Applied Kinesiology as "a system that evaluates our structural, chemical, and mental aspects by employing muscle testing with other standard methods of diagnosis." In addition, nutrition, body manipulation, diet, acupressure, exercise, and education are used to help restore balance and maintain well-being. During assessment, the applied kinesiologist individualizes each diagnosis and treatment, and determines which therapy, or which combination of therapies, will be most effective for each patient. By properly matching the patient's condition with the most effective therapy, applied kinesiology provides a "best fit algorithm," creating the possibility of higher rates of effectiveness in treating illness.

Because part of the kinesiologist's role is to diagnose (according to regulations set by each state), practitioners must be licensed in a medical discipline. It therefore requires more education than the Feldenkrais Method, which is similar but does not incorporate diagnosis. Most practitioners are chiropractors; some are naturopathic or allopathic doctors, osteopaths, or dentists. All use kinesiology as a complementary technique only. Nurses are generally excluded from practice if they do not have the necessary amount of training hours required for diagnostic licensure.

Periodicals
Applied Kinesiology Review
Contact the International College of Applied Kinesiology

Training Programs
International College of Applied Kinesiology (ICAK)
Resonant Kinesiology Training Program
P.O. Box 905
Lawrence, KS 66044-0905
(913) 542-1801

The ICAK provides a clinical and academic arena for investigating, substantiating, and propagating the aspects of applied kinesiology that are pertinent to the relationships among structural, chemical, and mental factors in health and disease and to the relationship between structural faults and the disruption of homeostasis exhibited in illness. The college supports the Foundation for Allied Conservative Therapies, a research organization dedicated to evaluating the clinical efficacy of applied kinesiology. The college certifies diplomates—who in turn offer a 100-hour kinesiology training program to qualified health providers—in the United States and Europe. Contact the college for a current schedule.

Resonant Kinesiology Training Program
41 Main Street
Burlington, VT 05401
(802) 860-2814

Resonant kinesiology is a style of body-mind work based on the educational rather than the medical model. A resonant kinesiologist serves as a resourceful participant in a client's learning by the use of touch, sound, and movement, which evoke growth and healing. Practitioners need not be medically trained. Founded in 1989, the training program is offered in two formats: a one-year workshop series for health professionals and a more in-depth two-year program entitling a graduate to practice resonant kinesiology independently.

REBIRTHING

Originated by Leonard Orr, rebirthing (also known as "conscious connected breathing" and "energy breathing") is a simple form of gentle breathing that stimulates repressed thoughts and feelings related to an individual's birth, family, and sexual history. As with Holotropic Breathwork, this type of breathing

stimulates and brings to consciousness suppressed (and therefore unresolved) emotional trauma from an individual's past. In addition, affirmations help clients release negative thought patterns while simultaneously stimulating more healthy ones. During most sessions, clients follow a specific breathing regime while the practitioner supportively supervises.

Sessions are typically done on a one-on-one basis. More advanced forms include hot and cold water rebirths, eye gaze, and group sessions. The technique is used worldwide by a variety of healers, including self-employed mental-health professionals, nurses, and midwives. The therapy is used independently and as an adjunct technique (often combined with integrative therapy, massage, and energy work). Training programs include weekend workshops or (if you are geographically restricted) instruction given by a certified rebirther from your area.

—Mike Phelps, a rebirther, contributed to this introduction.

Training Programs
Each of the following three organizations offers slightly different training styles in rebirthing. All of them can provide a list of teachers who practice in different regions of the United States. Contact each for more specific information.

Life Is Here International
Route 1, Box 12A
Afton, VA 22920
(703) 456-8655

Loving Relationships Training (LRT)
P.O. Box 1465
Washington, CT 06793
(800) 468-5578
LRT was developed by Sondra Ray.

Rebirth International
Philadelphia Rebirthing Center
1027 69th Avenue
Philadelphia, PA 19126
(215) 424-4444

REFLEXOLOGY

First established by William H. Fitzgerald, a physician at the turn of the century, and later developed by Eunice D. Ingham in the early 1930s, reflexology is a science based on the observation that parts of the exterior body correspond to all of the glands, organs, and internal parts of the body. Reflexology maps the body into zones (as does acupuncture) and concentrates on the massage of the foot, which is considered a microcosm of the entire body. It is considered a form of bodywork similar to acupressure (in fact, foot charts used by practitioners of reflexology are virtually identical to those used in acupressure text books), and is especially useful in reducing stress-related disorders.

Reflexology is used most by holistic health practitioners, including some who are licensed in another modality. A reflexologist charges $20 to $30 per treatment.

Training Programs

International Institute of Reflexology (IIR)
5650 First Avenue North
P.O. Box 12642
St. Petersburg, FL 33733
(813) 343-4811
Founded in 1974 by Eunice Ingham's nephew, the institute offers two-day seminars and a certification program. Despite the institute's disapproval, some graduates of IIR programs have formed their own private training programs.

ROLFING

Rolfing is a type of structural integration and form of bodywork developed by Ida Rolf. The technique involves applying deep hands-on pressure to loosen the fascia (the connective tissue surrounding and penetrating the muscles), which ultimately enables the body to properly restructure itself. Research conducted at the University of California, Los Angeles, and the University of Maryland offers evidence that Rolfing creates a more efficient use of the muscles, thereby allowing the body to conserve energy, reduce chronic stress, and alter the body structure.

Following Ida Rolf's long-term relationship with the Esalen Institute in the 1960s, she established the Guild for Structural Integration (now the Rolf Institute of Structural Integration) in 1970; by 1979, more than 200 Rolfers were practicing across the United States.

The basic training program lasts approximately two years and leads to a certificate in Rolfing. Many Rolfers pursue additional certification as an advanced Rolfer, which permits them to teach Rolfing movement integration. The majority of practitioners work for themselves; however, a few work with other health-care providers in hospitals and rehabilitation centers. Treatments are generally given in ten 60-minute sessions, and practitioners charge from $60 to $100 per session.

Training Programs

Rolf Institute of Structural Integration
P.O. Box 1868
Boulder, CO 80306
(303) 449-5903; (800) 530-8875
The Rolf Institute provides Rolfing training and continuing education workshops. It also acts as a membership and advocacy organization. Prospective candidates must have a college degree and be a member of the American Massage Therapy Association, or equivalent. The institute publishes a Rolfing Training School Catalog ($2.50). Training is also available in Canada, Europe, Brazil, Australia, and Japan.

ROSEN METHOD

The Rosen Method™ developed by Marion Rosen uses gentle, nonintrusive touch to invoke relaxation. The technique consists of touching tense muscles with equal pressure applied by the practitioner. As muscles relax and the breath deepens, feelings, attitudes, and memories held in the body begin to surface. Together, the practitioner and client talk about what is happening in the body during the client's experience. Although this method may seem like a body-centered psychotherapy, it is considered by its founder to be more a form of bodywork than a type of psychotherapy.

Training Programs

Rosen Center
5337 College Avenue, Suite 255
Oakland, CA 94618
(510) 653-9113
Founded in 1983, the center offers a four-year, 350-hour certificate training program.

SPECIFIC HUMAN ENERGY NEXUS THERAPY (SHEN)

SHEN℠ is a physio-emotional release therapy consisting of gentle touch on or near the body. SHEN practitioners are trained to work with the emotional energy field (also called the chi field, or the biofield) that is said to both permeate and surround the physical body. This field is involved in the production of sensations we call emotions. The chi field, then, can be a major factor in emotional dysfunction and contributes to those disorders often called psychosomatic or physio-emotional. The SHEN practitioner works to unlock the effects of contractility and to release debilitating emotions, particularly those held traumatic emotions that affect either psychological or physical functioning. SHEN therapy is an energy field intervention, or "energybody" work, and is considered by its practitioners to be different from traditional bodywork.

The association trains and certifies all SHEN practitioners. A small number of health-care providers use SHEN as their primary technique, but others (including nurses, psychotherapists, counselors, physical and occupational therapists, massage therapists, deep tissue workers, and physicians) use it to augment and accelerate conventional Western medical and psychological treatments and approaches.

Training Programs

International SHEN Therapy Association
P.O. Box 801
Edmonds, WA 98020
(206) 542-6199
Founded by Richard Pavek, the association holds SHEN Training Intensives in the United States, Canada, and Europe. There are three levels of training, including the

Certified SHEN Practitioner Internship Program. Training is open to laypeople and professionals.

SOMA BODYWORK

The word soma is derived from ancient Greek and refers to the integration of the body, mind, and spirit, or the totality of being. Founded by Bill Williams, Ph.D., and Ellen Gregory, Ph.D., in 1978, soma bodywork is a neuromuscular body-mind therapy that structurally balances the body while integrating the nervous system. Changes in structure are accomplished primarily through the manipulation of fascia (connective tissue) and muscles, while neurological work is done on both physiological and psychological levels. It is less intrusive and more focused on psychosomatic issues than Rolfing, and it does not treat symptoms per se but works with the entire human system so that, through proper alignment, the body structure becomes more disease-resistant and functions more appropriately.

People with conditions such as chronic back pain, arthritis, asthma, scoliosis, and headaches, as well as those with physically taxing careers, such as athletes and dancers, find the therapy helpful. Most practitioners use it as a primary modality, and many have counseling backgrounds.

Training Programs
Soma Institute
730 Klink Street
Buckley, WA 98321
(206) 829-1025
The Soma Institute provides training in somatic education and bodywork leading to certification; licensure is available in Washington State. There are associations of practitioners in Washington and Florida. The soma training program is considered more experiential than the Rolfing program.

SOMATOSYNTHESIS

Somatosynthesis, developed by Clyde W. Ford, D.C., a chiropractor and therapist, is an integrated body-based therapy that employs the tools of somatic therapy (touch, movement, and body awareness) to promote physical, emotional, and spiritual health. The technique seeks to guide an individual to deeper levels of meaning, including emotional barriers that limit full expression. It is often used to help address post-traumatic disorders following sexual, physical, and emotional abuse.

Somatosynthesis draws on Western and non-Western healing traditions. Beside encompassing teachings from the spiritual and healing traditions of Africa and the East, the therapy's philosophy is based on theories developed by William James, Roberto Assagioli, Carl Jung, Wilhelm Reich, Milton Erickson, and Daniel Palmer. Somatosynthesis is employed by a variety of healing arts practitioners including chiropractors, physicians, psychotherapists, and massage therapists.

—*The staff at the Institute for Somatosynthesis Training and Research contributed to this introduction.*

Training Programs
Institute for Somatosynthesis Training and Research
P.O. Box 3056
Bellingham, WA 98227
(206) 398-9355
Training is conducted through two-day and week- and year-long workshops held throughout the United States and Europe.

TRAGER

Developed by Milton Trager, M.D., psychophysical integration (popularly called Trager work) is a form of bodywork aimed at loosening restrictions in the joints. A Trager practitioner uses gentle, nonintrusive movements to reach and release the psychic roots of physical restrictions, facilitating deep relaxation, increased mobility, and mental clarity. In order to show that effortless movement is possible without the aid of a practitioner, clients are taught a series of dance-like movements called mentastics following each session. People in fields as disparate as massage and bodywork, sports, education, and the performing arts learn and practice Trager.

The Trager Institute, founded in 1980, offers a six-month certification program. Training consists of a six-day beginning, a five-day intermediate, and a six-day anatomy and physiology program. Elective courses are also offered to meet continuing education requirements. Instruction is given in selected areas around the United States, Canada, and Europe.

Training Programs
Trager Institute
33 Millwood
Mill Valley, CA 94941-2091
(415) 388-2688
The Trager Institute provides the certification program in Trager psychophysical integration and mentastics movement education. Training is conducted throughout North America and Europe. The Trager Institute is accredited by the California Nursing Continuing Education Board and the Florida State Massage Board.

TRIGGER POINT MYOTHERAPY

Myotherapy evolved in the late 1970s from Trigger Point Injection therapy, which was developed by Janet Travell, M.D., a professor of pharmacology at the George Washington University Medical School. As a noninvasive, hands-on therapeutic program for the relief and control of dysfunction and myofascial pain(myo meaning "muscle"; fascial, "muscle covering"), myotherapy has since been established as an effective independent therapy.

A trigger point is a hyperirritable area within a taut band of muscle found only (it is currently presumed) in people who have suffered from muscle injuries. The therapy consists of identifying perpetuating factors (e.g., vitamin deficiencies, improper alignment, or anatomical problems); employing myo-massage and passive stretch techniques, including the placement of direct pressure on trigger points; and teaching corrective stretching exercises to clients.

There is an implicit connection between techniques used in trigger point myotherapy and Eastern therapeutic traditions such as acupressure and shiatsu. They differ, however, in that myotherapy is based on the medical model and investigates predisposing factors to illness as part of its treatment program. For this reason, myotherapy is best suited for rehabilitation and injury patients.

Myotherapists are knowledgeable in the areas of musculoskeletal anatomy, kinesiology, and stretch/corrective exercise. However, because they are not medical diagnosticians, myotherapists must rely on medical referrals given by a state licensed physician, chiropractor, or dentist before beginning a treatment plan.

Practitioners work in a range of settings, including hospitals and pain clinics, and with private practice physicians. They receive third-party insurance when they are physician-referred; they charge anywhere from $40 to $150 per hour, depending on the experience and geographic location.

Training Programs

National Association of Trigger Point Myotherapists (NATPM)
Richard Finn, C.T.P.M., President
1675 Genoa Street
Aurora, CO 80011
(303) 367-9368

The National Association of Trigger Point Myotherapists certifies individuals and also, in a constant and understandable desire to advance the field, seeks the establishment of licensure. The NATPM certifies practitioners upon completing a two-year training program and passing a national exam (Certified Trigger Point Myotherapist, C.T.P.M.). Prerequisites include a background in anatomy, physiology, nutrition, and psychology. The association also publishes a directory of training programs and a journal.

Trigger Point Myotherapists National Certification Board
Professional Testing Corporation
1211 Avenue of the Americas, 15th Floor
New York, NY 10036
(212) 852-0400

YOGA THERAPY

As spiritual practices become increasingly recognized for their transformative and healing properties, yoga continues to find increasing acceptance within mainstream therapies. For example, recent research studies have successfully incorporated yoga postures or meditation into programs for treating such ailments as coronary artery disease and asthma. In addition, the National Institutes of Health have recently funded research on whether yoga breathing techniques reduce symptoms of obsessive-compulsive disorders and whether weekly yoga sessions help addicts enrolled in a methadone treatment program.

Different systems of yoga, and the beliefs associated with them, are as varied as human nature itself. The same goes for the variety of yoga traditions taught in the United States, each offering an idiosyncratic philosophy, practice, and goal. Some traditions focus on yoga's religious and mystical aspects, others emphasize secular, practical ends like fitness; still others focus on the breath, seated meditation, chanting, or devotional practices. While the pursuit of any method of yoga should challenge its practitioner, beginning students should seek an approach that is basically compatible with their worldview. A person who tends to be hyperactive may have difficulty with methods that emphasize stillness, while a person who dislikes physical movement may find methods that emphasize rigorous physical exercise equally incompatible. Hence, the first step for an aspiring student is to explore different traditions of yoga, seeking one with which he or she resonates and feels both philosophically and physically comfortable.

Common to all traditions of yoga, however, is an emphasis on personal practice. One does not become a teacher of yoga, or a yoga therapist, without first becoming a yoga practitioner. A part of any training program should always emphasize the continua-

tion of personal experience. The aspiring teacher is well advised to avoid programs that advertise: "Learn to teach yoga in a weekend! No prior experience of yoga required!" Likewise, instructors who state that yoga practice is good for their students, but no longer necessary for them, are likely to be held in low regard by their peers.

Because most experienced teachers see their yoga classes (by the very definition of yoga) as therapeutic, and because many work one-on-one with at least some clients, it is not surprising that some training programs explicitly refer to their work as "yoga therapy" rather than just the practice of yoga. A main difference in this approach is the incorporation of verbal dialogue, which often addresses mind-body ailments, during individual sessions.

There are a number of regional yoga associations around the United States providing yoga teachers with informative seminars and a chance to hone their skills. These same associations are considering the establishment of an accrediting body that would issue a teaching certificate.

—Carol Cavanaugh, who has developed curricula for yoga teacher training courses since 1978 and has trained yoga teachers since 1984, contributed to this introduction.

Associations

California Yoga Teachers Association
Yoga Journal
2054 University Avenue, Suite 302
Berkeley, CA 94704
(510) 841-9200

International Association of Yoga Therapy
Larry Payne, President
4150 Tivoli Avenue
Los Angeles, CA 90066
(310) 306-8845

Contact the association for a listing of yoga therapy training programs.

Iyengar Yoga Association of the United States
P.O. Box 603
Pine Valley, CA 91962
Correspondence offered only by mail.

Contact the association for a list of yoga teachers certified to teach this method.

New York Yoga Association (NYYA)
Unity in Yoga
Leslie Kaminoff
151 First Avenue, Suite 92
New York, NY 10003
(212) 420-9642

Organizations
Integral Yoga International
Route 1, Box 1720
Buckingham, VA 23921
(804) 969-4925

The goal of Integral Yoga is to assist individual's in realizing the spiritual unity behind the diversity in creation and in living harmoniously as members of one universal family. There are over 40 Integral Yoga Institutes and Integral Yoga Teaching Centers throughout the United States offering classes, workshops, and retreats in hatha yoga, meditation, nutrition, and stress reduction. Teacher training programs in hatha yoga, meditation, and raja yoga are offered regularly.

Yoga Research Society (YRS)
341 Fitzwater Street
Philadelphia, PA 19147
Correspondence offered only by mail.
The YRS encourages research in yoga and holds an annual conference.

Periodicals
Holistic Health Directory
New Age Journal
42 Pleasant Street
Watertown, MA 02172-2333
(617) 926-0200

Journal of the International
Association of Yoga Therapy
International Association of Yoga Therapy
Annual; $12.50

Yoga International Magazine
Himalayan International Institute
R.R. 1, Box 407
Honesdale, PA 18431
(717) 253-6241
Bimonthly; $15
Published by the Himalayan International Institute, this magazine offers essays and instruction regarding the practice of yoga.

Yoga Journal
2054 University Avenue, Suite 302
Berkeley, CA 94704
(510) 841-9200
Bimonthly; $18
Founded in 1975 by the California Yoga Teachers Association as a newsletter for yoga teachers, this magazine defines yoga as practices that aspire to union or communion with some higher power, greater truth, or deeper source of wisdom, as well as practices that tend to increase harmony of body, mind, and spirit. The focus is on mind-body approaches to personal and spiritual development, which include, other than hatha yoga, holistic healing, transpersonal psychology, bodywork and massage, the martial arts, Eastern spirituality, and Western mysticism. Its annual July/August issue includes a yoga teacher directory.

Training Programs
Himalayan International Institute
R.R. 1, Box 400
Honesdale, PA 18431
(800) 822-4547

Founded by Swami Rama, the institute offers a hatha yoga teachers' training program and publishes books on holistic health topics.

Integrative Yoga Therapy
305 Vista de Valle
Mill Valley, CA 94941
(415) 388-6569

This six-month program culminates in a Yoga Therapist certificate.

International Association of Yoga Therapy
See above.

Iyengar Yoga Institute of San Francisco
2404 27th Avenue
San Francisco, CA 94116
(415) 753-0909

Since 1975, the institute has conducted the nation's only two-year, state-certified training program for yoga teachers. The Iyengar method is known as being a strict and precise method of hatha yoga.

Kripalu Center for Yoga and Health
Box 793
Lenox, MA 01240
(800) 967-3577

The center was founded by yoga master Amrit Desai and is now the largest residential, holistic health educational facility in North America. The center offers month-long training programs emphasizing asanas (yoga postures) and personal growth, and recently held a symposium on yoga and psychotherapy.

Kripalu Center for Yoga, Meditation, and Personal Growth
2109 Walters Road
Sunnytown, PA 18084-0250
(215) 234-4568

This center offers programs in yoga therapy.

Mount Madonna Center
445 Summit Road
Watsonville, CA 95076
(408) 722-7175

The center offers yoga teacher training in Ashtanga yoga, taught by Baba Hari Dass and his students.

Phoenix Rising Yoga Therapy (PRYT)
P.O. Box 819
Housatonic, MA 01236
(800) 288-9642

Phoenix Rising yoga therapy is an integrated system of supporting and holding the body in positions based on classic yoga postures. Practitioners use verbal dialogue techniques in order to create conscious awareness, which in turn allows for the release of both physical and emotional tension. The PRYT offers a three-level certificate program in yoga therapy. College credit is available. Contact PRYT for a nationwide list of certified practitioners.

Yoga Institute
Prabhat Colony, Santa Cruz East
Bombay 400 055
India

Founded in 1918, the institute offers ongoing camps and training programs for teachers and students.

ZERO BALANCING
When a client commented after a session, "I feel so well balanced, like I'm zero, zero balanced," osteopath and acupuncturist Fritz Frederick Smith, M.D., decided to call his technique Zero Balancing. A synthesis of Western medicine, osteopathy, and Eastern theories of body energy including acupuncture, tai chi and yoga, Zero Balancing uses gentle manipulative techniques, such as touch and pressure, as well as movement to encourage the smooth flow of body energy and to enhance the body's own healing potential. Clients report feelings of well-being, harmony, a deep-

er connection with life, and a renewed sense of being centered and grounded.

Zero Balancing is not a system of therapy per se but rather a series of specific principles and skills based on Eastern and Western beliefs, which are used as an adjunct treatment in various healing professions. How it is specifically used depends on a therapist's training and type of licensure. Some use it in formal sessions, concentrating on improving the balance between body energy and structure; others incorporate its concepts into other specialty areas such as bodywork and acupuncture.

Like most of the somatic therapies listed in this guide, Zero Balancing is not a separately licensed therapy. Health-care professionals must practice such therapies through their licensed title (e.g., massage therapists, acupuncturists, etc.).

Training Programs
Zero Balancing Association
P.O. Box 1727
Capitola, CA 95010
(408) 476-0655

A certificate program is taught through the association, which requires a minimum of four levels of instruction given intermittently over a two- to three-year period.

SUBTLE ENERGY THERAPIES
Although the editors categorize polarity, Qigong, Reiki, and therapeutic touch as subtle-energy methods separate from other mind-body modalities listed in this section, it is important to remember that every somatic therapy, by its very holistic definition, implicitly recognizes many of the scientific principles developed from subtle energy research.

A subtle energy is described as a life force that "flows" through the body and psyche and that may be redirected by various mind-body techniques (most of them spiritually based); some have been practiced for thousands of years, like Qigong. Activating this energy, which is considered inherently therapeutic, gives rise not only to nonordinary states of consciousness but also to specific measurable psychophysiological responses.

A newly emerging field known as energy medicine examines subtle-energy phenomena such as self-regulation or other energy couplings between the mind and body. It has been documented, for example, that individuals are capable of generating and controlling electric forces that seem to influence their physiological and psychic systems. Conversely, low-level changes in magnetic, electric, electromagnetic, acoustic, and gravitational fields often have profound effects on both biological and psychic functioning, suggesting that energy emitted from the environment influences humans and animals in a variety of ways.

Just as it is difficult to measure subtle energy, it is also difficult to locate it within our current scientific paradigm. These energies have nevertheless been named and described by a host of divergent cultures, each with its own lexicon: chi, prana, ruach, ha, fohat, mana, etheric energy, orgone, odic force, and homeopathic resonance are just some examples. It is also recognized that Qigong, polarity, Reiki, and therapeutic touch, which are both new and old therapies, work with these same energies.

Some religious traditions, particularly of the East, believe that expansions of consciousness are related to changes in subtle energies, but this relationship remains open to question. The most advanced research in the field, which is taking place at the Menninger Foundation in Topeka, Kansas, suggests that subtle energies may not be part of the known physical fields as we understand them. It is hoped that through a better comprehension of subtle energies, both for therapeutic purposes and for the study of human potential, this emerging field of research will help reveal undiscovered depths of body, mind, and spirit interconnectedness while providing a much-needed bridge between modern science and the transpersonal dimensions of life.

Organizations
International Society for the Study of Subtle Energies and Energy Medicine (ISSSEEM)
256 Goldco Circle
Golden, CO 80401
(303) 278-2228

Organized in 1989 under the leadership of Elmer Green, Ph.D., of the Menninger Foundation, the purpose of ISSSEEM is to encourage the investigation of alternative medical practices, with the ultimate goal of integrating validated alternative medical practices into current conventional medical procedures. The society is concerned with the study of "informational systems and energies that interact with the human psyche and physiology, either enhancing or perturbing healthy homeostasis." ISSSEEM holds an annual conference and publishes *Subtle Energies: An Interdisciplinary Journal of Energetic and Informational Interactions*.

Periodicals
Bridges
Contact ISSSEEM.

Qi: The Journal of Traditional Eastern Health and Fitness
Insight Graphics, Inc.
P.O. Box 221343
Chantilly, VA 22022
(703) 378-3859; (800) 787-2600
Quarterly; $18.95
Contact ISSSEEM.

POLARITY THERAPY
Founded at the turn of the century by R. Stone, D.O., polarity therapy is a comprehensive set of methods based on the existence of human energy fields, which are believed to have a spiritual, emotional, and physical component. Many of these methods draw on the philosophy of Eastern somatic therapies such as Qigong and shiatsu. Polarity therapy's approach differs from acupressure and trigger point myotherapy, however, in that it integrates bodywork (its primary focus) with counseling, nutrition, and an exercise program.

Most polarity therapists are licensed or certified in some other discipline. They can be found working in private practice and counseling centers, and with physicians and chiropractors. There are two certification levels: the Associate

Practitioner of Polarity, which allows professionals in other fields to use polarity as a complementary technique; and the Registered Practitioner of Polarity, a more advanced form of certification enabling practitioners to use polarity as a primary technique. Both certificates require classes and hands-on experience. Polarity therapists charge from $35 to $75 an hour.

Associations
American Polarity Therapy Association (APTA)
2888 Bluff Street, Suite 149
Boulder, CO 80301
(303) 545-2080
The APTA provides a list of over 20 accredited training programs in the United States.

Periodicals
Energy
Quarterly; $50
Contact the APTA.

QIGONG (CHI KUNG)
According to historical records, some methods of Qigong (pronounced CHI-kung) have been practiced for at least 5,000 years, making it one of the oldest known therapies in the world. Qigong is the art and science of using breath, movement, and meditation to cleanse, strengthen, and circulate the life energy (called qi or chi). It produces effects that are similar to acupuncture but without the use of needles.

A Qigong teacher assesses the needs of the student and suggests particular movements, postures, breath practices, and meditation techniques that will assist the individual in self-healing or improving personal performance. This highly refined fitness system is similar to tai chi (a type of Qigong), except that most Qigong methods have fewer movements, are not martial arts oriented, and are focused on internal rather than external chi development.

A more advanced form of Qigong called external healing is used to assist the healing of others. This systematic technique includes the assessment of

chi in the patient or client and the subsequent projection of the practitioner's life energy through the fingers using gentle touch or noncontact treatment. The goal is to bring the chi energy of the recipient to a state of balance and health. When appropriate, the patient or client is typically taught how to perform Qigong techniques independent of a practitioner

In China, where the method has a long history, almost every hospital (including those geared to both Oriental medicine and Western approaches) sponsors a Qigong program. There are major Qigong research centers sponsored by the government health-care system in every major city, and it is estimated that over 100 million people practice Qigong daily. Meanwhile, American hospitals and community education programs have recently begun offering gentle forms of exercise (similar to Qigong) as part of their increasing attention to health maintenance. The National Institutes of Health, through the Office of Alternative Medicine, is currently researching the efficacy of Qigong for use in the West.

There are only a few training programs in the United States, most of which are informal. While there is no clearinghouse unifying practitioners, teachers, and training institutes, many American Qigong practitioners nevertheless claim that it is only a matter of time before the mainstream American health-care system discovers the benefits of Qigong. The technique is already being discussed in medical literature as a "self-applied health enhancement method," as is yoga and other noninvasive systems of health enrichment. In addition to the few training programs listed below, conference and retreat centers are beginning to offer Qigong workshops, as are individual practitioners.

—Ken Cohen, M.A., Ching Lee, Ph.D., and Roger Jahnke, O.M.D., all Qigong practitioners, contributed to this introduction.

Periodicals
Qi: The Journal of Traditional Eastern Health and Fitness
Insight Graphics, Inc.
P.O. Box 221343
Chantilly, VA 22022
(800) 787-2600
Quarterly; $18.95

Qigong Magazine
Contact the Qigong Institute.

Training Programs
Institute of Self-Initiated Healing
Roger Jahnke, L.Ac., O.M.D.
243 Pebble Beach
Santa Barbara, CA 93117
(805) 682-3230
Dr. Jahnke offers training programs in the conceptual foundations and practice of Qigong. Books and tapes on Qigong are also available.

Qigong Institute
East West Academy of Healing Arts
450 Sutter Street, Suite 2104
San Francisco, CA 94108
(415) 788-2227

Taoist Mountain Retreat Center
Ken Cohen, M.A.
P.O. Box 234
Nederland, CO 80466
(303) 258-7806
The Taoist Mountain Retreat Center, directed by Ken Cohen, one of the original spokespersons of Qigong in the United States, offers Qigong training and research both at the center and in various centers around North America. Advanced training, which leads to certification, takes approximately three years.

REIKI
Reiki, a Japanese word derived from *ray* ("divine wisdom") and *ke* ("life force energy"), is a healing technique that enhances the field of life force energy surrounding and infusing the physical body. The healing system incorporates both self-treatment and the treatment of others even without direct contact.

According to Reiki philosophy, life force energy is the primary source of direction and nourishment for the cells and organs of the body. Disturbances in this living field of energy or aura are thought to be the cause of most illness. A

Reiki practitioner acts as a medium by channeling life force energy through his or her hands at various positions on the body, or within the general aura of a client. The practitioner also taps into the client's core sense of well-being, or innate wisdom, to know exactly where to place his or her hands. By releasing these "energy blocks," Reiki helps restore the natural flow of life force, thus helping restore a person to physical, psychological, and spiritual health. (The resulting flow of energy helps explain why this therapy is often referred to as the Radiance Technique®.)

Reiki resurfaced in the late 19th century after Makao Usui, a Christian minister and teacher living in Japan, deciphered parts of the Buddhist sutras, a composite text outlining healing methods taught by the Buddha. His discoveries laid the foundation for modern Reiki, which was brought to the United States by Mrs. Hawayo Takata in 1935, and was later transmitted to 22 Reiki masters between 1970 and 1980, many of whom continue to teach today. There are approximately 1,500 Reiki masters and 150,000 practitioners worldwide. The ability to channel Reiki is not taught in the usual sense, but is simply transferred to the student by a Reiki master. There are two formal training programs in the United States.

—William Lee Rand of the Center for Reiki Training contributed to this introduction.

Organizations
Reiki Alliance
P.O. Box 41
Cataldo, ID 83810
Correspondence offered only by mail.
The alliance sets professional standards for teachers in the Mikao Usui System of Reiki.

Reiki Outreach International (ROI)
P.O. Box 55008
Santa Clarita, CA 91385
(805) 254-4800
ROI is an organization for all Reiki practitioners regardless of lineage, affiliation, or experience level, and sends "distant Reiki" to troubled spots around the world.

Periodicals
Radiance Technique Journal
Quarterly; $20
Contact the Center for Reiki Training

Reiki News
Quarterly; complimentary
Contact the Center for Reiki Training

Training Programs
Center for Reiki Training
29209 Northwestern Highway, Suite 592
Southfield, MI 48034
(313) 948-8112
The center establishes and maintains standards for teaching Reiki (based on Mukao Usui's system), certifies students and teachers, and acts as an educational link to the public. Classes leading to certification are taught around the United States.

Radiance Technique
Association International
P.O. Box 40570
St. Petersburg, FL 33743-0570
Correspondence offered only by mail.
This association is the educational and membership organization of the Radiance Technique®. It provides a geographical list of authorized instructors.

THERAPEUTIC TOUCH
Therapeutic touch was developed by Dolores Krieger, Ph.D., R.N., a New York University nursing professor, and Dora Kunz, R.N. It is derived from the ancient laying-on-of-hands technique, in that it uses the hands to read, direct, and balance the energy in a person's body with the intent to help or to heal. The technique includes assessing, clearing, mobilizing, directing, and rebalancing the energy field. Practitioners may or may not use light touch. The method also shares many of the same methodologies as external Qi healing and Reiki.

Therapeutic touch is being practiced by nurses in a wide variety of settings and with many different patient populations, including adult medical-surgical patients, sick newborns, dialysis patients, and senior citizens with medical conditions. Outcome studies offer evidence that therapeutic touch can increase human hemoglobin levels, induce physiologic relaxation, decrease anxiety and pain, and accelerate the healing of wounds. Research on the efficacy of this adjunct healing method continues to take place.

Therapeutic touch is taught through schools of nursing and hospital programs; continuing education credits are usually available. The National League for Nursing has furthered the application of therapeutic touch by developing a three-part videotape series that provides the basic content of an introductory course; Nurse Healers and Professional Associates has developed training guidelines that hospitals often follow. There is no certification available in therapeutic touch; however, if the technique is included in the standard curriculum for nurses, as is hoped, such separate recognition would become unnecessary. Also, the American Holistic Nurses Association offers certification in Healing Touch, a similar yet different modality (see Holistic Nursing).

Training Programs
Center for Human Caring
University of Colorado School of Nursing
4200 East Ninth Avenue
Denver, CO 80262
(303) 270-6157
The center provides information on training programs in therapeutic touch.

National League for Nursing
350 Hudson Street
New York, NY 10014
(212) 989-9393
The NLN accredits schools of nursing, sets standards of nursing education, and advances the nursing profession at the local, national, and international levels. It is also involved in promoting a "national health plan on behalf of the nursing community that assures affordable quality care to all Americans."

Nurse Healers and Professional
Associates (NHPA)
175 Fifth Avenue, Suite 2755
New York, NY 10010
(212) 886-3776
Incorporated in 1978, NHPA, a membership and advocacy group, is also a resource for health-care professionals interested in the Krieger/Kunz model of therapeutic touch.

SECTION IV

CREATIVE AND EXPRESSIVE ARTS THERAPY DEGREE PROGRAMS

In This Section:

➤ ART THERAPY

➤ DANCE THERAPY

➤ DRAMA THERAPY

➤ MULTIMODAL THERAPY

➤ MUSIC THERAPY

➤ POETRY THERAPY

➤ PSYCHODRAMA

➤ ADDITIONAL RESOURCES

➤ MOVEMENT THERAPY (SEE SECTION V)

CALIFORNIA INSTITUTE OF INTEGRAL STUDIES

A LTHOUGH THE IDEA OF COMBIN-ING ART AND THERAPY MAY STRIKE many today as novel, the relationship has a long history, dating as far back as the ancient Greek civilization. Virtually every culture, past and present, has devised some therapeutic use of the arts in healing rituals or ceremonies. In the first half of the 20th century, a number of people working independently developed what have become the separate fields of art, dance, drama, music, poetry, and psychodrama therapy. In the last decade a multidisciplinary or multimodal approach has also been developed, often referred to as expressive arts (or multimodal) therapy.

Each discipline seems to be following the same general path toward the development of licensure and independent certifying bodies, although at different rates. In fact, the evolution of the creative and expressive arts field is similar to that of many other mental health professions. It begins with the founding of a professional, nonprofit membership association, as well as public and private training programs. Next, the organization creates a title (called registration or certification). An independent certifying board is established

A COMPARISON OF EXPRESSIVE AND CREATIVE ARTS

	ART THERAPY	DANCE THERAPY	DRAMA THERAPY	MUSIC THERAPY		POETRY THERAPY		PSYCHODRAMA THERAPY	EXPRESSIVE ARTS THERAPY (MULTI-MODAL)
NATIONAL NONPROFIT PROFESSIONAL MEMBERSHIP ASSOCIATION	AATA	ADTA	NADT	NAMT	AAMT	NAPT		ASGPP	Committee in Progress
APPROVES TRAINING PROGRAMS	Yes	Yes	Yes	Yes	Yes	No, but approves mentors		Yes	No, but in progress
REGISTRATION TITLE (i.e., Professional Recognition from Peers)	A.T.R.	D.T.R. (entry level) A.D.T.R. (experienced)	R.D.T.	RMT	CMT	CPT	RPT	C.P. (entry level) T.E.P. (experienced)	Emerging
MASTERS DEGREE REQUIRED	Yes	Yes	Yes	No	Yes	No	Yes	Yes	Yes
BOARD CERTIFIED	No, but in progress	No	No	Yes	Yes	No	No	Yes	No
STATE LICENSURE	If your state licenses, it will be as a generic mental health, marriage-family-child, or other counselor. It is up to each state to decide whether the creative and expressive arts falls under that title. Some practitioners are licensed psychologists, social workers, nurse practitioners, or ministerial counselors.								
INSURANCE REIMBURSEMENT	In most cases, no (or not yet), unless you have a state license.								
WORK ENVIRONMENT	Agencies, Clinics, Community Centers, Counseling Centers, Hospitals, Private Practice, and Schools								

and state licensure secured. Finally, third-party health insurers recognize the profession as a legitimate practice. (There is often a positive correlation between holding a state license and eligibility to receive insurance reimbursement, although this is not always the case.) Thus the stages that help legitimize these and most mental health disciplines begin with demonstration of approval from a professional organization, and culminate in state recognition.

There are a number of states in which licensure in a related field (e.g., marriage, family and child counselor, psychologist, and social worker) includes the opportunity to practice a creative and expressive arts therapy. However, because of the wide and often confusing variation between therapies and state regulation, we encourage you to contact the relevant association for the most up-to-date information on the state in which you plan to practice. The chart above differentiates between the creative and expressive arts disciplines, and is meant to introduce you to the field as a whole.

FUTURE TRENDS: LICENSURE

Although there are 40 states that license mental health counselors, Massachusetts is the first state to recognize explicitly the creative and expressive arts as independent from other mental health disciplines. Professional associations or independent certification boards often help maintain licensure status, but each state regulates licensing laws independently.

The regulating board of Massachusetts, along with professional associations from many counseling modalities—such as marriage and family, pastoral, and creative arts counseling—sought a common ground on which certain education standards could be required of all counselors without sacrificing the unique properties of each therapy. Massachusetts then introduced the umbrella title, Mental Health Counselor (MHC), which includes the freedom to practice any type of creative and expressive arts therapy. Moreover, the new title helped simplify and consolidate the confusing array of mental health professions. Massachusetts's ability to widen its definition of counseling has left professionals from many disciplines optimistic that other states will follow.

The rising costs of health care coupled with the wide range of mental health disciplines may pressure other states to follow Massachusetts's lead. If so, future creative and expressive arts therapists may be required to receive training much like a general counselor, psychologist, or social worker, and then take additional training in a specialty.

FUTURE TRENDS: ARTIST AND THERAPIST

As mentioned, most creative and expressive arts therapies are following the traditional path toward integration within the established mental health field. However, some practitioners are critical of this development, claiming that in the process of seeking legitimacy (through tight regulation, more standardization, and most troubling of all, conformity to the Western medical model) each discipline will sacrifice many of its honored foundations: artistic creativity, freedom of expression, and a tolerance for the emergence of innovative healing approaches.

Each creative and expressive arts discipline is experiencing internal debate over these issues, and unless all of them reach a consensus in reference to the field's future directions, each discipline will separately have to make these difficult decisions. The debate within and between these fields was demonstrated at the American Art Therapy Association's national conference in 1993, where, on the one hand, a number of panels focused on the development of an independent certification board (a move toward standardization) while on the other, many interdisciplinary and nonspecialized presentations helped reflect the conference's title, "Common Ground: The Arts, Therapy, and Spirituality."

Shaun McNiff, an art therapist who presented at the conference, is one of the founders (along with Paolo Knill) of mulit-modal therapy, an expressive arts therapy that considers itself more interdisciplinary and all-encompassing. McNiff and Knill, both from Lesley College in Massachusetts, purport that the separation among the creative arts is an arbitrary distinction brought about by a larger societal trend toward specialization. The distinction, they believe, has little to do with the genuine practice of art in conjunction with therapy and is a potential disservice to the people for whom the therapy is meant. On the other hand, trends show that a growing number of traditionally mainstream licensed psychologists, psychiatrists, social workers, and counselors are adding multimodal expressive arts therapy to their healing repertoire, and successfully combining it with verbal psychotherapy.

—*Jack S. Weller, Rudolph Schaeffer Professor of Arts and Creativity and founding director of the expressive arts therapy program at the California Institute of Integral Studies, contributed to the development of this introduction and overall section.*

ART THERAPY

Art therapists, through an understanding of ordinary human behavior, psychopathology, and the counseling process, use the creation of graphic and plastic arts as a tool to foster the therapeutic expression of the self. They work with individuals and groups, and in settings such as hospitals and psychiatric centers.

After a candidate has completed an art therapy (or related) master's degree program and acquired two years of practical experience, the American Art Therapy Association (AATA) grants the A.T.R. (Registered Art Therapist) certificate. The AATA is in the process of developing an independent certification board.

Associations
American Art Therapy Association (AATA)
1202 Allanson Road
Mundelein, IL 60060
(708) 949-6064

The AATA was founded in 1969 and represents a membership of approximately 4,000 professionals and students. Contact the AATA for a listing of approved art therapy programs.

Periodicals
American Journal of Art Therapy
Vermont College of Norwich University
Montpelier, VT 05602
Quarterly; $27

Art Therapy: Journal of the American Art Therapy Association
Quarterly; $25

Contact the American Art Therapy Association.

Arts in Psychotherapy
Pergamon Press Journals Division
660 White Plains Road
Tarrytown, NY 10521-5133
(914) 524-9200
Five times a year; $60

NONDEGREE PROGRAMS
Harding Hospital
Clinical Internship in Art Therapy
445 East Granville Road
Worthington, OH 43015
(614) 785-7443

The Harding Hospital is a nonprofit comprehensive psychiatric center. Founded in 1916, the hospital has provided graduate education in art therapy since 1971. The internship is a master's level clinical training program in affiliation with the Lesley College Graduate School in Cambridge, Massachusetts. The program is approved by the American Art Therapy Association.

New England Art Therapy Institute
216-R Silver Lane
Sunderland, MA 01375
(413) 665-4880

Founded in 1981, the institute provides courses in art therapy and creativity for the general public and a certificate program for professionals in related fields.

Round Oaks Creative Center
3410 Ridge Road
Charlottesville, VA 22901
(804) 973-7543

Round Oaks offers programs in expressive arts and nondegree certificate programs.

DANCE THERAPY

Dance therapy is a profession that uses dance and movement as media for helping individuals develop, change, and function better physically, socially, mentally, and emotionally. Dance therapists work in rehabilitation, hospital, psychiatric, and pediatric programs that focus on issues such as chronic pain, substance abuse, recovery and traumatic experiences. Some also work with the physically challenged. Regardless of the setting, however, clients tend to have body-image problems that are not easily ameliorated within traditional talk-therapy modalities.

Graduates of programs approved by the American Dance Therapy Association (ADTA) are eligible for a D.T.R. (Registered Dance Therapist). The more advanced A.D.T.R. (Registered American Dance Therapist) is granted only after acquiring professional experience. According to ADTA, however, individuals with extensive dance and movement backgrounds may combine their experience with study in a related field (e.g., social work, psychology, or special education) as an alternative path toward earning certification.

Associations
American Dance Therapy Association (ADTA)
2000 Century Plaza, Suite 108
Columbia, MD 21044
(410) 997-4040

The ADTA is a membership and advocacy group that sets dance therapy eligibility standards. Contact the ADTA for a list of seven graduate training programs, including specific D.T.R. requirements. It publishes the *American Journal of Dance Therapy*.

Periodicals
American Journal of Dance Therapy
Plenum Press
233 Spring Street
New York, NY 10013-1578
Semiannual; $24

Contact Quarterly: A Vehicle for Moving Ideas
P.O. Box 603
Northampton, MA 01061
(413) 586-1181
Semiannual; $14

Supported in part by a grant from the New York State Council on the Arts, this publication focuses on dance and improvisation.

DRAMA THERAPY

Drama therapy is defined by the National Association for Drama Therapy as the systematic and intentional use of drama/theater processes to achieve psychological change and emotional growth. Drama therapists use a wide variety of drama/theater techniques, including role play, improvisation, theater games, storytelling, puppetry, performance, and reenactment of real life events and conflicts. Drama therapy capitalizes on the healing properties of play and pretend and tends to utilize the fictional mode as much as the more direct confrontational mode of psychodrama. Scenes enacted in drama therapy become personal and highly emotional over time, but the focus is generally on group process and group interaction, and on a gradual progression from the more distanced to the less distanced.

Aside from their training, drama therapists have a background in theater and in psychotherapy. Completion of an approved master's program plus 1,500 hours of paid work experience as a drama therapists leads to a D.T.R. (Registered Drama Therapist).

—Renee Emunzh, the director of the drama therapy program at the California Institute for Integral Studies, contributed to this introduction.

Associations

National Association for Drama Therapy (NADT)
2022 Cutter Drive
League City, TX 77573
(713) 538-1689
Established in 1979, NADT is a membership and advocacy group that sets drama therapy eligibility standards. Contact NADT for a list of training programs—New York University and the California Institute of Integral Studies are the only two—including specific D.T.R. requirements.

Periodicals

Journal of Group Psychotherapy, Psychodrama and Sociometry
Heldref Publications
1319 Eighteenth Street, N.W.
Washington, DC 20036-1802
(800) 365-9753
Quarterly; $40

NADT Newsletter
National Association for Drama Therapy
Semiannual; $10

MULTIMODAL THERAPY

The formation of the Institute for the Arts and Human Development, begun in 1974 at Lesley College in Cambridge, Massachusetts, represented a movement away from the tendency to fragment and specialize and toward a more multi-disciplinary approach to both training and working with clients. This perspective approaches healing from the belief that the whole person is best represented when he or she is allowed to express him- or herself fully in whichever arts modality is most appropriate.

Jack S. Weller, founding director of the Expressive Arts Therapy program at the California Institute for Integral Studies, explains that multimodal therapists "tend to avoid using art for diagnosis, and . . . are less interested in the clinical interpretation of the art product and more interested in the healing aspects of the artistic process." In other words, these types of programs emphasize the healing power of the creative artist in all of us, as well as teaching the art of being an effective expressive arts therapist.

As clients are often drawn to different creative arts modalities, a multimodal approach allows for a wider range of clientele, which is part of its appeal to psychotherapists and counselors. Because a clearinghouse-type association of multimodal training programs is still forming, we list only the programs our search uncovered.

Organizations

Creative and Expressive Arts Therapies Exchange (CREATE)
See Additional Resources in this section.

Creative and Expressive Arts Therapy Exchange West (CREATE West)
See Additional Resources in this section.

Expressive Therapists of New England (ETNE)
P.O. Box 960
Jamaica Plain, MA 02130
(617) 524-2782
The ETNE is a nonprofit advocacy organization that works toward the progressive development of the therapeutic use of the arts; the improvement of standards of practice and business conditions for expressive psychotherapists; the development of criteria for training expressive therapists; and the general advancement of the field. Besides supporting the licensing procedures within the New England states, the ETNE offers workshops, day-long and weekend conventions and educational resources.

International Network of Creative Arts Therapy Associations
See Additional Resources in this section.

National Expressive Therapy Association (NETA)
1441 Broadway, Suite 338
New York, NY 10018; or
1164 Bishop Street, Suite 124
Honolulu, HI 96813
(808) 524-5411 (x15)
Expressive therapy in this context is the same as multimodal therapy. The NETA serves as a membership and advocacy organization and provides certification in expressive therapy. It also publishes "Guidelines for Expressive Therapy Education" and "Programs in Expressive Therapy."

North American Expressive Arts Therapy Interim Committee
c/o Creative and Expressive Arts Therapies Exchange West
P.O. Box 641 246
San Francisco, CA 04164-1246
An ad hoc committee of leaders in the multimodal expressive arts therapy movement are in the process of forming a North American, nonprofit, democratic, professional membership organization.

ACADEMIC PROGRAMS IN
MULTIMODAL EXPRESSIVE ARTS
THERAPY IN ACCREDITED COLLEGES
OR UNIVERSITIES

**California Institute of
Integral Studies (CIIS)**
Expressive Arts Therapy Program
765 Ashbury Street
San Francisco, CA 94117
(415) 753-6100 (x250)

CIIS offers a certificate program that can be combined with its M.A. and Ph.D. programs in counseling, clinical psychology, and drama therapy. Emphasis is on developing approaches to multimodal expressive arts therapy. The certificate can also be completed by postgraduate continuing education students in year-round and summer retreat formats. An independent M.A. program in expressive arts is being developed.

John F. Kennedy University (JFK)
Expressive Arts Therapy Program
12 Altarinda Road
Orinda, CA 94563
(510) 254-0200

JFK offers a creative arts option to its M.A. counseling psychology program. The program emphasizes combining expressive arts therapy with diverse populations.

**Lesley College Graduate School:
Expressive Therapies Program**
Institute for the Arts and Human
Development
29 Everett Street
Cambridge, MA 02138-2890
(800) 999-1959 (x480)

Founded in 1975, Lesley has been a pioneer graduate program in the creative and expressive arts, especially in the multimodal approach. Its program offers an M.A. in expressive arts, with a specialization in art, dance, music or inter-modal expressive therapies.

NONDEGREE INSTITUTE
TRAINING IN MULTIMODAL
EXPRESSIVE ARTS THERAPY

Because the multimodal field is growing rapidly, programs and certificates often change. We recommend contacting the following training centers for information on their current programs.

**Art Spirit: Expressive Arts
Training Institute**
1295 Delaware Street
Berkeley, CA 94702
(415) 524-1633

Atira
8307 Plateau Road
Baileys Harbor, WI 54202
(414) 839-2530

Creative Artistic Training
2887 Shaw Road
Middle Grove, NY 12850
(518) 882-5487

**International School for Interdisciplinary
Studies Canada (ISIS)**
118 Wells Street
Toronto, Ontario M5R 1P3, Canada
(416) 539-9728

National Institute of Expressive Therapy
1164 Bishop Street, Suite 124
Honolulu, HI 96813
(808) 524-5411(x15)

Oasis Center
7463 North Sheridan
Chicago, IL 60626
(312) 274-6777

**Person-Centered Expressive
Therapy Institute**
P.O. Box 6518
Santa Rosa, CA 95406
(800) 477-2384

**Professional Training Program in
Expressive Arts Therapy (formerly TREAT)**
2033 Port Bristol Circle
Newport Beach, CA 92660
(714) 760-0115

Tamalpa Institute
P.O. Box 794
Kentfield, CA 94914
(415) 461-9479

Also see Nondegree and Postgraduate Training Programs.

MUSIC THERAPY

Music therapy uses music as a way of accessing emotions and experiences not easily accessible in conventional verbal psychotherapies. A music therapist often works with people who have trouble communicating verbally, such as the developmentally delayed, mentally challenged, and geriatric patients. There are two professional organizations for music therapy. The first, the American Association for Music Therapy (AAMT), is a spin-off of the second, the National Association of Music Therapy (NAMT).

The separation represents different philosophies of practicing music therapy: NAMT focuses on entry-level B.A. programs, while AAMT focuses on graduate M.A. programs. NAMT awards the title of M.T.R. (Registered Music Therapist); AAMT awards the title M.T.C. (Certified Music Therapist). According to some professionals in the field, NAMT's listing of approved schools is curriculum-based, whereas AAMT's listing is competency-based, that is, based on the degree of practical experience acquired.

A Certification Board administers a standardized test for both groups, which enables practitioners to add B.C. (Board Certified) to their title. This helps the profession garner recognition and societal legitimacy while providing another step toward state licensure. Because it was one of the first creative arts therapies to possess an independent certification board (psychodrama also has one), other therapies look to music therapy as an indicator of where the established field of creative and expressive arts may be moving.

Associations

**American Association for
Music Therapy (AAMT)**
P.O. Box 27177
Philadelphia, PA 19118
(215) 265-4006

The AAMT provides the M.T.C. (Certified Music Therapist) credential. Contact the association for a listing of AAMT-approved graduate programs. The group publishes a journal and sponsors conferences.

**Certification Board for
Music Therapists (CBMT)**
6336 North Oracle Road
Suite 326, Box 345
Tucson, AZ 85704
(800) 765-2268

The CBMT oversees the certification process for both the AAMT and the NAMT.

**International Society for
Music in Medicine (ISMM)**
Roland Droh, M.D., President
Contemporary Arts Building
3526 Washington Avenue
St. Louis, MO 63103-1093
(314) 531-9635

The ISMM is an advocacy group for the use of music in the practice of medicine. It publishes books and a journal, *The International Journal of Arts Medicine,* and also holds a conference approximately every three years.

National Association of Music Therapy (NAMT)
8455 Colesville Road, Suite 930
Silver Spring, MD 20910
(301) 589-3300

The NAMT provides the M.T.R. (Registered Music Therapist) credential. Contact the association for a listing of NAMT-approved graduate programs. NAMT publishes a journal and sponsors conferences.

Periodicals
International Journal of Arts Medicine
Semiannual; $20
Contact the International Society for Music in Medicine.

Journal of Music Therapy
Quarterly; $85
Contact the National Association of Music Therapy.

Music Therapy
Annual; $15
Contact the American Association for Music Therapy.

Others Relevant Periodicals
Contact your local library for availability.
Bulletin of Council for Research in Music Education
Contributions to Music Education
Journal of Research in Music Education
Medical Problems of Performing Artists
Music Perception
Music Therapy Perspectives
Psychology of Music
Psychomusicology
Update: Applications of Research to Music Education

NONDEGREE PROGRAMS
Bonny Foundation: An Institute for Music-Centered Therapies
2020 Simmons Street
Salina, KS 67401
(913) 827-1497

The Bonny Foundation, founded by Helen Bonny in 1988, is a nonprofit organization that provides resources and training in the therapeutic use of the arts for professional therapists. It offers complete training and credentialing in the Bonny Method of Guided Imagery and Music.

Institute for Music, Health and Education (IMHE)
P.O. Box 4179
Boulder, CO 80306
(303) 443-8484

The IMHE was established in 1988 by Don Campbell to provide leading-edge programs for those with an interest in the therapeutic and educational uses of sound and music. It offers independent and year-long training programs.

POETRY THERAPY
Poetry therapy employs poetry and other forms of evocative literature to achieve therapeutic goals such as promoting self-understanding, changing behavior and feelings, and enhancing mental and social well-being. Poetry therapy is used to maintain health as well as to treat emotional disorders and geriatric, family, and marital problems, and social maladjustments. Health-care professionals (such as M.D.s, M.S.W.s, and Ph.D.s) often augment their practice with techniques learned from poetry therapy. Thus it is used in a wide range of settings, including hospitals, schools, clinics, prisons, nursing homes, hospices, drug and alcohol addiction centers, and in individual and group private practice. The P.T.C. (Certified Poetry Therapist) practitioner has a bachelor's degree and 440 hours of supervised training, and functions as an assistant therapist, while a P.T.R. (Registered Poetry Therapist) practitioner possesses a master's degree in a clinical field and has undergone 975 hours of training. P.T.R.s also work with more difficult populations, act as primary practitioners, and often supervise P.T.C.s.

Associations
National Association for Poetry Therapy (NAPT)
P.O. Box 551
Port Washington, NY 11050

The NAPT is a membership and advocacy organization. Contact it for a list of NAPT-approved mentors and supervisors. It publishes a newsletter, *Museletter.*

Periodicals
Journal of Poetry Therapy
Human Sciences Press, Inc.
P.O. Box 735, Canal Street Station
New York, NY 10013-1578
(212) 620-8000
Quarterly; $32

PSYCHODRAMA
Psychodrama is a form of therapy founded by Jacob Moreno, M.D., that utilizes dramatic enactment and reenactment, primarily of real-life events and issues. Psychodrama tends to be individually focused; that is, it focuses on one person in a group at a time. Psychodramatists encourage clients to reenact events, including traumas and unresolved issues from their lives. Unlike the other creative and expressive arts, psychodrama is available only to students who have already completed a master's degree in a related field (e.g., counseling or social work); therefore, training in psychodrama is primarily conducted through private training centers and by individual trainers who conduct workshops. Certification is available through the American Society of Group Psychotherapy and Psychodrama.

Associations
American Society of Group Psychotherapy and Psychodrama (ASGPP)
6728 Old McLean Village Drive
McLean, VA 22101
(703) 556-9222

The ASGPP is a membership and advocacy organization that grants the titles, C.P. (Certified Practitioner) and T.E.P. (Trainer, Educator, and Practitioner) through the American Board of Examiners in Psychodrama, Group Psychotherapy and Sociometry. The organization also provides a list of nationwide trainers and institutes offering workshops.

Periodicals
Journal of Group Psychotherapy, Psychodrama and Sociometry
Heldref Publications
4000 Albermarele Street, N.W.
Washington, DC 20016
Quarterly; $40

ADDITIONAL RESOURCES

Associations

**American Occupational
Therapy Association, Inc.**
1383 Piccard Drive
Rockville, MD 20849-1725
(301) 948-9626

Although occupational therapy tends to deal with physical rehabilitation more than it does the expressive arts, some occupational therapists use art and music therapy to augment their practices. Most occupational therapists are licensed.

**Association of Schools of Allied
Health Professions (ASAHP)**
1101 Connecticut Avenue, N.W., Suite 700
Washington, DC 20036-4387
(202) 857-1150

The ASAHP is a membership and advocacy organization composed of various health professions. Although this organization has little contact with expressive and creative arts therapists, some members are music and art therapists.

**Creative and Expressive Arts Therapies
Exchange (CREATE Canada)**
238 Davenport Road, Suite 142
Toronto, Ontario M5R 1J6, Canada
Correspondence offered only by mail.

Established in 1989, CREATE is a membership organization open to therapists, educators, artists, and others interested in psychotherapy and the arts. The association is a network of individuals who are working (or have an interest) in the creative and expressive arts therapies. CREATE embodies all creative and expressive therapies—multi-model, art, music, drama, psychodrama, dance/movement, poetry, and so forth. Participation allows members to share resources and find strength through a sense of common purpose. Membership is open to all who are interested in the use of the expressive arts in therapy. The organization publishes a journal, *C.R.E.A.T.E.*; holds an annual conference; and is unrelated to CREATE West.

**Creative and Expressive Arts Therapy
Exchange West (CREATE West)**
P.O. Box 641246
San Francisco, CA 94164-1246
Correspondence offered only by mail.

Formerly the Artist-Therapists of Northern California, CREATE West was established in 1988 and maintains the same purpose of CREATE in Canada. CREATE West

emphasizes a supportive environment for members to share their particular approaches and experiences of the creative and expressive arts.

**International Network of Creative Arts
Therapy Associations**
Friesstrasse 24
CH - 8050 Zurich, Switzerland

This organization includes an international network of ten independent training institutes in eight European countries, including one in Israel and one in Canada. Administrative headquarters are in Zurich, Switzerland. Emphasis is on multimodal expressive arts therapy, but each institute emphasizes a particular modality. The curricula is coordinated so that students can include training with teachers at other institutes. Teachers, graduates and others gather each Spring for a symposium.

**National Coalition of Arts Therapies
Associations (NCATA)**
c/o American Dance Therapy Association
2000 Century Plaza, Suite 108
Columbia, MD 21044
(410) 997-4040

The coalition unifies the field and lobbies for the inclusion of the creative and expressive arts in health care legislation at the national and state level. It has held joint conferences in the past; however, plans for a future conference have yet to be announced.

Organizations

Center for Liturgy and the Arts
The Rev. J. Bruce Stewart, Director
4327 Ravensworth Road, 210
Annandale, VA 22003
(703) 941-9422

The center provides teaching, performing, and consulting services in the use of arts in worship.

**Peaceworks International Center for the
Dances of Universal Peace**
444 NE Ravenna Blvd., Suite 306
Seattle, WA 98115-6467
(206) 522-4353

The center, a nonprofit membership organization founded by Samuel Lewis, links the many worldwide dance circles through a registry of meetings and leaders, newsletters, archives and publications, and trainings. The Dances of Universal Peace use sacred phrases, chants, music, and movements from the many traditions of the earth to promote peace and integration within individuals and groups. Contact the center for a listing of regional networkers.

Periodicals

The Arts in Psychotherapy
Pergamon Press
660 White Plains Road
Tarrytown, NY 10521-5133
(913) 524-9200
Five times a year; $40

Healing
1050 Fulton Avenue, Suite 150
Sacramento, CA 95825
(916) 974-8686
Quarterly; $30

This publication offers a forum where health care professionals and patients can engage in a dialogue about the experience of healing illness—through stories, interviews, poetry, artwork, and photography.

International Journal of Arts Medicine
3526 Washington Avenue
Saint Louis, MI 63103-1093
(314) 531-9635
Semiannual; $20

This publication is the official journal of the International Arts Medicine Association and the International Society for Music in Medicine.

*Journal of the Creative and Expressive Arts
Therapy Exchange (CREATE Canada)*
118 Wells Street
Toronto, Ontario M5R 1P3, Canada
Annual; $12

GENERAL TRAINING CENTERS

Oasis Center
7463 North Sheridan
Chicago, IL 60626
(312) 274-6777

Founded in 1968, the Oasis Center offers certification in expressive arts (E.T.C.) through the National Expressive Therapy Association, as well as registration in Art Therapy (A.T.R.) and Psychodrama. It also offers a training program in psychodrama that meets the requirements of the certifying exam administered by the American Board of Examiners in Psychodrama, Group Psychotherapy and Sociometry.

Cuyamungue Institute
See Nondegree Training Programs.

SECTION V

NONDEGREE AND POSTGRADUATE TRAINING

In This Section:

➤ ESTABLISHED ALTERNATIVE FIELDS OF STUDY

Analytic (Jungian) Psychology, Hypnotherapy, Para- and Meta-Psychology, Psychoanalysis, Psychosynthesis, Shamanic Counseling

➤ INDEPENDENT TRAINING PROGRAMS

The Carl G. Jung Institute of New York, founded in 1973, was the first Jungian training center incorporated in the United States.

NUMEROUS NONCONVENTIONAL AND ALTERNATIVE HEALING METHODS ARE BEING TAUGHT TODAY. MOST OF these training programs have their origins outside the confines of professional schools and are either too brief, too unconventional or too "hands-on" to be found in academic settings. As a result, you will find that nondegree training is either provided by freelance teachers who travel around the country offering workshops at conference centers, holistic health facilities, and hotels, or is sponsored by independent centers located around the country.

The following programs are known for maintaining an innovative pedagogy, in part because they are free from the fetters that institutionalization often fosters. Circumventing the rigid structures of academic accreditation has its benefits, for students of these programs often find an overlap between personal growth and advancing their education. Furthermore, many students who have already earned graduate degrees and licensure in a mental health field (such as clinical psychology, clinical social work, counseling, or psychiatry) may only be interested in augmenting their practices and are not concerned with the thorny issues of accreditation. Upon the completion of a program, a certificate is commonly awarded by the teaching program in such areas as Shamanic counseling, Holotropic Breathwork™, body/somatic therapy, and Jungian psychology. Depending on one's existing profession, continuing education credits are usually available.

In general, nondegree programs offer practical experience, while degree programs primarily provide students with theoretical skills. However, trends show that an increasing number of nondegree and degree

ROBERT FUCCI, 1992

programs are beginning to complement each other—each offering an important yet different aspect of the training process. The Institute for Transpersonal Psychology (ITP), for example, offers independent study credit for nondegree training programs in the transpersonal field, including Creative Energy Options, the Foundation for Shamanic Studies, and Transpersonal Training in Holotropic Breathwork™. In addition, ITP and other transpersonal-oriented, degree-granting institutions (listed in Section I) are inviting freelance teachers and researchers—such as Christina Grof and Stanislav Grof, Michael Harner, and Jeanne Achterberg—to act as adjunct faculty members. These developments enrich students' experiences, help professionalize nondegree programs, and widen the focus of the host college, university, or institute. Importantly, they may also generate more psychospiritual research in the form of theses and dissertations.

CRITERIA FOR LISTING

Most programs listed in this section are for people who have completed a graduate program (or are currently in one). Prior experience relevant to the respective training program is encouraged but usually not required. We do not list centers whose primary mission is only self-help or personal growth, but rather focus on programs that offer professional training for those who wish to incorporate these techniques into their own practices. Some of these programs are conducted by freelance teachers who travel to various locations around the country where they are sponsored by local interest groups or conference centers. In such instances, we list the teacher's central facility or main address.

A NOTE ON CERTIFICATION, REGISTRATION, AND LICENSURE

CERTIFICATION, LICENSURE, AND REGISTRATION ARE ALL TYPES OF PROFESSIONAL CREDENTIALing. Certification is used by private, nongovernmental organizations to recognize individuals who have achieved the minimum entry-level skills necessary to practice. Certification is widely accepted by practitioners, employers, and consumers as a dependable indicator of quality and competence. Typically, the qualifications include education and successful completion of an examination sponsored by the training body. Licensure, however, is administered and regulated by individual states and is the most restrictive form of credentialing. If a mental health profession requires licensure, it is illegal for anyone not licensed to engage in that profession. Typically, only licensed providers are eligible to receive health insurance reimbursement for their services.

Registration (e.g., Registered Art Therapist, Registered Drama Therapist) represents a third credentialing category that can be thought of as a credentialing level between certification and licensure. It involves passing an exam and taking a specified curriculum developed by a professional association.

Established Alternative Fields of Study

Although the fields of study outlined in this section are nondegree and are often multidisciplinary in orientation, the editors feel that they are well enough established by virtue of their substantive history to warrant listing them by subject rather than by individual program name. Programs not fitting this criteria are listed next under independent training programs.

ANALYTIC (JUNGIAN) PSYCHOLOGY

Carl Gustav Jung (1875-1961), a Swiss psychiatrist, broke from Freud in 1913 and later founded the discipline of analytic psychology. By the 1980s, Jungian psychology had crossed the threshold from esoteric obscurity to mainstream popularity. This rapid growth has happened despite the fact that there is no centralized Jungian organization in the United States or any standardized requirements among the seven training institutes. Although the Jungian psychology of today has changed little since its inception, James Hillman, a contemporary neo-Jungian scholar, has developed a theory of archetypal psychology that represents the first departure from the traditional Jungian perspective (see the journal *Spring*).

In order to become a Jungian analyst, an individual must acquire a certificate from one of the many certifying training institutes in either the United States or abroad. Although admission requirements vary considerably, at least 100 to 250 hours of personal Jungian analysis and an advanced degree in social work, psychology, or psychiatry, or some other prior clinical training, are common prerequisites. The average analyst is 45 years old. Curricula at the various institutes also differ. Some institutes offer seminars and supervision on a weekly or monthly basis, with training lasting anywhere from three to six years.

Academic programs have shied away from offering specialized training in Jungian psychology preferring to focus on the development of theory and research. Texas A&M University and Pacifica Graduate Institute, however, offer unusual clinical psychology programs in that they allow students to specialize in depth psychology, which, by definition, incorporates Jungian concepts.

According to Jerome Bernstein, a Jungian analyst, there is some confusion outside the Jungian community regarding terminology. He notes that Jung referred to the field as "analytical psychology," whereas the term "Jungian analysis," which essentially describes the same thing, only became popular after Jung's death. Bernstein also notes that the term "Jungian therapist" is misleading to the general public, as it incorrectly implies that the person using the label has undergone all of the requisite training. When applicable, the term "Jungian-oriented therapist" is admissible, as it does not imply that the person is a Jungian analyst. Nevertheless, there are no licensing laws regulating the use of the word "Jungian," just as there is no regulation of the term "psychoanalysis."

The lack of a centralized Jungian organization in the United States is reflected by the fact that there are few national conferences. Chiron Publications sponsored a Jungian conference from 1981 to 1991, called Ghost Ranch, which produced papers still available through Chiron. Centerpoint sponsors an annual conference in the fall and publishes a newsletter listing events sponsored by regional Jungian organizations. Many major cities throughout the United States have Jungian societies that also sponsor lectures and maintain libraries; contact a Jungian Institute located near you.

Organizations

Center for Sacred Psychology
See Spiritual Direction.

Centerpoint
c/o The Education Center
6357 Clayton Road
St. Louis, MO 63117
(800) 427-2359
Founded in 1972, Centerpoint offers nondegree courses, publishes the newsletter *In Touch,* and sponsors an annual Harvest conference held in New Hampshire.

Fairfield County Jung Society (FCJS)
c/o Temenos Institute
See Conference Centers.
The FCJS at Temenos Institute sponsors lectures and courses about application of Jungian concepts to a number of mental health topics and fields.

Institute for the Study of Imagination (ISI)
4803 Yellowwood Avenue
Baltimore, MD 21209
(410) 367-3219
The ISI is a nonprofit organization founded in 1987 to foster imagination in all areas of life. Its activities are currently centered in Baltimore, Chicago, and western Massachusetts and include conferences, lectures, workshops, seminars, and ongoing programs in imagination studies. The ISI publishes *Primavera* and, in association with Lindisfarne Press, a book series featuring seminal works in the history, theory, and practice of imagination.

International Association of Analytical Psychology (IAAP)
c/o Tom Kirsch, M.D.
945 Middlefield Road
Palo Alto, CA 94301
(415) 521-7075
The IAAP, whose headquarters are located in Zurich, Switzerland, is a professional organization open to all certified Jungian psychoanalysts. This organization charters and certifies the various Jungian training institutes throughout the world and holds a congress every three years.

Journey into Wholeness (JIW)
See Retreat Centers under Kanuga conferences.
JIW combines Christian spirituality and the psychology of Carl Jung.

The London Convivium for Archetypal Studies
P.O. Box 417
London, NE3 6YE
England

Periodicals

Chiron Clinical Series
Chiron Publications
400 Linden Avenue
Wilmette, IL 60091
(708) 256-7551
The series consists of journal-type publications that focus on Jungian topics.

Film Analyst
2404 Narbonne Way
Costa Mesa, CA 92627-1424
Bimonthly; $7.50
This newsletter interprets modern and classic films from a Jungian perspective.

Harvest
Analytical Psychology Club
37 York Street Chambers
London WIH 1DE
England

In Touch
Centerpoint
33 Main Street, Suite 302
Nashua, NH 03060-2777
(603) 880-3020
Three times a year; $12
This national Jungian newsletter contains interviews and articles as well as a schedule of programs held at Jungian organizations around the United States and Canada. It also provides a list of regional Jungian societies across the United States.

Journal of Analytical Psychology
Routledge Subscriptions
ITPS Ltd., Department J.
Cheriton House, North Way
Andover, SP 10 5BE
England
0264 332424
Quarterly; $100

Jung at Heart
Inner City Books
Box 1271, Station Z
Toronto, Ontario M4T 2P4
Canada
(416) 927-0355
In addition to producing this Jungian-oriented newsletter, Inner City Books is the only publishing house devoted exclusively to the work of Jungian analysts.

The Library Journal
Carl Jung Institute of San Francisco
2040 Gough Street
San Francisco, CA 94109
(415) 771-8055
Quarterly; $36
This journal is dedicated to reviewing books relevant to Jungian readers.

Parabola
See Interdisciplinary Resources.

Psychological Perspectives
Carl Jung Institute of Los Angeles
10349 West Pico Boulevard
Los Angeles, CA 90064
(310) 556-2290
Biannual; $20

This Jungian journal seeks to integrate psyche, soul, and nature, offering essays, articles, short fiction, poems, visual art, and reviews.

Quadrant
C.G. Jung Institute of New York
28 East 39th Street
New York, NY 10016
(212) 697-6430

Round Table Review
Round Table Press
P.O. Box 475
Southeastern, PA 19399
Five times a year; $18.50

This newsletter includes current and noteworthy contributions to Jungian psychology.

Sphinx
P.O Box 417
London NW3 6YE
England

Spring: A Journal of Archetype and Culture
P.O. Box 583,
Putnam, CT 06260
(203) 974-3229
Semiannual; $20

TRAINING CENTERS

Avalon Institute
See Residential Psychology Degree Programs.

Carl G. Jung Foundation (CGJF)
28 East 39th Street
New York, NY 10016
(212) 697-6430

The CGJF offers educational programs for the lay public and maintains the Archives for Research in Archetypal Symbolism library.
See Residential Psychology Degree Programs.

Center for Advanced Studies in Depth Psychology
23 The Parkway
Katonah, NY 10536
(914) 232-0352

The center is devoted to a particular topic in analytical psychology each year. Participants may elect to stay in the pro-

gram for one year or longer. A certificate of completion is awarded at the end of each year, and credit for work done in the program has been granted by various university graduate programs. Admission requirements include two years of active psychotherapeutic work and an interview.

Dallas Institute of Humanities and Culture
See Independent Training Programs in this section.

Jungian Seminars
190 Westbrook Road
Essex, CT 06426-1511
(800) 258-3533
Programs: Jungian summer seminar in Britain; Jungian winter seminar in Switzerland

Pacifica Graduate Institute
See Residential Psychology Degree Programs.

Process Work Center of Portland
See Residential Psychology Degree Programs.

Texas A&M University
Department of Psychology
See Implicit Degree Programs.

TRAINING INSTITUTES

C.G. Jung Institute of Boston
283 Commonwealth Avenue
Boston, MA 02115
(617) 267-5984

C.G. Jung Institute of Chicago
1567 Maple Avenue
Evanston, IL 60201
(708) 475-4848

C.G. Jung Institute of Dallas
P.O. Box 7004
Dallas, TX 75209-0004
(214) 691-6835

C.G. Jung Institute of Los Angeles
10349 West Pico Boulevard
Los Angeles, CA 90064
(213) 556-1193

C.G. Jung Institute of New York
28 East 39th Street
New York, NY 10016
(212) 986-5458

C.G. Jung Institute of San Francisco
2040 Gough Street
San Francisco, CA 94109
(415) 771-8055

C.G. Jung Institute of Santa Fe
227 East Palace Avenue, Suite D
Santa Fe, NM 87501
(505) 983-2740

INTERNATIONAL INSTITUTES

In addition to the famous institute in Zurich, there are also institutes in Brussels, Belgium; Sao Paulo and Rio de Janeiro, Brazil; Paris, France; Stuttgart and Berlin, Germany; Milan and Rome, Italy; and Tel-Aviv, Israel. Contact one of the American institutes listed above for additional information.

C. G. Jung Institute of Zurich
Hornweg 28
8700 Kusnacht
Zurich Switzerland
01-910-53-23

Training at the Zurich Institute is not required for becoming a legitimate Jungian analyst, although Carl Jung's direct affiliation with it makes the institute an understandably prestigious choice. Training candidates need not hold an advanced degree; however such candidates are discouraged from entering the program because without an American license in a mental health discipline it is difficult to qualify for insurance reimbursement.

HYPNOTHERAPY

Hypnotherapy is any form of psychotherapy practiced in conjunction with hypnosis. It is thought of as an adjunctive treatment modality rather than a science or an independent treatment. Hypnosis is difficult to define precisely because of its many different applications. At its lowest common denominator, the technique involves the relationship between a hypnotist and another person, during which suggestions made by the hypnotist affects the person's cognition, perceptions, and memory.

Hypnotic trance states influence a wide variety of conditions, both physical and mental. The technique's more notable applications include helping clients to control pain, stop minor habit disorders, relieve depression, and reduce anxiety.

There appears to be little research on

the relationship between hypnotic trance states and psychospiritual techniques—such as the Grof's Holotropic Breathwork™ and Michael Harner's shamanic counseling practices, which, like hypnosis, induce non-ordinary states of consciousness and allow access to latent insights, feelings, and memories.

HISTORY

Hypnosis is not a new modality. The Celts and Druids practiced hypnosis. Ancient Egyptians used "sleep temples" in which curative suggestions were given, and many sections of the Bible allude to hypnotic phenomena.

Little attention, however, was given to hypnotic states until the early 16th century, when Paracelsus described how magnetic fields come from the stars and influence human behavior. In 1646, the German mathematician Kircher described a cure for "animal magnetism" (a natural force responsible for disease) using a process called "magneto therapeutics." Franz Mesmer (1734-1815), however, is considered to be the modern inventor of hypnosis as a treatment technique because he was the first to describe animal magnetism as a therapeutic tool. Working in a room containing a tub of iron filings known as a banquet, he walked in circles around his patients who sometimes entered into a stuporous trance state and were then allegedly cured of their afflictions. Mesmer's popularity resulted in an official investigation appointed by the king of France and headed by Benjamin Franklin. The commission concluded that any reported effects were due to imagination. Mesmer was denounced as a quack, and eventually died in obscurity in Switzerland.

Fortunately, Mesmer's discovery found a new life in England during the 1840s, when James Braid studied animal magnetism and coined the phrase "hypnosis," which he took from the Greek word *hypnos,* meaning "sleep." Later, after concluding that hypnosis was, in fact, a state of mental activity rather than sleep, he changed the term to

HOW TO FIND A HYPNOSIS TRAINING PROGRAM

UNLESS OTHERWISE NOTED, HYPNOTHERAPY ASSOCIATIONS HAVE A LIST OF TRAINing programs in hypnosis, and many of them also provide certification. Until state law mandates hypnosis as an adjunct technique that only licensed mental health professionals may utilize—and such a mandate is currently under discussion in many states—training programs may certify anyone, just as anyone can practice hypnosis. Because there are numerous certifying bodies (some more reputable than others), we have listed only those organizations that share a commitment to certifying practitioners who are already licensed mental health professionals. Contact individual organizations for a list of their specific requirements.

"monoideism." By this time, however, the term hypnosis was already popular among its users, and the word remains in use today.

James Esdaile, an English surgeon, later used hypnosis on all of his patients while in India during the middle 1800s. He performed 3,000 operations, 300 of which were major procedures, and discovered that the mortality rate dropped from 50 percent to 5 percent when the patients were in a hypnotic state. In addition, many of them recovered more quickly, had increased resistance to infection, and experienced greater comfort during the surgical procedure. Esdaile presented his findings to the Royal Academy of Physicians in London but was denounced as blasphemous because "God intended people to suffer."

In France, Hippolyte Bernheiam, a famous neurologist, was mortified that a local family physician was using hypnosis on a patient. Feeling only contempt, he visited the physician but was so over-

whelmed after observing the therapeutic effect of hypnosis that the two doctors collaborated, forming the famous School of Nancy, where Freud would later study. In 1885, another famous neurologist, Jean Martin Charcot, taught his students hypnosis in Paris. Freud studied under Charcot and later worked with Josef Breuer using hypnotic techniques. In 1895, Freud and Breuer published "Studies of Hysteria," in which hypnosis was used to discover the source of "conversion reactions." Although Freud's opinion of hypnosis vacillated throughout his life, the neo-Freudians were so entrenched in the new psychoanalytic movement that they mostly disregarded the benefits derived from hypnosis.

Hypnosis dropped into obscurity until World War II, when dentists began to use hypnosis with soldiers in combat situations. Spurred on by the studies of Clark Hull in the 1930s, interest in hypnotic phenomena continued to grow, and in 1955 the British Medical Association endorsed hypnosis as an acceptable method of treatment. In 1958, the American Medical Association recognized hypnosis as a therapeutic adjunct, and the American Psychiatric Association endorsed it in 1961. Despite its acceptance into the medical model, however, many physicians remain skeptical, mainly because of their misconceptions about its usefulness in the therapeutic process.

Hypnosis is being taught by many medical and dental schools, intern and residency programs, and in training programs located throughout the United States. Many psychologists also have incorporated clinical and experimental hypnosis into their practices. A number of research grants have been awarded to such institutions as the University of Pennsylvania and Stanford Medical School to investigate the efficacy of hypnotherapy.

—This introduction was adapted from an essay written by Charles B. Mutter, M.D., of the American Society of Clinical Hypnosis.

Associations

American Academy of Medical Hypnoanalysts (AAMH)
25W550 Royce Road
Naperville, IL 60565
(800) 344-9766

The AAMH is a membership, accrediting, and certifying organization. Members must have at least a master's degree or higher in one of the behavioral sciences such as medicine, psychology, social work, and/or theology. They must also devote 50 percent or more of their clinical practices to hypnoanalysis.

American Association of Professional Hypnotherapists (AAPH)
P.O. Box 29
Boones Mill, VA 24065
(703) 334-3035

Founded in 1980, the AAPH is a membership and advocacy organization. It publishes *Hypnotherapy Today*. Contact the association for a list of approved training programs.

American Council of Hypnotist Examiners (ACHE)
1147 East Broadway, Suite 340
Glendale, CA 91205
(818) 242-5378

Founded in 1980 by Gil Boyne, ACHE is a national organization that has certified more than 7,000 hypnotherapists, including numerous physicians, psychiatrists, psychologists, and representatives of the healing arts, counseling, and allied health professions. The first requirement in receiving a "certified hypnotherapist" or "certified clinical hypnotherapist" registration is possession of a valid state license as a psychiatrist, psychologist, marriage, family, and child counselor (MFCC), or clinical social worker. Examination and registration are done by regional examining boards, while certification is provided by the national parent body, ACHE.

American Guild of Hypnotherapists (AGH)
7117 Farnam Street
Omaha, NE 68132
(402) 397-1500

The AGH is a nonprofit professional organization. It conducts hypnosis training seminars for health professionals—chiropractors, physicians, psychologists, counselors, and nurses—sponsors a school accreditation program, and publishes the *Journal of Hypnotherapy*.

American Psychological Association (APA)
Continuing Education Department
750 First Street, N.E.
Washington, DC 20009
(202) 336-5500

The APA provides a list of approved continuing education "sponsors" that offer training in hypnotism (among other things) to psychologists (who are all licensed Ph.D.s). The APA does not certify hypnotists.

The American Society of Clinical Hypnosis (ASCH)
2200 East Devon Avenue, Suite 291
Des Plaines, IL 60019-9690
(708) 297-3317

The ASCH is an organization of professionals in the fields of medicine, dentistry, psychology, social work, and nursing who share scientific and clinical interests in hypnosis and who use hypnosis in their practices. ASCH does not approve programs or certify practitioners, but it does provide one of the most reputable training programs in the United States. The society also publishes *The American Journal of Clinical Hypnosis*.

International Medical and Dental Hypnotherapy Association (IMDHA)
4110 Edgeland, Suite 800
Royal Oak, MI 48073
(800) 257-5467

The IMDHA is a membership, advocacy, accrediting, and certifying organization. It is unique in that the IMDHA encourages the use of hypnotherapy with medical and dental populations. Contact the association for a list of approved training programs.

National Board for Certified Clinical Hypnotherapists (NBCCH)
8750 Georgia Avenue, Suite 125E
Silver Spring, MD 20910
(301) 608-0123

The NBCCH approves training programs and certifies hypnotherapists.

National Society of Hypnotherapists (NSH)
2175 Northwest 86th Street, Suite 6A
Des Moines, IA 50325
(515) 270-2280

The NSH is a nonprofit organization that advocates hypnotherapy as a separate and distinct profession. It also provides a directory to hypnosis organizations, conventions, and members ($7).

Society for Clinical and Experimental Hypnosis (SCEH)
6728 Old McLean Village Drive
McLean, VA 22101
(703) 556-9222

The SCEH is a professional membership organization that conducts education and training in the field of hypnosis. Like ASCH, it does not approve programs or certify practitioners; however, you may contact SCEH for further information on independent certifying bodies such as the American Board of Clinical Hypnosis, Incorporated; the American Board of Medical Hypnosis; the American Board of Hypnosis in Dentistry; the American Hypnosis Board for Clinical Social Work; and the American Board of Psychological Hypnosis.

Periodicals

The American Journal of Clinical Hypnosis
The American Society of Clinical Hypnosis
Quarterly; $30 (member)

Hypnotherapy Today
American Association of Professional Hypnotherapists
Quarterly; $55
(703) 334-3035

International Journal of Clinical and Experimental Hypnosis
The Society for Clinical and Experimental Hypnosis
Quarterly; $52 (member)

PARA- AND META-PSYCHOLOGY

The field of psychical phenomena is currently being investigated by researchers across many disciplines, including philosophy, psychology, and physics. Topics being studied include extrasensory perception (which consists of telepathy, clairvoyance, and precognition), psychokinesis, out-of-body experiences, near-death experiences, non-ordinary states of consciousness, dreams, apparitions, psychic healing, poltergeists, trance channeling, and reincarnation.

The following represents only a partial list of resources. Contact the Parapsychology Foundation for a copy of its "Guide to Sources of Information on Parapsychology" ($3) and the American

Society for Psychical Research for a copy of the booklet "Courses and Other Study Opportunities in Parapsychology" ($7).

Organizations

Academy of Religion and Psychical Research (ARPR)
P.O. Box 614
Bloomfield, CT 06002
(203) 242-4593

The ARPR encourages a cooperative exchange between clergy and academics in religion and philosophy as well as academics of all scientific and humanistic disciplines in the fields of psychical research. Spiritual Frontiers Fellowship, sponsored by ARPR, is an educational program that was formed to "sponsor, explore, and interpret the growing interest in psychic phenomena and mystical experience . . . whenever these experiences relate to effective prayer, spiritual healing, and personal survival." The academy also publishes a scholarly quarterly, *The Journal of Religion and Psychical Research.*

American Association of Professional Psychics (AAPP)
P.O. Box 2005
Ellicott City, MD 21042
(410) 750-0077

The AAPP is an education organization that also certifies professional psychics.

American Society for Psychical Research (ASPR)
5 West 73rd Street
New York, NY 10023
(212) 799-5050

The ASPR, founded in 1885, is the oldest psychical research organization in the United States and the second oldest in the world. The ASPR has served as an international information network for scientists, journalists, teachers, students, film makers, and other interested individuals. ASPR is a nonprofit organization that publishes a newsletter and a journal, and maintains a research library and archives. It offers a convenient reference "Courses and Other Study Opportunities in Parapsychology."

Association for Research and Enlightenment
See Research Institutes.

Foundation for Research on the Nature of Man (FRNM)
402 North Buchanan Boulevard
Durham, NC 27701
(919) 688-8241

Established in 1962, the FRNM is a nonprofit organization that seeks to explore

non-ordinary experiences that suggest underlying capacities as yet unrecognized in the domain of human personality. The Institute for Parapsychology, a division of the foundation and similar to the former Duke University Parapsychology Laboratory from which it evolved, conducts experimental research into apparent psychic (*psi*) ability. It publishes *Psi Today*.

International Association of Metapsychology (IAM)
7301-F Alicante Road
Colina de la Costa
La Costa, CA 92009
(619) 931-6969

The IAM, a nonprofit organization founded in 1980, originated from the Cosmosophy Society, which was founded in 1965. The association draws upon modern and ancient philosophies, broad religious concepts, academics, and recent scientific breakthroughs, and offers research and educational programs in metapsychology. The IAM also established the International Institute of Metapsychology.

Parapsychological Services Institute (PSI)
5575 B Chamblee Dunwoody Road, Suite 323
Atlanta, GA 30338
(404) 391-0991

A nonprofit organization founded in 1986, PSI offers education and counseling for those wishing to explore the meaning of psychic and spiritual experiences.

Parapsychology Foundation (PF)
228 East 71st Street
New York, NY 10021
(212) 628-1550

The PF was established in 1951 to encourage and support impartial scientific inquiry into the psychical aspects of human nature. The foundation is not a membership organization, nor is it a laboratory or a research center, but rather it impartially observes the many research and theoretical studies of parapsychology and offers assistance to scientists and universities engaged in understanding telepathy, clairvoyance, precognition, psychokinesis, and other psychic phenomena. Since 1951, the foundation has sponsored domestic and international conferences. PF provides a useful "Guide to Sources of Information on Parapsychology," a listing of international and American organizations and research centers, and it also offers an annual award for contributions to the field (see Research Institutes).

Parapsychology Sources of Information Psi Center (PSIC)
2 Plane Tree Lane
Dix Hills, NY 11746
(516) 271-1243

The PSIC collects, catalogs, and indexes books, journals, and other resources dealing with parapsychology and the transformation of consciousness. It also publishes a journal, *Exceptional Human Experience.*

Periodicals

Exceptional Human Experience
Parapsychology Sources of Information Psi Center
Biannual; $35

Journal of Near Death Studies
Human Sciences Press
233 Spring Street
New York, NY 10013-1578
(212) 620-8000
Quarterly; $32

Journal of Parapsychology
Foundation for Research on the Nature of Man
Quarterly; $35

Journal of Religion and Psychical Research
Academy of Religion and Psychical Research
Quarterly; $30 (membership)

Journal of Scientific Exploration
Pergamon Press
660 White Plains Road
Tarrytown, NY 10521-5133
(914) 524-9200
Quarterly; $40

Journal of the American Society for Psychical Research
American Society for Psychical Research
Quarterly; $25

Psi Today
Foundation for Research on the Nature of Man
Quarterly; $15

Research in Parapsychology
Scarecrow Press
52 Liberty Street
P.O. Box 656
Metuchen, NJ 08840

This journal reflects the abstracts and papers presented at the annual convention of the Parapsychological Association.

DOMESTIC NONDEGREE AND DEGREE PROGRAMS

Antioch University, Los Angeles
See Residential Psychology Degree Programs.

Antioch offers a clinical psychology specialization in parapsychology.

Association for Research and Enlightenment
P.O. Box 595
Virginia Beach, VA 23541-0595
(804) 428-3588

The association sponsors a psychic training seminar. Also see Research Institutes.

California Institute for Human Science (CIHS)
See Residential Psychology Degree Programs.

CIHS offers a Ph.D. in Clinical-Counseling Psychology with an optional specialization in parapsychology.

Institute for Parapsychology
Foundation for Research on the Nature of Man
P.O. Box 6847
College Station
Durham, NC 27708-6847
(919) 688-8241
Programs: Advanced parapsychology training; summer study

International Institute of Metapsychology
P.O. Box 234236
Leucadia, CA 92023
(619) 931-6969

This program leads to ordination as a minister who may practice pastoral counseling.
General Information: Private, nonsectarian, nonresidential
Degrees Offered: M.A., Ph.D.
Programs: Metapsychology (independent study)
Admission Requirements: Bachelor's degree preferred
Application Deadline: N/A
Contact Person: Director of Admissions
Tuition: $15/unit
Accreditation: Under the California Education Code
Year Established: 1980
Faculty: 7 advisory committee members

John F. Kennedy University (JFK)
See Residential Psychology Degree Programs.

JFK sponsors an Interdisciplinary Consciousness Studies program. Students can take up to six units of independent study in parapsychology.

Rosebridge Graduate School of Integrative Psychology
1040 Oak Gove Road, Suite 103
Concord, CA 94518
(510) 689-0560

The program in parapsychology should be fully operational by 1995.
General Information: Private, nonsectarian
Degrees Offered: M.A., Ph.D.
Programs: Parapsychology
Admission Requirements: Bachelor's degree
Application Deadline: Rolling
Contact Person: Director of Admissions
Tuition: $192/unit
Accreditation: State of California; WASC (pending)
Year Established: 1977
Faculty: Contact school

Saybrook Institute
See Nonresidential Psychology Degree Programs.

Saybrook offers master's and doctoral programs in human science psychology with a concentration in parapsychology. The program is directed by Stanley Krippner, Ph.D., a Parapsychological Association member.

West Georgia College
See Residential Psychology Degree Programs.

West George offers a clinical psychology specialization in parapsychology.

INTERNATIONAL NONDEGREE AND DEGREE PROGRAMS

Andhra University
Department of Psychology and Parapsychology
Visakhapatnam 530 003
India

Andhra offers a three-year Ph.D. program. Resident students have access to research facilities at the Institute for Yoga and Consciousness, which is affiliated with Andhra University.

Faculty for Bio-Psychical Sciences
Facauldade de Ciencias Biopsiquicas do Parana
Caixa Postal 7313
Curitiba - Parana
Brazil 80000

The program offers an 18-month (440-hour) clinical parapsychology study course designed for graduate students.

University of Edinburgh
Department of Psychology
7 George Square
Edinburgh EH8 9JZ
Scotland

Edinburgh offers an opportunity for graduate research leading to a Ph.D. in psychology with a concentration in parapsychology under the supervision of Professor Robert L. Morris, Ph.D., a Parapsychological Association member.

PSYCHOANALYSIS

Around the turn of the century Sigmund Freud developed a complex theory of human development, a method of investigation, and a specific mode of treatment called psychoanalysis, around which his theory of the unconscious is built. From his understanding of the human psyche, Freud introduced now-familiar concepts such as the ego, the id, the superego, defense mechanisms, transference (and countertransference), resistance, repression, narcissism, paranoia, and psychoneurosis. Psychoanalysis has remained unique among mental health methods and has developed into a comprehensive theory of mind, a psychotherapeutic procedure, and an educational process.

Despite the fact that there are various psychoanalytic perspectives—from Freud to Klein to Adler—the discipline itself remains a distinct and surprisingly cohesive field. For example, the field's non-academic orientation, post-graduate training programs, and intentional distinction from the disciplines of psychology, counseling, rehabilitation, clinical social work, and psychiatry provide common ground. There is also a shared commitment to analyzing each individual separately and to undergoing a personal psychoanalysis before functioning independently as an analyst.

One variant of psychoanalysis is known as self-psychology, developed by Heinz Kohut, M.D., a psychoanalyst who died in 1981. According to George Atwood, Ph.D., a professor at Rutgers University who is involved with the Institute for the Psychoanalytic Study of Subjectivity, self-psychology views everything in terms of the development and sub jective experience of the individual self, or what Atwood calls the "embeddedness of interpersonal contexts." This is in contrast to classical psychoanalysis, which views the psyche in terms of drive theory. Self-psychology's departure from traditional theoretical approaches such as these, in combination with its vital clinical application, has helped the movement become recognized in both professional and lay circles. However, given the theory's emphasis on empathy and caring (terms concurrently used in transpersonal psychology circles), it is somewhat surprising that the movement eschews an explicit spiritual dimension.

Psychoanalysis is less popular today that it was in the 1950s, and has become increasingly dislodged by psychotherapies that do things differently. For example, psychotherapy is performed with the client sitting up and facing the therapist, whereas a client undergoing psychoanalysis reclines, eyes closed. On the average, psychotherapy is conducted once a week over one or two years rather than four to five times a week over a four- or five-year period for psychoanalysis. Psychoanalysts usually charge from $60 to $150 per hour or session, depending on the analyst's experience. With most health insurance companies reducing the amount of reimbursement and the number of sessions per year, it is no wonder that, simply from a practical standpoint, the use of psychoanalysis continues to decline.

Two associations unify the psychoanalytic field: the International Federation for Psychoanalytic Education (IFPE) and the National Association for the Advancement of Psychoanalysis (NAAP). According to the American Board for Accreditation in Psychoanalysis (ABAP), a psychoanalyst is a graduate of a recognized training institute or program that meets the following criteria: at least 375 classroom hours, 300 hours of individual psychoanalysis, and 450 hours of supervised clinical experience. Training at any of the institutes can last anywhere from two to seven

years, and consists of weekly seminars plus personal analysis.

Certain psychoanalytic institutes have only recently waived the traditional M.D. requirement from their admission standards, although most programs still require at least a master's degree (and sometimes a Ph.D.) in an unspecified area. (Originally, the American Psychoanalytic Association renounced Freud's psychoanalytic tradition, which valued an intense education in the liberal arts, and adopted instead a policy restricting the practice of psychoanalysis to medical analysts only.) Students who meet the requirements established by the ABAP receive certification; however, because the field remains unregulated (and there are no apparent indications that this will change any time soon), most practitioners become licensed in and receive third-party insurance through a complementary field before specializing.

—Jeffrey Rubin, Ph.D., contributed to this introduction. He practices psychoanalysis and psychoanalytically oriented psychotherapy, and is an instructor in the Adult Psychoanalytic Training Program of the Postgraduate Center for Mental Health in New York City.

General Organizations

American Academy of Psychoanalysis
47 East 19th Street, 6th floor
New York, NY 10033-1323
(212) 475-7980

Founded in 1956, the academy aims to develop a dialogue among psychoanalysts and colleagues in other science and humanity disciplines. The academy advocates an acceptance of all relevant and responsible psychoanalytic views of human behavior, rather than adherence to one particular doctrine. It publishes the quarterly *Journal of the American Academy of Psychoanalysis.*

American Psychoanalytic Association (APA)
309 East 49th Street
New York, NY 10017
(212) 752-0450

The APA, founded in 1911, currently has a membership of about 3,000 analysts. It also includes accredited training institutes and affiliate psychoanalytic societies throughout the United States. Since its inception, it has been a member of the

International Psychoanalytic Association, the official representative of world-wide psychoanalysts. The APA is the most prestigious psychoanalytic association, and now admits nonmedical men and women drawn from various fields.

Committee on Psychoanalysis of the National Federation of Societies for Clinical Social Work (COP)
40 Arrandale Avenue
Rockville Centre, NY 11570
(516) 764-9726

The COP is a national advocacy group for Clinical Social Workers (CSW) who practice psychoanalysis and psychoanalytic psychotherapy. Just as Division 39 of the American Psychological Association represents psychologists with an interest in religion, so does the COP represent social workers interested in combining psychoanalysis with social work.

Institute for Psychoanalytic Training and Research (IPTAR)
1651 Third Avenue, Suite 201
New York, NY 10128
(212) 427-7070

Founded in 1958, the IPTAR was the first membership organization for nonmedical analysts. Even though the training institute was established in 1960, its curriculum is governed by a contemporary Freudian perspective.

International Federation for Psychoanalytic Education (IFPE)
340 Lewelen Circle
Englewood, NJ 07631-2021
(201) 569-2766

IFPE was established in 1991. Its goals include "supporting the educational and training endeavors of psychoanalysts from different perspectives and encouraging critical dialogue among representatives of those perspectives." Membership is open to individuals and organizations with an interest in psychoanalysis. IFPE publishes a newsletter and a directory of individual and institutional members.

National Association for the Advancement of Psychoanalysis (NAAP)
American Board for Accreditation and Certification
80 Eighth Avenue, Suite 1501
New York, NY 10011
(212) 741-0515

Ever since the early schisms in psychoanalysis, Freudians, Jungians, Adlerians, and other psychoanalytic schools have remained relatively fragmented. NAAP represents the first contemporary effort to reunite these schools of thought. NAAP was conceived in 1972 when institute faculties from the western, the southwestern, and the eastern United States met to discuss unification of the profession. NAAP sets educational standards, accredits training centers, accepts membership, and works toward the recognition of psychoanalysis as a distinct discipline. Contact NAAP for their "Directory of Psychoanalytic Training Institutes."

National Psychological Association for Psychoanalysis (NPAP)
150 West 13th Street
New York, NY 10011-7891
(212) 924-7440
   Founded in 1948 by Theodor Reik, the NPAP is an association of psychoanalysts dedicated to the advancement of psychoanalysis as a science and as a profession. The training institute of NPAP is the oldest and largest nonmedical program in the United States.

Periodicals
International Journal of Psychoanalysis
63 New Cavendish Street
London W1M7RD
England
Quarterly; $79

International Review of Psychoanalysis
Routledge Press
for the Institute for Psychoanalysis London
11 New Fetter Lane
London BC4P 4EE
England
Quarterly; $93

Journal of the American Academy of Psychoanalysis
American Academy of Psychoanalysis
Quarterly; $45

Journal of the American Psychoanalytic Association
American Psychoanalytic Association
Quarterly; $59

Modern Psychoanalysis
Center for Modern Psychoanalytic Studies
Semiannual; $15

Psychoanalysis and Contemporary Thought
International Universities Press
59 Boston Post Road
Madison, CT 06443
(203) 245-4000
Quarterly; $65

Psychoanalytic Dialogues: The Journal of Relational Perspectives
The Analytic Press
365 Broadway
Hillsdale, NJ 07642
(201) 666-4110
Quarterly; $42.50

Psychoanalytic Inquiry
The Analytic Press
365 Broadway
Hillsdale, NJ 07642
(201) 666-4110
Quarterly; $55

Psychoanalytic Quarterly
Psychoanalytic Quarterly, Inc.
175 5th Avenue, Room 517
New York, NY 10010-7799
Quarterly; $70

The Psychoanalytic Review
Guilford Publications
72 Spring Street
New York, NY 10012
(212) 431-9800
Quarterly; $35

Training Institutes
We have included schools of psychoanalytic thought that hold a humanistic orientation.

ADLERIAN
Alfred Adler Institute
1780 Broadway, Suite 502
New York, NY 10019
(212) 974-0431
   The institute was established in 1950.

EGO PSYCHOLOGY AND OBJECT RELATIONS
California Graduate Institute
Department of Psychoanalysis
1100 Glendon Avenue, Suite 1119
Los Angeles, CA 90024
(213) 879-1533

Institute for Expressive Analysis
325 West End Avenue, Apt. 12B
New York, NY 10023
(212) 362-5085

Washington Square Institute for Psychotherapy and Mental Health
41 East 11 Street
New York, NY 10003
(212) 477-2600

EXISTENTIAL
Westchester Institute for Training in Psychoanalysis and Psychotherapy
2 Sarles Street
P.O. Box 89
Mount Kisco, NY 10549
(914) 666-0163

GENERAL PROGRAMS
Center for Modern Psychoanalytic Studies
16 West 10th Street
New York, NY 10011
(212) 260-7050

Institute for Psychoanalytic Training and Research
1651 3rd Avenue
New York, NY 10128
(212) 427-7070

Metropolitan Institute
Training in Psychoanalytic Psychotherapy
336 Central Park West
New York, NY 10025
(212) 864-7000

New York University
Postdoctoral Program in Psychotherapy and Psychoanalysis
Department of Psychology
1 Washington Place, First Floor
New York, NY 10003
(212) 998-7890
   The student may select a systematic course of study in a Freudian, an interpersonal-humanistic, or a relational orientation.

The Program of Psychiatry and Religion at the Union Theological Seminary
3041 Broadway
New York, NY 10027
(212) 662-7100

Training Institute of NPAP
150 West 13th Street
New York, NY 10011
(212) 924-7440

The Westchester Institute for Training and Psychoanalysis and Psychotherapy
   See Existential Psychoanalysis.

SELF-PSYCHOLOGY
Institute for the Psychoanalytic Study of Subjectivity
Sanda Kaiersky, Ph.D., Coordinator of Training
344 West 23rd Street
New York, NY 10011
(212) 807-0023

Psychoanalytic Psychotherapy Study Center
31 West 11 Street, Suite 1B
New York, NY 10011
(212) 633-9162

The Training and Research Institute for Self-Psychology
Society for the Advancement of Self-Psychology
15 West 96th Street
New York, NY 10025
(212) 663-3508

Washington Square Institute for Psychotherapy and Mental Health
41 East 11th Street
New York, NY 10003
(212) 477-2600

PSYCHOSYNTHESIS

Psychosynthesis is based on "universal" principles that Italian psychiatrist Roberto Assagioli formulated from his integration of depth psychology and Eastern psychospiritual traditions during the early part of this century. Since then, psychosynthesis has become a recognized approach to self-help, counseling, and education.

The psychosynthesis model is widely applicable in counseling and related fields as a tool for psychological healing and personal transformation. Certificate programs teach psychosynthesis theory and methodology, the principles of holistic counseling, and the process of psychological and spiritual development.

In practice, psychosynthesis is an openly flexible framework that draws on a wide range of analytic, behavioral, humanistic, transpersonal, and spiritual principles. It is, however, designed to be used only as an adjunct technique. Psychosynthesis can be applied to such disparate fields as psychology, health and healing, addiction counseling, hospice work, education, body therapy, religion, the arts, organizational development, and international relations. Practitioners utilize an array of techniques including imagery, hypnotherapy, Gestalt, movement, assertion training, family systems work, breathwork, art therapy, journal writing, and meditation. Enabling clients to take responsibility for their own growth is a priority.

Since psychosynthesis is a non-regulated (i.e., no license required) therapeutic method, graduates are provided with a certificate indicating the completion of a program. The level of training to be obtained is dependent upon the manner in which psychosynthesis will be applied. The training of teachers, nurses, and physical therapists, for example, emphasizes incorporating a psychosynthesis perspective into their professional roles, while the training of psychotherapists involves a more hands-on understanding of psychosynthesis, including specific techniques to be used during therapy. Some non-residential degree programs and transpersonal graduate schools, such as the Institute for Transpersonal Psychology, offer partial credit upon completing a training program. Although psychosynthesis remains comparatively well organized in Europe, there is no central membership or clearinghouse organization in the United States.

—*Staff from Psychosynthesis Distribution, a mail-order book company, contributed to this introduction.*

ADDITIONAL RESOURCES

Psychosynthesis and Education Trust (PET)
92-94 Tooley Street, London Bridge
London SE1 2TH
England

The PET publishes the annually updated *International Psychosynthesis Directory* (available through Psychosynthesis Distribution).

Psychosynthesis Distribution (PD)
2871 West Ironwood Ridge Drive
Tuscon, AZ 85745
(602) 743-8881

PD is a mail-order book company whose catalog includes a comprehensive listing of psychosynthesis centers in North America, as well as a helpful overview of the field.

Periodicals

Psychosynthesis Lifeline: A Newsletter for the Psychosynthesis Community
The Psychosynthesis Resource Center
P.O. Box 3833
New Haven, CT 06525
Three issues a year; $20.00

TRAINING PROGRAMS
Concord Institute Program in Spiritual Psychology
P.O. Box 82
Concord, MA 01742
(508) 371-3206

Connecticut Institute for Psychosynthesis
2225 Main Street
Stratford, CT 06497
(203) 377-2421

Huntington Therapy Institute
2 Murray Court
Huntington, NY 11743
(516) 673-0293

Integrative Therapy Institute
c/o New York Open Center
72 Spring Street
New York, NY 10012
(212) 219-2527

International Association for Managerial and Organizational Psychosynthesis (IAMOP)
3308 Radcliffe Road
Thousand Oaks, CA 91360
(805) 492-4815

The major purpose of IAMOP is to encourage the application of psychosynthesis to managerial and organizational development. Summit University of Louisiana honors the IAMOP program with academic credit (see Nonresidential Psychology Degree Programs).

Kentucky Center of Psychosynthesis
436 West 2nd Street
Lexington, KY 40507
(606) 254-9112

New York Psychosynthesis Collective
P.O. Box 602
Wilton, CT 06897
(203) 762-9709

Psychosynthesis Center
P.O. Box 264
Uwchlan, PA 19480
(215) 458-8616

Psychosynthesis Institute of Minnesota
P.O Box 8171
St. Paul, MN 55108
(612) 341-3611

Psychosynthesis Institute of New York
70 West 11th Street, Suite 1E
New York, NY 10011
(212) 674-5244

Psychosynthesis International
P.O. Box 279
Ojai, CA 93024
(805) 646-7041

Psychosynthesis of Puget Sound
925 116th Avenue, N.E., Suite 241
Bellevue, WA 98004
(206) 450-9787

Synthesis Center for
Psychosynthesis Training
P.O Box 575
Amherst, MA 01004
(413) 256-0772

Synthesis Institute of San Diego
2615 Camino del Rio South, Suite 300
San Diego, CA 92108
(619) 291-4465

Vermont Center for Psychosynthesis
62 East Avenue
Burlington, VT 05401
(802) 862-8485

SHAMANIC COUNSELING

Over tens of thousands of years, our ancestors all over the world learned in their struggle for survival how to maximize extraordinary consciousness. The system they developed is known today as "shamanism," a term that comes from a Siberian tribal word for its healing practitioners. A shaman (pronounced SHAH-mahn) is a type of medicine man or woman who is able to journey to invisible worlds, most commonly recognized through the narratives of world mythology, in order to effect healing. These journeys are usually accessed by entering a non-ordinary state of consciousness, often using a monotonous percussion sonic or sound, such as drumming. Shamanism is a methodology, not a religion.

What we know today about shamanism comes from the last living bearers of this ancient human knowledge, the shamans of surviving tribal cultures scattered in remote parts of the world. Due to the destruction of indigenous peoples and their cultures, few aboriginal practitioners are left today. Westerners have only recently begun to discover shamanism's astonishing results in problem-solving and healing.

Practitioners of shamanism may have particular specialties or they may be involved in a full range of activities including divination, empowerment, and spiritual healing. The shaman believes that all things have a spirit—not only what we ordinarily think of as living beings, but also rocks, rivers, the sky, and the earth. Through working with the spirits of these beings (in a non-ordinary state of consciousness), the shaman effects healing, communes with nature, or gains important self-awareness or information about a member of the tribe or the community.

Contemporary shamans often work with people individually or on a case-by-case basis. Although most people are used to seeing them dressed with masks and costumes in their tribal community, many such practitioners find no need to do so; in fact, those same practitioners find that shamanic techniques work in clinical settings, including those of the creative and expressive arts.

Perhaps the most controversial (and enigmatic) aspect of shamanic work is that a shaman claims that he or she may heal another person through techniques performed while in a non-ordinary state of consciousness even though the individual may not believe in shamanism, participate in its techniques, or be present during a shaman's "journeying." Ethically speaking, however, the client should consent to any shamanic work performed for his or her benefit.

Techniques of a shaman include the extraction of spiritual entities that may be causing sickness and the retrieval of lost spiritual parts of an individual that may be making a person particularly vulnerable to disease. The techniques are usually used as a complement to more conventional healing techniques, although it has been known to be more effective where those conventional techniques have failed. In some instances, a therapist trains a patient or client to do shamanic healing for her- or himself.

Modern shamanism is practiced by a range of practitioners in various settings: physicians and nurses in hospitals, therapists in offices, and counselors in hospices.

Workshops and training programs include both international foundations and programs offered by individuals associated with a specific cultural tradition (such as Huichol as taught by Brant Secunda and Lakota as taught by Wallace Black Elk). The Foundation for Shamanic Studies (FSS), founded by anthropologist Michael Harner, Ph.D., teaches counseling techniques based on shamanic tradition and offers certification in Harner Method Shamanic Counseling to teach and counsel for shamanic divination on a one-on-one basis.

Some shamanic counselors practice without additional mental health experience, and insofar as shamanism is concerned, it has been suggested that the psychotherapeutic process may be more of an impediment than a benefit. More conventional counselors incorporate shamanism into their practices—some presenting it up front, others using the techniques but not referring to themselves as shamanic. Although it is difficult to forecast the future directions of shamanic counseling, the FSS would like to see this form of healing incorporated into modern treatment settings, as well as scientifically tested for efficacy and usefulness.

—Steve White, of the Foundation for Shamanic Studies, contributed to this introduction.

Associations and Organizations

Conference on the Study of Shamanism and Alternative Modes of Healing
Ruth-Inge Heinze, Ph.D.
2321 Russell Street, Suite 3A
Berkeley, CA 94705
Correspondence offered only by mail.

Institute of Noetic Sciences (IONS)
See Research Institutes.
IONS shares an interest in shamanism.

International Society for Shamanistic Research
Mihály Hoppál
1250 Budapest
P.O. Box 29
Hungary

Society for the Anthropology of Consciousness
See Interdisciplinary Resources.

The Spiritual Emergence Network (SEN)
See Interdisciplinary Resources.
SEN maintains an interest in the healing aspects of shamanism.

Periodicals

Anthropology and Consciousness
See Interdisciplinary Resources.

Shamanic News
10 Town Plaza, Suite 222
Durango, CO 81301
(303) 259-4027
Monthly; $16

Shamanism Newsletter
Foundation for Shamanic Studies
Semiannual; $30 (with membership)

Shaman's Drum: A Journal of Experiential Shamanism
P.O. Box 430
Willits, CA 95490
(707) 459-0486
Quarterly; $15
This magazine is published by the Cross-Cultural Shamanism Network and presents articles related to shamanism.

TRAINING INSTITUTES

Dance of the Deer Foundation
Center for Shamanic Studies
P.O. Box 699
Soquel, CA 95073
(408) 475-9560
Programs: Various pilgrimages and workshops in the United States, as well as trips to Mexico and Europe
The foundation was founded in 1979 by Brant Secunda and various Huichol shamans.

Foundation for Shamanic Studies (FSS)
P.O. Box 1939
Mill Valley, CA 94942
(415) 380-8282
Programs: Death and dying; shamanic counseling training; shamanism and shamanic healing training; soul retrieval training
This nonprofit educational organization was founded and is directed by Michael Harner, Ph.D. In addition to training, it also sponsors research concerning indigenous shamanic practices.

Independent Training Programs

The following nondegree programs provide training for professionals who seek to enhance their current practice. Most are applicable to health professionals, both alternative and conventional, as well as to lay people. Whereas academic degree programs and licensing exams emphasize more intellectual, theoretical, and perhaps methodical skills, the following nondegree programs allow graduates from both mainstream and psychospiritual graduate schools who are already well grounded in their discipline's theoretical traditions a chance to pursue experiential learning, personal growth, and inspiring topics.

Academy for Guided Imagery
311 Miller Avenue
Mill Valley, CA 94942
(415) 389-9324; (800) 726-2070
Programs: Certificate program in guided imagery
Founded in 1989, the academy's mission is to teach professionals in the counseling and health fields to use imagery in their practices. Drawing on related disciplines—including Eriksonian hypnosis, Jungian psychology, psychosynthesis, self-actualization, and ego-state psychology—the academy believes that the technique helps patients evoke the inner potential for growth and healing. The academy's certificate program includes 150 hours of clinically oriented training. Introductory programs are held throughout the United States.

Aletheia Heart Institute
1068 East Main Street
Ashland, OR 97520
(503) 488-0709
Programs: Four-year internship program; monthly seminars; personal health training; post-treatment of substance abuse
Founded in 1958 by Jack Schwarz as a nonprofit organization, Aletheia supports programs and research that synthesize the findings of science, the perspectives of philosophy and psychology, and the revelations of spirituality. Various programs provide tools and techniques for continued

growth, along with the underlying basis that enables a person to take control of his or her own life in a positive manner. All of the programs emphasize the mind-brain-body connection and assist the participant in applying developed tools to his or her daily life. The institute publishes a quarterly newsletter, *Discovery*.

American Imagery Institute
P.O. Box 13453
Milwaukee, WI 53213
(414) 781-4045
Programs: Death before life; Eastern and Western approaches to healing; healing from within; intensive training in guided imagery; world conference in guided imagery
Founded in 1983, the institute organizes workshops primarily in the field of imagery. Many workshop participants are counselors, nurses, psychologists, physicians, and social workers.

American Society of Alternative Therapists
85 Eastern Avenue
Gloucester, MA 01930
(508) 281-4400
Programs: Holistic health counselor certification; natural childbirth and parenting certification; psychic healing certification
Founded in 1990, the society is a nonprofit professional and educational organization intended to unite persons having a serious interest in alternative approaches to healing and wellness. Members include both professional and lay persons from eclectic scientific, philosophical, and spiritual orientations. The society sponsors certification programs and professional development workshops, monitors legislation impacting the field of alternative therapy, promotes community education projects to further public awareness and acceptance of alternative healing, and sponsors regional and state chapters.

Animas Valley Institute
54 Ute Pass Trail
Durango, CO 81301
(303) 259-0585
Programs: Training and apprenticeship programs for vision quest guides
A vision quest is a multi-day, earth-centered rite of passage enacted with a small group of fellow seekers. Founded in 1980 by psychologist Bill Plotkin, Ph.D., the institute also offers programs in sustainable living, creativity, and expressive movement.

Barbara Brennan School of Healing

P.O. Box 2005
East Hampton, NY 11937
(516) 329-0951
Programs: Introduction to healing science workshops; professional healing science training program

Founded by *Hands of Light* author Barbara Brennan in 1982, the school offers a four-year program in healing science. Studies include the anatomy and physiology of the human energy field, interpersonal energy interaction, perceiving an aura to determine the cause of illness, channeling, and various deep healing techniques. Five-day workshops are held five times a year in New York.

Beshara School of Intensive Esoteric Education

P.O. Box 422283
San Francisco, CA 94142
(415) 333-8403
Programs: Introductory courses; residential six-month course

Biofeedback Training Institute (BTI)

Stens Corporation
6451 Oakwood Drive
Oakland, CA 94611
(510) 339-9053; (800) 257-8367

The BTI offers a professional biofeedback certificate program in Berkeley, Los Angeles, Dallas, and Atlanta.

Cape Cod Institute

1308D Belfer
Albert Einstein College of Medicine
1300 Morris Park Avenue
Bronx, NY 10461
(718) 430-2307
Programs: Varying from summer-to-summer (i.e., Jungian psychotherapy: a critical synthesis; psychotherapy and spirituality; shorter term existential-humanistic psychotherapy)

The institute offers a summer-long series of courses on topics of current interest to mental health professionals. Although it sponsors numerous secular courses, the institute almost always offers at least three from a depth psychology and psychospiritual perspective. It also offers 21 week-long courses throughout the summer.

Center for Action and Contemplation

P.O. Box 12464
Albuquerque, NM 87195-2464
(505) 242-9588
Programs: Justice and peace work internship
Founded in 1987 by Richard Rohr, the center is interested in social change through a Christian faith perspective. Program topics include contemplation and liberation theology, Myers-Briggs/Enneagram workshops, activist dialogues, and spiritual direction.

Center for Attitudinal Healing

19 Main Street
Tiburon, CA 94920
(415) 435-5022
Programs: Attitudinal healing training workshop (level I, II); group facilitation training workshop

Attitudinal healing is based on the belief that it is possible to choose peace rather than conflict, and love rather than fear. The center was established in 1975 by Gerald Jampolsky, M.D., and supplements traditional health care through an environment in which children, youths, and adults faced with life-threatening illness actively participate in the attitudinal healing process. There are a number of similar independent centers located around the United States; contact the Tiburon center for more information.

The Center for Journal Therapy

Department 0-3, P.O. Box 963
Arvada, CO 80001
(303) 421-2298
Programs: Instructor certification training
Founded in 1985 by Kathleen Adams, M.A., L.C.P., the center teaches the art of journal writing to individuals, groups, and mental health professionals.

Center for Sandplay Studies

252 South Boulevard
Upper Grandview, NY 10960
(914) 358-2318
Programs: Sandplay training
Sandplay therapy was developed by Dora Kalff, a Swiss psychologist and close collaborator of C.G. Jung. The therapy combines aspects of play therapy, art therapy, and verbal therapy that enhance and often accelerate the therapeutic process. It is used with individuals, children, couples, and families and is amenable to the treatment of a wide variety of disorders.

Center for Studies of the Person

The Carl Rogers Institute of Psychotherapy, Training and Supervision
1125 Torrey Pines Road
La Jolla, CA 92037
(619) 459-3861
Programs: Certificate in client-centered therapy; La Jolla summer institute

The center comprises a group of professionals committed to person-centered values based on the principles developed through the research and practice of the late psychologist Carl R. Rogers, Ph.D. The didactic and experiential training and supervision program is designed for mental health professionals who are interested in developing and enhancing their knowledge, skills, and understanding of client-centered individuals, family, and group therapy. The center maintains the Carl Rogers Memorial Library.

Circle

400 Cote Lane
Missoula, MT 59802
(406) 542-2383
Programs: Specific programs and workshops change annually; contact Circle for more information

Circle offers residential programs in the art and practice of creating and sustaining sacred space.

Concord Institute

Box 82
Concord, MA 01742
(508) 391-3206
Programs: Certificate program in group leadership; certificate program in spiritual psychology; Concord Institute Summer School

This educational organization was founded in 1990 to help professionals of all kinds who want to expand and deepen their work within a comprehensive spiritual context.

Consciousness Research and Training Project

315 East 68th Street, Box 9G
New York, NY 10021
Correspondence offered only by mail.
Programs: Healing and self-healing seminars

These seminars work with a wide range of meditations and cognitive material that are linked with personal and transpersonal growth, consciousness theory and research, holistic health, and wellness.

Creative Energy Options (CEO)

909 Sumneytown Pike, Suite 105
Springhouse, PA 19477
(215) 643-4420
Programs: American Association for Marriage and Family Therapy supervision group; cross-cultural healing practices; expressive arts; In Search of Meaning; Power of Sound; studies in new therapies

Founded in 1984, the CEO is a therapeutic education center offering programs in transpersonal psychology, cross-cultural practices, and experiential techniques from a therapeutic intervention model.

Cuyamungue Institute (CI)
Route 5, Box 358A
Santa Fe, NM 87501
(505) 455-2749
Programs: Masked trance dance workshop combining ecstatic trance with the expressive arts

Founded in 1979 by anthropologist Felicitas Goodman, Ph.D., as a nonprofit institute, CI provides adjunct educational opportunities in anthropology, psychotherapy, ecology, and the arts. The institute utilizes ritual body postures and ecstatic trance in its training methods.

Dallas Institute of Humanities and Culture (DIHC)
2719 Routh Street
Dallas, TX 75201
(214) 871-2440
Programs: Public education; creative leadership seminars; spiritual psychology

Founded in 1980, the DIHC is a center for creative thought dedicated to the awakening of a sense of the sacred in the world through studies in literature, art, spirituality, psychology, architecture, city planning, and economics. The institute offers courses of study, seminars, and public conferences, generally from a Jungian perspective.

Dialogue House Associates
80 East 11th Street, Suite 305
New York, NY 10003-6008
(212) 673-5880
Programs: Progoff Intensive Journal®

Ira Progoff, Ph.D., developed the Intensive Journal method in the mid-1960s and founded Dialogue House to make the method available to the general public. Continuing education credits for counselors are available through various professional licensing associations.

The Education Center (EC)
6357 Clayton Road
St. Louis, MO 63117
(314) 721-7604

Since 1941, EC has been a cooperative network dedicated to designing, researching, and teaching the Socratic process of teaching. The center honors life experiences as steps on the journey toward meaning, wholeness, and transformation, and offers training programs through regional workshops and local training events.

Elizabeth Kübler Ross Hospice and Grief Counseling Program
Northern New Mexico Community College
El Rito Campus
El Rito, NM 87530
(505) 581-4501

Programs: Death education; home health aid training; hospice administration; hospice care; transpersonal grief counseling

Also see Northern New Mexico Community College under Residential Psychology Degree Programs.

Eupsychia
3930 West Bee Caves Road, Suites I-J
Austin, TX 78746
(512) 327-2795
Programs: Psychospiritual integration; integrative breathwork

Eupsychia, founded by Jacquelyn Small, M.S.W., in 1983, is a "new paradigm" educational and training institute that offers training and healing programs for health professionals and others seeking knowledge and experience of personal psychospiritual transformation. The institute attempts to bridge traditional and alternative approaches.

The Focusing Institute
731 South Plymouth Court, Suite 801
Chicago, IL 60605
(312) 922-9277
Programs: Certificate in focusing

Founded in 1985 as a nonprofit corporation, the theoretical basis for the method evolved from the work of Eugene Gendlin, Ph.D., of the University of Chicago (author of *Focusing*). The institute sponsors seminars, workshops, and classes; trains teachers in the focusing process; and conducts research into the method's efficacy. It also publishes a journal, *The Folio: A Journal of Focusing and Experiential Therapy.*

Foundation for A Course in Miracles
1275 Tennanah Lake Road
Roscoe, NY 12776-5905
(607) 498-4116
Programs: A Course in Miracles workshops

The foundation was founded in 1983 to augment *A Course in Miracles*—a copious, three-volume "curriculum" of spiritual development channeled by Helen Shuchman, Ph.D., and transcribed by William Thetford, Ph.D.

Foundation for Community Encouragement (FCE)
109 Danbury Road, Suite 8
Ridgefield, CT 06877
(203) 431-9484
Programs: Community building skills seminars; community building workshops; community continuity conference; public facilitator training

The FCE, a nonprofit educational foundation, was founded by M. Scott Peck, M.D., and teaches the principles and values of community to individuals, groups, organizations, and businesses. It publishes a quarterly newsletter, *Communiqué.*

Four-Fold Way Training
P.O. Box 2077
Sausalito, CA 94966
(415) 331-5050
Programs: Year-long foundation training; Four-Fold Way training; six-day foundation training; twelve-day in-depth training

Founded by Angeles Arrien, Ph.D., these educational programs explore indigenous wisdom, cross-cultural values, and experiential practices gleaned from ancient and modern ways.

Grief Recovery Institute
Loyola Marymount University
8306 Wilshire Boulevard, Suite 21-A
Beverly Hills, CA 90211
(800) 334-7606; (213) 650-1234
Programs: Grief Recovery™ certificate program

Grof Transpersonal Training
20 Sunny side Avenue, Suite A-314
Mill Valley, CA 94941
(415) 383-8779
Programs: Holotropic Breathwork™ workshop; certification seminar

In 1976, Christina Grof and Stanislav Grof, M.D., developed the practice of Holotropic Breathwork™, a comprehensive approach to self-exploration that integrates the physical, psychological, and spiritual dimensions of human experience. The technique helps people access many levels of human experience, including unfinished issues from one's postnatal history, sequences of psychological death and rebirth, and the entire spectrum of transpersonal phenomena.

The name holotropic (from the Greek word *holos,* meaning "whole," and *trepein,* meaning "to move in the direction of") literally means "moving toward wholeness." This approach is based on the spontaneous healing potential of non-ordinary states of consciousness, which are induced by breathing techniques and evocative music. Focused release work and mandala drawing are additional elements used in the healing process.

Guild for Psychological Studies (GPS)
2230 Divisadero Street
San Francisco, CA 94115
(415) 931-0647
Programs: Various seminars and workshops

Since 1952, the GPS has offered seminars on the process of becoming a "value-centered" individual. Emphasis is on religious, psychological, mythological, and literary texts.

Healing Circle Center
Crystal Road
Colmar, PA 18915
(215) 822-0729
Programs: Three-year holistic therapy training

Ute Arnold developed the Unergi© Method, a dynamic system of touch, movement, and verbal therapy, creative expression, and contact with nature that helps integrate the body, mind, emotion, and spirit. The program brings together Fritz Perls's Gestalt Therapy, Feldenkrais awareness movements, the Alexander Technique, Rubenfeld Synergy®, nature, and art.

Heartwood Institute
220 Harmony Lane
Garberville, CA 95542
(707) 923-2021
Programs: Hypnotherapy; transformational studies

Also see Retreat Centers, Addiction Counseling, and Interdisciplinary Somatic Therapies.

Helen Palmer Workshops
1442A Walnut Street, Suite 377
Berkeley, CA 94709
(510) 843-7621
Programs: Aikido; Enneagram workshops; intuition training workshops

Founded and directed by Helen Palmer, the center's three main objectives are to engage in and promote intuition research; to provide training for people who want access to intuition as a source of information for their lives; and to offer professional training to those who wish to apply this work to their area(s) of interest.

The Hendricks Institute
409 East Bijou Street
Colorado Springs, CO 80903-3414
(719) 632-0772
Programs: Hendricks Method of Body-Mind Integration

The institute offers programs that help mental health professionals develop themselves in order to better serve their clients.

Himalayan Institute (HI)
R.R. 1, Box 400
Honesdale, PA 18431
(800) 822-4547
Programs: Seminars for counselors and therapists; Hatha Yoga teachers' training

Since its establishment in 1971 by Swami

Rama, HI has been dedicated to helping individuals develop themselves physically, mentally, and spiritually. All the institute programs—educational, therapeutic, research—emphasize holistic health, yoga, and meditation as tools to help achieve these goals.

Hippocrates Health Institute
1443 Palmdale Court
West Palm Beach, FL 33411
(407) 471-8876
Programs: Hippocrates Health Educator

Founded in 1981, this six-month certificate program offers educational experiences in five principal areas of personal and career development: lifestyle and nutritional education, apprenticeship experience, self-actualization, opportunities in related holistic disciplines, and career placement opportunities.

Institute for Dialogical Psychotherapy (IDP)
Executive Plaza Building
225 Stevens Avenue, Suite 101
Solana Beach, CA 92075-2058
(619) 481-8744
Programs: Dialogical psychotherapy certificate

The IDP, founded in 1984, arose out of a desire expressed by a number of psychotherapists to apply Martin Buber's philosophy of dialogue (the I-Thou relationship) to the practice of psychotherapy. This approach to psychotherapy rests upon the belief that our interconnectedness with others is at the core of human existence.

Institute for International Connections (IIC)
200 South Sherman Street
Denver, CO 80209
(303) 733-6878
Programs: Family therapy training; social welfare services; business management and consultation

The IIC, founded in 1989 as a nonprofit corporation, seeks to contribute to the massive cultural change occurring in Eastern Europe as experienced on individual, family, and cultural levels. With colleagues from Europe, the IIC offers cross-cultural training and internships in psychology, social work, education, and management consultation, and works to develop models for the workplace, schools, and institutions that enhance creativity and self-esteem. It publishes a newsletter, *The Paper Connection.*

Institutes of Religion and Health
The Blanton-Peale Graduate Institute
3 West 29th Street
New York, NY 10001-4597
(212) 725-7850
Programs: Marriage and family residency; Master of Professional Studies; pastoral psychotherapy and pastoral studies program (see Pastoral Counseling); psychotherapy residency

The American Foundation of Religion and Psychiatry was founded in 1937 when the late Smiley Blanton, an eminent New York psychiatrist, was contacted by the famous Reverend Dr. Norman Vincent Peale for help with the large number of people coming to him for counseling during the Depression years. The Academy of Religion and Mental Health was started by the Rev. George Christian Anderson, Paul Tillich, Gordon Allport, and William C. Menninger in 1954. It was created to provide a forum for interested clergy, psychiatrists, and other medical, social, and behavioral scientists to discuss the relationship of health and behavior and its relevance to issues of faith and wholeness.

The two organizations were merged in 1972 to form the Institutes of Religion and Health, which includes the Blanton-Peale Graduate Institute. The institute offers a postdegree psychotherapy program for ordained and nonordained individuals of all faiths that emphasizes the integration of psychotherapy and spirituality. The institute's main focus, however, is the professional training of clergy in the art of pastoral psychotherapy. It publishes the quarterly *Journal of Religion and Health.*

Integrative Therapy Institute
c/o New York Open Center
83 Spring Street
New York, NY 10012
(212) 219-2527
Programs: Integrative Therapy certificate program; psychosynthesis certification

This program offers a three-year in-depth education for human service professionals who wish to incorporate psychospiritual and holistic perspectives into their professional work.

The Journey School (JS)
4219 Magnolia Street
New Orleans, LA 70115
(504) 899-2335

Founded 1988, JS offers weekend workshops that focus on the mythology of the "ancient mysteries" and how they relate to psychological and spiritual truths.

Kripalu Center for Yoga and Health
Box 793
Lenox, MA 01240
(800) 967-3577
Programs: Holistic health, yoga, meditation, bodywork, spiritual attunement

The center was founded by eminent yoga master, yogi Amrit Desai and is now the largest residential holistic health educational facility in North America. Also see Retreat Centers.

Kripalu Center for Yoga, Meditation and Personal Growth
2109 Walters Road
Sunnytown, PA 18084-0250
(215) 234-4568
Programs: Same programs as above

Mid-Life Directions
45 Poe Avenue
Vailsburg, NJ 07106
(201) 373-6118
Programs: Professional training program in Mid-Life Directions; workshops and retreats

Anne Brennan, Ph.D., and Janice Brew, Ph.D., founded Mid-Life Directions in 1981 in response to Carl Jung's complaint that people are "wholly unprepared to take the step into the second half of life." The organization promotes the personal and spiritual growth of adults through education, publishing, training, consulting, workshops, retreats, and seminars.

The Monroe Institute
Route 1, Box 175
Faber, VA 22938
(804) 361-1500
Programs: Gateway; Guidelines; Life Span 2000; Lifeline

Founded by Robert Monroe, the institute offers programs in the Hemi-Sync™ learning system, a sound-based technology that teaches techniques to enhance perception beyond the five senses, as well as to facilitate out-of-body experiences.

The Mystery School
Box 3300
Pomona, NY 10970
(914) 354-4965
Programs: Varies each year

Founded and directed by Jean Houston, Ph.D., the school offers various weekend and year-long programs that incorporate sacred psychology, history, music, theater, anthropology, philosophy, theology, science, and metaphysics.

The New Seminary
7 West 96th Street, Suite 19B
New York, NY 10025
(212) 866-3795
Programs: Jewish spiritual guides/rabbinical ordination; correspondence programs; interfaith ministry, levels I and II; Kabbalistic healing and visual meditation

See Jewish Theological Training for more information.

Nine Gates
220 Redwood Highway, Suite 61
Mill Valley, CA 94941
(415) 927-1677
Programs: Nine Gates Training

Founded and directed by Gay Luce, Ph.D., the training program incorporates concepts developed from the ancient mystery schools.

Pendle Hill
Wallingford, PA 19086
(215) 566-4507
Programs: Biblical studies; literature and the arts; Quakerism; religious thought and spiritual practice; social concerns

Founded in 1930 by members of the Religious Society of Friends, this Quaker center roots its educational philosophy in equality, simplicity, harmony, and community.

Phoenicia Pathwork Center
Programs: Eva Pierrakos's teachings; weeklong intensive; workshops; process groups; retreats

See Retreat Centers.

Quest
Center for Spiritual Wholeness
Grace Cathedral
1051 Taylor Street
San Francisco, CA 94108
(415) 776-6611

Quest offers courses, conferences, and unique spiritual experiences in three broad areas: knowledge of self; healing; and wholeness through service. Four pathways are emphasized to reach these three areas: re-envisioning the mystical tradition, finding the sacred through creativity, and rediscovering the feminine in the divine. Spiritual direction groups are also offered to help integrate one's experiences.

Riverside Institute
4660 Kenmore Avenue, Suite 307
Alexandria, VA 22304
(703) 751-5646
Programs: Exploring One's Own Sacred Landscape; Integrating the Analytic and the Spiritual in Dynamic Psychotherapy;

Object-Relations Theory as a Spiritual Lens.

The institute is a group of four psychodynamically oriented psychotherapists who have developed a method of including the spiritual dimension of their patients' lives in the experience of psychotherapy. Based upon object-relations theory, and utilizing the construct of the God Object, this method provides a means of understanding "the patient's unconscious connection to the ultimate." Through courses and supervision, the institute trains therapists to recognize and utilize unconscious representations of the ultimate in the practice of psychotherapy.

Round Oaks Creative Center
3410 Ridge Road
Charlottesville, VA 22901
(804) 973-7543
Programs: Mari Course in Mandala Assessment; Sandtray training

School for Esoteric Studies (SES)
425 Madison Avenue, Suite 1903(c)
New York, NY 10017
(212) 755-3027
Programs: Preliminary course; additional lessons

Established in 1956 by former associates of Alice A. Bailey, SES is led by a core teaching staff at its New York City headquarters. The school emphasizes meditation, study, and service. Students usually start with the first of three preliminary lessons based on Bailey's book *A Treatise on White Magic*, which teaches, among other themes, the "laws of spiritual psychology as distinguished from mental and emotional psychology." Following the preliminary course is a series of 12 lessons on integration and fusion that takes approximately two-and-a-half years. The school is nonsectarian, and tuition is based on an individual's ability to pay.

The School of Spiritual Psychology
Transformations Incorporated
4200 West Good Hope Road
Milwaukee, WI 53209-2250
(414) 351-5770
Programs: Master of Spiritual Psychology certificate; various workshops and seminars

Servant Leadership School (SLS)
Church of the Savior
1640 Columbia Road, N.W.
Washington, DC 20009
(202) 328-7312
Programs: Servant Leadership I & II

Neither a seminary nor a school of social work, SLS was founded to combine these two forms of education and to enable people to explore and develop servant leadership (that is, their potential for service to the poor). The school hopes to train servant leaders who will contribute to social transformation and social justice, and offers various ecumenical, multiracial, multicultural workshops and classes.

Sevenoaks Pathwork Center
Route 1, Box 86
Madison, VA 22727
(703) 948-6544
Programs: Pathwork Transformation

The center is a school for spiritual development, emphasizing the importance of proceeding through all the levels of personal and spiritual transformation work. The foundation of the Pathwork program is a series of lectures originally delivered over a 22-year period through the channel of a spiritual teacher named Eva Peirrakos. The Pathwork process is a blend of spiritual and psychological elements, and includes specific forms of meditation and prayer, as well as physical and emotional work referred to as Core-Energetic. Also see Conference Centers.

Sound Listening and Learning Center
2701 East Camelback Road, Suite 205
Phoenix, AZ 85016
(602) 381-0086
Programs: Ear-Voice Connection; listening training program; Power of Sound; Rubenfeld Synergy® Method; School for Listening to Self and Soul; Structure of Intellect; Tomatis method; Total Quality Listening

The Tomatis method is a system of sound stimulation and audio-vocal training developed by Alfred Tomatis, M.D., to improve the functioning of the ear and increase motivation and desire for communication. The program also aims to explore the relationship among sound, self, and soul. The center works with both children and adults.

The Spiritual Emergence Network
P.O. Box 548
Corte Madera, CA 94976-0548
(415) 924-8345
Programs: Saturday workshops; Spiritual Emergence Syndromes (9-month certification)

The training is designed for licensed therapists, clergy, and transpersonal psychology graduate students but is open to interested laypersons as well. The training

program encompasses the full spectrum of spiritual emergence syndromes, including recognizing, understanding, and working with individuals going thorough spiritually transformative experiences.

Tamalpa Institute
P.O. Box 794
Kentfield, CA 94914
(415) 461-9479
Programs: Foundation of the Life/Art Process; Self-Portraits Exploration of the Body Parts; Facilitation skills; Halprin practitioner training; community outreach; healing arts

Tamalpa Institute, cofounded in 1978 by Anna Halprin and Daria Halprin Khalighi, is a movement-based expressive arts center.

Touching Spirit
Elizabeth K. Stratton, M.S.
131 East 95th Street
New York, NY 10128
(212) 410-7340
Programs: Four year certification training program

Touching Spirit®, a laying-on of the hands and "psychic attunement" technique developed by Elizabeth K. Stratton, M.S., is a healing system that deepens spiritual growth as it leads to physical, emotional, and mental healing.

Transformational Arts Institute
1380 Pacific Street
Redlands, CA 92373
(909) 798-4453
Programs: A Vision Quest; "Imagination's Wisdom," by Edith Sullwood, Ph.D.; Four-Fold Way training by Angeles Arrien, Ph.D.; men's group with Hugh Redmond, Ph.D.; various seminars and workshops

Founded by Hugh and Nancy Redmond in 1980, the institute focuses on integrating the psychological, spiritual, and creative realms of human experience within a transformational context.

Wainwright House
260 Stuyvesant Avenue
Rye, NY 10580
(914) 967-6080
Programs: Guild for Spiritual Guidance; various programs

Wainwright House, a nonprofit, nonsectarian educational organization, is a learning center dedicated to awakening consciousness in the mind, body, spirit, and the community as a whole. With special

focus on interdisciplinary programming, the center provides seminars, conferences, and ongoing courses in spirituality, psychology, personal growth, health, the arts, global issues, and business leadership. Its mission is to act as a bridge to develop and maintain dialogue between new frontiers of thought and the traditional religious, scientific, medical, educational, and business establishments. Wainwright House is also considered a conference center.

Westbrook University
404 North Mesa Verde
Aztec, NM 87410
(505) 334-1115
Programs: Ayurveda; bach flower remedies; hair mineral analysis; herbology; homeopathy; iridology; nutritional counseling

See Nonresidential Psychology Programs.

SECTION VI

A SAMPLING OF RECENT THESIS AND DISSERTATION TOPICS
(FROM PSYCHOSPIRITUAL DEGREE PROGRAMS)

CALIFORNIA INSTITUTE OF INTEGRAL STUDIES

IN THIS GUIDE, WE MAKE A DISTINCTION BETWEEN "EXPLICIT" PSYCHOspiritual graduate programs and those that offer "implicit" opportunities for study in the psychospiritual field. The former are located in institutions that overtly address the nexus of psychotherapy (or psychology or counseling) and spirituality (or religious studies). The latter are in institutions with more traditional curricula where students have nonetheless incorporated psychospiritual topics into their degree programs.

Below we list some of the titles of theses and dissertations written by students pursuing degrees at explicit psychospiritual institutions. Following this section, in Implicit Degree Programs, we offer a sampling of theses and dissertations on psychospiritual topics written by students in more traditional programs. Both sets of information should give you a flavor of the kind of research that has been approved and executed at these institutions. We remind you that they are only partial lists. For copies of these dissertations, call University Microfilms International at 1-800-521-0600.

Topic: **Absence and Presence: The Poetic Depiction of Religious Psychology in Soren Kierkegaard**
School: Emory University/Candler School of Theology
Program: Department of Theology and Personality
Author: Brian Barlow

Topic: **Buddhist Vipassana Meditation and Daily Life: Effect on Cognition, Affect, Awareness, and Acceptance**
School: California Institute of Integral Studies
Program: Clinical Psychology
Author: Barbara Easterlin, Ph.D.

Topic: **Communities: An Exploratory Study of the Existential and Transpersonal Dimensions of a Psychological Sense of Community as Found in the Community Building Workshop**
School: Institute of Transpersonal Psychology
Program: Transpersonal Psychology
Author: David Goff, Ph.D.

Topic: **Compassion and the Psychotherapist**
School: California Institute of Integral Studies
Program: Counseling Psychology
Author: Joanne Braun, Ph.D.

Topic: **Creative Selves-in-Relation in Taoist T'ai Chi and Dance Movement Therapy: The Dance of Original Goodness**
School: Antioch New England Graduate School
Program: Dance/Movement Therapy and Counseling Psychology
Author: Felicia Leighton, M.A.

Topic: **Creativity as a Bridge Between the Individual, Community, and Environment**
School: John F. Kennedy University
Program: Interdisciplinary Consciousness Studies
Author: Amy Ione, M.A.

Topic: **A Critique of the Disease Concept of Alcoholism**
School: Harding University Graduate School of Religion
Program: Christian Counseling
Author: Donald Brock, M.A.

Topic: **Drama Therapy and Ritual: A Study of Drama Therapy's Potential for Creating an Environment Conducive to the Production of Ritual**
School: California Institute of Integral Studies
Program: Drama Therapy
Author: Mary Lou Atkinson, M.A.

Topic: **The Dreaming Body: A Case Study of the Relationship Between Chronic Body Symptoms and Childhood Dreams According to Process-Oriented Psychology**
School: Institute of Transpersonal Psychology
Program: Transpersonal Psychology
Author: Alan Strachan, Ph.D.

Topic: **The Essence of Meditation: A Dialogical-Hermeneutical-Phenomenological Conceptual Encounter**
School: California Institute of Integral Studies
Program: East-West Psychology
Author: Tempril Zunka, Ph.D.

Topic: **The Evolution of Consciousness and Moral Imperative**
School: John F. Kennedy University
Program: Interdisciplinary Consciousness Studies
Author: David Borsos, M.A.

Topic: **Journey to the Heart of God: A Study of Dreamwork Used in Spiritual Direction**
School: Ecumenical Theological Center
Program: Doctor of Ministry
Author: Carol Vaccariello, D. Min.

Topic: **Profiles of Christian Contemplation: A Numerically Aided Qualitative Study of Prayer**
School: California Institute of Integral Studies
Program: East-West Psychology
Author: Kurt Van Kuren, M.A.

Topic: **Psychological Variables as Predictors of Women Staying in or Leaving Religious Communities**
School: California School of Professional Psychology
Program: Clinical Psychology
Author: Carmelita Centanni, Ph.D.

Topic: **Relationship of Cultural and Family Background to Dependency-Conflict and Need for Power Among Alcoholic Roman Catholic Priests**
School: California School of Professional Psychology
Program: Clinical Psychology
Author: Michael Doyle, Ph.D.

Topic: **Religious Issues in Psychotherapy: A Qualitative Analysis**
School: Antioch University/New England Graduate School
Program: Clinical Psychology
Author: Maria Goldstein, Psy.D.

Topic: **The Role of Spirituality in Recovery from Drug and Alcohol Addiction**
School: California Graduate School of Psychology
Program: Marriage, Child and Family Counseling
Author: Douglas Cooper, Ph.D.

Topic: **Sacred Sign Dance: A Creative and Therapeutic Integration of Language, Movement, and Spirituality**
School: Antioch New England Graduate School
Program: Dance/Movement Therapy and Counseling Psychology
Author: Beverly Miller, M.A.

Topic: **The Speech of the Grail: An Initiation for Practitioners of Helping, Educational and Pastoral Professions Derived from *Parzival* by Wolfram von Eschenbach**
School: Union Institute
Program: Spiritual Psychology and Oral Tradition
Author: Linda Sussman, Ph.D.

Topic: **Ultradian Rhythms in Self-Actualization, Anxiety, and Stress-Related Somatic Symptoms**
School: California Institute of Integral Studies
Program: Clinical Psychology
Author: Darlene Osowiec, Ph.D.

SECTION VII

DEGREE PROGRAMS ACKNOWLEDGING AN IMPLICIT SPIRITUAL CONTENT

In This Section:

➤ IMPLICIT PROGRAMS BY DISSERTATION TOPIC

➤ ADDITIONAL IMPLICIT PROGRAMS

CALIFORNIA INSTITUTE OF INTEGRAL STUDIES

IN ORDER TO LOCATE THOSE ACADEMIC INSTITUTIONS WHERE STUDENTS have written dissertations or theses on psychospiritual topics, we conducted a computer search (using 300 search words) of all the doctoral dissertations and master's theses filed during 1991, 1992, and 1993. Below we list a representative selection listed by author, academic institution, and catalog number. Anyone wishing to order copies may call University Microfilms International at 1-800-521-0600. When you order, you need to cite the GAX (the reference number) and author. You may also read brief summaries of each in *Dissertation Abstracts International,* which is available in most academic and large public libraries.

Because many of the theses or dissertation topics we discovered were written at more conventional colleges or universities, we make the (implicit) assumption that there is a department mentor who has knowledge of the topic or, at the very least, was interested enough in the subject to support the graduate student's independent research. You may want to find out more about the programs that interest you by contacting each institution.

IMPLICIT PROGRAMS BY DISSERTATION TOPIC

California School of Professional Psychology, Berkeley/Alameda
10005 Atlantic Avenue
Alameda, CA 94501
(510) 523-2300
Title: Meditation, Rest, and Sleep Onset: A Comparison of EEG and Respiration Changes (1993)
Author: Karen Hempel Naifeh, Ph.D.
GAX: 93-12789

California State University, Fresno
Department of Health Sciences and Nursing
5150 North Maple Avenue
Fresno, CA 93740-0057
(209) 278-2191
Title: The Spiritual Concerns of Clients in a Psychiatric Day Treatment Program (1992)
Author: Maye Annette Thompson, M.S.
GAX: 13-52899

California State University, Long Beach
Long Beach, CA 90840
(213) 985-4111
Title: An Analysis of Shamanistic Approaches in Clinical Psychology (1992)
Author: Mary Mills, M.S.
GAX: 13-49911

Chicago School of Professional Psychology
806 South Plymouth Court
Chicago, IL 60605
(312) 786-9443
Title: Personal Epistemologies of Substance Abusers (1992)
Author: Timothy William O'Brien, Psy.D.
GAX: 93-11256

Fairleigh Dickinson University
Department of Psychology
270 Montross Avenue
Rutherford, NJ 07070
(201) 460-5267; (800) 338-9903
Title: Gender Differences in Empathy and Separation-Individuation: An Investigation of Self-in-Relation Theory (1993)
Author: Ellen Dee Fenster-Kuehl, Ph.D.
GAX: 93-24135

George Fox College
414 North Meridian
Newberg, OR 97132
(503) 538-8383
Title: Relationship Between Personality and Spiritual Gifts (1991)
Author: Kenneth John Stone, Ph.D.
GAX: 93-04473

Miami University
Department of Psychology
Oxford Campus
Oxford, OH 45056
(513) 529-2531
Title: Role Relationships: A Methodology for Exploring Shared Universes of Meaning (1993)
Author: April Faidley, Ph.D.
GAX: 93-34484

Michigan State University
Department of Psychology
250 Administration Building
East Lansing, MI 48824-1046
(517) 355-8332
Title: Existential Theory, Ego Development, Purpose in Life, and Death Anxiety Among Older Adults (1992)
Author: Charles Elias Gutierrez, Ph.D.
GAX: 93-14678

New York University
New York, NY 10011
(212) 998-1212
Title: Mythopoetic Music Therapy: A Phenomenological Investigation into its Application with Adults (1992)
Author: David Rafael Gonzalez, M.A.
GAX: 92-37753

Pacific Graduate School of Psychology
935 East Meadow Drive
Palo Alto, CA 94303
(415) 494-7477
Title: Working with Shadow: A Jungian Perspective on Child Abuse and Its Treatment (1992)
Author: Larry Isaacs, Ph.D.
GAX: 93-07507

Pepperdine University
400 Corporate Pointe
Culver City, CA 90230
(213) 568-5606
Title: The Potential of Musical Sound in Psychotherapy: Interdisciplinary Synergy Toward a Comprehensive Paradigm of Health Psychology (1991)
Author: Jeannine Lemare Calaba, Psy.D.
GAX: 93-01155

Purdue University
West Lafayette, IN 47907
(317) 494-6067
Title: A New Theory of Forgiveness (1992)
Author: Michele Killough Nelson, Ph.D.
GAX: 92-29170

Regent University
1000 Centerville Turnpike
Virginia Beach, VA 23464-9800
(804) 523-7400
Title: Prayer Form Preference and Temperament Type: A Correctional Study (1992)
Author: Carol Dee Hepburn, M.A.
GAX: 13-49802

University of Arizona
Division of Educational Psychology
Tucson, AZ 85721
(602) 621-7825
Title: An Empirical Study of the Relationship Between Spirituality-Related Variables and Depression in Hospitalized Adults (1992)
Author: Debra Sue Brauchler, M.S.
GAX: 13-48467

University of La Verne
Department of Education and Guidance and Counseling
1950 Third Street
La Verne, GA 91750-4443
(909) 593-3511; (800) 876-4858
Title: A Comparison of the Frequency and Effectiveness of Contacts with Holistic Versus Traditional Counselors as Perceived by High School Sophomores (1992)
Author: Patrick Joseph Castagnaro, Ed.D.
GAX: 94-00161

University of Massachusetts
Department of Education
Boston, MA 02125-3393
(617) 287-5800
Title: A Qualitative Case Analysis of Mindfulness Meditation Training in an Outpatient Stress Reduction Clinic and Its Implications for the Development of Self-Knowledge (1992)
Author: Saki Frederic Santorielli, Ph.D.
GAX: 92-33158

University of Mississippi
Department of Health Sciences and Nursing
University, MS 38577
(601) 232-7226
Title: Effects of Therapeutic Touch on Perception of Pain and Physiologic Measurements from Tension Headache in Adults: A Pilot Study (1993)
Author: Carolyn Dollar, M.S.N.
GAX: 13-53981

University of North Texas
Department of Psychology
P.O. Box 13797
Denton, TX 76203-3797
(817) 565-2681
Title: Psychosocial and Spiritual Factors
Affecting Persons Living with HIV and
AIDS (1993)
Author: Tamara Lynn Elkins, Ph.D.
GAX: 94-01138

Univeristy of Rochester
Department of Health Sciences and
Nursing
Rochester, NY 14627-0251
(716) 275-3221
Title: Living with Asthma: A
Phenomenological Search for Meaning
(1992)
Author: Barbara Cull-Wilby, Ph.D.
GAX: 93-26608

University of South Carolina
Columbia, SC 29208
(803) 777-4137
Title: The Effects of Yoga Training on
Concentration and Selected Psychological
Variables in Young Adults (1992)
Author: Anna Parker Williams, Ph.D.
GAX: 92-37784

University of South Dakota
Department of Psychology
414 East Clark
Vermillion, SD 57069-2390
(605) 677-5434
Title: Inner Healing Prayer: The Therapist's
Perspective (1993)
Author: Clare Catherine Rossiter, Ed.D.
GAX: 94-01985

University of Southern Mississippi
Box 5025, Southern Station
Hattiesburg, MS 39406-5025
(601) 266-4604
Title: The Relationship of God-Construct
and God-Image, Emotional Attachment
Style, and Worldview Orientation to
Psychological Health (1992)
Author: James Truett McLaughlin, Ph.D.
GAX: 92-39409

**Virginia Polytechnical Institute and
State University**
5088 Derring Hall
Blacksburg, VA 24061-0436
Title: Adult Survivors of Incest and Non-
Victimized Women's Evaluation of the Use
of Touch in Counseling (1992)
Author: Suzanne Torrenzano, Ed.D.
GAX: 92-37159

Wright Institute
2728 Durante Avenue
Berkeley, CA 94704
(510) 841-9230
Title: Object Relations and Images of the
Divine (1992)
Author: Sharon Swedean Muhlenkort
GAX: 92-28363

ADDITIONAL IMPLICIT PROGRAMS

In the process of compiling this guide,
the editors noted a few programs that
had faculty who informally indicated
interests in psychosocial fields or that
occasionally offered courses on psychospiritual topics. Unfortunately, the
course catalogs of these programs do
not provide such details.

California Graduate Institutes
1122 East Lincoln Avenue, Suite B200
Orange, CA 92665
(714) 637-5404

Carleton University
Department of Sociology and
Anthropology
1125 Colonel By Drive
Ottawa, Ontario K1S 5B6
Canada
(613) 788-2600
    Professor Charles Laughlin's interest is
in transpersonal anthropology.

Pacific Graduate School of Psychology
935 East Meadow Drive
Palo Alto, CA 94303
(415) 494-7477
    Advanced classes include topics such as
psychoanalysis, and existential, interpersonal, and Jungian psvchotherapy.

Spalding University
Office of Graduate Admissions
851 South Florida Street
Louisville, KY 40203-2188
    Barbara Williams, Ph.D., a faculty mem-
ber of the psychology department, is a
member of the Association of Transpersonal Psychology.

Texas A&M University
Department of Psychology
College Station, TX 77843-4235
(409) 845-7146
    Professor David Rosen of A&M's clinical
psychology program works with graduate
students interested in a Jungian approach
to psychology.

University of Hawaii at Manoa
School of Social Work
2500 Campus Road
Honolulu, HI 96822
(808) 956-8111
    Past courses have included the relation-
ship between Native Hawaiian healing and
social work.

University of Kansas
Department of Psychology
426 Fraser
Lawrence, KS 66045
(913) 864-4131
    The University of Kansas offers a Ph.D.
in Clinical, Child and Social Psychology.
Some courses include a humanistic and
transpersonal perspective.

University of Southern Mississippi
Department of Psychology
Southern Station, Box 5025
Hattiesburg, MS 39406-5025
(601) 266-4604
    Larry Gates, Ph.D., a faculty member,
holds an interest in psychospiritual topics.

SECTION VIII

RESEARCH INSTITUTES AND ASSOCIATIONS RELEVANT TO THE PSYCHOSPIRITUAL FIELD

FETZER INSTITUTE

THE FOLLOWING IS A LIST OF ORGANIZATIONS AND INSTITUTIONS INVOLVED IN TRANSPERSONAL AND HOLISTIC research. After inquiring into the center's research activities, students and professionals may want to consider applying for grants, submitting their own research, or inquiring about employment opportunities.

The Academy of Religion and Psychical Research
P.O. Box 614
Bloomfield, CT 06002
(203) 242-4593
See Para- and Meta-Psychology.

Association for Past-Life Research and Therapies(APRT)
P.O. Box 20151
6825 Magnolia Avenue, Suite D
Riverside, CA 92506
(909) 784-1570
The APRT, founded in 1980, is an international association of practitioners and lay persons interested in researching and promoting the use of alternative healing therapies, particularly past-life regression therapy. The association publishes a quarterly newsletter and the annual *Journal of Regression Therapy*, sponsors two educational conferences per year, and occasionally presents seminars and training workshops.

Association for Research and Enlightenment (ARE)
P.O. Box 595
Virginia Beach, VA 23541-0595
(804) 428-3588
The ARE was founded in 1931 to preserve, research, and make available the readings of Edgar Cayce, most of which have to do with psychic issues, meditation, dreams, reincarnation, and prophecy. As an open-membership research organization, it continues to index and catalog Cayce's writings, to initiate investigation and experiments relevant to his ideas, and to promote conferences, seminars, and lectures. The association also publishes a magazine, *Venture Inward*, and sponsors academic programs through its affiliation with Atlantic University (see Residential Psychology Degree Programs).

Association for the Sociology of Religion (ASR)
Marist Hall, Room 108
Catholic University of America
Washington, DC 20064
(202) 319-5447

The ASR is an international scholarly association that seeks to advance theory and research in the sociology of religion. The association encourages and disseminates research relevant to the study of religion. The association's journal is the only English-language publication devoted to the sociology of religion.

Association for the Study of Dreams (ASD)
P.O. Box 1600
Vienna, VA 22183
(703) 242-8888

Incorporated in 1984, ASD is a nonprofit, international, multidisciplinary organization dedicated to the pure and applied investigation of dreams and dreaming. Its purposes are to promote awareness and appreciation of dreams in both professional and public arenas; to encourage research into the nature, function, and significance of dreaming; to advance the application of the study of dreams; and to provide a forum for the eclectic and interdisciplinary exchange of related ideas and information. The ASD holds an annual conference and publishes a journal, *Dreaming*, and a newsletter.

Barre Center for Buddhist Studies
See Buddhist Theological Training.

The Cambridge Institute of Psychology and Religion (CIPR)
98 Clifton Street
Cambridge, MA 02140
(617) 492-1130

The CIPR is a private teaching and research organization that deals with historical, philosophical, and contemporary issues related to psychology, especially where they have a bearing on matters of inner exploration, self-knowledge, religious awareness, and personal growth. The institute maintains contact with Division 36 of the American Psychological Association, (the Psychology of Religion), as well as scholars who are interested in psychology such as members of the American Academy of Religion.

The Center for Advancement in Cancer Education
300 East Lancaster Avenue, Suite 100
Wynnewood, PA 19096
(215) 642-4810

The center is a nonprofit information, counseling, and referral agency that offers resources for cancer prevention and nontoxic, holistic approaches as adjuncts or alternatives to conventional cancer treatments.

Center for Alternative/Complementary Medicine
See Allopathic Medicine.

Center for Ecumenical Marian Studies (CEMS)
St. Mary's University
One Camino Santa Maria
San Antonio, TX 78228
(210) 436-3991

Founded in 1992, the CEMS is a national center that studies Mary, the mother of Jesus. The center collects and disseminates information on Mary in the ecumenical movement, and discusses Mary's role in the feminist movement and in popular culture. The center maintains a library collection; sponsors symposia, classes, speakers, art and music; and publishes a collection of symposia and a newsletter.

The Center for Frontier Sciences (CFS)
Temple University
Ritter Hall 003-00 / Room 478
Philadelphia, PA 19122
(215) 204-8487

The CFS was established in 1987 to coordinate information exchange, networking, and education about issues of science, medicine, and technology. The center aims to encourage greater openness to novel scientific claims in areas such as bioelectromagnetics, the mind-matter interrelationship, complementary medicine, and new energy technology. As an integral part of a major university, high academic standards are maintained in reviewing new claims, and new questions are raised to help facilitate research breakthroughs. Scientists and scholars interested in the frontier sciences (defined as areas of science not yet mainstream) are invited to become affiliates of the center. Affiliates receive *Frontier Perspectives*, a journal published by the center, and invitations to various events.

Center for Mind-Body Studies
See Allopathic Medicine.

Center for the Study of Religion and American Culture
Purdue University at Indianapolis
425 University Boulevard, Room 344
Indianapolis, IN 46202-5140
(317) 274-8409

Founded in 1989, the center serves as a national research institute and as a communications hub for people interested in the ways in which religion and other features of American culture intersect. It offers seminars and workshops to college and university teachers and encourages ongoing examination through fellowship programs, opinion polls, and open discussions.

The Center for Theology and the Natural Sciences (CTNS)
2400 Ridge Road
Berkeley, CA 94709
(510) 848-8152

The CTNS, an affiliate of the Graduate Theological Union, is dedicated to advancing dialogue and interaction between Western theological traditions and the natural sciences. The center fulfills this goal through long- and short-term research projects, teaching, and communications such as public forums and the *CTNS Bulletin*, a scholarly publication.

Common Boundary
5272 River Road, Suite 650
Bethesda, MD 20816
(301) 652-9495

Common Boundary sponsors a $1,000 annual award for an outstanding dissertation/thesis in the psychospiritual field. It will administer an award for research or projects relevant to the relationship between ecology and psychospirituality beginning in 1995.

Esalen Institute
Highway One
Big Sur, CA 93920
(408) 667-3000

Esalen Insitute sponsors research pertinent to the field of human potential and growth. Also see Conference Centers.

Foundation for the Advancement of Innovative Medicine (FAIM)
See Allopathic Medicine.

Friends World Committee for Consultation (FWCC)
Section of the Americas
1506 Race Street
Philadelphia, PA 19102
(215) 241-7250

The FWCC oversees the Elizabeth Ann Bogert Memorial Fund which provides grants of up to $500 to individuals involved in the study and practice of Christian mysticism.

Heffter Research Institute
See Transpersonal Psychiatry.

Institute for Ecumenical and Cultural Research

P.O. Box 6188
Collegeville, MN 56321-6188
Correspondence offered only by mail.

Since its founding in 1967, the Institute for Ecumenical and Cultural Research has sought to discern the meaning of Christian identity and unity in a religiously and culturally diverse nation and world, and to communicate that meaning for the mission of the church and the renewal of human community. The institute is committed to research, study, prayer, reflection, and dialogue in a community shaped by the Benedictine tradition of worship and work. It encourages constructive and creative thought not only in theology and religious studies, but also in the humanities, natural sciences, and social sciences as they relate to the Christian tradition, including the interplay of Christianity and culture.

Institute for Interdisciplinary Research (IIR)

2828 3rd Street, Suite 11
Santa Monica, CA 90405-4150
(310) 396-0517

The IIR is a nonprofit educational organization that seeks to recover the lost unity of Renaissance learning while affirming transcendental values and faith. It publishes the *Journal of Interdisciplinary Studies*, an international journal of interdisciplinary and interfaith dialogue (co-sponsored by the International Christian Studies Association).

The Institute for the Study of Health and Illness (ISHI)

Commonweal
P.O. Box 316
Bolinas, CA 92924
(415) 868-2642

The ISHI is a professional development institute for health professionals who wish to devote all or part of their practice to serving people with life threatening illnesses. One of the fundamental assumptions of the institute's work is that people cannot function as healers without examining their lives in depth. The curriculum is directed towards practicing and teaching professionals in the fields of medicine, nursing, psychology, and social work.

The Institute for the Study of Human Knowledge (ISHK)

P.O. Box 176
Los Altos, CA 94023
(415) 948-9428

As a nonprofit educational institution dedicated to publicizing useful research on the mind—particularly research that is overlooked by mainstream science—the ISHK works at the frontier of psychological research, especially where there is a need to explain new discoveries and their practical applications. The institute offers seminars, a book service, tapes, and a newsletter.

Institute of Formative Spirituality

Duquesne University
Pittsburgh, PA 15282
(412) 434-6388

The discipline of formative spirituality addresses the need for a comprehensive approach to the foundations, dynamics, and conditions of harmonious spiritual living. Within the discipline of formative spirituality, the institute has founded a science of formation with its own methods of research that, according to the institute, meet the standard requirements of any legitimate science.

Institute of Noetic Sciences (IONS)

475 Gate Five Road, Suite 300
Sausalito, CA 94965
(415) 331-5650

The IONS, founded in 1973, is a research foundation, an educational institution, and a membership organization. The institute is committed to the development of human consciousness through scientific inquiry, spiritual understanding, and psychological well-being. The "noetic sciences" involve an interdisciplinary study of the mind and its diverse ways of knowing. The IONS provides seed grants for cutting-edge scientific and scholarly research; organizes lectures; sponsors conferences; and publishes books, journals, and research reports by leading scientists, philosophers, and scholars. It also supports a variety of networking opportunities, member research projects, and local member group activities. Its quarterly journal, *Noetic Sciences Review*, offers discussion of emerging concepts in consciousness research, the mind-body connection, and the changing worldview in science and society. The institute is in the process of preparing a list of meditation researchers and the work they are doing, which will serve graduate students who seek meditation-oriented research projects and mentors.

The Islamic Academy

See Islamic Theological Schools.

Islamic Research Foundation for the Advancement of Knowledge (IRFAK)

7102 Shefford Lane
Louisville, KY 40242-6462
(502) 634-1395

The IRFAK, a nonprofit educational, research, and charitable organization, encouraging free thinking and opposing viewpoints in order to help re-establish the tenants of Islamic civilization. It funds awards and grants to research projects relevant to Islamic traditions. An International Congress will be held in 1995.

The John E. Fetzer Institute

9292 West KL Avenue
Kalamazoo, MI 49009
(616) 375-2000

The Fetzer Institute, founded in 1963, is a nonprofit educational organization that promotes the research and dissemination of low-cost, scientifically tested health-care methods that utilize the principles of mind-body phenomena. The aim of the institute is to expand the development of health-care approaches in which all dimensions of the mind, from the emotional to the spiritual, are applied to the health of the body. The institute publishes *Advances: The Journal of Mind-Body Health* and sponsors a fellowship program, Fetzer Fellows, for outstanding researchers in the mind/body/spirit field. It also sponsors a "teacher formation" program in Kalamazoo, a spiritually-oriented training program for teachers (contact Parker Palmer, Berea College, at 606-986-2787).

The Joseph Campbell Archives and Library

Pacifica Graduate Institute
249 Lambert Road
Carpinteria, CA 93013
(805) 969-3626

Joseph Campbell's lengthy association with Pacifica included frequent lectures and conferences during the last two decades of his life. The library is part of the Center for the Study of Depth Psychology, an independent nonprofit organization. Among the holdings are comprehensive notes on all areas of world mythology from Campbell's 38 years of teaching at Sarah Lawrence College. Major sections of the library cover sacred traditions from all regions of the world, including anthropology, folklore, and mysticism.

Louisville Institute for the Study of Protestantism and American Culture(LISPAC)

Dissertation Fellowship Program
1044 Alta Vista Road
Louisville, KY 40205-1798
(502) 895-3411

The LISPAC was founded in 1990 as a center for research and leadership education on mainstream Protestantism. The institute seeks to nurture inquiry and conversation regarding the character, problems, contributions, and prospects of the historic institutions and stances of American Protestantism, with particular interest in comparative and contextual studies. During each academic year, the institute supports up to 10 doctoral research fellowships (with a stipend of $10,000) to promising scholars whose dissertation work addresses these issues.

Menninger Foundation
P.O Box 829
Topeka, KS 66601-0829
(913) 273-7500

The Menninger Foundation was founded in 1925 to treat severe mental illness; since then it has become an internationally recognized training center for mental-health professionals. While most of its $60 million annual budget goes toward mainstream research, the foundation exhibits an openness to nonconventional healing methods for promoting positive mental health. This is demonstrated by its pioneering work in biofeedback as well as its current research on meditation, subtle energy, and nonconventional healing (research curiously titled "physical fields and states of consciousness").

Two recent studies include "Anomalous Electrostatic Phenomena in Exceptional Subjects" and "EEG Amplitude, Brain Mapping, Percent Synchrony in and between a Bioenergy Practitioner and Client during Healing." Menninger offers a psychiatric residency program, through which some students have demonstrated transpersonal interests (see Transpersonal Psychiatry). The Menninger Foundation also sponsors an annual invitational conference known as the Council Grove. Begun in 1969 by Alyce Green, Ph.D., and Elmer Green, Ph.D., the conference aims to bring together consciousness pioneers from all disciplines within a supportive and provocative environment.

Mind-Body Medical Institute
See Allopathic Medicine.

Monterey Institute for the Study of Alternative Healing Arts (MISAHA)
400 Virgin Avenue
Monterey, CA 93940
(408) 646-8019

The MISAHA is a scientific research organization dedicated to broadening knowledge of alternative healing methods and mind-body connections. The new program will attempt to establish the efficacy of alternative healing treatments by measuring "whatever is measurable between the healer and recipients by means of physical and physiological instrumentation and methodologies."

Multidisciplinary Association for Psychedelic Studies (MAPS)
See Transpersonal Psychiatry.

National Institutes of Health
Office of Alternative Medicine (OAM)
Building 31, Room B1-C35
Bethesda, MD 20892
(301) 402-2466

The OAM was established by Congress in 1992. Areas of investigation include, but are not limited to: diet, nutrition, and lifestyle changes; mind/body control such as biofeedback and guided imagery; traditional and ethnomedicine, including acupuncture, native American medicine, and traditional Oriental medicine; energetic therapies including therapeutic touch and Qigong; and bioelectromagnetic applications, including diagnostic and therapeutic applications of electromagnetic fields. Research grants are available. The office organizes occasional conferences and publishes a free newsletter, *Alternative Medicine.*

Paramann Programme Labs
Jamal N. Hussein, Ph.D., Director
P.O. Box 310087
Al-Mahatta
Amman Jordan

Started ten years ago by a group of scientists in different fields of medicine and experimental physics, this research project studies paranormal immunities to pain, bleeding and infection as demonstrated by extraordinary persons such as swamis and gurus (also known as fakirs).

Parapsychology Foundation (PF)
228 East 71st Street
New York, NY 10021
(212) 628-1550

The PF offers an annual award of $3,000 to an author working on a manuscript pertaining to the science of parapsychology.

The Pre- and Perinatal Psychology Association of North America (PPPANA)
1600 Prince Street, Suite 509
Alexandria, VA 22314-2838
(703) 548-2802

The PPPANA is an educational, non-profit organization dedicated to the exploration of the psychological dimensions of human reproduction and pregnancy, and the mental and emotional development of the unborn and newborn child. It sponsors an annual conference.

Preventive Medicine Research Institute
See Allopathic Medicine.

Princeton University
School of Engineering/Applied Science
Princeton Engineering Anomolies Research (PEAR)
C-0 131 Engineering Quadrangle
P.O. Box CN5263
Princeton, NJ 08544-5263
(609) 258-5950

The PEAR Center, located at Princeton University, studies the role of conciousness in the establishment of physical reality. The center inaugurated the Academy of Consciousness Studies summer program in 1994 (sponsor by the Fetzer Institute), intended to introduce young scholars to the emerging field of conciousness research.

The Religious Research Association (RRA)
The Catholic University of America
Marist Hall, Room 108
Washington, DC 20064
(202) 319-5447

The RRA's goals are to increase understanding of the function of religion in persons and society through application of social-scientific and other scholarly methods; to promote the circulation, interpretation, and use of the findings of religious research among religious bodies and other interested groups; to cooperate with other professional societies, groups, and individuals interested in the study of religion; and to aid in the professional development of religious researchers. The association also publishes the *Review of Religious Research,* a quarterly journal.

Sharp HealthCare
3131 Berger Avenue
San Diego, CA 92123
(619) 541-6730

Directed by physician and mind-body researcher Deepak Chopra, this research center investigates the effect of the mind on physical health. A recent grant received from the National Institutes of Health will allow the institute to study the effectiveness of Ayurvedic and Western medicine in programs that encourage human wellness. It also offers seminars designed for professionals and lay persons.

The Society for the Scientific Study of Religion
Purdue University
Sociology Department
1365 Stone Hall
West Lafayette, IN 47907-1365
(317) 494-6286

The SSSR was founded in 1949 by scholars in religion and social science (mainly sociology). Its purpose is to stimulate and communicate significant scientific research on religious institutions and religious experience. Membership includes subscription to the *Journal for the Scientific Study of Religion*. The society also sponsors an annual conference.

Spindrift
P.O. Box 5134
Salem, OR 97304-5134
Correspondence offered only by mail.

Spindrift is a private, nonprofit corporation dedicated to education and research in the area of spiritual healing. The organization is nondenominational.

Stone Center for Developmental Services
Wellesley College
Wellesley, MA 02181
(617) 235-9669

The center, dedicated in 1981, is developing programs aimed toward the following goals: research in psychological development among peoples of all ages; service demonstration and research projects that will enhance psychological development of college students; and service research and training in the prevention of psychological problems. The Stone Center is best known for conducting research in feminine psychology. Research projects include: "Empathy and the Mother-Daughter Relationship," by J. Jordan; "The Meaning of 'Dependency' in Female-Male Relationships," by I. Stiver; and "The Self-in-Relation: A Theory of Women's Development," by J. Surrey.

Study Project in Phenomenology of the Body (SPPB)
Elizabeth A. Behnke, Ph.D., Coordinator
P.O. Box 0-2
Felton, CA 95018
(408) 335-2036

The SPPB is a research venture and networking organization devoted to studying the body and bodily experience in their "invariant structures and their historical and cultural variations." The SPPB is phenomenological in orientation but interdisciplinary in scope. It is based not only on the study of texts about the body, but on the careful observation of bodily experience itself. The project publishes a semiannual newsletter.

Touch Therapy Institute
See Bodywork and Massage.

The Upledger Institute
11211 Prosperity Farms Road
Palm Beach Gardens, FL 33410-3487
(407) 622-4334

The Upledger Institute, an educational and clinical research center, integrates naturopathic techniques with conventional and well-proven health-care methods. Also see Cranio-Sacral Therapy.

SECTION IX

CONFERENCE CENTERS

KAREN PREUSS © 1993

CONFERENCE CENTERS ALLOW HELPING PROFESSIONALS TO TAKE PART IN MEANINGFUL DIALOGUES WITH THEIR COLLEAGUES, EXPAND THEIR knowledge of other healing methods, and maintain a sense of community within a field whose work environment is often isolated. Also, holistic conference centers are often the first forums for discussion of innovative ideas and techniques that have not yet found their way into the more conventional educational channels. Many conference centers have facilities for silent retreats just as many retreat centers offer some educational programs. Conference centers often provide work-exchange and scholarship programs.

Abode of the Message (AM)

R.D. 1, Box 1030-D, Shaker Road
New Lebanon, NY 12125
(518) 794-8090

The AM is a residential Sufi community with an educational purpose. Founded in 1975, the organization offers retreats, seminars, and evening classes. The Sufi Order School for Mystical Studies at the Abode was founded in 1987 with the specific purpose of presenting the Sufi teachings of Pir-O-Murshid Inayat Khan, founder of the Sufi Order of the West, and of his son and successor, Pir Vilayat Inayat Khan.

Aleph: Alliance for Jewish Renewal

7318 Germantown Avenue
Philadelphia, PA 19119
(215) 242-4074

The Alliance for Jewish Renewal came into existence through a merger of P'nai Or Religious Fellowship and the Shalom Center. Its mission is to provide programs and activities to help enhance participants' spiritual lives while familiarizing them with the Jewish Renewal life paths. Aleph sponsors retreats, seminars, conferences, and other programs for the general public, as well as nondegree educational programs in Jewish studies. Aleph enthusiastically welcomes participants regardless of age, gender, sexual orientation, ethnic origin, spiritual background, or level of Jewish education. The organization publishes *New Menorah, a Journal of Jewish Renewal.*

Applewood Center

121 Dundas Street East
Belleville, Ontario K8P 1C3, Canada
(613) 967-8520

Formed in 1982, the Applewood Center offers workshops and conferences to help thoughtful adults explore issues of personal life and inner development. Defining itself as a "catalyst for discovery," the center offers programs with a wide range of topics, including sexuality and spirituality, science and religion, creativity, relationships between men and women, the meaning of dreams, and ecology.

Association of Holistic Healing Centers (AHHC)

109 Holly Crescent, Suite 201
Virginia Beach, VA 23451
(804) 422-9033

The AHHC, a membership organization founded in 1990, is dedicated to providing opportunities for individuals and groups involved in the healing arts to work together toward a more integrated health care methodology that bridges traditional and complementary practices. Its goals include the creation of healing centers that support this vision.

Avalon Institute

3985 Wonderland Hill
Boulder, CO 80302
(303) 443-4363

Avalon offers contemplative retreats and summer education programs. It also offers training programs in Jungian and archetypal psychotherapy. See Residential Psychology Degree Programs.

Breitenbush Hot Springs Retreat and Conference Center

P.O. Box 578
Detroit, OR 97342
(503) 854-3314

Breitenbush offers workshops as well as individual retreats.

Center for Action and Contemplation (CAC)

P.O. Box 12464
Albuquerque, NM 87195-2464
(505) 242-9588

The CAC works to actively engage in transforming society from a faith perspective. It offers conferences, retreats, workshops and lectures.

City of God

R.D. 1, Box 319
Moundsville, WV 26041
(304) 845-7539

The City of God was founded in 1968 as a Vaisnava (worshipers of Vishnu or Krishna) community. Since then, the community has expanded their facility to include a retreat center. (According to the editors' research, they are the only Hindu retreat center in the United States.)

Claymont Society

Route 1, Box 279
Charles Town, WV 25414
(304) 725-4437

The Claymont Society was founded in 1975 as a community and school to promote the principles of continuous education and integrated human development. In 1985 Claymont Court Seminars, sponsored by the society, was established to host and facilitate retreats, workshops, and seminars.

Common Boundary

5272 River Road, Suite 650
Bethesda, MD 20816
(301) 652-9495

Common Boundary, a nonprofit educational organization, has been holding an annual conference on the relationship of spirituality, psychology, and creativity since 1980 in Washington, D.C. It also publishes the bimonthly magazine *Common Boundary*, sponsors a $1,000 annual award for the most outstanding dissertation/thesis in the psychospiritual field, and publishes this *Graduate Education Guide,* with periodic updates. It will administer an award for research or projects relevant to the relationship between ecology and psychospirituality beginning in 1995.

Esalen Institute

Highway One
Big Sur, CA 93920
(408) 667-3000

Esalen was founded in 1962 as a nonprofit educational center and soon after found itself a pioneering representative of the human potential movement. Esalen offers seminars, workshops, and invitational conferences in the area of personal and social transformation. Esalen offers certification courses in Esalen massage and a month-long certification course in hypnotherapy; all other courses are nondegree programs.

Friends Conference on Religion and Psychology

97 Gunderman Road
Ithaca, NY 14850
Correspondence offered only by mail.

This organization sponsors an annual conference on the East Coast.

Full Circle Center for Holistic Studies (FCCHS)

1332 Talbot
Huntington Woods, MI 48070
(801) 541-3033

The FCCHS serves to bring people of all ages, cultural, ethnic and spiritual backgrounds together to develop a deeper understanding of the interrelationship between spirituality, psychology, ecology, and creativity. It offers various workshops.

High Wind Association
W7136 County Road U
Plymouth, WI 53073
(414) 528-7212

The High Wind Association, founded in 1977 as a nonprofit educational organization, is dedicated to developing models and ideas of sustainability by which people can live in harmony with one another and with nature. High Wind offers year-round conference and retreat facilities, but most of its programs are concentrated in the summer. The association publishes *Windwatch*, a semiannual journal detailing the life and ideas of the High Wind community.

Hollyhock Farm
See International Conference and Retreat Centers.

Institute for the Study of Natural Systems (ISNS)
P.O. Box 2460
Mill Valley, CA 94942
(415) 383-5064

The ISNS sponsors The Spirit of Place symposiums that seek to bridge modern and ancient cultures in search of new and better ways to create an ecologically sustainable society.

Institute of Noetic Sciences
See Research Institutes.

Interface
55 Wheeler Street
Cambridge, MA 02138-1168
(617) 876-4600

Interface is an educational center founded in 1975 to explore those trends in health, personal growth, science, and religion that excite and encourage people to seek new ways of living, expand personal horizons, and join with others to help create a better world. Interface offers lectures, courses, workshops, and conferences that reflect its focus on health and integration of body, mind, and spirit.

International Transpersonal Center
38 Miller Avenue, Suite 160
Mill Valley, CA 94941
(415) 388-7788

The center is still in its conceptual phase under the leadership of Stan and Christina Grof and a board of directors. It will be an international community dedicated to facilitating the application of new scientific paradigms that recognize the fundamental unity underlying all of humanity

and the material world. According to the center's description, its mission will be to "explore the transpersonal perspective in the integration of education, psychology, scientific research, addictions, spiritual practice, the arts, ecology, politics, and other areas of human life."

Kalani Honda Conference and Retreat Center
R.R. 1, Box 4500
Pahoa, HI 96778
(808) 965-7828

Kalani Honda was founded in 1980 as an intercultural conference center devoted to supporting physical, spiritual, and emotional healing, the arts, and traditional Hawaiian culture. The center is a multicultural, shared living community that presents a spectrum of educational events including workshops, conferences, and retreats.

Kanuga Conferences
Postal Drawer 250
Hendersonville, NC 28793
(704) 692-9136

Kanuga is a nonprofit corporation affiliated with the Episcopal Church. The center sponsors conferences, educational programs, retreats, and summer camps. The "Journey into Wholeness" conference integrating Christianity and Jungian psychology is held annually at this location.

Keys Institute
P.O. Box 3150
Key Largo, FL 33037-8150
(305) 451-3519

The Keys Institute is a human potential center that sponsors retreat workshops. The institute, a nonprofit and nondenominational organization, offers a variety of programs, providing opportunities for exploration, discovery, healing, and adventure.

Kirkridge
R.R. 3, Box 3402
Bangor, PA 18013-9359
(215) 588-1793

Founded in 1942 by the late John Oliver Nelson, a Presbyterian minister and former Yale Divinity School professor who was inspired by the Christian community on the Scottish island of Iona. The name "Kirkridge" derives from the Scottish word for church, "*kirk*," and the center's location on the Appalachian ridge. It offers ongoing workshops, lectures, seminars and retreats on topics of Christian and Jewish spiritual perspectives for clergy and lay persons.

Merritt Center
P.O. Box 2087
Payson, AZ 85547
(602) 474-4268

Merrit Center is a renewal and conference center. Past workshops have included "Women's Journey," "Spiritual Psychodrama," and "The Last Original Power Intensive."

National Havurah Committee (NHC)
P.O. Box 2621
Bala Cynwyd, PA 19004-6621
(215) 843-1470

Havurah, meaning "fellowship" in Hebrew, is a dynamic form of Jewish community that emerged as a force for Jewish renewal in the late 1960s. It is transdenominational in that the organization attempts to bridge the differences between Reformed, Reconstructionist, Conservative, and Orthodox Judaism. The NHC conducts national summer institutes and week-long gatherings for intensive study, discussion, celebration, and community living.

New College of Berkeley (NCB)
Center for Christian Studies
2606 Dwight Way
Berkeley, CA 94704-3029
(510) 841-9386; (800) 383-9387

The NCB offers weekend workshops, lectures, and a summer institute.

New York Open Center
83 Spring Street
New York, NY 10012
(212) 219-2527

The New York Open Center is a nonprofit holistic learning center that was founded in 1984 by Walter Beebe and Ralph White. Located in Soho in downtown Manhattan, the center offers a broad array of programs in all aspects of the emerging spiritual, holistic, and ecological worldview, including a three-year program in Integrative therapy for those seeking training in alternative approaches to couseling. Program formats include weekend workshops, ongoing courses, and evening lectures and concerts. As a prototype of the urban holistic learning center, NYOC also offers workshops on how groups can start holistic centers in their own towns or cities.

Oasis Center
7463 North Sheridan Road
Chicago, IL 60626
(312) 274-6777

The center's purpose is to provide an environment where people can involve themselves in various processes of personal development that may lead to more fulfilling lives and greater appreciation of human values. It also offers training for individuals who desire to work with others toward this end.

Ojai Foundation
P.O. Box 1620
Ojai, CA 93024
(805) 646-8343

Founded by Joan Halifax, Ph.D., Ojai offers weekend workshops, group retreats, educational programs and ceremonies.

Omega Institute
260 Lake Drive
Rhinebeck, NY 12572
(800) 862-8890

Omega Institute for Holistic Studies was founded by the Sufi Order of the West in 1977 with a handful of participants and a few weekend classes. In 1982 the institute purchased a former summer camp in the rural woodlands of the Hudson Valley, 90 miles outside of New York City. Programs at Omega are varied and include new ideas in health, psychology, family and relationships, the creative arts, sports, spiritual understanding, and global studies. It also sponsors an annual conference.

Openway
R.R. 10, Box 105
Charlottesville, VA 22903
(804) 293-3245

Founded in 1983 by Graciela Damewood, Openway is a nonprofit healing center offering transpersonally oriented workshops.

Peace Valley
H.C. 65, Box 73B
Caddo Gap, AR 71935
(501) 356-2908

Peace Valley is a new conference center that also offers workshops and retreats. Its vision is "to provide a healing place for awakening unconditional love, reverence for all life, and spiritual purpose through experiencing a joyous and cooperative relationship between the human race, the earth, and God."

Rim Institute
404 North 4th Avenue, Suite 152
Tuscon, AZ 85705
(602) 623-6277

The Rim Institute, a nonprofit educational and research organization, is a catalyst for the expansion of inner consciousness and its relationship to outer realities through the exploration of the spiritual, psychological, physical, and planetary dimensions of being human. The institute offers various workshops and weekend retreats to meet its goals.

Rowe Camp and Conference Center
Kings Highway Road
Rowe, MA 01367
(413) 339-4954

Rowe Conference Center, founded in 1973 in the Berkshires of western Massachusetts, is committed to creating a space where the sacred enters into the everyday, and where personal, social, and spiritual transformation is encouraged and experienced. Most of Rowe's various programs are in the form of weekend workshops.

Sevenoaks Pathwork Center
Route 1, Box 86
Madison, VA 22727
(703) 948-6544

Sevenoaks offers various programs that integrate spirituality and psychology. Also see Nondegree and Postgraduate Training Programs.

Shenoa Retreat and Learning Center
P.O. Box 43
Philo, CA 95466
(707) 895-3156

Shenoa's vision is "to create a center for renewal, education and service dedicated to the positive transformation of [the] world." The center offers various workshops, retreats, and family gatherings.

Spring Hill of Ashby
Spring Hill Road
P.O. Box 130
Ashby, MA 01431
(800) 550-0244

Spring Hill's workshops focus on applying the principles of physical, emotional and spiritual health to participants' personal life struggles.

Taos Institute
Box 4628, Camino De La Placita
Taos, NM 87571
(505) 751-1232

The Taos Institute is a center for dialogue, inquiry, and consultation aimed at achieving more humane and ecologically viable forms of relationship—from the level of daily intimacies, to local communities and organizations, and onward to the global community. The institute offers conferences, consulting, and workshops. Future conferences may include "From Conflict to Community" and "Postmodern Organizational Processes."

Temenos Conference Center
685 Broad Run Road
West Chester, PA 19382
(215) 696-8145

Temenos is a service of the Swedenborgian Church and offers retreats, conferences, and various workshops.

Temenos Institute
29 East Main Street
Westport, CT 06880
(203) 227-4388

The name Temenos comes from the Greek language and refers to the sacred precinct where drama was performed for the purpose of what is now considered spiritual, emotional and psychological transformation. The institute offers workshops, lectures, films and courses that represent different modals of depth psychology. Some are of special interest to mental health professionals.

Vallecitos Mountain Refuge
Tides Foundation
1807 Second Street, Suite 10
Sante Fe, NM 87501
(505) 988-4714

Vallecitos, established by Grove T. Burnett and Linda M. Velarde, is dedicated to awakening and cultivating the spiritual dimension of environmental and social activism in our society. All applicants must have at least ten years of experience as an activist working for environmental or social justice, and the endorsement of the organization which employs them or with which they work closely. Accepted applicants are awarded full fellowships. Vallecitos will be holding its second annual meditation retreat for environmental leaders in 1994 (also by invitation).

Wainwright House

See Nondegree and Postgraduate Training Programs.

Wildflower Lodge Conference Center

P.O. Box 670

Paulden, AR 86334-0670

(800) 448-9187

William Brugh Joy, M.D., Ph.D., founded Wildflower in 1988 as a center for transformation, meditation, healing and personal growth.

Wise Woman Center

P.O. Box 64

Woodstock, NY 12498

(914) 246-8081

The center offers various workshops focusing on women's spirituality and health, herbal medicine, shamanic skills, death and dying, the healing power of sound, and psychic skills.

Woodstock Center for Healing and Renewal (WCHR)

P.O. Box 127

Woodstock, NY 12498

(914) 679-2638; (800) 398-2630

Founded in 1992 by Elat Chayyim, the WCHR brings together a network of people to facilitate individual healing and renewal in a manner that links the individual to broadening circles of social, political, and ecological transformation. The center explores the richness of Jewish spiritual heritage together with other traditions. In addition to week-long seminar classes, a broad range of healing services are available, such as massage therapy, yoga, reflexology, and nutritional counseling.

SECTION X

RETREAT CENTERS

In This Section:

➤ MAJOR RETREAT CENTERS

➤ GUIDEBOOKS TO RETREAT CENTERS

FRANCIS GEORGE

THERE IS A BELIEF WITHIN THE TRANSPERSONAL AND HOLISTIC field that by following a spiritual path and attending to one's own psychological growth, one is better able to facilitate healing in others. Retreat centers offer mental health professionals (and others) the opportunity for rejuvenation, personal exploration, and firsthand experience of a spiritual practice. Listed below are some of the most popular retreat centers throughout the United States. The length of retreat programs and the corresponding rates vary considerably. Check with the individual center, and consider that many centers offer work-exchange and scholarship programs. Also note that some holistic conference centers utilize retreat space as well. You may want to consult one of the guidebooks listed at the end of this section for more detailed information.

MAJOR RETREAT CENTERS

Anabasis
1084 South Briggs Avenue
Sarasota, FL 34237
(813) 365-5245; (800) 329-5245

This retreat center offers massage, meditation, biofeedback, yoga, and exercise classes.

Campion Renewal Center
319 Concord Road
Weston, MA 02193
(617) 894-3199

Campion, a Jesuit-sponsored retreat house, was founded in 1972. The staff is committed to adapting the spiritual exercises of St. Ignatius to help people of all faiths grow in a contemplative relationship with God, and to develop lay leaders who will act as companions to others along the same path.

Center for Spiritual Awareness
P.O. Box 7
Lakemont, GA 30552
(404) 782-4723

The center offers meditation retreats in the northeast Georgia mountains from May to September.

Center for Spiritual Development
96 Milton Road
Rye, NY 10580
(914) 967-7328

The center offers various programs in spirituality.

Chinook Learning Center and Retreat Facility
P.O. Box 57
Clinton, WA 98236
(206) 321-1884

Chinook was founded in 1972 as a contemplative learning center. As a nonprofit educational organization committed to creating a sustainable future for the planet, Chinook shares and stewards its resources in a way that demonstrates and teaches the sacred interconnection of Earth, Spirit, and all living things. Chinook offers individual retreats, work retreats, and internship programs.

Chrysalis House
Contemplative Outreach, Ltd.
235 Bellvale Lakes Road
Warwick, NY 10990
(914) 986-8050

Chrysalis House is a Trappist monastery and center for contemplative living under the guidance of Fr. Thomas Keating. It is affiliated with the Archdiocese of New York and offers formation in centering prayer and contemplative living.

City of God
R.D. 1, Box 319
Moundsville, WV 26041
(304) 845-7539

Since 1968, Swami Bhaktipada and an expanding group of more than 300 men and women have worked to establish a spiritual sanctuary and a place of pilgrimage for people of all faiths. Sisters and brothers of the community offer weekend retreats.

Dayspring Retreat Center
11301 Neelsville Church Road
Germantown, MD 20876
(301) 428-9348

Sponsored by the Church of the Savior in Washington, D.C., Dayspring offers silent retreats.

Feathered Pipe Ranch
P.O. Box 1682
Helena, MT 59624
(406) 442-8196

The Ranch offers retreat-style workshops on topics such as astrology, yoga, women's wisdom, and shamanism.

Four Winds Institute
Route 7, Box 124 RLB
Santa Fe, NM 87505
(505) 983-2272

The purpose of the Four Winds Institute is to stimulate and encourage awareness of self, a connection to nature and the world, and relationship to a higher power. The four areas of study at the institute include creativity, balance, the feminine, and listening. The institute has no religious affiliation.

F.R.E.S.H. Renewal Center
P.O. Box 219
Augusta, MO 63332
(314) 228-4548

Fellowship Renewing Experience, Strength and Hope (FRESH) Renewal Center, founded in 1990, is dedicated to a spiritual renewal process in which individuals recovering from addictions and their families can find sanctuary, support, and personal growth. The center follows the 12-Step recovery program.

Green Gulch Farm Zen Center
1601 Shoreline Highway
Sausalito, CA 94965
(415) 383-3134

Green Gulch Farm is a Buddhist practice center in the Japanese Soto Zen tradition, and offers training in Zen meditation.

Heart of Stillness Retreats
P.O. Box 106
Jamestown, CO 80455
(800) 748-0919; (303) 459-3431

Heart of Stillness Retreats, founded in 1993, offers individuals, families, and small groups opportunities for spiritual growth and development through silence and meditation. Retreats range from a few days to a number of weeks, or longer. The center has a Jewish affiliation.

Heartwood Institute
220 Harmony Lane
Garberville, CA 95542
(707) 923-2021

Heartwood provides resources for attaining higher physical, psychological and spiritual well-being. Besides offering an array of somatic nondegree training programs (e.g., massage, polarity, and shiatsu), Heartwood conducts various personal growth retreats, often within an educational framework. Also see Nondegree and Postgraduate Programs, Addiction Counseling, and Somatic Therapy-General Programs.

Insight Meditation Society (IMS)
Pleasant Street
Barre, MA 01005
(508) 355-4378

Founded in 1975 by Jack Kornfield, Ph.D., Joseph Goldstein, and Sharon Salzburg, the society is a nonprofit retreat center whose purpose is to foster the practice of Vipassana (insight) meditation and to preserve the essential teachings of Theravada Buddhism. The IMS offers a year-round program of intensive meditation retreats and various opportunities for volunteer service.

Karma Triyana Dharmachakra (KTD)
352 Meads Mountain Road
Woodstock, NY 12498
(914) 679-5906

This monastery and retreat center is the North American seat of His Holiness the Gyalwa Karmapa, head of the Karma Kagyu school of Tibetan Buddhism. Founded in

1978, the center offers traditional Buddhist training and education as transmitted by meditation masters of the Kagyu lineage since the 10th century. It publishes the quarterly newsletter *Densal*.

Karme-Choling
Barnet, VT 05821
(802) 633-2384

The center was founded in 1970 by Chogyam Trungpa Rinpoche, a Buddhist meditation master who was formerly the abbot of the Surmang monasteries in Tibet. Chogyman, also known as Vidyadhara, taught throughout Europe and North America; he also founded The Naropa Institute, Shambhala Training, and Vajradhatu, an international Buddhist church.

Kripalu Center for Yoga and Health
P. O. Box 793, West Street
Lenox, MA 01240
(413) 448-3400

Kripalu Center is a nonprofit, volunteer organization founded in 1972. Staff live and work full-time at the center, practicing the spiritual teachings of yoga as modeled and taught by Yogi Amrit Desai, the center's founder. Dedicated to promoting personal and spiritual growth, the center provides humanitarian service and education based on the yogic principle that harmony of the body and mind are central to inner growth. The center offers programs in yoga, self-discovery, spiritual attunement and meditation, bodywork, and health and wellness.

Lama Foundation
P.O. Box 240
San Cristobal, NM 87564
(505) 586-1269

The foundation was incorporated in 1968 with the intention of creating a center for the awakening of consciousness and the integration of body, mind, and heart. During its first 25 years it has been an ecumenical monastery, a transitional community, and a retreat center. Retreats offer instruction in a wide array of spiritual traditions including Sufi, Buddhist, Jewish, Hindu, Christian, and Native American.

Lindisfarne Mountain Retreat
Crestone Mountain Zen Center
P.O. Box 130
Crestone, CO 81131
Correspondence offered only by mail.

Lindisfarne offers retreats devoted to exploring the relationship between Buddhist thought and practice and Western

philosophy and psychology. See the Lindisfarne Association in Interdisciplanary Resources.

Maria Wald Retreat House
c/o Precious Blood Convent
P.O. Box 97
Shillington, PA 19607
(215) 777-1624

Maria Wald Retreat House is named after a Trappist abbey in Germany. The house offers hospitality to those who wish to make arrangements for guided, directed, or private days of prayer. Day and evening programs or group weekend retreats may be scheduled throughout the year. A recent workshop focused on the Enneagram.

Metivta: A Center for Jewish Wisdom
Los Angeles Hillel Council
6233 Wilshire Boulevard
Los Angeles, CA 90048
(213) 934-7066

This center offers various programs throughout the year that promote studies in Jewish spirituality.

Mount Madonna Center
445 Summit Road
Watsonville, CA 95076
(408) 847-0406

Mount Madonna Center for the Creative Arts and Sciences is a community designed to nurture the creative arts and the health sciences within a context of spiritual growth. The center is inspired by Baba Hari Dass and is sponsored by the Hanuman Fellowship, a group whose talents and interests are unified by the common practice of yoga. Personal and group retreats as well as weekend programs are available. The center also maintains a work-study program.

Mountain Light Retreat Center
R.T. 2, Box 419
Crozet, VA 22932
(804) 978-7770

The center offers meditation and massage programs in the Blue Ridge mountains of Virginia.

Northeast Zen Centers of the Kwan Um School
Most of the following centers offer a format that combines retreat and workshop experience with meditation practice.

Cambridge Zen Center
199 Auburn Street
Cambridge, MA 02139
(617) 576-3229

International Head Temple
99 Pound Road
Cumberland, RI 02864
(401) 658-1464

New Haven Zen Center
193 Mansfield Street
New Haven, CT 06511
(203) 787-0912

Zen Center of New York
400 East 14th Street, Apartment 2E
New York, NY 10009
(212) 353-0461

The Benedictine Monastery
Pecos, NM 87552
(505) 757-6415

The Benedictine monastic community has been offering group retreats since its inception in 1955. It also offers workshops on a regular basis.

Phoenicia Pathwork Center
P.O. Box 66
Phoenicia, NY 12464
(914) 688-2211

Pathwork is a spiritual path of purification and transformation concerned with self-responsibility, self-knowledge, and self-acceptance. The practice is based on 258 lectures given over 20 years by a spirit entity known as the Guide, and transmitted through Eva Pierrakos. The Phoenicia Center is the largest of a number of Pathwork communities around the world.

Pocket Ranch Insitute
P.O. Box 516
Geyserville, CA 95441
(707) 857-3359

Pocket Ranch Institute was created by Barbara Findeisen, M.F.C.C., in 1986 as both a retreat and psychological healing center. The Woodlands Program is a 12-bed short-term adult residential treatment center for people experiencing emotional crisis or life disruption. Licensed by the state of California and staffed 24 hours a day, the Woodlands is an alternative to hospitalization. Intensive workshops and self-directed retreat programs are also available.

Red Mountain Lodge
Route 1, Box 140
Crowley Lake, CA 93546
(619) 935-4560

Incorporated in 1992, Red Mountain Lodge offers two- to seven-day intensive workshops devoted to the study of spirituality and consciousness. Most workshops emphasize experiential work and are limited to about 25 people. Topics include shamanism, holistic health and healing, Kabala, and the "new physics."

Resources for Ecumenical Spirituality (RES)
P.O. Box 2
Mankato, MN 56002
(507) 387-4276; (417) 754f-2562

RES, founded in 1987, is a Minnesota-based nonprofit organization that fosters mutual understanding among religious faiths through shared spiritual practice and dialogue. It sponsors retreats, colloquia, publications, and other projects related to spiritual practice and study.

Satchidananda Ashram-Yogaville
Route 1, Box 120
Buckingham, VA 23921
(804) 969-3121

Founded in 1979, this spiritual center located in the foothills of the Blue Ridge Mountains in central Virginia sponsors programs, including workshops and retreats, in Hatha Yoga, Raja Yoga, meditation, and vegetarian cooking—all based on the Integral Yoga teachings of Sri Swami Satchidananda, the founder of the Integral Yoga Institute.

Shenoa Retreat and Learning Center
P.O. Box 43
Philo, CA 95466
(707) 895-3156

Inspired by Findhorn in Scotland (see International Resources), Shenoa is a retreat and learning center for groups, families, and individuals. The center includes a garden, a land stewardship program, and work-study and community-outreach programs. Shenoa currently works with the Daily Bread Project of Berkeley to provide fresh organic produce to feed the hungry. Programs offered include courses on Carl Jung, Joseph Campbell, dreamwork, and sustainable agriculture.

Southern Dharma Retreat Center
Route 1, Box 34H
Hot Springs, NC 28743
(704) 622-7112

Southern Dharma Retreat Center, founded in 1978, is a nonprofit foundation whose purpose is to offer silent group meditation retreats led by teachers from a variety of spiritual paths. The center is located in the North Carolina mountains about an hour from Asheville.

Spirit Rock Center
Insight Meditation West
P.O. Box 909
Woodacre, CA 94973
(415) 488-0164

Spirit Rock Center offers insight meditation retreats that are designed for both beginning and experienced meditators. The center is nonsectarian, although the ethics and traditions of Buddhist psychology offer guidance. Advisors include the Venerable Thich Nhat Hanh, Ram Dass, and Stan and Christina Grof.

Spiritual Life Institute
1 Carmelite Way
Crestone, CO 81131
(719) 256-4778

The Spiritual Life Institute, founded in 1960 by William McNamara, O.C.D., with a mandate from the visionary Pope John XXIII, is a small ecumenical Roman Catholic monastic community of men and women who embrace a life of contemplative solitude according to the Carmelite ideal. There are two hermitages open for private retreats to those who want to go "into the desert and pray" (Luke 5:16). The institute also publishes a newsletter and the quarterly magazine *Desert Call*.

St. Benedict Center
P.O. Box 5070
Madison, WI 53705
(608) 836-1631

St. Benedict Center is an ecumenical retreat and conference facility. The focus of all educational offerings is personal spiritual transformation and growth. Personal retreat experiences and spiritual direction are also available year-round. Program themes focus on creativity and spirituality; how to live a simpler, more balanced life; watercolors and clay as tools for self-discovery; journaling; spiritual friendship; and peace and justice issues.

Temenos at Broad Run Conference and Retreat Center
685 Broad Run Road
West Chester, PA 19382
(215) 696-8145

Established in 1986, Temenos is a service of the Swedenborgian Church. Temenos sponsors programs for psychological and spiritual growth directed toward integration of body, mind, and spirit. Regular offerings include healing arts, dream sharing, family relationships and communication, couples retreats, creative expression, inner child work, Holotropic Breathwork™, world community, Creation

Spirituality, Universal Peace Dances, and Swedenborgian spiritual perspectives.

Upaya Foundation
1404 Cerro Gordo Road
Santa Fe, NM 87501
(505) 986-8518

Founded by Joan Halifax, Ph.D. (also the founder of the Ojai Foundation), Upaya is a Buddhist study and retreat center.

Zen Center
300 Page Street
San Francisco, CA 94102
(415) 863-3136

The Zen Center offers retreats and workshops at both the center and Green Gulch Farm (see listing in this section), an affiliated monastic community in Sausalito.

Zen Center of Los Angeles (ZCLA)
923 South Normandie Avenue
Los Angeles, CA 90006
(213) 387-2351

The ZCLA has both a city and mountain center (see below). The city center includes a meditation hall and a residential community of about 35 committed Zen practitioners, whose practice is aimed at integrating meditation with family and career life. A 90-day retreat emphasizing everyday life is held during the winter months. It also publishes *Ten Directions*.

Zen Mountain Center
P.O. Box 43
Mountain Center, CA 92561
(714) 659-5272

The Zen Mountain Center offers various retreats during the spring, winter, and fall months.

Zen Mountain Monastery
Box 197, South Plank Road
Mount Tremper, NY 12457
(914) 688-2228

The Zen Mountain Monastery offers a year-round program of weekend and week-long retreats on a wide variety of topics. All retreats are conducted within an ongoing Zen training matrix that includes dawn and evening meditation, Zen Buddhist services, work practice, and talks—given by Abbot John Daido Loori, who founded the center in 1980, or senior Zen students—that help clarify the common ground between Zen and the topic of that particular retreat. Past topics have included mysticism and science, psychology, wilderness survival, martial arts, and social action. The monastery also publishes the quarterly journal *Mountain Record*.

GUIDEBOOKS TO RETREAT CENTERS

Buddhist America: Centers, Practices, Retreats (1990)
By Don Moreale
John Muir Publications
P.O. Box 613
Sante Fe, NM 87504

Catholic America: Self Renewal Centers and Retreats (1989)
By Christian Meyers
John Muir Publications
P.O. Box 613
Sante Fe, NM 87504

A Guide to Monastic Guest Houses (1989)
By J. Robert Beagle
Morehouse Publishing Company
70 Danbury Road
Wilton, CT 06897

Healthy Escapes: 240 Spas, Fitness Resorts and Cruises (1990)
By Fodor's Travel Publications
East 50th Street
New York, NY 10022

Retreat Ministry Centers in the U.S. and Canada (1990)
By Retreats International
P.O. Box 1067
Notre Dame, IN 46556

Sanctuaries: A Guide to Lodgings in Monasteries, Abbeys, and Retreats of the United States: Northeast (1991)
By Jack and Marcia Kelly
Belltower/Crown Publications
201 East 50th Street
New York, NY 10022

Sanctuaries: A Guide to Lodgings in Monasteries, Abbeys, and Retreats of the United States: The West Coast and Southeast (1992)
By Jack and Marcia Kelly
Belltower/Crown Publications
201 East 50th Street
New York, NY 10022

Transformative Adventures, Vacations and Retreats: An International Directory of 300+ Host Organizations (1994)
By John Benson
New Millennium Publishing
P.O. Box 3065
Portland, OR 97208

Travelers Guide to Healing Centers and Retreats in North America (1989)
By Martine Rudee and Jonathan Blease
John Muir Publications
P.O. Box 613
Santa Fe, NM 87504

SECTION XI

INTERNATIONAL RESOURCES

In This Section:
➤ TRANSPERSONAL DEGREE PROGRAMS
➤ ORGANIZATIONS
➤ CONFERENCE AND RETREAT CENTERS
➤ PERIODICALS

Skyros Institute and Center, Greece

THE FIELD OF TRANSPERSONAL PSYCHOLOGY HAS GROWN FROM A SMALL GROUP OF PSYCHOLOGISTS AND PSYCHIatrists meeting in the San Francisco Bay Area in the early 1960s to a multidisciplinary movement that has attracted thousands of people from all over the world.

Dissemination of the transpersonal perspective abroad has been accomplished largely by the meetings of the International Transpersonal Association (ITA). Conferences have been held in Reykjavik, Iceland; Inari, Finland; Belo Horizonte, Brazil; Boston, Massachusetts; Melbourne, Australia; Bombay, India; Davos, Switzerland; Kyoto, Japan; Santa Rosa, California; Eugene, Oregon; Atlanta, Georgia; Prague, Czechoslovakia; and, in 1994, Killarney, Ireland.

Recognizing the application of the transpersonal perspective to their own fields, anthropologists, educators, physicians, biologists, physicists, systems theorists, economists, ecologists, theologians, journalists, and artists have joined psychologists and other mental health professionals in their enthusiasm for and commitment to developing a comprehensive transpersonally oriented and inclusive worldview.

While there are, as yet, only a few formal graduate degree programs in transpersonal psychology outside North America, there are individuals around the globe sharing these interests and developing transpersonal programs in their respective regions. Despite the obvious barriers of language and culture, we hope this composite sample of international resources will help bridge the worldwide movement toward more holistic perspectives in all fields.

—Patricia Ellerd, Ph.D., President of the International Transpersonal Association, contributed to this introduction. She was also the senior editor of the Graduate Education Guide, *first edition.*

TRANSPERSONAL DEGREE PROGRAMS

Beshara School of Intensive Esoteric Education
Chisholme House
Roberton, Roxburghshire TD9 7PH
Scotland

Goetheanum School of Spiritual Science
P.O. Box 134
Dornach CH-4143
Switzerland
This school is affiliated with Rudolf Steiner and the Anthroposophical Society.

International College of Psychical and Spiritual Sciences
P.O. Box 1445
Station H
Montreal, Quebec HUG 2N3
Canada

Laban Center for Movement and Dance
Laurie Grove, New Cross
London SE14 6NH
England
The center offers a master's degree in dance and movement therapy.

Regents Park College
Oxford OX1 2LB
England
Regents has recently inaugurated a Ph.D. program in psychotherapy.

Schumacher College
The Old Postern
Dartington, Devon TQ9 6EA
England
Founded by E.F. Schumacher, the college is an international center for ecological and spiritual studies.

The Skyros Institute and Center
92 Prince of Wales Road
London NW5 3NE
England

Training in Process-Oriented Psychology
Fitzeltrasse 10
Zurich CH 8038
Switzerland
Process-oriented psychology is a psychotherapeutic paradigm developed in Zurich, Switzerland, with helpers in many parts of the world. It has its roots in the analytical psychology of C. G. Jung and shares with it the basic attitude that the

process in which a client finds him- or herself is fundamentally right and should be encouraged, since it contains the seeds of personal development.

Trinity College, Bristol
Senate House
Bristol BS8 ITH
England
Bristol offers an advanced diploma in implicit religion in conjunction with the Network for the Study of Implicit Religion (NSIR). See the NSIR under Organizations in this section.

University of Guadalajara
Mtro. Ramón Gallegos Nava, General Coordinator
Av. Hidalgo 1755
Col. Landrón de Guevara, C.P. 44600
Guadalajara, Jalisco
Mexico
As a result of the "New Paradigms of Sciences" conference in 1993, the Mexican government and the University of Guadalajara have approved funds to start a Frontier Sciences program that will drive the diffusion of the new paradigms in gestation. This program represents the first transpersonal department in Latin America.

ORGANIZATIONS

Applewood Center
See Conference Centers.

Asociacion Transpersonal Espanola
Manuel Almeñoro
Fernaneo VI 17, 2o Derecha
Madrid, 28004
Spain

Associação Transpessoal Dà Amárica Do Sul
Rua Barata Ribeiro, 163 - cj 02
São Paulo SP CEP 01308
Brazil

Association of Jungian Analysts
Flat 3 Eton Avenue
London NW3
England

Associazione Italiana Di Psicologia Transpersonale (AIPT)
Via Callalto Sabino 21
Rome 00199
Italy
AIPT was founded in 1989.

Australian Transpersonal Association
P.O. Box 11, Phillip Mall
West Pymble New South Wales 2073
Australia

British Society for Music Therapy
69 Avondale Avenue
East Barnet, Herts EN4 8NB
England

Eurotas (European Transpersonal Association)
c/o Monique Tibergien
Place de la Neuville, 3
B-1348 Louvain-la-Neuve
Belgium

Institute of Cultural Affairs
Rue Amedee Lynen 8
1030 Brussels
Belgium
The institute works toward building a future global vision that emphasizes, among other things, personal development and a better understanding of economic and ecological systems.

Institute of Jainology
31 Lancaster Gate
London W2 3LP
England
Jainism is one of the three religions of the world that originated in India. The term "Jain" means a follower of the "Jinas" (Spiritual Victors), human teachers who through their own efforts are believed to have attained "Kevalajnana" (omniscience or infinite knowledge). The estimated population of the Jains is 10 million. They practice "Ahimsa" (nonviolence) and are strict vegetarians.

International Center for Science, Culture and Consciousness
15, Institutional Area
Lodhi Road
New Delhi 110 003
India

International College of Spiritual and Psychic Sciences
1974 de Maissonneuve West
Montreal, Quebec H3H 1K5
Canada
(514) 937-8359
Programs: Personal, Spiritual and Psychic Development; East-West Spirituality and the Quest for Universal Human Value in the World's Religions; New Paradigms of Science and Human Culture in Consciousness Studies, Parapsychology and Paraphysics; and Pastoral Studies for an Inter-Faith Ministry.

International Transpersonal Association (ITA)
20 Sunnyside, A257
Mill Valley, CA 94941
(415) 383-8819

The ITA is distinguished from its sister organization, the Association for Transpersonal Psychology also located in California, by its international orientation and multidisciplinary field of interests. Members share a commitment to developing a comprehensive, transpersonally oriented, and inclusive worldview. The association holds a conference every two years in various locations around the world. Simultaneous translations are available in the major languages.

Japanese Association of Transpersonal Psychology/Psychiatry
6-7-1 Nishi-shinjuku, Shinjuku-ku
Tokyo 160
Japan

Based in the Tokyo Medical Hospital, the association offers research programs and educational training programs in transpersonal psychology and psychiatry.

Martinus Cosmology Center (MC)
Mariendalsvej 94-96
DK-2000 Frederiksberg
Denmark

The MC in Copenhagen was established in 1932 in order to make Martinus's literature available. The Cosmology is described as a spiritual science describing and analyzing the spiritual laws of life. There is no sect or association around which Martinus Cosmology is organized.

Network for the Study of Implicit Religion
Winterbourne Rectory
58 High Street
Winterbourne BS17 1JQ
England

The purpose of the network is to provide opportunities for the study of implicit religion within three main headings: academic, educational, and ecclesiastical. It sponsors the Denton Conferences, which represent all the religious studies and social science disciplines, and offers an advanced diploma in implicit religion in conjunction with Trinity College, Bristol.

Psychopolitical Peace Institute (PPPI)
Gehrenhof
CH 8712 Staefa
Switzerland

Through research, development, and application of new paradigms, the PPPI supports the transformation of individuals and organizational and societal values. It offers a three-year training program in Zurich in Body/Psychosynthesis and Transpersonal Psychology.

Scientific and Medical Network (SMN)
Lesser Halings
Tilehouse Lane
Denham, Uxbridge, Middlesex UB9 5DG
England

The SMN cosponsored the first Mystics and Scientists Conference in 1978. It is an informal international group consisting mainly of qualified scientists and physicians, with a seasoning of psychologists, engineers, philosophers, and other professionals. The network, founded in 1973, questions the assumptions of contemporary scientific and medical thinking. By remaining open to intuitive and spiritual insights, it claims to foster a climate in which science as a whole can adopt a more comprehensive and sensitive approach.

Society of Ordained Scientists
55 St. John Street
Oxford OX1 2LQ
England

CONFERENCE AND RETREAT CENTERS

Skyros Institute and Center
92 Prince of Wales Road
London NW5 3NE
England

Skyros (also known as Atsitsa) is an international holistic health and fitness center on the Greek island of Skyros. The institute offers workshops and various training programs.

Bethlehem Retreat Center
2371 Arbot Road
Nanaimo, British Columbia V9R 5K3
Canada

Center for Spiritual Growth
580 Chapel Street
Ottawa, Ontario K1N 7Z8
Canada
(613) 236-8855

Findhorn Foundation (FF)
Cluny Hill College, Forres
Morayshire IV26 ORD
Scotland

Founded in 1962, the FF is an international spiritual community. It holds a series of conferences and publishes the magazine *One Earth.*

Frankfurter Ring (FR)
Kobbachstr.12
D-6000 Frankfurt 50
Germany

Founded in 1969, the FR promotes the development of human potential by organizing weekend and week-long courses, lectures, and conferences.

Hollyhock Farm
Box 127, Manson's Landing
Cortes Island, British Columbia VOP 1KO
Canada
(604) 935-6533

Laban Center for Movement and Dance
See Transpersonal Degree Programs in this section.

The London Convivium for Archetypal Studies
P.O. Box 417
London, NE3 6YE
England

Loyola House
Guelph Center of Spirituality
P.O. Box 245
Guelph, Ontario NIH 6J9
Canada
(519) 824-1250

National Retreat Association
Liddon House
24 South Audley Street
London W1Y 5DL
England

Plum Village, Meyraa
47120 Loubés-Bernac
France

This retreat center was founded by the Vietnamese Buddhist monk Thich Nhat Hanh.

PERIODICALS
Rates are shown for the cost of an international subscription.

Human Potential: Psychology for Developing Humans
5 Layton Road
London N1 OPX
England
Quarterly; $22

I-to-I Magazine
92 Prince of Wales Road
London NW5 3NE
England
Quarterly; $34
    I-to-I publishes articles having to do with
the needs of the whole person, be they
material, emotional, spiritual, physical,
social, or environmental.

Inward Path
North American Office:
New Frontier
101 Cuthybert Street
Philadelphia, PA 19106
(215) 627-5683
    Written in English, this Russian maga-
zine addresses issues of human
development.

International Journal of
Transpersonal Psychology
P.O. Box 5513
Stafford Heights, Queensland 4053
Australia
Published irregularly; $45

Kindred Spirit
Foxhole, Dartington,
Totnes, Devon TQ9 6EB
England
Quarterly; $23

New Renaissance
Weisenauer Weg 4
D-6500 Mainz 42
Germany
Quarterly; $14
    The magazine is a forum for progressive
and holistic discussion on local and global
concerns, and represents Renaissance Universal, a membership and networking
organization.

Resurgence
Salem Cottage
Trelil, Bodmin
Cornwall PL30 3HZ
England
Bimonthly; $36
    This international magazine promotes
the ideas of author and thinker E.F.
Schumacher.

Studies in Spirituality
Kik Pharos Publishing House
P.O. Box 130
8260 AC Kampen
Netherlands
Annual
    Published by the Titus Brandsma Insti-
tute in the Netherlands, this new journal
includes scholarly articles on spirituality
and mysticism, and promotes spirituality as
an academic discipline.

The Way: A Review of
Contemporary Christian Spirituality
Heythrop College
11-30 Cavendish Square
London WIM 0AN
England
Quarterly; $26.50

SECTION XII

INTERDISCIPLINARY RESOURCES

In This Section:

➤ ORGANIZATIONS AND INSTITUTES

➤ PERIODICALS

➤ TAPE-RECORDING COMPANIES

ORGANIZATIONS AND INSTITUTES

This chapter includes organizations, associations, institutes, and training centers relevant to the psychospiritual field but without a sufficiently specific focus to belong within any single section or chapter.

American Anthropological Association
Society for the Anthropology of Consciousness (SAC)
4350 North Fairfax Drive, Suite 640
Arlington, VA 22203
(703) 528-1902 (Ext. 3005)
　　The SAC is an interdisciplinary organization concerned with cross-cultural, experimental, experiential, and theoretical approaches to the study of consciousness. The primary

areas of interest include (altered) states of consciousness, religion, possession, trance, and dissociative states; ethnographic studies of shamanistic, mediumistic, mystical, and related traditions; indigenous healing practices; linguistic, philosophical, social, and symbolic studies of consciousness phenomena; and psychic (psi) phenomena, including their roles in traditional cultural practices and applications such as in psychic archaeology. It publishes the newsletter *Anthropology of Consciousness*.

American Humanist Association (AHA)
P.O. Box 1188
Amherst, NY 14226-7118
(716) 839-5080

The AHA promotes naturalistic humanism, a philosophy which holds that human beings determine the moral principles by which they live. The AHA publishes *The Humanist*, a bimonthly magazine of critical inquiry and social comment, and *Free Mind*, the association membership magazine.

Association for Religion and Intellectual Life (ARIL)
College of New Rochelle
New Rochelle, NY 10805-2308
(914) 654-5425

The ARIL, an interreligious group, hopes to have an impact not just on university campuses but also on the ways in which ideas find their way into the broader community. ARIL sponsors an annual three-day conference and the Coolidge Research Colloquium, a month-long interreligious program in Cambridge, Massachusetts. It also publishes the journal *Cross Currents*.

Brahma Kumaris World Spiritual University (BKWSU)
1609 West Chase Avenue
Chicago, IL 60626
(312) 262-2828

In the course of 50 years, the BKWSU has expanded from its beginnings in Pakistan to become an international organization with some 1,500 centers. Activities include sponsoring major projects to promote the International Years of Youth and Peace, and organizing conferences, concerts, lectures, and training workshops in hospitals, schools, universities, prisons, and youth and community centers.

Center for Educational Guidance (CEG)
P.O. Box 445
North San Juan, CA 94950
(916) 292-3623

The CEG is an emerging center for holistic and spiritual education.

Center for Faith and Science Exchange (CFSE)
93 Anson Road
Concord, MA 01742
(508) 369-1464

The CFSE was organized in 1989 for the purpose of stimulating cooperation between the religious and scientific communities in order to address societal and global problems to which each community offers unique resources. The center is a Program Affiliate of the Boston Theological Institute, a consortium of nine seminaries and theological schools in the greater Boston area.

Center for Psychology and Social Change
1493 Cambridge Street
Cambridge, MA 02139
(617) 497-1553

The center aims to work with community and corporate leaders, parents, educators, social planners, and journalists to promote a new consciousness as a means of changing human behavior and to define a new psychology for sustainability. The special focus of the center is to explore the role human consciousness plays in building a sustainable world peace. The center is affiliated with the Harvard Medical School at Cambridge Hospital and publishes the newsletter *CenterPiece*.

Center for Sacred Psychology (CSP)
Box 643, Gateway Station
Culver City, CA 90232
(310) 838-00279

The CSP is a group of psychotherapists and spiritual directors with a Jungian orientation, focusing on service to those in the helping professions. The center offers personalized intensive experiences and occasional workshops.

Center for the Study of the Spiritual Foundations of Education
Teachers College, Box 132
Columbia University
New York, NY 10027
(212) 678-3987

The center seeks to provide a forum within mainstream American education where control questions about the nature of an education for the whole human being can be raised and pursued. The center attempts to explore the imaginative, ethical, aesthetic, and spiritual capacities that our times require, and to find ways in which our educational and social institutions can nourish and reflect those capacities.

Center for Women and Religion (CWR)
Graduate Theological Union
2400 Ridge Road
Berkeley, CA 94709
(510) 649-2490

The CWR, founded in 1970 as a nondenominational and interfaith center of the Graduate Theological Union, has as its goals to end sexism and to promote justice for women in religious institutions.

The Center for Women, the Earth and the Divine (CWED)
114 Rising Ridge Road
Ridgefield, CT 06877
Correspondence offered only by mail.

The CWED is dedicated to exploring what parallels exist between the imagined and the actual treatment of women and the earth, and how images of the Divine relate to the experiences of women and the earth. CWED initially examined these relationships within the Christian tradition and is now also looking at these same issues in other traditions such as Hindu, Jewish, Buddhist, and Muslim. As an educational organization, CWED makes its work available to the public through talks, workshops, written materials, and retreats.

Center for Yoga and Christianity
P.O. Box 2615
Monterey, CA 93940
Correspondence offered only by mail.

Founded in Ecuador in 1972, the center is devoted to a holistic development of modern humanity in its three main aspects: physical, mental, and spiritual. The center offers lectures, workshops, and classes in the areas of world religions, mysticism, spirituality, and yogic techniques and holds an annual international congress in Ecuador.

Circle Sanctuary
P.O. Box 219
Mount Horeb, WI 53572
(608) 924-2216

Circle Sanctuary provides a guide to pagan groups, sanctuary circles, and pagan arts. Its quarterly newsletter, *Circle Network News*, and its newspaper, *Circle*, contain educational information and networking resources for Wiccans (practitioners of earth-based religion or witchcraft), pagans, and other nature-religion practitioners worldwide. Its school for priestesses is open only to women.

Covenant of the Goddess (CG)
P.O. 1226
Berkeley, CA 94704
Correspondence offered only by mail.

The CG is a Wiccan religious organization with members in North America, Europe, and Australia. Wicca, or Witchcraft, is a life-affirming, earth- and nature-oriented religion that sees all of life as sacred and interconnected. Established in 1975, CG is an umbrella organization functioning to increase cooperation and mutual support among Wiccans and to secure legal protections enjoyed by members of other religions. In recent years the organization has turned its attention and resources to sponsoring spiritual and educational conferences; correcting negative stereotypes; promoting positive media portrayals and interfaith outreach; and providing for the needs of its members and their families with disaster relief, health insurance, and legal assistance in instances of discrimination.

The Eagle Connection
57 Scenic Road
Fairfax, CA 94930
(415) 457-4513

The Eagle Connection is an alliance of organizations and individuals working for personal, communal and global transformation through a cross-cultural and spiritual exploration. Founding co-directors Jo Imlay and John Broomfield, Ph.D., disseminate information on individuals and groups developing imaginative holistic solutions to critical educational, social, economic, health, and environmental problems. They also teach workshops on these topics throughout North America. Membership is by subscription ($25/year) to the bimonthly newsletter the *Eagle Connector.*

The EarthSpirit Community (ESC)
P.O. Box 365
Medford, MA 02155
Correspondence offered only by mail.

The ESC is a Boston-based collective that coordinates a nationwide network of people following earth-centered spiritual paths. Their spiritual practices are rooted in the ancient traditions of pagan, pre-Christian Europe that have at their core a respectful awareness of the sacredness of the earth. EarthSpirit works to develop pagan concepts and attitudes for living in the present age, to encourage communication and understanding among people of different traditions and ideologies, and to educate the general public concerning earth-centered spirituality.

Fellowship in Prayer (FIP)
291 Witherspoon Street
Princeton, NJ 08542-9945
(609) 924-6863

Incorporated in New York City in 1950, FIP is a nonprofit, interfaith organization whose purpose is to promote the practice of prayer and meditation. The organization publishes *Fellowship in Prayer*, a bimonthly interfaith journal (subscriptions are free) with an international readership in over 80 countries. Fellowship in Prayer sponsors events that deepen an individual's relationship to prayer and to traditions other than one's own. In 1989 and 1990, for example, Fellowship in Prayer sponsored concerts of "Sacred Music—Sacred Dance" by Tibetan Buddhist monks; in 1991, it offered a series of Native American sweat lodges, led by a Native American medicine woman trained in the Lakota tradition. FIP has also sponsored a "World-wide Day of Prayer and Meditation to help heal Mother Earth."

The Forge Institute for Spirituality and Social Change
Hunter College Program in Religion
695 Park Avenue
New York, NY 10021
(212) 772-4987

Founded in 1992, the institute seeks to bring the knowledge and practice of spirituality into the mainstream, and to bring the lessons and techniques of the spiritual life into the wider social and political dialogue. It holds an annual conference addressing spirituality and social change.

Global Alliance for Transforming Education
P.O. Box 21
Grafton, VT 05146
(802) 843-2382

The alliance is working toward a broad-based vision for the future of education. This vision is founded on organizing principles that focus on human development, experiential learning, global citizenship, earth literacy, freedom of choice, and a participatory democracy. The alliance's statement, titled, *Education 2000: A Holistic Perspective*, calls for redefining the role of the educator, honoring students as individuals, and advocating a deep sense of connection to others and to the earth.

The Institute for Bio-Spiritual Research (IBSR)
6305 Greeley Hill Road
Coulterville, CA 95311-9501
Correspondence offered only by mail.

The IBSR is an international network of several thousand people—parents, coun-selors, health care providers, hospice volunteers, clergy and sisters, teachers, therapists, retreat house staffs, and spiritual guides. The institute's mission is to develop a transcultural psychological foundation for healthy spiritualities that are solidly grounded in the body's processes. Through an easily learned process called focusing, the institute believes that individuals are able to open themselves to body awareness—hence, the term "bio-spirituality." The institute, which is nondenominational, offers training programs, publications, audio and videotapes, focusing retreats, six-day intensives, and an annual conference.

The Institute on Religion in an Age of Science (IRAS)
P.O. Box 341
Quakertown, NJ 08868
(314) 935-6836

The IRAS, founded in 1954, is a nondenominational society with two purposes: to formulate dynamic relationships between science and the goals and hopes of humanity as expressed through religion; and to state human values and contemporary knowledge in such universal terms that they may be understood by all peoples, whatever their cultural background and experience. Membership is open to those who have an interest in religion, philosophy, and the natural and social sciences. The IRAS sponsors a week-long conference and publishes a scholarly journal called *Zygon.*

International Assembly of Spiritual Healers and Earth Steward Congregations (SHES)
6040 35th Avenue, N.W.
Seattle, WA 98107-2620
(206) 783-3410

Each SHES congregation is an autonomous group of two or more people who have joined together to promote their own personal spiritual growth and holistic integration. The assembly's purpose is to assist SHES and other individuals interested in tolerating, respecting, recognizing, opening, preserving, and protecting the rights to follow any of the many spiritual pathways; observing mutual respect and peace wherever possible; and facilitating their works of earth stewardship. It publishes the *Shes Gazaette.*

International Association for Near-Death Studies (IANDS)
P.O. Box 502
East Windsor Hill, CT 06028-0502
(203) 528-5144

The IANDS is the world's only organization devoted to scientifically grounded exploration of the "near-death experience." Representing five continents, its membership includes researchers and professionals interested in near-death experience. It publishes the quarterly *Journal of Near-Death Studies* and sponsors a conference.

International Society for Scientific Exploration (ISSE)
Stanford University, ERL 306
Stanford, CA 94305-4055
(415) 725-2333

The ISSE is interested in the discussion and research of anomalous phenomena that lie outside the conventional disciplines of science. Most members are professional Ph.D. and M.D. researchers in such fields as physics, astronomy, chemistry, biological sciences, engineering, and medicine. The society publishes the *Journal of Scientific Exploration.*

Interspecies Communication(IC)
273 Hidden Meadow Lane
Friday Harbor, WA 98250
Correspondence offered only by mail.

IC was founded in 1978 to promote a better understanding of what is communicated between human beings and other animals (especially dolphins and whales) through music, art, and ceremony. Its methods consist of integrating the arts and the sciences with a strong emphasis upon environmental preservation. IC publishes a newsletter.

The Isthmus Institute
4221 Renaissance Tower
Dallas, TX 75270
(214) 742-5700

The institute's mission is to provide an educational forum for participants to explore the interactions between scientific and spiritual approaches to reality. It holds an annual conference on such topics as "Science-Spirit-Nature: A New Paradigm for the Planet."

Joseph Campbell Foundation (JCF)
P.O. Box 457
Madison Square Station
New York, NY 10159-0457
(212) 678-0545

The JCF, founded in 1990, is a nonprofit membership organization seeking to formulate a mythopoetic response to contemporary literalism and cultural retrenchment. The foundation preserves, protects, and perpetuates Campbell's work

by publishing his books and cataloging his papers and recorded lectures; promotes mythological education; and sponsors conferences, workshops, and seminars.

The Lindisfarne Association
c/o Dean's Office
Cathedral Church of St. John the Divine
1047 Amsterdam Avenue
New York, NY 10025
Correspondence offered only by mail.

Lindisfarne is an association of individuals devoted to the study and realization of a new planetary culture. Lindisfarne brings together religious leaders, scientists, ecologists, architects, artists, and business people to enjoy the creative work of imagining and building a new world culture. Although its headquarters is located at the Episcopal Cathedral Church of St. John the Divine, the Lindisfarne Association is a nondenominational and independent, not-for-profit, educational corporation. The association offers conferences, concerts, lectures, exhibitions, poetry readings, and public workshops, and it supports a publishing house (The Lindisfarne Press), a newsletter (*Annals of Earth*), and the Lindisfarne Mountain retreat center.

Millennium Institute
1611 North Kent Street, Suite 204
Arlington, VA 22209
(703) 841-0048

Formally called the Institute for 21st Century Studies, the Millennium Institute is a nonprofit organization founded in 1983 to promote long-term integrated global thinking. Its programs construct frameworks for action by nourishing a worldwide network of individuals and organizations.

Miracle Distribution Center (MDC)
1141 East Ash Avenue
Fullerton, CA 92631
(714) 738-8380

MDC, a nonprofit organization, was founded in 1978 by Beverly and Richard Hutchinson to help make the teachings of *A Course in Miracles*—a copious, three-volume "curriculum" on spiritual development channeled by Helen Shuchman, Ph.D. and transcribed by William Thetford, Ph.D. to aid Course students in their practice of its transformational principles. The center publishes the bimonthly newsletter *The Holy Encounter.*

National Hospice Organization (NHO)
1901 North Moore Street, Suite 901
Arlington, VA 22209
(800) 658-8898

The NHO offers referrals to over 1,900 local hospice groups, most of which incorporate a spiritual framework into their work. It also publishes a magazine called *Hospice.*

Our Ultimate Investment
P.O. Box 1868
Los Angeles, CA 90068
(213) 461-8248

This nonprofit organization founded in 1977 by Laura Huxley is dedicated to the nurturing of the possible human by educating and informing the public of scientific research and humanistic ideals relating to the preparation for conception, pregnancy birth, and the first five years of life.

Person, Culture and Religion (PCR)
See Spiritual/Religion Degree Programs, General Associations.

Psychopolitical Peace Institute (PPPI)
150 West 80th Street, Suite 6C
New York, NY 10024
(212) 362-6915

Founded in 1989, the PPPI derives its name from the Greek words *psyche* ("soul") and *politae* ("action"). Through research, development, and application of new paradigms, PPPI supports change and transformation of individual, organizational, and societal values. There is a related institute in Zurich, Switzerland (see International Resources).

Resource Center for Redesigning Education
Ron Miller, Ph.D., President
P.O. Box 818
Shelburne, VT 05482
(802) 865-9752

Founded in April 1993, the center aims to facilitate a deeper rethinking of the role of schooling in the emerging postindustrial world. Its goal is to encourage dialogue among diverse educational perspectives leading toward democratic, learner-centered, holistic understandings of education. The center sponsors workshops, retreats, and conferences, and publishes *Great Ideas in Education.*

San Francisco Center for Meditation and Psychotherapy (SFCMP)
1719 Union Street
San Francisco, CA 94123
(415) 567-8404

The SFCMP is an association of individual psychotherapists who share an interest in the practice of meditation and a commitment to exploring the relationship between psychotherapy and spirituality.

Society for Chaos Theory in Psychology and the Life Sciences (SCTPLS)
P.O. Box 53
Waterbury Center, VT 05677
(410) 479-2631

Chaos theory is used as an umbrella term for the newly emerging approaches to studying nonlinear, interdependent systems, such as dynamical systems theory, catastrophe theory, and self-organization theory. The society is a gathering place for individuals who are applying the concepts and methods of modern nonlinear dynamics to their field—whether it be psychology, neurophysiology, economics, or sociology. The society's goal is to promote the growth and development of nonlinear concepts in disciplines outside of physics and mathematics.

Spiritual Emergence Network (SEN)
5905 Soquel Drive, Suite 650
Soquel, CA 95010
(408) 464-8261

The SEN, an information and referral service, was founded in 1980 by Christina Grof, a pioneer in the documentation and treatment of people experiencing spiritual emergencies, in response to an increasing worldwide demand from people experiencing intense non-ordinary states of consciousness, psychospiritual crisis, and the transformative processes of spiritual emergence. Volunteers who staff the phone lines—most of whom have experienced their own spiritual emergence/emergency—refer inquiries to organizations and individual practitioners who are trained to assist people in the spiritual emergence process.

Women's Alliance for Theology, Ethics and Ritual (WATER)
8035 13th Street, Suites 1,3, & 5
Silver Spring, MD 20852
(301) 589-2509

WATER is a feminist educational center that began in 1983 as a response to the need for serious theological, ethical, and liturgical development for and by women. It publishes a quarterly newsletter.

World Future Society (WFS)
7910 Woodmont Avenue, Suite 450
Bethesda, MD 20814
(301) 951-0394

The WFS holds conferences, seminars, and other programs relevant to the study of alternative futures. It also publishes the bimonthly magazine *The Futurist*.

World Research Foundation
15300 Ventura Boulevard., Suite 405
Sherman Oaks, CA 91403
(818) 907-5483

Founded in 1984, the purpose of the foundation is to locate, gather, codify, evaluate, classify, and disseminate all information dealing with health and the environment, including both ancient and current data from traditional and nontraditional medicine. Library searches tend to contain complementary, alternative, nontraditional, and natural therapeutics.

PERIODICALS

This chapter includes periodicals that are relevant to the modalities outlined in this guide but too general or multidisciplinary to fit within any one section or chapter.

JOURNALS
American Indian Culture and Research Journal (AICRJ)
University of California at Los Angeles
American Indian Studies Center
3220 Campbell Hall
405 North Hilgard Avenue
Los Angeles, CA 90024-1548
(310) 825-7315
Quarterly; $20

The *AICRJ* provides an interdisciplinary research forum for scholars and innovators in the area of historical and contemporary American Indian life and culture. Original scholarly papers are invited on a broad range of issues. While encouraging innovative ideas, the editor favors articles that demonstrate rigorous and thorough research in an interdisciplinary context.

American Indian Religions (AIR)
Center for Academic Publication
Stanford University Branch, Box 5097
Stanford, CA 94309-5097
Quarterly; $30

AIR is an interdisciplinary journal devoted to the study and advancement of the religious traditions of American Indians. This publication brings together a diverse group of individuals who are interested in understanding and promoting the sacred traditions of American Indians, including, but not limited to, scholars, lawyers, journalists, politicians, poets, and activists.

Anima: The Journal of Human Experience
1053 Wilson Avenue
Chambersburg, PA 17201-1247
(717) 267-0087
Semiannual; $9.95

Topics include philosophy, psychology, spirituality, and mythology from the perspective of feminism and goddess religion.

Chrysalis
139 East 23rd Street
New York, NY 10010
(800) 366-7310
Three times a year; $20

This interdisciplinary journal is published by the Swedenborg Foundation (see Theological Training).

Crone Chronicles: A Journal of Conscious Aging
P.O. Box 81
Kelly, WY 83011
(307) 733-5409
Quarterly; $18

Founded in 1989 to "activate the archetype of the Crone," or the third aspect of the ancient Triple Goddess (Maiden/Mother/Crone), this grassroots publication is written by and for wise, older women who are challenging cultural stereotypes.

Cross Currents
Quarterly; $25

Sponsored by the Association for Religion and Intellectual Life, *Cross Currents* is a scholarly journal covering interreligious issues (see Interdisciplinary Organizations).

Dreaming
Association for the Study of Dreams
See Research Institutes.
Quarterly; $70 ($44 student)

This journal investigates all topics germane to dreams and dreaming.

The Empty Vessel: A Journal of Contemporary Taoism
996 Ferry Lane
Eugene, OR 97401-3349
(503) 345-8854
Quarterly; $20

This publication is dedicated to the exploration and dissemination of Taoist philosophy and practice.

Fellowship in Prayer
291 Witherspoon Street
Princeton, NJ 08542
(609) 924-6863
Bimonthly; complimentary

The purpose of *Fellowship in Prayer* is to promote the practice of prayer among all religious faiths whose fundamental belief is in God regardless of race, creed, or color. The journal publishes articles on prayer, meditation, spiritual experience, and religious faith and practices.

Feminism and Psychology
Sage Publications
P.O. Box 5096
Newbury Park, CA 91359
(805) 499-0721
Three times a year; $41

The Folio: A Journal for Focusing and Experiential Therapy
Focusing Institute
731 South Plymouth Court, Suite 801
Chicago, IL 60605
(312) 922-9277
Quarterly; $50

Frontier Perspectives
Center for Frontier Sciences at Temple University
See Research Institutes.
Semiannual; $25

Frontier Perspectives is a scholarly journal devoted to novel claims and the frontier issues of medicine, science and technology.

Holistic Education Review (HER)
Holistic Education Press
P.O. Box 328
Brandon, VT 05733-0328
(802) 247-8312
Quarterly; $35

The *HER* aims to stimulate discussion and application of all person-centered educational ideas and methods. Articles explore how education can encourage the fullest possible development of human potentials and planetary consciousness. The publisher believes that human fulfillment, global cooperation, and ecological responsibility should be the primary goals of education, and this journal inquires into the historical, social, and philosophical issues that have prevented these goals from further development.

Image: A Journal of the Arts and Religion
3100 McCormick Avenue
Wichita, KS 67213
(316) 942-4291 (x256)
Quarterly; $30 (membership)

The International Journal of Psychology of Religion
Journal Subscription Department
Lawrence Erlbaum Associates, Inc.
356 Broadway
Hillsdale, NJ 07642
(201) 666-4110
Quarterly; $35

Journal for the Scientific Study of Religion
Society for the Scientific Study of Religion
See Research Institutes.
Quarterly ; $28 (student $12)

This scholarly journal is devoted primarily to the study of religion from the perspective of the social sciences.

Journal of Esoteric Psychology
Seven Ray Institute
128 Manhattan Avenue
Jersey City Heights, NJ 07307
(201) 798-7777
Semiannual; $28

The *JEP* clarifies and disseminates the principles of esoteric psychology and the ageless wisdom. It provides a forum for exploration of all aspects of the esoteric sciences. Articles cover a variety of topics such as the soul, meditation, the esoteric constitution of the human being, healing, holistic education, mythology, and academic esoteric research.

Journal of Feminist Studies in Religion (JFSR)
Scholars Press
P.O. Box 15399
Atlanta, GA 30333-0399
(404) 727-2320
Annual; $18

The *JFSR* is a channel for the dissemination of feminist scholarship in religion and a forum for discussion and dialogue among women and men of differing feminist perspectives.

Journal of Interdisciplinary Studies (JIS)
Institute for Interdisciplinary Research
See Research Institutes.
Annual; $15

The *JIS* is an international journal of interdisciplinary and interfaith dialogue. It is co-sponsored by the International Christian Studies Association.

Journal of Near-Death Studies (JNDS)
Human Sciences Press
P.O. Box 735
Canal Street Station
New York, NY 10013-1578
(212) 620-8000
Quarterly; $36

The *JNDS* publishes articles on near-death experiences and related phenomena,

such as out-of-body experiences, death-bed visions, and comparable experiences occurring under other circumstances. It investigates the empirical effects and theoretical implications of such phenomena as they inform our understanding of human consciousness and its relation to the life and death processes.

The Journal of Psychology: Interdisciplinary and Applied (JP)
Heldref Publications
1319 Eighteenth Street, N.W.
Washington, DC 20036-1802
(202) 296-6267; (800) 365-9753
Bimonthly; $95

The *JP* publishes a variety of research and theoretical articles in the field of psychology, emphasizing articles that integrate divergent data and theories, explore new avenues for thinking and research, or present criticisms of the present status of the behavioral disciplines.

Journal of Religion and Health
Institute of Religion and Health
Human Sciences Press
233 Spring Street
New York, NY 10013-1578
Quarterly; $49

This publication covers primarily Judeo-Christian aspects of religion and psychology. It is published by the Institute of Religion and Health—one of the earliest pastoral training and counseling programs—which was founded in 1937 by the Reverend Norman Vincent Peale and psychiatrist Smiley Blanton (see Pastoral Counseling).

Journal of Scientific Exploration (JSE)
Stanford University, ERL 306
Stanford, CA 94305
(415) 593-8581
Quarterly; $30

The *JSE* is an independent professional journal published in the United States and Germany covering new approaches in physics and medicine. It also offers constructive criticism of orthodox science and medicine.

Journal of Spiritual Formation
Institute of Formative Spirituality
Duquesne University
Pittsburgh, PA 15282
(412) 396-6026
Three times a year; $18

This journal includes articles from a wide variety of disciplines and fields, such as religious and theological studies, psychology, sociology, the natural sciences, the arts, and literature, as well as the broad field of spirituality. (Also see Research Institutes.)

Journal of Women and Religion
Center for Women and Religion
See Interdisciplinary Organizations.
Annual; $20

MindField: A Quarterly Source Journal for Consciousness
MindField Publishing
270 Madison Avenue
New York, NY 10016
Quarterly; $19.50
This journal is a digest of excerpts from currently published books on philosophy, psychology, physics, cosmology and spirituality.

Noetic Sciences Review
Institute of Noetic Sciences
See Research Institutes.
Quarterly; $35 (membership)

Pilgrimage: Reflections on the Human Journey
Pilgrimage Press
Route 1, Box 188M
Highlands, NC 28741
Correspondence offered only by mail.
Five issues a year; $24
This journal is mainly written for and by therapists and people in therapy. The publication began as a mostly pastoral counseling journal, but has widened its scope in recent years to include the personal experience of psychotherapy of all kinds.

Psychological Perspectives
Carl Jung Institute of Los Angeles
See Nondegree and Postgraduate Training Programs, Analytic Psychology.

Psychoscience: The Journal of Theoretical Psychiatry
P.O. Box 7176
Loma Linda, CA 92354-0689
(909) 799-7651
Semiannual; $15
Psychoscience is considered a new theory of mind, in part propounded by the late physicist David Bohm who was in turn influenced by Jiddu Krishnamurti.

Religion and American Culture: A Journal of Interpretation
Indiana University Press
601 North Morton
Bloomington, IN 47404
(812) 855-9449
Semiannual; $15

Published by the Center for the Study of Religion and American Culture (see Research Institutes), this scholarly journal explores the interplay between religion and other spheres of American culture.

Review of Religious Research
Religious Research Association
See Research Institutes.
Quarterly; $22 (student $12)
This scholarly journal embraces many methodological approaches and theoretical perspectives. Although concentrated on specific topics, articles illuminate larger patterns, implications, or contexts of American life, and are devoted to promoting an ongoing, scholarly discussion of the nature, terms, and dynamics of religion in America.

ReVision: Journal of Consciousness and Change
Heldref Publications
1319 Eighteenth Street, N.W.
Washington, DC 20036-1802
(202) 296-6267; (800) 365-9753
Quarterly; $28
Since 1978, ReVision has provided a unique forum for new paradigm thinkers, countercultural intellectuals, philosophically inclined spiritual seekers, transpersonally oriented social activists, undogmatic exponents of the perennial wisdom, constructive postmodernists, and other kindred minds.

Sociological Analysis: A Journal in the Sociology of Religion
Association for the Sociology of Religion
See Interdisciplinary Organizations.
Quarterly; $25 (student $10)

Soundings: An Interdisciplinary Journal
University of Tennessee
306 Aconda Court
Knoxville, TN 37996-0530
(615) 974-8252
Quarterly; $18
This journal encourages scholars to challenge the fragmentation of modern intellectual life and to turn the best and most rigorous methods of the different academic disciplines toward the common good in human affairs.

Studia Mystica
Robert Boenig, Editor
Department of English
Texas A&M University
College Station, TX 77843
(409) 845-8318
Annual; $24.95
This academic journal is born out of the belief that the mystical experience is extra-

ordinary, yet universal, limited to no one cultural or religious tradition, an experience to be approached with delicacy, vigor, and a measure of boldness. Poetry, prose, fiction, essay, and other art forms are as important to the journal as scholarly articles, to the extent that they evoke the immediacy and fragility of the mystical experience.

Syzygy: Journal of Alternative Religion and Culture (JARC)
Center for Academic Publications
160 North Fairview Avenue, Suite D282
Goleta, CA 93117
(805) 683-0633
Quarterly; $30
The JARC publishes articles on communal and utopian groups, identity groups, spiritualism, new thought, occultism, neopaganism, astrology, UFO groups, and related phenomena.

Transpersonal Review
21821 Burbank Boulevard, Suite 143
Woodland Hills, CA 91367
(818) 888-6690
Biannual; $40
The Transpersonal Review covers transpersonal studies in psychology, philosophy, religion, medicine, and the arts.

Voices: The Art and Science of Psychotherapy
The American Academy of Psychotherapists
Guilford Press
72 Spring Street
New York, NY 10012
(800) 365-7006; (212) 431-9800
Quarterly; $32
This journal is largely written by and for psychotherapists belonging to the Academy. Topics are usually addressed briefly and in a first-person format by the authors.

Zygon: Journal of Religion and Science
The Institute on Religion in an Age of Science
Blackwell Publishers
Subscriber Services Coordinator
238 Main Street
Cambridge, MA 02142
(800) 835-6770
Quarterly; $35 (students $26)
Zygon explores the relationship between religious beliefs and philosophies and the theories and findings of modern-day science in order to illuminate issues of human purpose and moral direction in contemporary life.

MAGAZINES AND NEWSLETTERS

Alternative Medicine
National Institutes of Health
Office of Alternative Medicine
Building 31, Room B1-C35
Bethesda, MD 20892
(301) 402-2466
Bimonthly; complimentary subscription

Alternative Medicine is the official bimonthly newsletter of the Office of Alternative Medicine (see Research Institutes).

Annals of Earth
Lindisfarne Association
See Interdisciplinary Resources
Three times a year; $15

This newsletter is concerned with ecological conservation, right livelihood, and alternative forms of global development, as well as philosophy and the arts.

Anthropology of Consciousness
American Anthropological Association
See Interdisciplinary Organizations.
Quarterly; $30

This newsletter represents a division of the American Anthropological Association.

At the Crossroads
P.O. Box 112
St. Paul, AR 72760
(501) 677-2235
Quarterly; $24

This magazine explores the relationship between feminism, spirituality, and science.

Atlantis: The Imagery Newsletter
4016 Third Avenue
San Diego, CA 92103
(619) 298-7502
Bimonthly; $35

Brain Mind and Common Sense
Interface Press
Box 4221
4717 North Figueroa Street
Los Angeles, CA 90042
Correspondence offered only by mail.
Monthly; $45

Founded by Marilyn Ferguson, author of the *Aquarian Conspiracy*, this several-decades-old newsletter reports on research dealing with the mind-body interface.

Circle Network News
Circle Sanctuary
See Interdisciplinary Organizations.
Quarterly; $15

Common Boundary
5272 River Road, Suite 650
Bethesda, MD 20816
(301) 652-9495
Bimonthly; $22

This magazine explores the relationship of spirituality, creativity, and psychotherapy. Its format includes feature articles, interviews, essays, and departments that cover psychospiritual trends and innovations; reviews of books, videos, and audio tapes; and first-person accounts of spiritual journeys. The publication supports an ongoing dialogue on the spiritual dimensions of psychotherapy and the psychological aspects of spiritual growth. The magazine sponsors a psychospiritual thesis/dissertation award of $1,000 and publishes an essay based on the winning entry in the magazine. It will administer an award for research papers or projects relevant to the relationship between ecology and psychospirituality beginning in 1995.

Communiqué
Foundation for Community
Encouragement
See Nondegree and Postgraduate Training Programs.

Convergence
One Sanborn Road
Concord, NH 03301
(603) 225-3720
Five issues a year; $12.50

This publication describes itself as a magazine for "personal and spiritual growth and holistic health."

Creation Spirituality
160 East Virginia Street, Suite 290
San Jose, CA 95112
(408) 286-8505
Bimonthly; $20

This magazine, edited by Matthew Fox, is the voice of the Creation Spirituality movement, which strives to awaken mysticism, revitalize Western religion and culture, and promote social and ecological justice by mining the wisdom of ancient spiritual traditions and the insights of contemporary science. The philosophy Creation Spirituality teaches pantheism, the belief that divinity permeates all things, and honors women's wisdom and the cosmologies of Native cultures around the planet.

Gnosis
P.O. Box 14217
San Francisco, CA 94114-0217
(415) 255-0400
Quarterly; $20

This publication explores the inner spiritual traditions of Western culture.

Healing
The Health Communication Research Institute
1050 Fulton Avenue, Suite 105
Sacramento, CA 95825
(916) 483-1583
Quarterly; $30

This magazine focuses on communication in the healing relationship.

Health
475 Gate Five Road, Suite 225
Sausalito, CA 94965
(415) 332-5866
Seven times a year; $24

This magazine offers articles on maintaining good health.

The Humanist
American Humanist Association
See Interdisciplinary Organizations.
Biannual; $25

Intuition
925 Church Street
San Francisco, CA 94114
(415) 550-1627
Quarterly; $15

This magazine presents articles, profiles, and interviews on topics relevant to the development and application of intuition.

Magical Blend
1461 Valencia Street
San Francisco, CA 94110
(415) 821-9190
Quarterly; $17

Magical Blend's purpose is to chart the course of society's fundamental transformation currently taking place and to assist the individual in coping with this process. The magazine does not endorse one path to spiritual growth but attempts to explore many alternative possibilities for transforming the planet.

Miracles Magazine
The Miracles Community Network
P.O. Box 418
Santa Fe, NM 87504-0418
(505) 989-3656
Quarterly; $21.95

This magazine is published by the Miracles Community Network, a nonprofit corporation, and features stories of healing and the work of contemporary healers. It is also affiliated with the Foundation for Inner Peace, which publishes *A Course in Miracles.*

Natural Health (formerly East-West Journal)
17 Station Street, Box 1200
Brookline, MA 02147
(617) 232-1000
Bimonthly; $24

This magazine provides information on alternative approaches to health and encourages readers to rely on remedies that facilitate the body's natural healing capacities.

New Age Journal
42 Pleasant Street
Watertown, MA 02172-2333
(617) 926-0200
Bimonthly; $24

Founded twenty years ago by Peggy Taylor, Eric Utne and others, this publication is a natural lifestyle magazine for the conscious consumer. Issues include a mix of features, departments in the areas of natural health and wellness, personal growth, the environment, spirituality, and social change.

New Dimensions Radio Journal
New Dimensions Foundation
P.O. Box 410510
San Francisco, CA 94141-0510
(415) 563-8899

Since 1973, New Dimensions Radio has been "transforming culture and freeing it of destructive misinformation" by inviting radio listeners to tune into weekly interviews with leading thinkers in psychology, mythology, human values, business, spirituality, health, science, politics, ecology, philosophy, and the arts. In addition to membership fees, the Foundation supports its work by revenue generated from the sale of audio tapes of its radio interviews. This publication offers articles and lists audio tapes of radio interviews that are for purchase.

Night Vision: A Dream Journal
P.O. Box 402
Questa, NM 87556
(505) 586-0863
Quarterly; $12

This publication explores dreaming from various cultural and spiritual perspectives, including visionary, shamanic, and lucid dreams.

Of a Like Mind
P.O. Box 6021
Madison, WI 53716
Correspondence offered only by mail.

This newspaper is dedicated to bringing together women following spiritual paths. Its focus is on women's spirituality, goddess religions, paganism, and earth connections from a feminist perspective.

Parabola: The Magazine of Myth and Tradition
656 Broadway
New York, NY 10012
(212) 505-6200
Quarterly; $22

Parabola covers the world's myths, folklore, and spiritual heritage by addressing such topics as humor, forgiveness, addiction, sadness, the body, guilt, demons, and pilgrimage.

Sagewoman: A Quarterly Magazine of Women's Spirituality
Bookpeople Publications
7900 Edgewater Drive
Oakland, CA 94621
(510) 632-4700
Quarterly; $23.80

Sagewoman is dedicated to helping women explore the spiritual energy within themselves.

Science and Religion News
65 Hoit Road
Concord, NH 03301
(603) 226-3328
Quarterly; $9.50

This newsletter covers the science and religion field, and includes information on upcoming conferences, recent publications and articles, news from societies in the field, speakers and topics at recent conferences, and reactions from scholars.

Seeds of Unfolding
Cafh Foundation
168 West Kerley Road
Tivoli, NY 12583
(914) 757-5451
Three times a year; $10

This magazine is published by Cafh Foundation, a nonprofit organization whose purpose is to assist in the spiritual development of all persons. The articles in *Seeds* present ideas for spiritual growth from various cultures for the development of consciousness and new ways of thinking. Besides publishing *Seeds*, Cafh Foundation sponsors conferences, retreats, and discussions on spiritual topics in various cities around the United States.

Shambhala Sun
1345 Spruce Street
Boulder, CO 80302
(303) 422-8404
Bimonthly; $20

Founded in 1978, Shambhala Sun is a Buddhist-oriented publication that presents teachings, political and social commentary, arts and aesthetics, and views on business, lifestyles and personal development.

The Sun
107 North Roberson Street
Chapel Hill, NC 27516
(919) 942-5282
Monthly; $30

The Sun is a literary magazine that frequently covers topics that appeal to those interested in psychospiritual subjects.

Utne Reader
1624 Harmon Place, Suite 330
Minneapolis, MN 55403
(612) 338-5040
Bimonthly; $18

This magazine is the *Reader's Digest* for twenty, thirty-, and forty somethings. It offers articles originally published in the alternative press that center around a different theme each issue. Many of the psychospiritual periodicals listed here are often excerpted.

Woman of Power Magazine
P.O. Box 2785
Orleans, MA 02653
(508) 240-7877
Quarterly; $7.50

Founded in 1984, this nonprofit, 88-page magazine celebrates the international visions of feminism, spirituality, and politics that are transformational, creative, growth-centered, and empowering.

Yoga Journal
2054 University Avenue, Suite 302
Berkeley, CA 94704
(510) 841-9200
Bimonthly; $21

Founded in 1975 by the California Yoga Teachers Association as a newsletter for yoga teachers, this magazine defines yoga as practices that aspire to union or communion with some higher power, greater truth, or deeper source of wisdom, as well as practices that tend to increase harmony of body, mind, and spirit. The focus is on mind-body approaches to personal and spiritual development, which include, other than hatha yoga, holistic healing, transpersonal psychology, bodywork and massage, the martial arts, Eastern spirituality, and Western mysticism.

TAPE-RECORDING COMPANIES

The following companies offer audio tapes (often recorded at workshops, conferences or lectures) covering topics such as psychology, spiritual traditions, relationships, mythology, creativity, holistic health, and methods of healing.

Big Sur Tapes
P.O. Box 4
Tiburon, CA 94920
(800) 688-5512
Recordings include teachers such as Stan Grof, Anne Armstrong, Ram Dass, Joseph Campbell, Angeles Arrien and others who have presented at the Esalen Institute over the last two decades.

Credence Cassettes
115 East, Armour Boulevard
Kansas City, MO 64111
(816) 531-0538
Credence began in 1973; most of its recordings are oriented in the Catholic tradition.

Dharma Communications™
P.O. Box 156DC, South Plank Road
Mt. Tremper, NY 12457
(914) 688-7993
Dharma Communications™ is a nonprofit educational corporation dedicated to providing resources pertinent to the challenges and opportunities encountered by spiritual practitioners within Buddhist and other religious traditions.

Dharma Seed Tape Library
P.O. Box 66
Wendell Depot, MA 01380
(800) 969-SEED
The Dharma Seed Tape Library originated in 1983 to provide a resource of meditative instruction, guidance and inspiration by teachers who conduct retreats at the Insight Meditation Society in Massachusetts.

Dolphin Tapes
P.O. Box 71
Big Sur, CA 93920
Correspondence offered only by mail.
Dolphin Tapes records psychospiritual topics taught by various teachers, including Jack Kornfield, Huston Smith, Carl Rogers, and Angeles Arrien.

Hanuman Foundation Tape Library
524 San Anselmo Avenue, 203
San Anselmo, CA 94960
(415) 457-8570
The Foundation distributes audiocassettes and videotapes of workshops, lectures and meditations by Ram Dass and other Dharma teachers.

Menninger Video Productions
P.O. Box 829
Topeka, KS 66601-0829
(913) 273-7500; (800) 345-6036
Affiliated with the Menninger Foundation (see Research Institutes), this company provides educational material regarding mental health.

New Dimensions Foundation
P.O. Box 410510
San Francisco, CA 94141-0510
(415) 563-8899
See also *New Dimensions Journal* under Interdisciplinary Periodicals.

Quantum Link
8665 East Miami River Road
Cincinnati, OH 45207
19800) 531-9283
Quantum Link offers "psychoacoustic" audio tapes.

**The Sound Horizons &
New York Open Center Audio Collection**
83 Spring Street
New York, NY 10012
(212) 219-2527
This tape collection consists of recordings made during New York Open Center workshops by teachers such as Jeanne Achterberg, Robert Bly, Deepak Chopra, and Thich Nhat Hanh.

Sounds Photosynthesis
P.O. Box 2111
Mill Valley, CA 94942
(415) 383-6712
Sounds Photosynthesis offers audio cassettes of intellectuals and health practitioners who focus on alternative theology and therapies.

Sounds True
735 Walnut Street
Boulder, CO 80302
(800) 333-9185
Sounds True has over 300 audio tapes from speakers including Clarissa Pinkola Estés, Sogyal Rinpoche, Marion Woodman, Stephen Levine, and Thomas Moore.

World Research Foundation (WRF)
15300 Ventura Boulevard, Suite 405
Sherman Oaks, CA 91403
(818) 907-5483
The WRF offers audio and videotapes concerned with "New Directions For Medicine." Examples include Qigong, Ayurvedic medicine, and wellness (see Interdisciplinary Organizations).

WHAT YOU NEED TO KNOW ABOUT ACCREDITATION

Plus:
➤ REGIONAL ACCREDITING ASSOCIATIONS
➤ OTHER ACCREDITING BODIES

THE UNITED STATES HAS NO FEDERAL MINISTRY OF EDUCATION OR OTHER CENTRALIZED AUTHORITY EXERCISING SINGLE NATIONAL CONTROL OVER educational institutions in this country. Individual states assume varying degrees of control over education, but in general, institutions of postsecondary education are permitted to operate with considerable independence and autonomy. Consequently, the character and quality of American educational institutions vary widely.

The practice of accreditation arose in the United States as a means of conducting nongovernmental, peer evaluation of educational institutions and programs. Private educational associations of regional or national scope have adopted criteria reflecting the qualities of a sound educational program and have developed procedures for evaluating institutions or programs to determine whether or not they are operating at basic levels of quality.

The following essay is adapted from an article first printed in the ninth edition of *Bear's Guide to Non-Traditional College Degrees.* After it, we list accrediting bodies relevant to some of the programs outlined in this guide. Also note the Key to Accrediting Organizations, page xix.

ACCREDITATION IS PERHAPS THE MOST complex, confusing, and important issue in higher education. It is surely the most misunderstood and the most misused concept—both intentionally and unintentionally. In selecting a school, there are three important things to know about accreditation: what it is, why it may be important for certain situations, and what are the different kinds of accrediting associations?

WHAT IS ACCREDITATION?

Quite simply, accreditation is a validation—a statement issued by a group of persons who are, theoretically, impartial experts in higher education—that a given school, or department within a school, has been thoroughly investigated and found worthy of approval.

Accreditation is a peculiarly American concept. In every other country in the world, all colleges and universities are either government operated or given the right to grant degrees directly by the government. In the United States, accreditation is an entirely voluntary process, done by private, nongovernmental agencies. As a result of this lack of central control or authority, both worthy and unworthy accrediting agencies have evolved, along with recognized ones and unrecognized ones, legitimate and phony ones.

When a school says, "We are accredited," that statement alone means nothing. The question must always be asked, "Accredited by whom?" Unfortunately, many consumer-oriented articles and bulletins simply say that one is much safer dealing only with accredited schools—but do not attempt to unravel the complex situation. The wrong kind of accreditation can be worse than none at all, and some accrediting agencies may be as illegitimate as the schools they approve.

Normally a school wishing to be accredited will make application to the appropriate legitimate accrediting agency. After substantial preliminary investigation to determine that the school is operating legally and is running legitimately, it may be granted correspondent status. Typically this step will take anywhere from several months to several years more and, when completed, does not imply any kind of endorsement or recommendation but merely indicates that the first steps on a long path have been taken.

Next, teams from the accrediting agency, often composed of faculty of already accredited institutions, will visit the school. These "visitations," conducted at regular intervals throughout the year, are to observe the school in action and to study the copious amounts of information that the school must prepare relating to its legal and academic structure, educational philosophy, curriculum, financial status, planning, and so forth.

After these investigations, and normally at least two years of successful operation (sometimes a great deal more), the school may be advanced to the status "candidate for accreditation." Being a candidate means, in effect, "Yes, you are probably worthy of accreditation, but we want to watch your operation for a while longer." This "while" can range from a year or two to six years or more. The great majority of schools that reach candidacy status eventually achieve full accreditation. (The terms "accredited" and "fully accredited" are used interchangeably.)

Once a school is accredited, it is visited by inspection teams at infrequent intervals (every five to ten years is common) to see if it is still worthy of its accreditation. The status is always subject to review, should new programs evolve or any significant developments,

positive or negative, occur in the life of the school.

THE IMPORTANCE OF ACCREDITATION

Although accreditation is undeniably important to both schools and students, its importance is undermined and confused by three factors:

1. There are no national standards for accreditation. What is accreditable in New York may not be accreditable in California. The demands of the groups

---

A school's accreditation status can help identify clearly illegitimate or unsatisfactory institutions.

---

that accredits schools of chemistry may be very different from those of the people who accredit schools of forestry.

2. Many very good schools (or departments within schools) are not accredited. This may be by their own choice (since accreditation is a totally voluntary procedure) or because they are too new (all schools were unaccredited at one time) or too experimental (many would say too innovative) for the generally conservative accreditors.

3. Many very bad schools claim to be accredited—but always by unrecognized, often nonexistent accrediting associations, often of their own creation.

Still, accreditation is the only widespread system of school evaluation that we have. A school's accreditation status can be helpful to the potential student as a means of identifying clearly illegitimate or unsatisfactory institutions. While many good schools are not accredited, it is very unlikely that a very bad or illegally operating school is authentically accredited. (There have been exceptions, but they are rare.) In other words, authentic accreditation is a pretty good sign that a given school or program is legitimate. But it is important to remember that lack of accreditation need not mean that a school is either inferior or illegal.

Authentic accreditation is important

because there are very few laws or regulations anywhere governing the establishment of an accrediting association. Anyone can start a degree mill, then turn around and open an accrediting agency next door, give the school its blessing, and begin advertising "fully accredited degrees."

The crucial question, then, is this: Who accredits the accreditors? There are two agencies, one private and one governmental, that have responsibility for evaluating and approving or recognizing accrediting agencies.

The Council on Postsecondary Accreditation (known as COPA) is a nationwide nonprofit corporation formed in 1975 to evaluate accrediting associations and award recognition to those found worthy. Within the U.S. Department of Education is the Eligibility and Agency Evaluation Staff (EAES), which is required by law to "publish a list of nationally recognized accrediting agencies which [are determined] to be reliable as to the quality of training offered." This is done as one measure of eligibility for federal financial aid programs for students. The EAES also has the job of deciding whether unaccredited schools can qualify for federal aid programs, or their students for veterans' benefits. This is done primarily by determining whether credits from any given unaccredited school have been accepted by at least three accredited schools. If they have, then the unaccredited school is recognized by the Department of Education for that purpose.

ACCREDITATION AND NONTRADITIONAL EDUCATION

One of the frequent complaints leveled against the recognized accrediting agencies is that they have, in general, been slow to acknowledge the major trend toward alternative or nontraditional education. A few years ago, the Carnegie Commission on Higher Education conducted research on the relationship between accreditation and nontraditional approaches. Their report, written by Alexander Mood, confirmed that a serious disadvantage of accreditation is "in the suppression of innovation. Schools cannot get far out of line without risking loss of their accreditation—a penalty which they cannot afford."

Also, the report continues, "loss of accreditation implies that the curriculum is somewhat inferior and hence that the degree is inferior. Such a large penalty tends to prevent colleges from striking out in new directions.... As we look toward the future, it appears likely that accrediting organizations will lose their usefulness and slowly disappear. Colleges will be judged not by what some educational bureaucracy declares but by what they can do for their students. Of much greater relevance would be statistics on students satisfaction, career advancement of graduates, and data like that."

Faced with such high-power criticism, some accrediting agencies sponsored (with a major grant from the Kellogg Foundation) a large-scale study of how the agencies should deal with nontraditional education. The findings in the four-volume report of this investigation were similar to the Carnegie report. The accreditors were advised, in effect, not to look at the easy quantitative factors (percentage of doctorate-holders on the faculty, books in the library, student-faculty ratio, acres of campus, etc.) but rather to evaluate the far more elusive qualitative factors, of which student satisfaction and student performance are most crucial.

In other words, if the students at a nontraditional, non-residential university regularly produce research and dissertations that are as good as those of traditional schools, or if graduates of nontraditional schools are as likely to gain admission to graduate school or high-level employment and perform satisfactorily there, then the nontraditional school may be just as worthy of accreditation as the traditional school.

Accrediting agencies move slowly. Various committees and commissions are studying this Kellogg report (and others like it), and perhaps some of the recommendations will one day be implemented. Most nontraditional schools are not holding their collective

breath awaiting such action, although eventually either it must come or, as the Carnegie report predicts, the traditional accreditors will fade away.

APPROVED ACCREDITING AGENCIES

There are six regional associations, each with responsibility for schools in one region of the United States and its territories. Each has the authority to accredit an entire college or university. There are also about 80 professional associa-

---

For some jobs professional accreditation is more important than regional accreditation.

---

tions, each with authority to accredit either specialized schools or specific departments or programs within a school.

Thus it may be the case, for instance, that the North Central Association (one of the six regional associations) will accredit Dolas University. When this happens, the entire school is accredited, and all of its degrees may be called accredited degrees, or more accurately, degrees from an accredited institution. Or it may be the case that the art department of Dolas University has been accredited by the relevant professional association, in this case the National Association of Schools of Art. If this happens, then only Dolas art majors can claim to have accredited degrees.

CONCLUSIONS

If an accredited degree is important to you, the first question to ask is, "Has the school been accredited by one of the six regional associations?" If the answer is no, then the next question is, "Has the department in which I am interested been accredited by its relevant professional association?" For some jobs (psychology and nursing are two good examples), professional accreditation is more important than regional accreditation. In other words, even if a school is

accredited by its regional association, unless its graduate psychology department is also accredited by the American Psychological Association, its degrees will be less useful for the graduates hoping to enter the field of psychology.

There is a final confusion in this matter: Some accrediting agencies are officially recognized by the United States Department of Education, some are recognized by the Council on Postsecondary Accreditation (the private nongovernment agency), some are recognized by both, and some by neither. There are situations where it is important to know which national agency has recognized an accreditor, although by and large if either one has, that is good enough. Unrecognized agencies may or may not be legitimate. Each of the approved accreditors will gladly supply lists of all the schools (or departments within schools) they have accredited and those that are candidates for accreditation and in correspondent status. They will also answer any questions pertaining to any school's status (or lack of status) with them.

Regional Accrediting Associations

Middle States Association of Colleges and Schools
3624 Market Street
Philadelphia, PA 19104
(215) 662-5606
    States include Delaware, District of Columbia, Maryland, New Jersey, New York, and Pennsylvania.

New England Association of Schools and Colleges
Sanborn House
15 High Street
Winchester, MA 01890
(617) 729-6762
    States include Connecticut, Maine, Massachusetts, New Hampshire, Rhode Island, and Vermont.

North Central Association of Colleges and Schools
159 North Dearborn Street
Chicago, IL 60601
(312) 263-0456
    States include Arizona, Arkansas, Colorado, Illinois, Indiana, Iowa, Kansas, Michigan, Minnesota, Missouri, Nebraska,

New Mexico, North Dakota, Ohio, Oklahoma, South Dakota, West Virginia, Wisconsin, and Wyoming.

**Northwest Association of
Schools and Colleges**
3700-B University Way, NE
Seattle, WA 98105
(206) 543-0195
States include Alaska, Idaho, Montana, Nevada, Oregon, Utah, and Washington.

**Southern Association of
Colleges and Schools**
1866 Southern Lane
Decatur, Georgia 30033-4097
(800) 248-7701
States include Alabama, Florida, Georgia, Kentucky, Louisiana, Mississippi, North Carolina, South Carolina, Tennessee, Texas, and Virginia.

**Western Association of
Schools and Colleges**
Mills College, Box 9990
Oakland, CA 94613
(415) 632-5000
States include California and Hawaii.

Other Accrediting Bodies

Many professional associations also support independent accrediting bodies that approve educational programs relevant to its profession and, in some instances, certify individual practitioners.

**Accrediting Agency
Evaluation Branch (AAEB)**
Higher Education Management Services
Office of Postsecondary Education
U.S. Department of Education
Washington, DC 20202-5171
(202) 708-7417
Contact the AAEB for information about its accrediting process.

Commission on Recognition (COR)
1 Dupont Circle, NW, Suite 305
Washington, DC 20036
(202) 452-1433
The COR assumed the functions of the Federation of Regional Accrediting Commission of Higher Education and the National Commission on Accrediting in 1975. It is a nongovernmental organization intended to foster and facilitate the role of accrediting agencies in promoting and ensuring the quality and diversity of American postsecondary education. The council recognizes, coordinates, and periodically reviews the work of its member accrediting agencies, determines the appro-

priateness of existing or proposed accrediting activities, and performs other related functions.

**Higher Education Institutional
Eligibility Branch (HEIEB)**
Division of Eligibility and Certification
Debt Collection and Management
Assistance Service
Office of Postsecondary Education
U.S. Department of Education
Washington, DC 20202-5323
(202) 708-4913
Contact the HEIEB for information about the eligibility of degree-granting postsecondary institutions.

**Occupational/Vocational
Eligibility Branch (OVEB)**
Division of Eligibility and Certification
Debt Collection and Management
Assistance Service
Office of Postsecondary Education
U.S. Department of Education
Washington, DC 20202-5323
(202) 708-4913
Contact the OVEB for information about the eligibility of nondegree-granting vocational schools and programs.

THE POSSIBLE EFFECTS OF HEALTH-CARE REFORM ON CONVENTIONAL AND ALTERNATIVE THERAPIES

A N IMPORTANT CONCERN FOR MENTAL HEALTH PRACTITIONERS, BOTH CONVENTIONAL AND ALTERNATIVE, IS HOW HEALTH-CARE REFORM WILL AFFECT THEIR fields. Currently, health insurance companies (known as third-party payers) have the authority to determine which diagnoses and types of therapists receive reimbursement. However, with major reforms on the horizon, there

soon will be a fourth party entering the equation (in addition to the therapist, the client, and the insurance company); namely, the federal government. Due to the wide variety of legislative proposals and the politically heated debate that has ensued, the future configuration of national health care remains unclear as of this writing. Nevertheless, the unpredictable future of the mental health profession has not prevented policy experts such as Bryant Welch, J.D., Ph.D., senior policy advisor for the American Psychological Association (APA), from making a few speculative conclusions based on the legislation currently under consideration by Congress.

According to Dr. Welch, Congressional debate has centered more upon the economics of health care than on the individual and societal benefits of various therapies in use today. The federal government is not concerning itself with the more narrow questions—like the efficacy of alternative versus conventional therapies—but is focused on developing a general health-care policy that includes the mental health field. This focus is intended to establish a model for mental health care based on three essential questions: (1) Should mental health modalities such as psychotherapy be covered benefits? (2) If so, who should have the greatest access

to this care? And (3) to what extent should they have access to it? Answers to these questions may still be several years away as preliminary indications suggest that individual state governments, or perhaps a federally elected health-care board, will determine the degree to which the federal guidelines are implemented.

In all probability, regional health-care alliances (made up of health-care providers, patients, and citizens, and managed by the federal government) will oversee managed-care operations at the state or regional level. In addition, partially regulated health-care conglomerates, called health maintenance organizations (HMOs), will work with regional alliances and "manage" the distribution of benefits so as to conserve costs. HMOs focus on primary and preventive health care and, whenever possible, discourage the use of expensive specialists; HMO members pay an annual fee rather than fees for individual services. Some HMOs are already in existence. In fact, large segments of the mental health community, excluding the field of psychology, favor managed care for a variety of complicated reasons, often political and economic in nature. For example, many psychiatric hospitals are affiliated with managed-care operators.

HMOs may begin using lower-cost providers (e.g., social workers) for some mental health services such as psychotherapy, which has traditionally been considered primarily the psychologists' and psychiatrists' domain.

In order for HMOs to make a profit and successfully compete against one another under a federally mandated health-care system, they will seek to contain costs. One cost-cutting strategy may be to restrict benefits that are considered unnecessary or too expensive. (Not allowing consumers full access to benefits they consider essential is one of the more contentious issues among policy makers.)

Dr. Welch suggests a number of other possible consequences. First, HMOs may make available only a small number of providers in each profession (e.g., physicians, psychologists, physical therapists), thereby limiting the pool from which recipients choose their providers. Such a strategy would allow HMOs to increase the number of clients seen by each provider. Second, HMOs may employ providers who perform services at a lower cost, creating (in theory at least) healthy competition. Finally, HMOs, in a steadfast effort to contain costs, may place value on modalities that treat ailments most quickly (e.g., brief therapy and crisis intervention).

As for health-care providers who choose not to join an HMO or who are not accepted into the provider pool but remain in a fee-for-service private practice, their services would now cost more to their clients than those of HMO-member therapists. In short, these factors have led the APA to support a comprehensive health-care plan that ensures what it sees as adequate mental health services, no matter the system of administration.

If these speculations by Dr. Welch prove accurate, HMOs may consider the traditional long-term practice of psychotherapy a financial liability and so may either limit the amount of body therapy and psychotherapy allowed or provide incentives to therapists who place emphasis on short-term care, or both. HMOs may also begin using lower-cost providers (e.g., social workers) for some mental health services such as psychotherapy, which has traditionally been considered primarily the psychologists' and psychiatrists' domain. In addition, if HMOs are not required in the federal legislation to limit their contracting to regulated professions (such as clinical psychology, clinical social work, marriage and family therapy, mental health counseling, psychiatric nursing, psychiatry, and substance-abuse counseling), then each state could instead elect a "free market" approach and let the HMOs contract with the least costly mental health professions. Such a move could be a boon to the unregulated alternative professions such as somatic therapy, pastoral counseling, and the creative and expressive arts therapies, which claim to provide effective treatments at a relatively low cost.

ALPHABETICAL INDEX

SCHOOLS, PROGRAMS, ASSOCIATIONS, ORGANIZATIONS, AND PERIODICALS LISTED IN THIS DIRECTORY

GEOGRAPHICAL INDEX

SCHOOLS, PROGRAMS, AND
RETREAT AND CONFERENCE CENTERS
LISTED IN THIS DIRECTORY

Animas Valley Institute, 123
Jamestown
Heart of Stillness Retreats, 145
Morrison
Colorado Christian University, 46
Nederland
Taoist Mountain Retreat Center, 102

CONNECTICUT
Enfield
New England School of Homeopathy, 74
Essex
Jungian Seminars, 114
Farmington
University of Connecticut, 16
New Haven
New Haven Zen Center, 146
Ridgefield
Center for Women, the Earth and the
    Divine, 154
Foundation for Community
    Encouragement, 125
Stratford
Connecticut Institute for
    Psychosynthesis, 121
Washington
Loving Relationships Training, 96
West Hartford
Saint Joseph College, 58
Westport
Temenos Institute, 48, 142
Wilton
New York Psychosynthesis Collective, 121

DISTRICT OF COLUMBIA
Washington
Catholic University of America, 36
Center for Mind-Body Studies, 69
Free Catholic Church in the Greater
    Washington Area, 54, 56
George Washington University, 24
Georgetown University, 71
Servant Leadership School, 127
Shalem Institute for Spiritual
    Formation, 50

FLORIDA
Key Largo
Keys Institute, 141
Miami
Commission on Massage Training
    Accreditation/Approval, 87
Naples
Walden University, 31
Orlando
Hindu University of America, 60
Palm Beach Gardens
Upledger Institute, 94, 138

Sarasota
Anabasis, 145
St. Petersburg
International Institute of Reflexology, 97
Tallahassee
Core Institute of Massage Therapy and
    Structural Bodywork, 94
West Palm Beach
Hippocrates Health Institute, 126

GEORGIA
Atlanta
Emory University, 24, 56
Georgia School of Professional
    Psychology, 24
Carrolton
West Georgia College, 28
Decatur
Columbia Theological Seminary, 46
La Verne
University of La Verne, 132
Lakemont
Center for Spiritual Awareness, 145

HAWAII
Hilo
Greenwich University, 30
Honolulu
National Institute of Expressive
    Therapy, 108
University of Hawaii at Manoa, 133
Pahoa
Kalani Honda Conference and Retreat
    Center, 141

IOWA
Fairfield
College of Maharishi Ayur-Veda Health
    Center, 83
Maharishi International University, 25
Iowa City
On the Way, 50
University of Iowa, 37

ILLINOIS
Bourbonnais
Olivet Nazarene University, 48, 58
Chicago
American Islamic College, 62
Brahma Kumaris World Spiritual
    University, 154
Center for Religion and Psychotherapy of
    Chicago, 45
Chicago School of Professional
    Psychology, 23, 132
Chicago Theological Seminary, 45, 56
Focusing Institute, 95, 125
Illinois School of Professional
    Psychology, 25

Institute for Spiritual Leadership, 50
Loyola University of Chicago, 47
McCormick Theological Seminary, 36, 57
Mind-Body Medical Institute/Mercy
    Hospital, 70
Oasis Center Center, 110
Oasis Center, 108, 142
University of Chicago, 28, 37, 59
Deerfield
Trinity Evangelical Divinity School, 58
Dekalb
Northern Illinois University, 26
Evanston
C. G. Jung Institute of Chicago, 114
National-Louis University, 39
Park Ridge
Lutheran General Hospital, 47
Schaumburg
College of Chaplains, 42
University Park
Governors State University, 39
Wheaton
Wheaton College Graduate School, 59

INDIANA
Donaldson
Graduate Theological Foundation, 46, 50
Indianapolis
Center for the Study of Religion and
    American Culture, 135
Christian Theological Seminary, 45, 56
Muncie
Ball State University, 82
Notre Dame
University of Notre Dame, 28
Richmond
Earlham School of Religion, 46
West Lafayette
Purdue University, 132

KANSAS
Lawrence
International College of Applied
    Kinesiology, 96
University of Kansas, 133
Salina
Bonny Foundation: An Institute for Music-
    Centered Therapies, 109
Topeka
Menninger Clinic, 16
Menninger Foundation, 137

KENTUCKY
Lexington
Kentucky Center of Psychosynthesis, 121
Louisville
Islamic Research Foundation, 136
Louisville Institute for the Study of
    Protestantism and American
    Culture, 136

PSYCHOSPIRITUAL DISSERTATION AND THESIS AWARD

COMMON BOUNDARY'S ANNUAL PSYCHOSPIRITUAL AWARD PROGRAM RECOGNIZES OUTSTANDING DISSERTATIONS AND THESES THAT ADDRESS THE INTERRELATIONship of psychotherapy, spirituality, and creativity. Students whose doctoral dissertations or master's theses (or the academic equivalent) are officially accepted during a given calendar year are invited to apply by December 31st of that year. The award is announced in June of the following year. The author will receive an award of $1,000, and her or his essay will be printed in *Common Boundary* magazine.

Entrants are requested to send a two-page, double-spaced, typewritten description of their dissertation or thesis. Five authors will be selected by the Common Boundary staff to write a 10-page essay based on their research and findings. A panel of judges will then choose the winning essay. Decisions will be made on the basis of the originality and creativity of the essay and its relevance and contribution to the field of psychospirituality.

PANEL OF JUDGES:

Daniel Goleman, Ph.D., is the contributing behavioral science writer for *The New York Times* and author of *The Meditative Mind* and *Vital Lies, Simple Truths.*

John McDargh, Ph.D., is an associate professor in the Department of Theology at Boston College and the author of *Psychoanalytic Object Relations Theory and the Study of Religion: On Faith and the Imaging of God.*

Belleruth Naparstek, L.I.S.W., B.C.D., is an adjunct faculty member at Case Western Reserve University's Mandel School of Applied Social Sciences and author of the *Health Journeys* guided imagery tape series and the book *Staying Well with Guided Imagery.*

Frances Vaughan, Ph.D., is a psychotherapist in private practice, author of *Awakening Intuition* and *The Inward Arc,* and co-editor (with Roger Walsh) of *Paths Beyond Ego: Transpersonal Dimensions in Psychology; Accept This Gift; A Gift of Peace* and *A Gift of Healing.*

Miles Vich is the editor of the *Journal of Transpersonal Psychology* and executive director of the Association for Transpersonal Psychology.

PLEASE SEND ENTRIES TO:
Common Boundary
Dissertation/Thesis Award
5272 River Road, Suite 650
Bethesda, MD 20816
(301) 652-9495

To Submit a Resource for Prospective Inclusion in Future Editions:

PLEASE SEND DETAILED INFORMATION TO:
Common Boundary
Graduate Education Guide
—Additions/Changes
5272 River Road, Suite 650
Bethesda, MD 20816

Book Order Form

Please send me ____copy/copies of the *Common Boundary Graduate Education Guide* at $19.95 plus $3.50 shipping and handling for each copy (international air-mail orders add $16 for S & H) to the address below. Expect two to four weeks for order processing and delivery (shipment is via first-class mail).

Name _____

Address _____

City _____ State _____ Zip _____

Mail form with check or money order to:
Common Boundary, Dept. GEG, 5272 River Road, Suite 650, Bethesda, MD 20816